Russia

&

Asia

by the same author

The Art of Central Asia
Beyond the Oxus
Monuments of Central Asia
Archaeology and Architecture of Afghanistan

In Czech:
V srdci Asie (The Heart of Asia) travel
Smrt Tamerlanova (The Death of Tamerlane) novel
Klec (The Cage) novel
Navrat nezadouci (Return Undesired) stories
Strach (Fear) poems

RUSSIA

&

ASIA

Nomadic & oriental traditions in Russian History

E D G A R   K N O B L O C H

ODYSSEY BOOKS & GUIDES

Odyssey Books & Guides is a division of Airphoto International Ltd.
903 Seaview Commercial Building, 21–24 Connaught Road West, Sheung Wan, Hong Kong
Tel: (852) 2856-3896; Fax: (852) 2565-8 004
E-mail: info@odysseypublications.com; www.odysseypublications.com

Distribution in the USA by
W.W. Norton & Company, Inc.,
500 Fifth Avenue, New York, NY 10110, USA
Tel: 800-233-4830; Fax: 800-458-6515
www.wwnorton.com

Distribution in the UK by
Cordee Books and Maps, 3a De Montfort St.,
Leicester, LE1 7HD, UK
Tel: 0116-254-3579; Fax: 0116-247-1176
www.cordee.co.uk

Russia & Asia

ISBN: 978-962-217-785-7 Library of Congress Catalog Card Number has been requested.

Grateful acknowledgment is made to the following:
Illustrations courtesy of **Magdalena Beranová**, *Slovane*, (Librí, 2000) 60, *Studien zum Burgwall von Mikulčice IV* (Archeologický Ústav av čk Brno, 2000) 76, 81, 82, 84, **Den Barsboldt**, published in the book *Mongolové* (The Mongols) by **Ivana Grollova** and **Veronika Zikmundova** (Triton Books, 2001), 95, 145, 148, 154.

Photography courtesy of **Edgar Knobloch** II, III, IV top, V, VIII, IX top, X, XI, XVIII, XXIV bottom; *Europas Mitte um 1000 Katalog* (Theiss, 2000, Stuttgart) VII bottom, IX bottom left and right; **Keith Macgregor** XIX; **Masha Nordbye** (*Moscow and St Petersburg*, Odyssey Books and Guides, 2004) XII, XIII, XIV, XV, XVI–XVII, XX–XXI, XXIII; **Ivanov Viktor Semenovich** XXII; **Mikhail Klimentyev/PA Photos** XXIV top; **The Hermitage** (St Petersburg) I, IV bottom, VI; **The Russian State Museum** (St Petersburg) VII top.

Managing Editor: Bijan Omrani
Design: Sarah Lock
Cover design: Au Yeung Chui Kwai
Maps: On the Road Cartography

Production and printing by
Twin Age Ltd, Hong Kong
E-mail: twinage@netvigator.com
Manufactured in Hong Kong

contents

Part 3 MUSCOVY RUSSIA

Part 4 IMPERIAL RUSSIA

Part 5 SOVIET RUSSIA

A – THE STATE

Maps & iLLustrations

COLOUR PLATES

Acknowledgements

My thanks should go, first and foremost, to my University teachers, Professors Bohuš Tomsa and Miroslav Boháček from the Faculty of Law, and Professors Jan Rypka and Felix Tauer, from the Philosophy Faculty of the Charles University in Prague, who inspired and stimulated my interested in Political Theory, Economics and Oriental Studies, mainly the History of the Middle East.

Professors Richard Pipes, Felipe Fernández-Armesto, Martyn Bond, Z.A.B. Zeman, K.V. Malý and others commented kindly on my manuscript and encouraged me to pursue my research.

Mr. Magnus Bartlett, my publisher, showed considerable courage in publishing a book of such controversial nature. Mr. Bijan Omrani, my editor, helped enormously to bring the text up-to-date, to include the latest publications in the field, and to introduce some useful explanations and additions to make the book more accessible to wider readership.

Throughout my work, which stretched over almost forty years, I had the benefit of the cooperation of my wife, Eva, who being a librarian, supplied me with all the necessary literature, accompanied me on my travels and acted not only as my diarist, record-keeper, etc., but she also read the manuscript in all its numerous phases and, thanks to her critical approach, various inconsistencies and inadequate formulations could be avoided.

I am also grateful to the publishers, Basil Blackwell for their permission to quote from their book, Letiche-Dmytryshin, *Russian Statecraft: the Politica of Iuri Krizhanich*. I have also used quotations from the book *A Message from Moscow*, but the author being Anonymous I can only express my thanks in this way.

"… for foreign barons and counts [Poland was] a half-Asiatic corner of Europe … Muscovy and the Ukraine were completely Asiatic."

Taras Bulba, Nikolai Gogol, p. 128
(translation by Peter Constantine, New York, 2004)

Preface

Before World War I, in 1910, Professor Thomas G. Masaryk, who later became the first president of Czechoslovakia, published a three-volume study under the title 'Russia and Europe'. This was misleadingly translated into English as The Spirit of Russia. The original title correctly showed Masaryk's intention to analyse European influences and traditions in Russian history and, especially, in its literature and political thought. This selective and limiting approach clearly indicates that Masaryk was well aware that there were also other influences and traditions which would provide explanation of other facets of Russian history in which a Europe-only approach could not succeed.

Previous attempts to come to terms with the enigma of Russian history were almost exclusively based on European-style approaches, literary analyses, studies of historical and political sources, etc. In short, their approach was similar to Masaryk's. 'Kremlinologists' tried to make sense of the utterances of political personalities and find some significance in the order Soviet bigwigs presented themselves on May-Day platforms. My approach had to be different. Oriental influences could only rarely be found in literature and hardly ever in contemporary political speeches. I had to concentrate on economic realities as far as these could be reconstructed for the earlier periods, use analogies with similar conditions where documentation or evidence was available, find models of Russian institutions in neighbouring countries East and West, and above all try to find what of the Asian heritage persisted in current Russian thinking and, consequently, in the aims and methods of Russian government. Some parts of my text were drafted during the Soviet era, and to keep its actuality, I left it in the present tense wherever it seemed useful.

It should be emphasised that this essay is not a course of Russian history, but merely an attempt to trace nomadic and Oriental traditions and to explain them as far as possible. To show that the widely accepted idea of a highly developed 'splendid' civilisation of early Russia is no more than a myth, it has been necessary to analyse the economic and social conditions of Kievan Russia in some detail.

Oriental influences in the Russian system of government, or in its way of life, have not escaped the attention of observers and scholars. Peresvetov in the sixteenth, Krizhanich in the seventeenth and Pososhkov in the eighteenth century saw the model government in Turkey except for some reservations mainly concerning religion. Travellers were struck by the country's Oriental appearance, from Herberstein, Fletcher and Olearius to Jenkinson, Korb and Custine. Chaadaev saw Russia as an Oriental despotism supported by an Oriental cult, in Chicherin's view Oriental despotism served as a model for Russia, while Plekhanov and, curiously, Lenin dreaded the reintroduction to Russia of the state ownership of all land, which they labelled alternatively 'Aziatchina' and 'Kitaishchina'. Kliuchevskii described basic aspects of Russian government and society of the mid-eighteenth century as 'characteristic features of states of an Oriental Asiatic structure, even if decorated by a European façade'. Russian poets Blok and Yesenin proudly called themselves 'Scythians' or 'Asians'[1].

Modern scholars were also well aware of Oriental elements in Russian history, but whereas the Soviet ones invariably tried to minimize or downright deny them, most Western scholars believed they were introduced only by the Mongols and were gradually squeezed out by the influence of Europe. Muscovy Russia would thus appear to be the most 'Asiatic' period of Russian history, whereas with Peter the Great Russia became gradually integrated into a wider framework of European civilisation[2].

In this way post-revolutionary Russia and the Soviet system could not be seen as continuation of earlier history; it had to be laboriously explained as an 'aberration' or 'deviation' based on some kind of 'specifics' found rather arbitrarily in the economy, social conditions or political situation of the twentieth century. Very few scholars were ready to see an uninterrupted, continuous evolution of economy, society and statecraft from pre-Mongol, and indeed pre-Kievan period to the present.

In 1948–49, after the communists seized power in Czechoslovakia, my teacher Professor Bohuš Tomsa gave a series of lectures at the Law Faculty of Prague on the 'ideology of totalitarian regimes' covering with considerable courage fascism, nazism and communism. He was promptly dismissed, but continued his work with a small group of his graduate students in the form of a private, or clandestine, seminar. He was arrested in 1956 and brought to trial, and the manuscript of his book was impounded. The trial eventually ended in acquittal, but the manuscript was never published.

I was at that time working on the social and economic background of these regimes, but being involved in the trial and expecting a house search, I destroyed all of my notes and drafts. I started again, but some years later when I prepared my escape to the West I had to destroy everything again. In England, the first draft of this book was ready in 1974, but my publisher rejected it after his supposedly academic reader labelled it 'hysterical cold war propaganda'. It was a sufficiently discouraging reception to make me drop the idea for another twenty years. Maybe after the disappearance of the 'untouchable' Soviet system and a full century after Masaryk's seminal work there is at last time to approach this fascinating side of Russian history from the hitherto unexplored and 'unacceptable' angle[3].

I can only hope that this updated and expanded version will now be judged on its merit without political hindsight, and that it will be treated in a more dignified way than its predecessor nearly a generation ago.

E. K.

introduction

The Fourth Civilisation

Traditionally, when speaking of Asian civilisations, there are usually three that spring to mind – the Arabo-Persian, the Indian and the Sino-Japanese. There is, however, the vast north of the continent which also had, since time immemorial, a distinct civilisation of its own: the nomadic one. And yet, this had never been acknowledged as such mainly for two reasons. First, all three others were sedentary agrarian civilisations with all the usual attributes such as literature, monumental architecture, painting and sculpture, and a tangible testimony of their character provided both in written and archaeological evidence. And they all considered the nomads from the steppes to be 'barbarians', uncivilised, brutal and more often than not unmentionable. The second reason was, or still is, that the nomads left hardly any traces of their own past. They had no script and therefore no literary records, chronicles or commentaries.

They had no permanent dwellings and therefore left no archaeological evidence apart from some tombs often difficult to date and interpret. The character of their civilisation has to be reconstructed from secondary evidence – chance remarks or comments in chronicles and historical records, frequently biased and hostile, occasional treaties and agreements concluded with the nomads, some elements in art pointing to steppe origins, commercial links reconstructed from archaeological finds, etc. Another method is using comparison with existing nomads and, wherever possible, with a way of life in similar economic and climatic conditions elsewhere.

We have to admit that, until very recently, literary and archaeological analyses were the main tools of modern historiography. Economic and sociological criteria and methods were rarely applied even where well-documented and developed civilisations were the subject. So, due to the absence of literature and archaeology, the nomads were again dismissed as 'uncivilised' and more often that not simply ignored.

Early Tribal Migrations 10th – 7th century BC

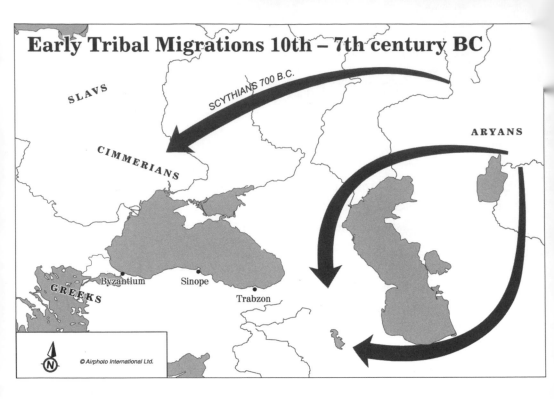

SLAVS

SCYTHIANS 700 B.C.

CIMMERIANS

ARYANS

GREEKS

Byzantium   Sinope

Trabzon

N

© Airphoto International Ltd.

Early Tribal Migrations 7th – 2nd century BC

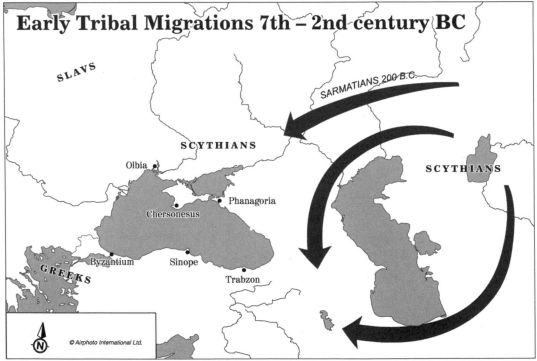

SLAVS

SARMATIANS 200 B.C.

SCYTHIANS

SCYTHIANS

Olbia

Phanagoria

Chersonesus

GREEKS

Byzantium   Sinope

Trabzon

N

© Airphoto International Ltd.

freedom & security
the early societies

When discussing the conditions of life in a primitive society of hunters and gatherers, two elementary points must be considered. First, man is a natural predator. Second, in order to survive, he cannot live alone. He must be a part of a group, a 'pack' which enables him to hunt for game and to protect himself against natural dangers and rival and hostile groups. The group thus becomes the provider of elementary security. But a group cannot consist of equal and independent individuals. That would mean endless quarrels and anarchy and exclude all possibility of concerted and organised action. Group life must therefore include a certain hierarchy and, eventually, some division of labour. A strongman would be chosen as leader or would seize the leadership because of his strength, prowess or cunning. In order to maintain his position, he would surround himself with an inner circle of trustworthy followers whom he would reward for their services and protection. To obtain the wherewithal for this reward, he would extract the means from the rest of the group – the outer circle. This method would be repeated on every level of clan, tribe or some higher grouping up to the level of a primitive 'state'.

The strongman or chieftain may be chosen by the 'elders', but would have no responsibility towards his 'electors'. His power would be circumscribed only by custom or (religious) belief. If he provoked enough dissatisfaction within the group, he would be deposed by force. In this way the members of the group obtained their security and help in their search for food against obedience to the leader and the 'payment' of contribution towards the maintenance of the 'inner' circle. A rudimentary hierarchy and a primitive system of taxation will thus emerge. The notions of freedom and security will appear in stark contradiction. Absolute freedom, i.e. liberty of movement and action, would be possible only outside the group. But without the group survival would be as good as impossible.

Within each community security was provided by kinship. Members of the family or clan protected each other and avenged collectively any crime committed against a member. On the other hand they were collectively responsible for any crime committed by a member. A blood feud *(vendetta)* or the collection of blood money *(wergeld)* was a matter for the whole clan. The freedom of action of each member was correspondingly restricted and had to conform to the collective action.

Evidently, most people in these primitive societies were neither slaves nor serfs. It is therefore tempting to call them 'free'. But if we define freedom, according to its Western and modern notion, as an individual's capability to decide for himself, to determine, within the law, his own moves, and to choose his own priorities, then this seems to be far away from the reality in which these societies had to live. Strict conformity, obedience and submission were *de rigueur* where life within a group was concerned. Exclusion meant death in hostile environments. So freedom and security may be regarded as mutually exclusive. And security, being more important for the survival of the individuality, the very notion of freedom and also that of individuality would be alien to people of those days. This changed dramatically with the appearance of early agriculture.

In essence, there were two possibilities. In the 'slash-and-burn' system of farming in forested lands the peasants were still living in small groups helping each other to clear the land, build their huts, etc. But although they shifted their dwellings and cultivated plots every few years, they were tied to their fields. Their requirement of security was therefore fundamentally different from that of a mobile group of hunters. They also became so to speak 'sitting ducks' for predators. So in order to survive, they needed to 'make a deal' with another group that would provide the necessary protection. Naturally, this was not necessarily a voluntary deal. More likely some predatory group would extract tribute from the peasants and prey on them in a parasitic manner. The peasants, dependent on their fields for their livelihood, were defenceless until, at a higher stage of development, they became capable of forming larger groups and to live in fortified settlements. Two different classes thus appear: subject peasants and dominating warriors. Simultaneously, the older stratification between a strongman-leader with his retinue and the outer circle of subservient members continued to exist within each class.

A different situation emerged where agriculture was based on artificial irrigation. On the one hand, much higher productivity of irrigated land made larger settlements possible. These, in turn, were permanent and did not require any periodic shifting. On the other hand, the digging of canals, their maintenance and distribution of water required large investments both in manpower and material, and a strong centralised system of government that would be able to enforce the required discipline and to extract the necessary contributions. The warrior class would thus split into bureaucracy organising labour and extracting taxes, and the military providing the required security. The peasants in this type of society became a much more important source of income than in the slash-and-burn system. They were therefore subject to much tighter supervision and to a much more complex system of labour and fiscal dues which, to some authors, symbolize the meaning of 'oriental despotism'. It is in this type of society, in connection with permanent dwellings and field labour, that a third category or class of people emerged – the slaves. They were either prisoners of war, hereditary slaves or individuals enslaved for various legal reasons (debt, punishment, etc.).[1]

The mobile warrior caste dominating the slash-and-burn peasants soon discovered, in places as diverse as Black Africa and Kievan Russia, that part of their subject population could be profitably creamed off and sold as slaves to hungry slave markets in other areas. The 'despotic' regimes running irrigated agriculture had unlimited need for slaves both for labour and for services.

Yet, another type of community was that of the nomads. Here again we can distinguish several varieties. The sea nomads, a special kind (they do not husband any flocks), move along the coast or even across some stretches of the sea following the fish as they still do, for example, on the east coast of India. There are the goat and sheep breeding nomads who shift their camps on the edges of deserts and mountains in search of pastures. They can still be seen in various parts of the Middle East. Although their society is tribal, they move in small communities and their tribal cohesion is usually rather loose. The most important type are the cattle breeding nomads of the Eurasian steppe who alone were capable of forming large groupings of tribes creating from time to time empire-size formations.

Their civilisation was different and in many ways certainly primitive, but it had a clearly defined pattern. Their social organisation, their laws, discipline and above all their military skill, both tactical and strategic, led them to some spectacular successes; sometimes, as in the time of Chinghiz-khan, they showed signs of real statesmanship and ability to organise vast empires efficiently. However, they never possessed the capacity to develop this civilisation. In spite of their mobility (or perhaps because of it), their civilisation was always static.

The lack of permanent homes did not encourage the nomads to create things of a permanent nature. This prevented them from exploiting the achievements and experiences of the previous generations, forcing them to learn all the basic skills again and again from the very beginning. Apart from the simplest personal belongings, they never developed a sense of property. There was very little to own, therefore practical communism was natural and easy, and there was no temptation to accumulate riches except by looting. There was no individualism: discipline was the accepted way of life. Because there was nothing to own and nothing to accumulate, there was also no inducement for progress.

The skills of the nomads were exclusively physical, not intellectual. Their spiritual ambitions never reached beyond primitive shamanism, and when they needed a script for administering their empires they had to borrow it from their subjects. Having no individual land possession, the organisation of nomadic life – and taxation – could not be based on land ownership or fields. The only effective way of assessment was by heads, which implied an organisation by units, similar to that of modern armies, with chiefs being, quite naturally, military commanders at the same time.[2]

In a way, the nomadic society resembled that of the hunter-gatherers.

There was a division between the nomadic élite and a subject population on which the élite would prey parasitically. Socially, the nomadic society was one of equals with the exception, of course, of the chieftain and his retinue. All of them were hunters and herdsmen in peace and warriors in wars or raids. As will be shown, the only division was based on rank. The horse-riding and cattle-breeding nomads had only a limited use for slaves in their own society, but gathered large numbers of them in raids on neighbouring agricultural communities merely to use them as 'walking merchandise' in their trade with settled communities. The same would apply to Viking raids on the shores of Western Europe and the Mediterranean.

For the steppe nomad security had a different aspect and different requirements than for a peasant. Not being tied to a field or a stable home, the security of the nomad lay in his mobility over vast expanses of land. This had deep repercussions in his attitude to land and fixed property in general, but primarily in the need for advance warning and fast movement. Information gathering, or spying, and an iron discipline were therefore the prime essentials of a nomadic society. Needless to say, any kind of freedom as independence from the leader's command had to be totally absent.

In their fragile and defenceless camps in open steppes the nomads had to accept danger as a permanent feature of their lives. To counter it they developed some distinct characteristics of their own. First, they turned vast stretches of the steppe into buffer zones which separated them from potential enemies. The consequence was their attitude to land – they considered it valueless in itself, but indispensable precisely for the purpose of security; any infringement of its integrity, however minute, immediately acquired the character of a threat, and was treated as a matter of life and death. Second, the security of the community depended on adequate intelligence both outside and inside the community. The prime purpose of the external intelligence was to provide advance warning of a possible attack; internal intelligence was designed to prevent subversion and treason. Both were treated with the same obsessive importance as the integrity of the land.

Spying and informing were accompanied by their correlates – suspicion and fear. Every outsider represented a potential enemy; every insider represented a potential traitor. Paradoxically, the security of the community thus brought with it a basic, if latent, insecurity of the individual who had to live with these suspicions and fears. Third, a successful defence demanded a high degree of mobility. This, in turn, could be achieved only if every member of the community was ready to move instantly without being attached to some particular possession or interests of his own, and if everybody was willing to obey the command of his superior. More often than not the enemy was to be avoided and tricked into ambush rather than faced in battle. The aim was to survive by destroying the enemy: and for this aim every means was acceptable. The fourth characteristic of the nomadic society was the command structure and the discipline that accompanied it.

The impact of all these upon the individual was considerable. He had to react in uniformity and conformity with all others. He was conditioned to obey without hesitation and to kill without scruples. Submissiveness and mental inertia dominated his personality. He was a collective being adapted to and conditioned by the circumstances he and his community had to live in. The community concerned with its own security developed certain organs and certain policies to safeguard it. There was a network of spies and informers reporting to the authorities at various levels. There were others who kept watch on foreigners and other suspects, and yet others whose job was to protect those in command and enforce their authority.

The command structure required that no rival command centre would be tolerated; anything approaching political opposition presented a threat to security and had to be eliminated forthwith. For reasons of security, power had to be absolute and the person at the top – the ruler – must have been in command of all security forces. This was likely to bring about a breakdown of security in the time of succession before new loyalties and new command had been established. At the same time the security forces – the power apparatus – were likely to influence the succession. In fact, under the nomadic system of power structure peaceful succession was seldom possible. Ample evidence may be found, for example, in the history of Turkey with its numerous depositions, assassinations, palace coups as well as, on the other hand, the Fratricide, the Kafes and other methods used to reduce or eliminate the challenge to the existing power holder.

As a rule, the mobility of the individual had to be restricted partly for economic reasons – men being considered the property of the ruler – and partly for the sake of security; if the command structure and the control of every individual had to remain effective, the movements of individuals had to be subject to command and closely supervised. Free movement had to be discouraged and eventually punished. This is quite understandable if we realize that everybody was part of a defence system and as such had to remain constantly within the reach of his commander.

Security reasons also demanded that whole peoples were sometimes removed from their homelands and resettled elsewhere. This method has been used by other empires and states as well and cannot be described as specifically nomadic; the nomads, however, used it with some degree of perfection. In a purely nomadic empire it was easy to send a disloyal tribe to some remote pastures surrounded by loyal territories.[3]

The principles of security as described above required an egalitarian society with no other distinction than military rank. To achieve the uniform reaction necessary for an efficient military operation, all individuals had to be equal in their obedience or subjection to the command. At the same time the mental inertia (the product of the command system) did not turn into the individual's disadvantage only when all were treated equally. It can be said that the system produced equality and was supported by it. Inequality or privilege of any kind would lead to a breach in the command structure and could eventually become a threat to security. Equality provided a certain rough justice, which made total subjection bearable and even enjoyable, especially for those conditioned to have as little individuality as possible. Absolute equality was, of course, difficult to maintain; in the course of time differences appeared in wealth, in social status, in various precedents and a privileged class would gradually emerge. Nomadic societies did not escape this development.

The basic difference between the Western and the Eastern (including nomadic) concept of freedom is that in the East man is regarded as being the property of the ruler, while in the West he is believed to be an independent being responsible for himself and endowed with a free will. Even if some philosophical schools denied such a free will of an individual, the Greek political system, the Roman law and Judaeo-Christian morality were all based on the belief that the individual is capable of distinguishing between right and wrong, good and evil, and consequently may be held responsible for his acts. The pivot of this thinking is the individual; the state is seen as a human creation and not some mystical entity with a supernatural existence of its own.

In the East the situation is quite the opposite. The duty of the individual is to obey. To distinguish between right and wrong and to decide upon the course of action is the task of the ruler who is identified with the state. The responsibility of the individual for his doings is therefore much narrower, restricted only to whether or not he conformed to the orders of the ruler. The state exists independently of the people and the law is the expression of the ruler's will.

The question of freedom becomes crucial in two points. First, as a heritage of Roman law, the individual in the West had certain rights, for example, to own, buy or sell things, to inherit, to marry, etc., and within the framework of these rights he could insist that his choice was respected by others and protected by law.

In the East any 'free area' could be filled arbitrarily by the ruler's will; the state could step in at any moment to direct the individual the way it decreed. Therefore there could be no 'right' of the individual and his actions could be protected by law only as long as it suited the state.

In Islam a man was considered free when he was not a slave. This narrow, negative and purely legal definition is about as far as Eastern thinking ever got in this field. This is not surprising considering the relation between the individual and the state: there was hardly room for anything else. Physical, personal freedom existed as a fact and not as a legal right. Deprivation of it was therefore not a legal punishment but an extra-legal device used for various, mostly political purposes.[4]

A distinction must be made between slavery, as it is generally understood, with an individual being private property of another individual, and a system in which all individuals were equally owned by the state personified by the ruler.

The society of the nomads

The Eurasian steppe zone, stretching from the lower Danube to the Yellow River in China, served from time immemorial as a huge reservoir of nomadic tribes, which from time to time inundated the border regions of civilised countries such as China, Iran and the Mediterranean area. The Scythians themselves came to the Pontic steppe from beyond the Volga River; in the second century BC the Sarmatians replaced the Scythians in South Russia. Beginning in the fourth century AD the nomadic world of Eurasia was in a state of almost perpetual flux, one wave pressing westwards after another. In the fourth and fifth centuries Turkish and Mongol tribes such as the Huns took the lead followed by the Avars and Khazars in the sixth and seventh centuries, the Pechenegs from the ninth to eleventh centuries, and the Kumans in the eleventh and twelfth centuries. The climax came with the Mongol invasion in the thirteenth century.[5] The migration of the Kalmyks to lower Volga in the seventeenth century was probably the last important movement on a large scale.

There were agricultural communities in the fringe areas between the steppe and the forests – in the so-called wooded steppe or forested steppe – where it was relatively easy to till the ground and where timber as a building material could be easily obtained. There were similar communities along the rivers in the steppe as well, but they used clay for their huts instead of timber.

These peasants were no match for the fighting skill of the nomads, and the nomads had no difficulty in subduing them. They ruled over them and extracted tribute from them; on the other hand, they also depended heavily on their products. 'The Scythian Empire may be described sociologically as a domination of the nomadic horde over neighbouring tribes of agriculturists.'[6] The same applied to the Khazars and to the Golden Horde. The structure of the Khazar state followed the traditional pattern of the nomadic empires of Eurasia – a horde of horsemen controlling neighbouring agriculturist tribes. Interest in trade added a peculiar feature to the character of their power.[7] Therefore a certain symbiosis existed between the nomads and their settled subjects – the nomads assuming a somewhat parasitic role.[8]

We may assume that, ethnically, the bulk of the peasant population in southern and central Russia was Slav from the times of the Scythians. The Slavs west of Kiev were subject to West Slavic, German and Roman influence, while east of Kiev they were strongly affected by the Iranian civilisation. There was not the same physical cleavage between steppe nomadism and agriculture that there was between the intensive agriculture of China and the extensive steppe economy of Mongolia. In South Russia the centre of gravity of the chieftains and rulers was unstable. 'At times it paid the ambitious chief to rely primarily on the following of pastoral tribesmen using their mobility and military potential to raid farming populations. At other times, it paid the ruler to associate himself with a fortified urban centre of power. An essential instability underlay the whole structure and the source of instability was among the nomads.'[9]

A comparison between the Russian fringe of the steppe and the Chinese fringe reveals the operation of two different modes of social history. On the Chinese fringe there existed a harsh cleavage between terrain that responded best to the intensive economy of irrigated agriculture and terrain that responded best to the extensive economy of pastoral nomadism. The two economic forms and the social structures based on them were so incompatible that they never merged with each other. On the Russian fringe there was a more gradual transition from arid steppe, which encouraged pastoralism, to rainfall steppe, which encouraged livestock economy in conjunction with rainfall agriculture. Conditions facilitated a transitional spread from 'pure' nomadism to a society of the Cossack type in which people lived in houses, but nevertheless were ready to migrate from one place to another.

The Russian extensive rainfall agriculture, capable of being combined with the grazing of livestock and with the exploitation of the forest, 'rapidly, though superficially, conquered enormous territories'. The Russian could carry on his general farming wherever he pleased, while for the Chinese it was an economic absurdity to farm intensively except within the cellular pattern of cities at a short distance from each other, each with its surrounding unit of closely cultivated land.[10] The intensive Chinese agriculture is bound up with a social order which is never successful without a close settlement, crowded villages and frequent towns. The extensive Russian agriculture is possible in isolated wilderness settlements with mixed pastoral and agricultural economy, which makes the transition from nomadic life much easier.[11]

The economy of the steppe had two main components – the animal husbandry of the nomads, in which milk presented the principle item, and the agriculture of the sparse peasant communities existing in places where the soil and climate permitted farming. The steppe provided the nomads with excellent grazing grounds and, moreover, communication between families and clans was fast and easy. Writing about present-day Mongols, O. Lattimore[12] finds that the essential thing about the nomads is not that they do move but that they can move.

The pastures required for their herds had to be enormous and had to be so combined that they provided suitable grazing both in summer and in winter. The allocation of these grounds, as well as the regime of water – a scarce commodity in most areas – required an organisation and authority over and above the family and clan unit. A tendency to larger units was therefore inherent in this system. Friction over pastures and access to water must have been frequent. Expanding the grazing grounds or moving over to other ones because of drought or other natural catastrophes was possible only at the expense of another tribe. To seek protection against such infringements, or to enforce their own expansion, tribes were compelled to form larger and larger units – groups of tribes, nations or even groups of nations. The essential unit of the pastoral nomadic tribe was the clan of blood kinship. Such clans did not wander haphazardly herding their livestock. They laid claim to definite pastures and to the control of routes of migration between pastures. War was a normal concomitant of their pastoral life.

The ordinary mobility of the nomad, arising out of his everyday life, could

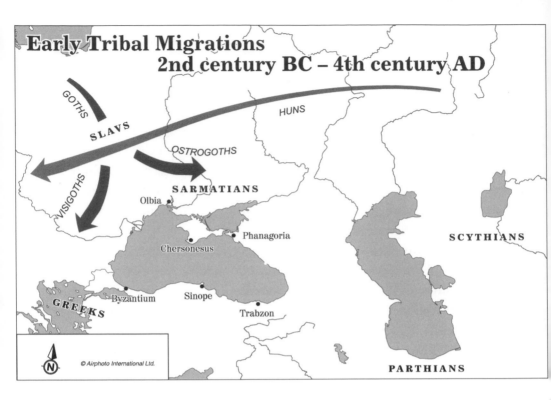

Early Tribal Migrations
2nd century BC – 4th century AD

GOTHS

SLAVS

HUNS

OSTROGOTHS

VISIGOTHS

SARMATIANS

Olbia

Phanagoria

Chersonesus

SCYTHIANS

GREEKS

Byzantium

Sinope

Trabzon

N

© Airphoto International Ltd.

PARTHIANS

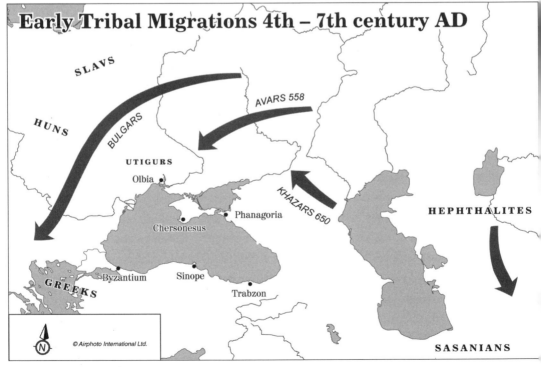

Early Tribal Migrations 4th – 7th century AD

SLAVS

AVARS 558

HUNS

BULGARS

UTIGURS

Olbia

KHAZARS 650

HEPHTHALITES

Phanagoria

Chersonesus

GREEKS

Byzantium

Sinope

Trabzon

N

© Airphoto International Ltd.

SASANIANS

be converted into military mobility with no special expense. The townsman and the farmer could not withdraw to evade attack; the nomad could.[13] On the face of it, this may have been an advantage for a subject who tried to escape his master. But there was a powerful device working against him. He was constantly watched by all his comrades. Each unit was collectively responsible for all its members. Collective responsibility exercised through the headmen of subordinate groups was the device for controlling this mobility. If one fled, the headman and all the others were responsible. These two principles, discipline and collective responsibility, formed a system in which each individual was inextricably intertwined.[14]

The circulation of goods within the nomadic economy seems to have been minimal. A reason for it may be found in the fact that private ownership was restricted to the bare minimum of personal belongings. There was no land to be owned and no houses to be furnished. All land was the property of the khan. The attitude to land ownership and landholding was probably the most significant feature of nomad thinking. Land was limitless and did not produce any economic value. Its only use was for grazing. It was therefore considered economically valueless. At the same time it acquired a mystical and sacred value totally abstract and detached from any particular plot, district or region. It was given to the people by God, and the khan, as God's trustee, was the sole owner. This is how Carpini characterised the khan's power: 'Let it be known further that everything is the emperor's property, so that nobody dares to say: This is mine and that is his, but everything belongs to the emperor, things, cattle and men. Quite recently the emperor issued an explicit law on this.'[15]

The organisation of the nomads was fairly simple. The twelfth–thirteenth century Mongols are the best-known example. Their sovereign (the khan or kagan) was surrounded by a group of *nokers* (corresponds to the Russian *'druzhinniki'*, members of an élite guard) and he acted as an absolute ruler with unlimited powers. The Eurasian empire was an association of clans and tribes on which the imperial authority and institutions were superimposed. The khan's clan held a position of honour. The khan was the head of the army, and the army formed the backbone of administration. Military organisation was based on decimal principle: greater family corresponded to a unit of ten, a clan to a unit of hundred, and a tribe to a unit of a thousand.[16] The commanders of the highest units, the *noyons*, had a privileged position comparable to that of the field marshals and generals in European armies, and more often than not had their own group of *nokers* around them. The bulk of the society were simple warriors who had to perform various services for their commanders, for instance, supply them with fuel, shear their sheep, and milk their cows and mares. These services may have been exacted in return for the allocation of grazing grounds, which probably led some observers to see in them an analogy with European feudalism. At the bottom of the society were the slaves, usually members of conquered tribes or peoples.

The nomadic transferable huts or yurts – according to Vernadsky, the Turkish word '*iurt*' means 'clan'– were usually built on a skeleton of poles covered with felt or hides. They could be easily dismantled and put together again. Another type could be put on a cart and transferred without dismantling. There was no furniture and the only equipment consisted of blankets and furs, some pottery, a few pieces of metalware – cauldrons, pans, knives – and eventually one or two caskets or chests with some clothing and other personal belongings. Theft was drastically punished, often by death.

Having this picture in mind, there can be no surprise that any idea of progress was completely alien to the nomadic society. Material incentives did not exist, apart from looting. Contacts with outside and more advanced communities were practically nil, and the pace of life in the perennial rhythmic movements was so monotonous and leisurely that the very notion of time seemed to be absent from it. This may well be the main reason why all our records of the nomads show the same picture, astonishingly similar even in minute details, in spite of being separated by two thousand or more years and by seven or eight thousand miles.

Poverty – or at least as we understand it – was at the very root of nomadic society. It is the poor nomad who is the pure nomad.[17] When the nomads modified their economy, their society and above all the status of their chiefs, they became vulnerable. The chiefs and nobles became less effective in their original functions because they became attached to new vested interests in trade, in levying of new kinds of tribute and in the taxation of new and non-nomadic agricultural and urban subjects. In times of defeat, on the contrary, the nomadic society got nearer to the sources of its true strength. 'Poverty sharpens the hunger for war of the whole people.'[18] Just as with freedom, it is likely that in respect of poverty and wealth the nomads had entirely different values from us. There was greed, of course, and an urge to plunder, but it was hardly motivated by any developed sense of ownership. Everybody being poor – and equally poor – nobody was actually feeling poor, envious or inferior. This egalitarian mentality was greatly helped by the military discipline, which implied privileges only on the basis of rank and, to some extent, of birth, but not of wealth.

The tax system was clumsy and inflexible, and whenever it was necessary to obtain some additional means, or perhaps replace the dwindling revenue from the existing sources, a raid was the easiest and, in fact, the only way to obtain them. 'That is why the economy of the steppe [...] was never rich enough to make a foundation for stable, centralised empire.'[19] But the purpose of plunder was not only financial or economic. It was a regular, organic, not an exceptional feature of the nomadic life. It was indispensable to hold the whole social structure together. Disengagement from the pursuit of plunder was unthinkable. The whole system of discipline and command would collapse and the central authority of the khan would disintegrate. This dual purpose of plunder raids can be detected, for instance, behind the periodic campaigns of the Ottoman Turks up to the end of the seventeenth century. The failure of these campaigns was probably the main cause of the decline of the Ottoman Empire.

The religion and the ideology of the nomads consisted of two principal creeds: the sky-worship and the sun-worship.

For some of the nomads, particularly those of Turkish and Mongol origin, the sky was the source of monarchic power. The khan ruled 'by the authority of Eternal Sky'.[20] He was believed to have been given this authority to rule over all people under the sky. As there was only one sky and the power to rule could only be bestowed upon one man at a time, it was clear that the chosen man could claim universal power. By this simple logic the idea of the universal empire was born. A chieftain could only assume the title 'khan' or 'kha-khan' when he succeeded in vanquishing and subduing all neighbouring tribes. His own tribe then felt quite naturally superior to others and his own role as 'the chosen arm of Heaven' was confirmed. But in general the khan was not regarded as a god or a divine person.

As Vernadsky puts it: 'The characteristic trait of each nomad empire was the feeling of universality which guided their builders. Each nomadic empire was a world state, potentially, or more than that – a cosmic monarchy.'[21] The urge to universal authority and universal order was a significant psychological factor in the growth of the nomadic empire. The reason for it will become evident when we recall the nature of the nomadic life, as it has been described above. In a military society authority and discipline must be absolute or it would break down. Everything outside the realm of authority represents a challenge and a threat and must be eliminated. It is the necessity to keep the authority absolute and the fear of a challenge that can be found behind the ideology of 'universality'.

Under the sky-worship system the election of the khan by an assembly, the *kuriltay*, was indispensable, even if it was sometimes a mere formality. The consent of the electors did not extend beyond the one act of appointing the ruler. It was not a principle of government. Once elected, the khan assumed unlimited power using fear as his main instrument; and his electors resumed their positions in the war machine according to their ranks, subject to the chief's command and ruled by fear as everybody else. Government by consent means ultimately a partial renunciation and sharing of power. Where all power is embodied in a single individual with universal aspirations, any consent becomes unthinkable.

The sun-worship was a little more complicated, although it was aimed towards the same goal. The khan was not given his power directly by the Sun, but claimed a personal relationship with the Sun-god. Either he was his direct descendant or he received a mystic investiture and ruled by the authority of the god.[22] The worship of the Sun-god or the God of light (Mithra) was common among the Iranians. Under the sun-worship the dynastic principle appeared fully justified. No election, no consent was necessary to enthrone the ruler. The birth itself contained the right.

In Persia, with the establishment of the Persian Empire, the sun-worship ideology became the root of the divine right and divine origin of the King of Kings.

The idea of a universal empire is here again reflected in the title 'King of Kings'. But the bearer of this title sees himself as god and an equal to gods. And because his origin is divine, his own descendants will enjoy the same right to rule as himself.

The Persian concept of king-god had some profound implications which were not limited to Persia. The person of the king was not human anymore. He was sacred, a superman and had to live up to it. The King of Kings was subject to no authority on earth. Being equal to God, he was the supreme and infallible judge and creator of legal as well as moral norms and the final interpreter of both. An elaborate ceremonial had to be introduced to inspire reverence and awe. Humility of the subjects had to be stressed to enhance the superiority of the ruler. Not to destroy this image, the ruler had to live in a strict seclusion and appear in public only occasionally and with suitable pomp. It was no wonder that this model played an important role in Byzantium, which, for centuries, was in constant touch with Persia; Persian traditions were deeply rooted in all its Asian provinces.

Due to the influence of Christianity, the Kingdom of Heaven replaced the claim for the domination of the temporal world. The idea of a universal empire, however, survived and found its expression in the concept of Christ the Ruler – Pantocrator – whose deputy on Earth was the emperor. In Byzantium there was no question of the emperor equalling God. Although his person was sacred, he was human and therefore subject to errors of judgement and to sin. His authority in affairs of state could not be challenged, but in spiritual matters the final authority was the Church. The emperor was himself head of the Church and he could appoint and dismiss the patriarch and the bishops. But, in theory at least, they were the interpreters of God's will and they had the authority to criticise the emperor's behaviour and even take him to task if he violated the law of the Church or, in their eyes, disobeyed the will of God.

After the collapse of Sasanian Persia the idea of the universal empire was passed on to the rulers of Islam, who regarded themselves as lawful heirs of Persia. Islam was, like Christianity, a proselytising religion, but unlike it and more in line with the original nomadic concept its programme was temporal conquest and world domination. The caliph's position was similar to that of the Byzantine emperor as far as his authority and power were concerned, but the religious aspects of it were more pronounced. The Omayyad and early Abbasid caliphs were theocratic rulers equally interested in the expansion of Islam and in the extension of their temporal holdings. The idea of Islamic universalism gradually faded when the caliphs were left with only nominal authority in religious matters, while effective political power was wrested from them. The last traces of Islamic universalism can be found in the ideology of the Ottoman Turks after the fall of Constantinople. The sultans regarded themselves as heirs of the emperors, and being at the head of a legal and theological hierarchy, they considered it their sacred duty to conquer the world for Islam.

The nomads in russian history

Russian historiography had to cope with several problems. By its geographical location and despite its enormous size Russia is a country on the fringe of three cultural entities or civilisations. Traditionally, it has been treated as part of Europe – the reason being, partly, the ethnic origin of the major part of its population, the Slavs, partly the closeness of its contacts, political, cultural, military, with nineteenth century Europe, and partly, perhaps mainly, the European character, at the same period, of its educated class and above all, its writers, musicians and historians. Some influence in the Middle Ages of the other cultural entity, Byzantium, has been acknowledged in religion and the arts, but its successor, the Ottoman state, has never been given any role except that of a military foe. And yet, for Muscovy Russia, from the mid-fifteenth century onwards, Constantinople of the Muslim sultans was no less an attractive model or partner as it had been under the emperors – except religion, of course.

The influence of Islam emanating from Persia can be detected in various fields even before that, but it was never allowed to play a role in the interpretation of Russian history. It will come as no surprise that under these circumstances the influence of the other large civilisation – that of the nomads – has been consistently overlooked or worse, denied. The century and a half of the Mongol domination has been acknowledged, but it has been treated merely as an episode without importance or consequences.[23] The existence of the nomads in earlier times in eastern and southern fringe territories or inside Russia proper has never been admitted. This omission is to some extent linked with the idealisation or, indeed, glorification of the earliest period of Russian history, the period of Kiev. The reason for this somewhat uncritical approach may be seen in the nineteenth century romanticism and twentieth century nationalism, for which a glorious and distant past was an important boost of national identity and pride.

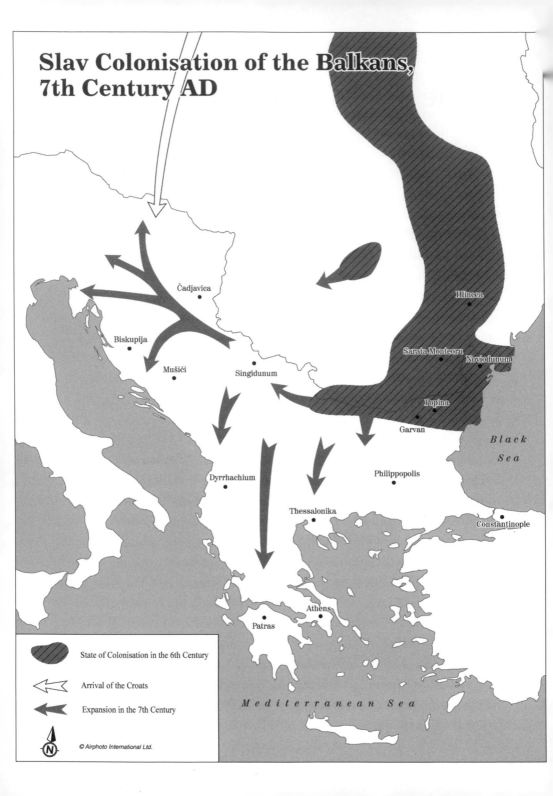

Slav Colonisation of the Balkans, 7th Century AD

Čadjavica

Hlincea

Biskupija

Sarata Monteoru

Noviodunum

Mušići

Singidunum

Popina

Garvan

Dyrrhachium

Philippopolis

Black Sea

Thessalonika

Constantinople

Athens

Patras

Mediterranean Sea

State of Colonisation in the 6th Century

Arrival of the Croats

Expansion in the 7th Century

N

© Airphoto International Ltd.

For this purpose the available literary documents, mainly Byzantine, the conversion to Christianity and the architectural monuments from the period were all interpreted as proofs of a high, even splendid cultural standard. Nevertheless, archaeological evidence is scanty and would not readily confirm this theory; nor would comparison with another Slav empire of that time, Great Moravia, whose archaeological exploration has been much more thorough and systematic than that of Russia. It was only with recent economic analyses concentrating mainly on the productivity of agriculture[24] that questions began to be asked whether such glorious empire could exist within the means it had at its disposal.

The interpretation of the earliest period of Russian history – the period between the late ninth and early thirteenth century commonly known as Kievan Russia – presents some formidable problems. Literary sources are rare, and only a few of them can be described as either indigenous or first-hand. Local or indigenous sources belong almost exclusively to the later part of the period, to the twelfth and thirteenth centuries. Earlier ones come mostly from foreign observers or compilers, Arabs, Jews and Persians. Byzantine chronicles contain a fair amount of information but most of it must be treated as second-hand. The same applies to some scattered references in West European annals.

Archaeological excavations have yielded few artefacts that can be considered with certainty as being products of local craftsmen or artists. The available publications of relatively recent dates seem to combine nationalist and Marxist bias with a tendency to introduce certain preconceived ideas into the interpretation of the finds.

Folklore and the origin of certain words and names can occasionally help, yet art, which elsewhere would be a major contribution to the understanding of the spirit of the period, can help only a little – so much it was in thrall to Byzantine traditions and values.

Faced with this situation, scholars inevitably resorted to the use of analogies, which, although acceptable in principle, is nevertheless a method fraught with danger. Understandably, it was almost exclusively Western Europe, which was used as a parallel or a model for the reconstruction of

Kievan civilisation.

In this way certain views became established, such as:

– that Kievan Russia was an under-populated country with an abundance of fertile agricultural land;
– that its economy was dominated by trade and that a developed urban civilisation existed;
– that certain social institutions, both urban, like the *veche*, and rural, like the *mir*, had essentially a 'democratic' character;
– and that before the Mongol invasion the population including the peasantry was 'free' – by which is mainly understood the absence of coercive domination, but often implying some legal safeguards against such domination.

A closer scrutiny would reveal that these views have been arrived at without considering the basic economic prerequisite: the available supply of food. The situation of agriculture in relation with the climate, geography and available technology therefore forms the starting point of this study.

Furthermore, much of the information which is available comes from Novgorod of the thirteenth century or later, but it has been rather indiscriminately applied to the entire realm of Kievan Russia and to the whole period spanning more than three centuries. In fact, the situation of Novgorod was altogether different from Kiev. It lay much nearer to the Baltic than to the Black Sea and had much closer contacts with Scandinavia, the Teutonic Knights and the Hanseatic towns than with the steppe nomads, Byzantium and Islam. These differences as well as, for example, the steppe element in the economy of Kiev and the fur trade in that of Novgorod are taken into account.

Finally, in view of the differences in geography, climate and cultural traditions, analogies with Western Europe seem out of place in many ways. Where appropriate, a different set of analogies has been used. The Great Moravian Empire of the ninth and tenth century had a similar geography to Kiev and similar economic conditions. It was also populated by Slavs. Recent archaeological excavations were carried out by modern methods, scrutinised in international conferences and published in a well-documented form. Forest farming and transport in Scandinavia in the sixteenth to eighteenth centuries, with a similar climate and soil conditions, had to grapple with similar problems as their Kievan counterparts. The same applies, *mutatis mutandis*, to the problems North American settlers encountered when they reached the zone of the prairies.

For the problems of society and government the Middle East provides closer parallels than Western Europe in such questions as land tenure, fiscal systems and the general relationship of the rulers and the subjects. Byzantium and later Ottoman Turkey often provided models for Russian institutions.

The nomads, who were for centuries the immediate neighbours of the Russians, also left their mark in the economy, in the social system and, especially, in the field of the military.

The Vikings were probably still nomads when they became the upper class in the Slav lands, and their civilisation was in a way superimposed over that of the sedentary peoples. Again, there was mutual influence: the Vikings were absorbed in the peasant mass, gradually adopting their way of life, accepting their language and customs but at the same time many of the nomadic values persisted, especially among the rulers. In the second half of the tenth century the Prince of Kiev, Svyatoslav, lived more like a nomad chieftain. 'He carried with him neither wagons nor kettles, and boiled no meat, but cut off small strips of horseflesh, game or beef and ate it after roasting it on coals. Nor did he have a tent, but he spread out a piece of saddlecloth under him and set his saddle under his head.'[25]

When a prince died, his favourite horse was buried with him. This practice continued some time after conversion of the Russes to Christianity. There are indications that human sacrifices were still taking place under the rule of Prince Vladimir (Saint Vladimir).[26]

Up to the end of the twelfth century, steppe nomads remained a constant threat on the south-eastern flank of Kievan Russia. In spite of that this period may be described as one with reduced nomadic influence. The settled population was increasing and several lines of forts were built, mostly along

Earliest Slav States, 9th Century AD

ESTONIANS

FINNISH TRIBES

Novgorod

Pskov

Suzdal

Bulgar •

BULGARS

Riazan

SLAV TRIBES

Vladimir

Chernigov

Prague

Passau •

Bratislava Nitra

Pereiaslav

Salzburg

Nagyszentimilkos •

PECHENEGS

KHAZARS

Zadar •

Black
Sea

Constantinople •

BYZANTINE EMPIRE

Great Moravia – Core size
Kievan Russia at the end of the 9th Century
Croatia at the middle of the 10th Century
Kievan Russia at the end of the 10th Century
Great Moravia at the end of the 9th Century
Empire of the Bulgars, 9th – 10th Century

N

© Airphoto International Ltd.

northern banks of steppe-rivers in order to protect the country against attacks. Similar fortified lines were still built by the Russians in south and east Russia as late as the eighteenth and early nineteenth centuries.[27] Numerous towns developed in this period, generally wooden fortresses with markets. A thin layer of townspeople – an urban middle class – began to emerge.

The Mongol invasions of 1221 and 1239–43 marked a reversal of this trend. They may have had an episodic character in themselves, but they influenced for centuries to come the entire development of Russian society. First, the defences against the steppe had broken down and the population in their numbers were driven into forests. Only the north-western part of the country with Novgorod and Pskov was spared. Trade was reduced to zero and the urban middle class, skilled craftsmen and merchants, virtually disappeared. The peasants, whether in the steppe borderland or in the forests, became more than ever dependants of their lords.

The nomadic notions of man ownership and personal bondage now extended more than before into the forested regions and the upper layer of society, just on the verge of accepting the values of a settled civilisation, was now again directly exposed to the influence of the nomads, their new overlords. For more than two hundred years the Russian princes with their retinues journeyed regularly to the Mongol headquarters on the Volga, received their investiture from them and delivered the tribute. These encounters were not always as humiliating as Carpini witnessed,[28] but had no doubt a profound influence on the Russians. It was not only 'barbarisation', as some authorities call it, but a gradual acceptance of the Mongol views and values which reversed the trend of evolution back where it was before the first attempts of Christianisation.

In this respect it can be said that Muscovy, when it emerged in the late fifteenth century as the dominant power in Russia, was a true successor of the Mongols. Yet it was not quite as some authorities have seen it.

The break with Kiev was not so complete and not so absolute. The settled, urban and 'civilised' elements were weakened and some of them eradicated, but the urban elements were only very sporadic and extremely weak before and the largest segment of the settled population, the peasants, was hardly touched by 'civilisation'. On the other hand, nomadic traditions and values became once more dominant and so strengthened that they were able to survive the Mongol domination for centuries.

This was by no means the end of the nomad story. After the victory of 'the forest over the steppe' came the colonisation of the steppes. And again, for centuries, the mixing with nomads continued, first, in the east on the Volga and between the Volga and the Urals. Then in the south in the Ukraine, east and west of the Dnieper until the fluid boundary was met by the Turks north of the Black Sea. The Turks were driven south and the boundary was pushed further until the coast was reached and Crimea annexed. There are no statistics and nobody can tell how many genuine nomads were included among the Russian population since the great drive south in the late sixteenth century. But from the late fifteenth century onwards, the rapid expansion and continuous wars taxed the resources of the government and the people to the breaking point and the authorities resorted to land grants linked with military service. The idea was that the servicemen would be supported by their estates. (The new *pomestie* was an adaptation of the older *kormlenie* and was modelled on the Turkish *timar*.)

It is known that an ever-increasing number of Mongols, some of whom had not even been converted to Christianity, became members of this so-called service gentry.[29] Some of them later held important positions and one, Boris Godunov, even became tsar (1598–1605).

There were noble families in Russia of Tartar and Mongol and other 'tribal' origin, and the process of mingling was even wider among the common people. It may well be said that the Cossaks, who formed the vanguard of this southern drive on the Dnieper as well as on the Don, were nearer in their way of life to their nomadic foes than to their peasant brethren who followed them. The nomads first retreated before the advancing Russians, but after the conquest of the Khanates of Kazan (1552) of Astrakhan (1556) and of Crimea (1783) they became subject to the rule of the tsar. On the Volga 'settled colonisation was still more retarded by the habitual raids of the Nogai Tartars, of the much more tightly organised Buddhist Kalmyks and of the Muslim nomad Bashkirs of the Middle Urals who struggled against Russian subjection right down to the end of the eighteenth century'.[30] Gradually, the nomads succumbed to settled life while further away the struggle with other tribes went on. It is reckoned that by 1920, 30 million out of the total population of 140 million were still nomads or semi-nomads.

The seLjuks & the russians

When the Seljuk Turks began their advance into Armenia and Anatolia, early in the eleventh century, they had already become acquainted with the urban population and highly developed civilisation in the Central Asian oases and in northern Iran. In the later half of the century, after the battle of Manzikert (1071) they established their capital in Erzurum and began to penetrate into the Anatolian high plateau pushing as far as Konya and establishing the Sultanate of Rum. It is interesting to compare the Seljuk sultanate with the contemporary principality of Kiev and the so-called Rus kaganate (the last prince bearing the title 'kagan' was Yaroslav the Wise, who died in 1054).

The Russians, just like the Seljuks, were a warrior élite preying parasitically on a settled farming population. But where the Russians had to extract their tribute from poor semi-migratory Slavs practising slash-and-burn agriculture and hunt among them for slaves, the Seljuks could prey on an efficient and a relatively well organised farming population with well established, mostly irrigated agriculture. Unlike the Russians, they had experience with towns, the word for which they took over from Persian *(shahr-shehir)*. From the Persians and the Byzantines they learned how to administer and tax their domains. They had at their disposal Koranic law and experienced Persian administrators and lawyers.[31]

As we can see both in Iran and Anatolia, the art and architecture of their period had reached a high level of sophistication and some aspects of it, like the monochrome architectural ornaments, must be rated among the supreme achievements of the Islamic art. The Russians of Kiev, on the other hand, had only their nomadic tribal traditions in administration, taxation and justice to fall back on. In certain fields, like religion, they borrowed from Byzantium. Their cities, few in number and small in size, were still hardly more than the old burgwalls.[32]

The only trading cities with genuinely urban population in touch with the Hanseatic cities in the Baltic were Novgorod and Pskov in the north-west but they were the first to be destroyed by the advancing Muscovy. Whatever experience there was with administration, taxation and justice in settled communities it was obliterated by the Mongols, who imposed their own nomadic ways on the whole country.

Carrying this comparison a step further, it becomes evident that when the successors of the Seljuks, the Ottoman Turks, began their push in the fourteenth century westwards across the Hellespont and into the Balkans, they were infinitely better equipped to run a centralised unitary state than were the Grand Princes of Muscovy when they embarked in the fifteenth century, after a century and a half of Mongol domination, on the fast expansion of their empire.

Summary to Introduction

The most important element in the nomadic way of life was the constant presence of danger. Not only was the climate harsh and the living conditions precarious; above all, there was a permanent risk of hostile incursions of other nomadic tribes, with not only looting and killing, but also the occupation of vital pastures and interruptions of migration routes. Security was therefore the prime requirement to which every aspect of life had to be subordinated.

Mobility and discipline were the main, indeed, the only means of guaranteeing an acceptable degree of security. The inevitable consequence was the lack of individual values and a strong sense of equality in submission to the leader.

Another consequence was the static character of nomadic civilisation, a way of life which did not change significantly over two thousand years. The skills required were essentially martial, not intellectual. The creative genius of the people which, with the lack of permanent homes, could not find outlets in architecture, painting or sculpture, found them instead in some lesser arts, such as textiles, embroidery, some metalwork and also music and dance.

The leadership of the group was usually, though not always, based on election, or sometimes, consent obtained by other means, but the elected chief, khan or kagan, was an absolute ruler, the sole owner of the realm, of the land and people alike, with no responsibility towards his electors. His power was, ideologically, based on the sky or on the sun. And there being only one sky and one sun, this resulted, quite naturally, in the idea of a monopoly of power and a world, or universal, empire. Among the sun-worshippers, the affinity with the sun-god soon appeared. The king was the son of the god, he became deified himself, and his descendants assumed power through their relationship with him. Thus, the idea of the dynasty appeared, something that among the sky-worshippers remained unknown. If there was succession within a family, it was based more on tribal seniority than filiation – and even that had to be confirmed by an election.

Part 1

KIEVAN
RUSSIA

Soil and Agriculture in Russia

URAL MOUNTAINS

P O D Z O L S

Saint Petersburg

Ufa

Moscow

Minsk

R. Volga

Ural River

Kiev

C H E R N O Z E M S

DESERT SOILS

Aral Sea

R. Dniester

Caspian Sea

Black Sea

CAUCASUS MTS.

N

© Airphoto International Ltd.

Chapter 1

Agriculture
&
the Production of Food

The key problem of the earliest period of Russian history from the ninth to the mid-thirteenth century – as indeed of the later periods and up to the present – is the production of food.

It is generally assumed that the bulk of the population lived on farming while a minority lived on hunting, fishing and gathering in the forests of Central and North Russia. It is also generally assumed that this agricultural activity was sufficient to support not only the sedentary communities, but also to produce a surplus which could keep large armies of mercenary cavalry in the field for indefinite periods. It is necessary, for the sake of this study, to look at these assumptions more closely.

The climate and soil are of decisive importance for agriculture. There is sufficient rainfall not to make artificial irrigation in any way necessary. The average annual precipitation ranges from 6 inches in the steppe to 20–25 inches in the west and north-west.[1] However, the rain often comes at the wrong time.[2] On the other hand, the growing season is relatively short varying between four months in the north-west, five and a half months in the central areas and about six months in the steppe.[3]

As for the soil, in the forest zone it is known as the *podzol*, which is 'sandy, clayish or stony in composition, with a low humus content and deeply leached'.[4] It can be and is farmed, but without fertiliser it gives relatively low crop yields. It requires deep ploughing to be of any use.[5] In part of the wooded steppe and through much of the steppe proper the prevailing soil is the fertile black earth or *chernozem*.[6] Only in the dry steppe, which is the semi-arid region in the south-eastern corner of European Russia, the soil is less fertile than the *chernozem*, but if artificial irrigation is employed, it can give high returns.[7]

Ploughing with a two-pronged sokha.
(From a 16th century miniature drawing by A. V. Chernetsov, 1972)

Another important factor which must be taken into consideration is the extent to which the soil could be worked with the implements available at the time. The soil in the forest is light enough to be scratched with a hoe or a wooden plough, which needs little pulling power. It can even be pulled by man. The implements used in the forest zone of Russia were, most probably, a wooden hook,[8] a forked wooden hoe or *sokha*,[9] and a wooden plough called *ralo*.[10] An iron ploughshare seems to have been known, at least in some areas.[11] As for pulling power, oxen were most probably used. The widely accepted belief that the horse was the main animal used for ploughing is open to serious doubts. First, it is easier to sustain cattle on open grazing in the forest than horses. Second, in winter cattle can be fed with straw and turnips, whereas horses require grain and hay. Third, oxen, even of a small breed, can provide greater pulling power than horses and can be put more easily into harness. The soft leather collar known in ancient times tended to interfere with the horse's breathing and made it suitable only for pulling light carts, chariots or sleighs. The stiff collar resting on the horse's shoulders became known only in the later part of the period, although it might have been known in certain parts of Asia earlier than in Europe. There were no such problems with oxen where the yoke could be tied to their horns. Consequently, at least in Western Europe, the horse began to replace the oxen only after the tenth century[12] and if White is to be believed, it took another two centuries before this happened in Russia.[13]

The problems were considerably more complex in the steppe. The soil there is very hard and in order to break it much more sophisticated implements and a good deal of pulling power were needed. 'Deep-rooted sod offers stout resistance to the plough and unless the turf can be effectively turned over and buried deeply enough to smother the native vegetation entirely, grass-roots will send up fresh shoots in the spring to crowd out young grain.'[14] To turn a deep furrow completely over, a mouldboard plough was needed. To pull such a plough through tough matted grass required a force several times as great as did the small scratch plough.[15] In America, when the settlers came to the edge of the prairies early in the nineteenth century, wooden and cast-iron ploughs of the time could not cut through the deep and thick prairie sod. A much larger and much heavier plough had to be invented in order to break and turn the sod. But the soft soil stuck to the rough iron making the plough so heavy that a team of six oxen could scarcely pull it. The solution was steel, which could be sharpened and polished smoothly. The first steel plough was made in 1823.[16]

According to McNeill, 'ploughs technically capable of penetrating the grasslands were not unknown in Pontic and Danubian Europe [...]. In the thirteenth century pioneers from Western Europe brought back the mouldboards into Transylvania [...].'[17] But it was a much more expensive implement which required altered field shape, new property concepts and

larger plough teams, so Magyars, Slavs and Rumanians saw no compelling reason to imitate the Germans.[18] Ploughs with metal ploughshares, or more often with wooden shares reinforced by metal became 'less rare' in the Carolingian period. The heavy plough with a fore-carriage, an asymmetric mouldboard and two handles is illustrated in the iconography of France and England in the eleventh century, but apparently reached Germany and Italy only in the fourteenth century.[19]

In Russia the acquisition of the stiff horse-collar and the mouldboard plough made the large-scale colonisation of the steppe possible, but this only happened in the latter part of the seventeenth century. No doubt, some farming in the steppe existed in the Kievan period, but it was restricted to patches of soft soil which was easily cultivable.[20] Until quite modern times the grassland grainfields had the proportion of gardens.[21] Cross[22] believes that at the end of the reign of Yaroslav the Wise (mid-eleventh century) the steppe was 'colonised' some 200 kilometres south of Kiev. This may well apply only to the security of agricultural settlements based on the cultivation of suitable patches or river beds rather than to a continuous cultivation of the grassland.

In the forests arable land was obtained by cutting down the trees and by burning the undergrowth. This was technically easy. The ashes fertilised the soil, which for a number of years could then be sown; the time varied from two to eight years depending upon fertility. When it was exhausted it was allowed to go back to forest. An estimated twenty five to forty years were necessary for the field to recover its fertility.[23] This is known as slash-and-burn, or the *podseka* system. In the forest-steppe and steppe zone new land for tillage was more difficult to obtain as easily workable patches were fewer and not necessarily within an easy distance. There was no fertilising by ashes and the fields were exhausted rather more quickly. When they were abandoned they were allowed to go to grass and could be used as pastures.

Tretiakov[24] believes that soil conditions in the forests were less favourable for farming than in the steppe, but he does not discuss the technological problems of the matter. His view is obviously based on Grekov's;[25] according to him, a single ploughing of the steppe soil can give crops for several years.

The experience of a Kazakh settlement in the region of Torgay in the nineteenth century is cited as evidence, but nothing is said about the soil, irrigation, etc. (in my view this case should be treated with extreme caution and it should certainly not be generalised and applied to the Kievan period). Blum[26] speaks only of 'continuous cropping' of a field for several years. Once exhausted, it was left for an indeterminate number of years while other fields were used.

Both systems required periodical shifting of settlements. This fact led some scholars to the conclusion that neither the *podseka* nor the field-grass husbandry *(Brachlandwirtschaft)* was compatible with a sedentary way of life. According to Pokrovsky, the entire population migrated continuously from one place to another. Only much later were the peasants tied to the land.[27] Tretiakov believes that from the eleventh century the population lived in permanent rather large settlements.[28] Fields were regularly worked and field boundaries were fixed.[29] Although *Pravda Russkaya* is cited as evidence, it is not explained how did this comply with the migratory character of the *podseka* system, especially when, according to the same author, evidence of a three-field rotation system does not begin before the fifteenth century.[30] It seems that, for Tretiakov, the *podseka* system ended with the introduction of ploughing. Yet, without crop rotation and manuring, the soil could hardly be re-fertilised by simple fallowing on a year-to-year basis. A *'lesnoy perelog'*, used in some areas until the eighteenth and nineteenth century, consisted of exploiting a field for 3–4 years followed by a 10–16 years rest.[31]

It is worth noting that the slash-and-burn technique was used in America at an early stage of colonisation in the seventeenth and eighteenth century. In Scandinavia, in parts of north-central Sweden and in Finland, it survived until the end of the eighteenth century and in some parts of Russia well into the nineteenth century.[32]

Lack of meadows available for haymaking made it impossible to feed livestock in winter. The resulting lack of manure led to reduced crops.[33] In fact, crops were so low that, for example, in Sweden butter was used to pay for grain.[34] The basic crop in Kievan Russia was probably rye, which also 'happens to be the cereal crop with the lowest yields'.[35] In Sweden rye sown into the ashes gave crops for two years.[36] Millet apparently gave the best yields.[37] Wheat was probably grown in the Pontic littoral from ancient times, but it is unlikely that it was grown in the south-Russian steppe. W. Rubruck mentions rye and millet at the banks of the Don in 1255 and says: 'wheat does not grow here very well'.[38] Oats were probably introduced at a later period. Its absence during the early stage could have hampered the breeding of horses in areas where outdoor grazing in winter was impossible.[39] From these preliminary considerations the following conclusions can be drawn:

1) The bulk of the farming had to be done in forested areas. Farming in the forest-steppe or feather-grass steppe belt was limited to areas or patches of softer soil. In the short-grass steppe it was still more restricted. In view of this, some established opinions should be treated with caution (for example, Grekov's and Vernadsky's belief that three-field farming was known in Kievan Russia, which Pokrovsky and Tretiakov place only in the fifteenth or sixteenth century[40], or that the south of Russia served as a granary for the north[41]).

2) The yields of such farming were necessarily very low. According to Pipes, the average Russian ratios in the Middle Ages were about 1:3. This 'means an annual doubling rather than tripling of the sown seed, because each year one of every three grains harvested must be set aside for seed. It also means that one acre of arable out of every three has to be devoted to seed production [...]. It may be said that civilisation begins only where one grain of seed multiplied itself at least five times; it is the minimum surplus which determines whether a significant proportion of the population can be released from the necessity of raising food to pursue other occupations.'[42]

D. Treštík in his comments on agriculture in Bohemia in the tenth–twelfth centuries believes that the yields were even more modest despite the fact that the climate and the soil conditions were generally more favourable. 'The average harvest was perhaps two grains for each grain sown [...and] animal husbandry gave equally low yields.'[43] It must be assumed that Russian agriculture remained on subsistence level at least until the end of the Middle Ages. According to McNeill, it entered the commercial stage only with the introduction of the mouldboard plough and the horse-collar and with the colonisation of the steppe in the late seventeenth century.[44] Hellie gives the 1:3 ratio for the seventeenth century with an increase in the yield ratios coming only around 1850.[45]

Under those conditions the farmer was able to produce enough grain to feed himself and his family and to save enough for the next year's sowing. There was little, if anything, left to support non-farming population of any size whether by means of a tribute, or by means of markets. An interesting calculation is given by Pipes[46]; it shows that because of the short farming season Russian agriculture required more manpower than elsewhere to produce the same result. 'Any job requiring x workers y days of full time to complete, will – if it must be done in $\frac{1}{2}$y time – require 2x workers.' This is no doubt true; but to provide the average food supply per head the yields thus obtained would have to be doubled. As this was technically impossible the result of Pipes' equation would be not only great intensity of work and pooling of resources,[47] but also half rations of food for everybody. As the work has presumably been done in half the time, the question arises what did the entire labour force do and eat for the rest of the year?

3) There are differences of opinion among scholars as to the importance of agriculture in the economic context of the period. For example, Kliuchevsky and Roshkov maintained that agriculture (sc. farming) did not represent the dominant economic activity of the population, while Grekov (and Khvoyko before him) finds a number of reasons to believe that it was.[48] There is evidence that among early Slavs (Czechs, Moravians, Poles) agriculture was a subordinate activity. The Slavs, for example, did not learn from the Germans to use the heavy wheeled plough[49] nor was 'Slavonic' economy stimulated to conquer fresh soil in order to extend arable farming.[50] With the low productivity of farming, the fiscal importance of land was minimal. In other words, if there was little or no surplus of agricultural produce, the lords' or princes' interest in tribute rent was correspondingly low. So the population was subjected to multifarious compulsory services, but was under no obligation to aim at maximum production of cereals.[51]

Excess labour supplies were not used but sold in bulk – as slaves.[52] This provides the answer to the question raised under point No. 2 above.

4) Some authors (Grekov, Tretiakov) base their conclusions concerning the economy and society of Kievan Russia on the assumption that land was cheap and plentiful and that there was a permanent shortage of labour. In fact, the supply of land had its natural limitations due to the soil, nature of the terrain, distances and technology. Because of the farming technique, in the *podseka, perelog* and *fieldgrass* systems, much more had to be available than was actually farmed. If, for example, a *podseka* plot could give crops for 2–3 years and then had to rest for 10–20 years, it means that there had to be, on average, five to seven times more arable available than was needed to sustain the population.[52a] With the low yields then obtainable the acreage needed to provide the minimum supply of grain had to be fairly large – and five to seven times more had to be kept in reserve or in partial preparation all the time.

There is no evidence that, as Blum believes,[53] these wasteful systems were abandoned some time in the ninth century or even earlier; his assumption that the fields were distributed on a permanent basis and continuously worked does not agree with the migratory character implied by reliance on the *podseka*; if the two or three-field system really had become dominant, it is hardly conceivable that the old wasteful system would have survived until the eighteenth or nineteenth century.

5) We might ask why the excess labour supply – mentioned above in point No. 3 – had not been used for the expansion of the arable. It seems that under the circumstances expanding the arable would make little economic sense, as it could not solve the problem of the 'half-ration' yields. The equation would be something like this: to obtain a given yield in half the time, a double labour force is needed (cf. Pipes' equation above). In Year 1 this double labour force living on half rations farms Land A. In their spare time they prepare Land B for sowing in Year 2. But in Year 2 the same labour force (plus some natural increase) would have to work Land A and Land B at the same time. Clearly, the size of Land B could only be in proportion to the natural increase in the labour force and it would, at best, provide them with similar half-rations

turning them into excess labour force for the rest of the year. In addition, between Year 1 and Year 2 harvests this increase in labour forces would have to live off the rations of the original number.

6) From what had been said under 3, an altogether new element has to be introduced into the picture, namely a large section of non-farming population that had to be supplied with food the farming sector was unable to provide. Leaving aside for the time being the revenue raised by the slave trade (which will be dealt with below), it must be assumed that other sources of food had to be available to feed not only the various service classes or groups, but also the prince and his retinue and indeed whole armies which were more or less permanently in the field. Clearly, hunting, fishing, bee-keeping or collecting honey would not be sufficient. The only plausible answer to this question is the existence of a large sector of animal husbandry alongside with farming, especially cattle breeding, centred on the steppe area of the country.

7) If there occurs a natural increase in the population and the current surplus of food available from a given area of arable does not suffice, then the situation can be solved either by increasing the arable or by improving the yields. The limitations of the former and the technological impossibility of the latter have already been discussed. Instead, there came about the annual creaming off of the population surplus in the form of slave trade. The economic explanation of this phenomenon can only be that the sale of slaves brought the prince more revenue than a tribute levied on farming. The farming population was not considered as a source of revenue for the prince and of food for the non-farming population, but primarily as a breeding ground for slaves.

8) In view of the low productivity and overall low yields of agriculture it would seem that the total population of Kievan Russia would have to be fairly small.[54] If farming were the main source of food, the numbers of those not actively engaged in it would have to be tiny by any standards.[55] And yet we are told that large armies were repeatedly sent as far as Constantinople, and that numerous and populous towns existed along the main trade routes. Either of these two phenomena implies considerable numbers of people not

engaged in farming.

It can be taken for granted that the peasant population could not take part in military campaigns; the growing season being so short and intensive would not allow any withdrawal of manpower. At the same time winter campaigning was difficult, if not impossible, and the long distance expeditions were by no means limited to any 'off-season' period. How was it possible, then, that some 80,000 men were besieging Constantinople in 907 for more than a year without disrupting the precarious balance of domestic food production in any way? Equally, it can be assumed that these men were not assembled and trained just for the purpose of one campaign; more likely they were part of a warrior caste which lived off the country without ever being engaged in farming. In addition, a sizeable amount of food had to be made available each year to supply the caravan to Constantinople[56] and other commercial ventures of the sort. The journey to Constantinople lasted not less than six weeks[57] and the annual caravan must have numbered several thousand men – traders, slaves, escorts, etc.

9) Given the character of the country, the only adequate source of food as an alternative to agriculture could be animal husbandry. The nomads in the steppe practised cattle breeding on a large scale since time immemorial. Animal husbandry provides a perfect answer to all the questions raised above. Neither the climate nor the soil conditions would affect it. It would provide ample food for the warrior class or caste as well as for the various service groups. It would provide a ready supply of food 'on the hoof' for caravans and armies, and it would make large numbers of men available at any time for slave-hunting raids and for military campaigns.

This would, of course, constitute a different way of life for that part of the population engaged in animal husbandry. If we accept the idea of cattle breeding as an alternative source of food, then pastoral nomadism would have to be acknowledged to have existed alongside farming. There is nothing new or special in the co-existence of these two economic and social formations. The symbiosis of the nomads and the peasants is an age-old phenomenon. Not only did the nomads rely for their subsistence on pastureland, but also on ready supplies of agricultural produce. 'The tendency of the nomad to shift towards an agricultural mode of life brought the steppe of Eurasia into an intimate relationship with the wooded steppe and the Black Sea coast [...]. The resultant interest, compounded of envy and contempt, which the Eurasian nomad showed for the farmer and merchant, underlies much of the human drama in the medieval history of Eastern Europe.'[58] The Scythian Empire may be described sociologically as a domination of the nomadic horde over neighbouring tribes of agriculturalists.[59] Nomadic peoples depended economically on neighbouring peoples for supplies of agricultural products and handicrafts.[60] The structure of the Khazar state shows the traditional pattern of the nomadic empire of Eurasia – a horde of horsemen controlling neighbouring agricultural tribes.[61]

10) The crucial fact is that by virtue of their way of life, their skills and their training, the pastoral nomads were the natural rulers, while the peasants were the subject class on which the nomads preyed regularly exacting from them tribute as well as slaves for the foreign markets. However, it would be wrong to regard the nomads as regular producers of an excess food supply. They were not producers at all. Their economy based essentially on milk was parasitic, not productive.[62] They grazed their herds and flocks and took from them what they needed, but they did not cultivate them. They treated their peasant subjects exactly in the same way.[63] Nevertheless, they had the potential to provide extra food when necessary by slaughtering their animals, or by delivering them to their sovereign in the form of tax or tribute.[64] Given the necessary organisation and discipline, herds of animals could be brought at a given time to a given place to supply a large-scale venture like the aforementioned annual caravan or campaign. But there was no marketable food surplus. For reasons discussed below, the nomads never traded with food or with any other goods of their own production. They did not produce, grow or manufacture anything for trade despite the fact that they were great traders. The only items which they sold and which might be called 'products' were hides and, to some extent, also wool. But they fleeced and skinned their animals in the same way as they stripped and looted their peasants or

raided their neighbours. There is a functional difference in the mentality of a predator and a cultivator and these two are hardly compatible.

11) We may assume that the Pontic steppe between the estuaries of the Danube and the Don – and perhaps the Kuban peninsula as well – provided the winter pastures for the Russian cattle breeders. The Greek treaty of 945 seems to give some evidence of this.[65] When the southern steppe was lost to the Polovtsy, not only was the trade diverted to the Volga route, but there began a population movement towards the north-east, to the Volga-Oka basin where the conditions were similar to the Kievan area. A fringe of a steppe suitable for combining farming and cattle breeding could also be found here, but the climatic conditions were less favourable. In particular, winter grazing became more difficult and the cattle-breeding sector of the economy suffered.

The social changes which began to appear precisely in that period were no doubt connected with the basic changes in the economy. When the Mongol invasion in the thirteenth century deprived the Russians of the remaining steppe pastures, the consequences were even more pronounced. The displaced cattle breeders and their descendants roamed the country in search of food and it took several centuries before the sedentary population absorbed them. The notorious vagrancy of the Russian peasants may be seen as the last stage of this assimilative process.[66]

A similar process took place in the Great Moravian Empire, which was also located on the fringe between the forests and the steppe with a mixed agrarian and cattle-breeding economy. When the invading Magyars snatched the grazing grounds at the beginning of the tenth century, the centre of gravity moved to Bohemia, where a purely agrarian, forest-type economy has been exercised, and the state known as 'Great Moravia' ceased to exist.

12) On the face of it, the area of Novgorod could not produce high agricultural yields because of its climate and geographical location. This was the typical country of the 'grain consuming north', which had to be supplied by the 'grain producing south'.[67] It is believed that the necessary grain supplies came from the Volga-Oka region, and to some extent from the Baltic countries.[68] But Rybakov[69] speaks only of 'episodic imports of grain and flour'

71

from Volga Bulgaria and Western Europe; a poor harvest could quickly put Novgorod into dependence on the 'southern grain growing countries', and the Volga principalities were in a position to cut its supply route. The grain was rye and it was transported by boat and cart. This would mean that the supplying region lay further down the Volga, that the imports were not regular, and that their extent had to be limited because of transport problems. Consequently, the main food supplies had to come either from Northern Germany or Poland, or from local resources.

It is tempting to speculate that higher productivity of agriculture had been achieved by a combination of more efficient farming techniques and a different system of land tenure. If Grekov believes that three or two-field rotation systems were introduced in Russia in the eleventh or twelfth century,[70] this may have applied to Novgorod, where contacts with German merchants already existed and information of West-European farming techniques may have been obtained. Similarly, German law *(Sachsenspiegel)* may have been known and its long-term hereditary lease *(emphyteusis)* applied.[71] However, Pipes prefers the theory of grain imports.[72]

As an example of Soviet statistics, Beranová[73] quotes yields of 1:30–1:40 for slash-and-burn agriculture in the Kievan period and sometimes (exceptionally) 1:60, 1:70 and even 1:100. These yields would be equal to or even slightly superior to those of the most modern and most productive European and American farms.[74]

Chapter 2

sLave trade

Slave trading was by far the most important item in the economy of Kievan Russia. According to the sources of the period, large numbers of slaves were shipped annually to the markets of Constantinople via the Dnieper and, most probably, via the Volga to some other Middle Eastern markets as well. The trade continued after the Mongol occupation of Russia. Taken over by the Genoese merchants it came to an end only in the mid-fifteenth century with the fall of Constantinople.[1]

In connection with what has already been said about the Kievan economy, the slave trade poses several questions. The first concerns the source of the supply, in other words the origin of the slaves. Referring to historical sources, the slaves were coming from Russia ('[…] from Russia furs, honey and slaves'),[2] or were described as Slavs.[2a] But more often they are referred to merely as 'slaves' without giving any indication of their ethnic or local origins. On the other hand, apart from the distinction between the Russes and the Slavs, there is no sign that these slaves were in any way different from their captors. If this had been the case, then it is highly probable that the chroniclers would have hinted at it, one way or another. For example, the ethnic differences between the Finno-Ugrians or the Turkic nomads and the Slavs must have been so conspicuous that they would not have escaped the contemporary observer. Therefore it can be assumed that the slaves exported from Kievan Russia were Slavs and that they were ethnically not different from the 'Russians'. Rybakov[3] speaks of 'Russian slaves'. Elsewhere he says that the slave trade scattered Slavs to all parts of the Byzantine and Arab world.[3a]

The second assumption must be that these slaves could not be prisoners or captives from raids or campaigns waged by the Russians against other ethnic communities. There were probably not many raids on the Finno-Ugrian forest hunters; all the steppe nomads with whom the Russians fought both south and east were Turkic tribes, whether Khazars, Pechenegs, Kumans (Polovtsy) or others. There certainly must have occurred some intertribal feuding and fighting among the Eastern Slavs, but in the tenth–eleventh century Kiev it was hardly on a scale warranting a sufficient supply of this most valuable merchandise. And, more importantly, wars could hardly guarantee a regular supply of slaves for the annual shipment to Constantinople.[4] It seems probable that the demand for Turkic slaves on Byzantine and West European markets was negligible. Slaves were used predominantly for work or domestic services, for neither of which were the nomads any good. Their skills were essentially martial and a demand for them appeared only when they began to be used as soldiers.

A regular supply of slaves necessitates a permanently available source that could be tapped at regular intervals without much effort or risk. Such a source could only be Kiev's own peasant population, defenceless and sedentary. There is, in fact, literary evidence that this must, indeed, have been the case. Both the *Russian Primary Chronicle* and Constantine Porphyrogenitus describe how the Prince of Kiev and his retinue would start their tour, usually in November, of the Slavic tribes subject to tribute in order to collect it. This was known as *poludie* (touring the people).[5]

The prince may well have collected the tribute from the forest hunters in the form of furs, wax and honey. But this could hardly be the principal objective of such an expedition. This purpose is indeed contradicted by the fact that, according to some sources, only a minute part of the tribute was destined for the prince's own use.[6] Leaving aside the obvious argument that November is not the best time to collect furs – best furs are usually obtained in winter and should be therefore collected in spring – all three items usually mentioned as staple Russian exports are easily enough transportable. Nor was the scattered forest population likely to offer any serious resistance to the collection or exaction of the tribute. Why then did the prince have to undertake such a large-scale 'collection campaign' himself?

The tempting analogy with the West European habit of an itinerant princely court that journeyed round the country collecting taxes in kind would also be misleading for several reasons. First, the productivity of agriculture would hardly permit feeding a large group of people at any one spot for any length of time. Second, the population was too dispersed to allow for the surplus of food, if any, to be concentrated in sufficient quantities at places where the prince's retinue would halt. Third, the 'court' went on its rounds in winter only – a curious reason, if the collection of provisions were to be the main purpose, for river transport rather than sleighs was better suited for any bulk shipments (cf. below on transport). The time was equally unsuitable for the collection of grain tribute. If there were any grain, it would have to be collected immediately after the harvest. Therefore it seems that the *poludie* had an entirely different purpose: to exact tribute, but not of furs, wax and honey, and not of food, but of slaves. As a slave-hunting expedition it was undertaken at the right time and with the right means.

The peasant population was fully occupied during the growing and harvesting season, but when this was completed a part of it became 'surplus labour' that could be dispensed with until its place would be filled again next spring by natural increase. At the same time, from the prince's point of view, this surplus labour represented a 'dormant asset' that could and should be turned into profit. Economically, this manpower drain had to be carefully managed because the loss of too many hands would mean a reduction of arable and hence starvation. This would ultimately lead to the reduction of the revenue of the prince. On the other hand, the productivity of farming being as low as it was, the prince was not very interested in the expansion of the arable – except as a means of growing more slaves.

Expressed differently, what the peasant produced and what could be taken from him as tribute – his surplus production – was less than a slave would fetch on the market. If the slave trade was profitable, then the value of the peasant was not in his work as a farmer. For the prince – and it will be shown below that the power of the prince was absolute and any 'freedom' of the

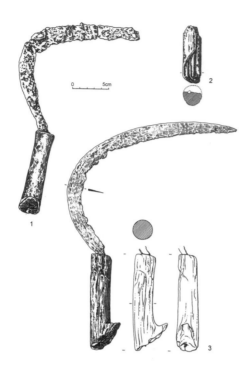

Sickles. Great-Moravian artefacts, excavated at Mikulčice, district Hodonin, Moravia.

peasants was a myth – the leading motive was the value of the people as slaves and producers of slaves rather than the value of land as a source of revenue derived from farm produce.

In abstract terms, the economic thinking of a slave-trader would be different from that of a landlord. In order to increase his revenue, the landlord is interested in expanding his holdings, in rationalising production and in increasing productivity. His serfs or tenants may be seen only as tools in this process, but when he sees that he can improve their performance, he will provide the right conditions for it. Feudal landlords in the West, hereditary possessors of their estates, understood this only too well. But the slaver's thinking is much more primitive. People being his merchandise, his interest is in getting as many of them as possible on the market and selling them for the best price. His 'husbanding' is therefore limited to providing 'breeding and grazing' grounds for his flock. It is a parasitic approach *par excellence* of the same kind as that of the pastoral nomads towards their herds of cattle. It should come as no surprise that the ruling élite in Kievan Russia should be slave-traders and nomads at the same time.

Turning back to the *poludie*, winter presented the most suitable time for its accomplishment, for the peasants were huddled in their huts and could not hide in the woods. The raiders on horseback and with sleighs could move rapidly from hamlet to hamlet without being confined to rivers and portages. The captured slaves needed no transport. If the expedition was a raid rather than a relatively peaceful collection of tribute, the provisioning of small and fast-moving raiding parties from local resources would become possible. This seems to be confirmed by Gardizi: 'Constantly 100 or 200 of them come to the Slavs and by force seize from them maintenance while they are there. From the Slavs many men go and serve the Russes in order that through their service they may be safe.'[7] It would seem that the differences between the hunters and the hunted was not based on any inter-tribal fighting nor on an ethnic difference – except that between the Russes and the 'Slavs'. More likely the division was that of the rulers and the subjects, the warriors and the farmers, the nomads and the peasants.

Although a certain amount of voluntary enslavement cannot be excluded – life in Constantinople, even that of a slave, would no doubt have its attraction – it must still be assumed that a large majority of the slaves had to be obtained with a certain degree of coercion. Even if there was nothing unnatural or degrading about slavery, people would be naturally and instinctively reluctant to leave their homes and the places they were accustomed to. Slavery was not abhorred on any moral and sentimental grounds, but it was certainly dreaded – and most probably also resisted – as a displacement, loss of security, cutting off local and personal ties, and as a step into the unknown. Racial and religious difference apart, Arab slave-hunting in Africa could probably provide a close enough parallel including the commercially motivated cooperation of local chieftains.[8]

A glut on the market could depress the price of slaves[9] and theoretically could also lead to an expansion of the arable. Pipes believes that such an oversupply must have provided 'a very strong inducement for the *apanage* princes and landlords to turn to the exploitation of land'.[10] This would be correct if agriculture were capable of producing a marketable surplus. But the same author admits that 'the main emphasis of the household economy of the *apanage* prince was not on growing cereals'[11] – which is obvious, as such emphasis could not bring any economic benefits. The solution suggested by Pipes for the unmarketable slaves was their use in the *promysly*, i.e. various cottage industries or crafts.

No doubt a certain number of slaves lived among the population not necessarily as the result of a collapse of foreign markets,[12] but as part of the prince's labour force called *kholopy*.[13] The prince's household certainly had craftsmen manufacturing arms, armour, harness, etc., for the army as well as the necessary artefacts for the prince and his court. But the nomadic economy was not geared to the use of slave labour, and the economic importance of slaves was negligible. If there were surplus slaves, it seems more likely that they were enrolled in the army. This practice persisted late into the sixteenth century.[14]

Slaves taken as prisoners of war were often ransomed and their slavery was therefore only temporary.[15] There were various legal grounds for enslavement, some involuntary, some voluntary, for example, as paying off debts or marrying a female slave.[16] The legal situation of the Kievan slaves had some basis in the *Pravda Russkaya*, which became a model of further law codes (or rather, compilations) – the *Sudebniki* – until the promulgation of a slavery code in 1597.[17] Although certain part of the laws in the *Pravda* was taken over from Byzantine sources, it must be assumed that until the enactment of the code of 1597 a large part of the relations between slaves and slave-owners, disputes between slaves, property and family questions were regulated by custom.

It is interesting to compare the word for 'slave' in Russian and in Old Czech, which is the same word: *'rab'*. In both languages the word for 'work' is derived from it, but in Russian *'robota'* means any work, while in Czech ordinary work is termed *'práce'* and *'robota'* means bonded work, *corvée*. Does it mean that in Russia there was no such thing as unbonded free work, only *corvée*?

There is ample literature on the subject of slavery, but, on the whole, it remains outside the scope of this essay, which is concerned with the wider economic and sociological relations between nomads and peasants in Kievan Russia.

Chapter 3

towns, crafts & commerce

The question of town and of urban dwellers in Kievan Russia is one of the most confusing and most difficult to answer satisfactorily. Their existence is attested by various annals of the period, but their numbers and their character are open to different interpretations. Blum[1] gives the numbers of individual towns identifiable from such annals as 24 in the ninth and tenth centuries, 62 more in the eleventh, another 120 in the twelfth, making a total of 206. In the thirteenth century only 32 are mentioned by name. As against this Vernadsky[2] mentions only three cities in the Dnieper Valley in the ninth century – Kiev, Chernigov and Pereiaslav, with Rusa in the north and Tmutorokan as a possible fifth. There is considerable confusion not only in the numbers of these 'cities' but equally as regards their populations. Some scholars who are conscious of the limiting effects of agriculture come to the conclusion that 'cities in Russia have never played a significant role in the nation's economy'[3] while others, like Kliuchevsky, who stress the importance of commerce are ready to accept them as commercial centres of prime importance.

There exists a certain correlation between the capacity of the farming population to produce a surplus of food and the number of non-farming population which could be supported by this surplus (see chapter 1, note 55). Another calculation can be made concerning the distances and the transport facilities available to get the product to the consumer. Some of the townspeople were, no doubt, part-time farmers, but their fields had to be within walking distance, say 7–8 kilometres, from their homes. The number of such homesteads and the area farmed by them therefore had a functional role in restricting the number of non-farmers inhabiting the settlement.

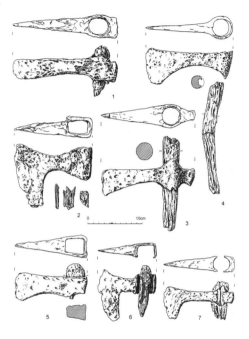

Axes. Great-Moravian artefacts from Mikulčice, Moravia.

Outlying villages were faced with the difficulties of transport in bringing their produce to market (see below).

It is also believed that the growth of a non-farming population stimulates increases in agricultural production.[4] It is argued that when the size of the non-farming population exceeds the amount of available food, more land will be cultivated until the requirements are met. The demand would thus encourage increases in supply. In the same vein, lack of demand would discourage yield improvements and lead to an absence of incentives. Pipes rather curiously argues that 'an agricultural surplus must be disposed of not to other farmers, but to people who themselves do not grow food [...]. Where an urban market is absent, little can be done with the excess grain except to distil it into spirits.'[5] Economically, a more correct answer would be that if there were no market, the surplus would be eliminated by the reduction of production, that is, by reduced acreage. However, this construction presupposes that there is surplus in the first place and that the agriculture is

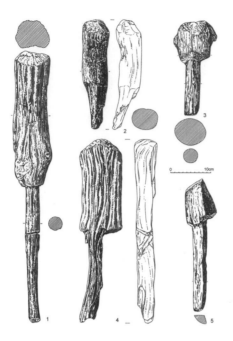

Wooden utensils (mallets).
Great-Moravian artefacts from
Mikulčice, Moravia.

capable of expanding and producing more when the demand appears. Elsewhere, Pipes himself comes to the conclusion that in the period of Kievan Russia there was hardly any surplus possible because of the climatic and technological conditions (cf. above). It has been shown in the preceding chapter that there were good economic reasons for the ruler to sell the available excess labour as slaves rather than encourage increases in acreage. Even if there was some demand in the form of an urban population, it is very likely that food supplies would not be available to meet it. The reverse is therefore more probable. Towns appeared and grew where the food supply existed, but they could grow only to the extent which that supply allowed.

The excavations of Great Moravian settlements of the ninth and tenth centuries have shown that the early Slav *burgwalls* were military camps laid out like towns; large fortified enclosures were destined as refuge for the population and their herds in time of danger, but most of the population were required to live outside the walls. The dwellings inside were destined only for the prince himself, or his lieutenant, and for the garrison represented, in practice, by the members of the prince's retinue and their followers. Sometimes there were also craftsmen working for the 'government', for example, slaves manufacturing arms and armour.[6] The principal function of such settlements was military, not economic. Originally, they were tribal settlements serving the area inhabited by one tribe or part of a tribe.

Gradually, with the emergence of a central or rather centralising power, they also acquired an administrative function serving as collection points for the tribute[7] (for the evolution of state and state power, see below). In the conditions of Kievan Russia the Slav *burgwalls* were most probably taken over by the Vikings and turned into such military-administrative centres inhabited by the warrior élite, while the peasants lived outside; the marketplace and the craftsmen's quarters were also located outside the fortification.[8] This would also explain the problem of food. The non-farming population was engaged in the collection of the tribute, which was, no doubt, collected in kind; therefore it had the necessary food supply at its disposal, especially as only a tiny fraction of the tribute had to be forwarded to the prince,[9] an additional reason why *poludie* as a tax-collecting expedition does not make sense.

In Kievan Russia the low density of population and the marginal character of its agriculture coupled with occasionally tricky and difficult transport would provide a very poor market for any craftsmen. It seems likely that home-made artefacts (wooden utensils, home-made clothes and shoes, etc.) satisfied most of the basic requirements. It is also likely that the peasants manufactured some of these artefacts on a semi-professional basis during the idle winter months. 'The mingling of agricultural and non-agricultural occupations [...] accounted [...] for a weak division of labour and the absence of highly skilled (that is, full-time) traders and artisans. For a long time it also inhibited the rise of a commercial and industrial culture.'[10] Blum, speaking of a later period, says that 'the demand for manufactured goods had been met primarily by peasant or slave artisans working on the manor, or in the commune, and producing for local needs. This practice [...] persisted and [...] artisans remained an important part of rural society into the twentieth century.'[11]

Rybakov was able to identify as many as sixty special crafts in some cities of the twelfth and thirteenth centuries.[12] In his major work, *Remeslo drevnei Rusi* (Crafts of Ancient Russia), this author divides the crafts into village crafts and town crafts. The former, producing simple and cheap goods, worked mainly on order, and supplied small areas of 10–20 km in diameter. The latter produced more sophisticated and more expensive goods for more demanding customers, and worked partly on order and partly for the market. They supplied areas of some 50–100 kilometres in diameter and, to some extent, also the export trade. This somewhat simplistic picture does not take into account the density of the population, nor its purchasing power, or the available supply of food and raw materials.[13]

The same author elsewhere[14] draws a picture of a village living on a natural economy in complete self-sufficiency. Local crafts cater for local needs and there is no dependence on imports or trade. Food, clothing and some indispensable utensils are made at home. A smith, a potter and one or two

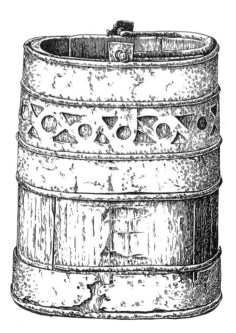

Pail. Great-Moravian, from Mikulčice, Moravia.

others will take care of the rest. Their production is minute, and their range of customers does not extend beyond their own village and perhaps the next one. This idea seems to clash with the assumption[15] that thousands of pedlars acted as middlemen between urban craftsmen and their distant customers. This admits the existence of internal trade and makes the self-sufficiency of the village somewhat less complete. Another problem to consider is the supply of raw materials. Although a potter may have found local supplies of clay fairly easily, the situation of the blacksmith was more complicated. Rybakov believes[16] that deposits of bog-iron were so frequent and evenly distributed that iron-smelting furnaces supplied areas with a radius of only 5–15 kilometres. Supplies to urban craftsmen are not discussed.

An economic analysis of the situation of crafts in villages and in towns would show that it is the number of households, rather than the area of a given diameter, which will determine the craftsman's market. If there are not enough households in the immediate neighbourhood, the craftsman will have to employ a pedlar to reach a wider range of customers. In this respect he will work 'for the market'. Conversely, purchasing power will also determine the range of customers.

мetaLLurgy

The problem of the availability of iron deserves a closer look. In Central and Western Europe the main sources of iron ore were mines in mountainous areas. There is no evidence of similar mines in Russia in the Kievan period and, indeed, much later. Rybakov himself speaks only of bog-ore that could be dredged from the floors of shallow lakes. It is improbable that such deposits were so frequent and so evenly spread as he believes. It is also highly probable that only limited quantities of ore could be obtained and that such deposits became quickly exhausted. This would mean that furnaces had to be abandoned and built elsewhere when a new deposit was found. So the metal would not be produced 'within a radius of 5–15 kilometres from the user', but would have been an important item of transport and trade.

As for the productivity of a medieval furnace, Czech scholars carried out experiments with a Great Moravian type of furnace (ninth–tenth century) not using bog-ore but quality ore from Sweden. The experiment took 17 hours, 8 hours of pre-heating using 50 kg of charcoal, 7 hours for the fusion and 3 hours for the re-heating of the product. Consumption was 1,036 kg of charcoal and 41 kg of hematite. The temperature reached 1,300–1,400 °C. Further treatment was necessary to separate the metal from slag. The result was about 5 kg of metal of which about 2 kg was suitable for forging. The hematite used contained 63 percent of iron.

Assuming that the Kievan furnaces were of a similar efficiency, this would give an idea of the proportion of ore to the final product and also of the quantity of fuel needed.[17] Therefore it must be assumed that every village blacksmith had to be supplied with his raw material by some tradesmen. Furthermore, this material was highly valuable and as such it was constantly re-worked and re-used. However, a blacksmith could only produce relatively simple utensils and tools; more sophisticated items (like arms and armour) required specialised, skilled craftsmen who would work for a range of different customers, most probably for the 'government'. (In 1405 Clavijo noticed that Timur had in the citadel of Samarkand 'over 1,000 craftsmen in permanent captivity who manufactured helmets, armour, crossbows and arrows'.)[18]

It seems more likely that the limited markets gave little incentive for specialisation of crafts for centuries to come. Artisans and other skills remained critically short in Russia until the eighteenth century.[19]

The distances and a low density of population hampered internal trade. Most of the goods manufactured for the market were distributed by itinerant pedlars (still active in the nineteenth century). Their suppliers were largely part-time farmers not necessarily living in towns. The purchasing power of the population, limited by the available food surplus it produced, was further restricted by the tribute exacted from it by the rulers. And yet Blum believes that extensive foreign trade gave a strong impetus to international commerce. 'The merchants travelled through the land to buy goods for export and to sell the wares they had imported […]. There was a mass demand for some of their merchandise, such as salt, metal articles and cheap jewellery.'[20]

Trade was in the hands of the prince and merchants and traders belonged to his *cheliad*, just like the craftsmen. According to Rybakov, merchants who were not bonded began to appear only in the late eleventh century.[21] Another economic reason for the growth of cities may have been long-distance trade but this is also open to doubt. The main trade routes and the goods that were shipped along them are fairly well documented, but little is known about the density of the traffic. It seems that Russian goods were shipped to Constantinople only once a year. The returning merchants most probably brought Byzantine products back to Kiev. There is no evidence of any other regular traffic between the two cities.

The trade between Novgorod and Gotland comprised mainly furs and cloth, but it belongs to a later period – from the mid-thirteenth century onward. The 'eastern trade route' via the Volga and the Oka to the Muslim markets in the Middle East is known to have existed, but the evidence of movements is scanty, and no cities in that area are mentioned before the late Kievan era when, because of the conquest of the steppe by the Polovtsy, the trade was diverted from the Dnieper route. The archaeological evidence is provided by hoards of Arabic and Persian coins found in Scandinavia;[22] Ibn Fadlan and Ibn Rusta[23] mentioned Rus merchants on the Volga in the tenth century, but from these sources it is difficult to assess the volume of goods, or the number of people engaged in this trade.[24] There also existed a 'Western route' from Kiev to Cracow, but again without much evidence as to the volume and density of commercial traffic it carried.[25]

There are three factors limiting the number of people economically connected with foreign trade: the demand for the goods produced, the amount of services required to bring them on market (this, in turn, depends to a large extent on the volume and density of the traffic), and the supply of food. From the history of other caravan routes (such as the Silk Road) it can be deduced that traffic follows the trail where food supplies can be obtained and where security risks are not prohibitive. When either food supplies or security break down, the traffic is re-routed.

The limitations of food supplies probably had a restrictive effect on commercial traffic along the trade routes from Russia. Normally, a settlement would grow at a place where the caravan had to stop for the night or for some technical reason like fords, rapids, etc. Yet there is no evidence of any settlement at the Dnieper rapids where, according to the sources, the caravan had to disembark and the boats were dragged overland. This operation certainly required several days.

Turning this negative evidence into reverse, the question is why did so many 'cities' appear at other places unconnected, it seems, with any kind of trade? The answer is twofold: first, no food could be grown around the Dnieper rapids. Second, the difficulties connected with obtaining supplies locally could have been the reason, or one of the reasons, why there was only one caravan a year. At other places where food could be grown locally its limited surplus would mean that settlements connected with the caravan trade would have to be very modest in size, just as the number of people engaged in running the caravans would also have to be modest.

The goods which are known to have been shipped along these routes support this assumption. Mostly, they were easily transportable and did not require large numbers of men to attend. All the evidence leads to the conclusion that the urban population connected with crafts and trade could not have been very large. Vernadsky, who bases his assumption partly on Constantine's description of the *monoxyla*, believes that the boats for the yearly caravan were assembled in Kiev each spring. 'Each year, in April and May, Kiev must have looked like a great shipyard.'[26] This raises two questions. Why had the boats to be assembled (or built) each year? It can only mean that the flotilla did not return to Kiev after its journey to Constantinople. Presumably, it was abandoned in the estuary of the Dnieper and the returning merchants proceeded overland with a caravan of pack animals. The reason for it could have been that hauling the boats upstream was too difficult or too dangerous and that a caravan was both cheaper, easier to handle and less vulnerable to attack. Unless, of course, the boats were in such a condition that they could not be used any more. The other question is what were the merchants returning with? Bulk cargo, like grain from the littoral, can be excluded because it would be difficult to transport. In any case, it would not be limited to only one shipment a year.

The goods purchased in Constantinople would have been mostly luxury items like cloths, jewellery, ivories, etc., and, perhaps mainly, arms and armour. All these would be easily transportable, but would also make the caravan a tempting target for raids. Therefore a reinforced protection would be called for and it may be assumed that some nomads were hired to provide it. It is understandable that when the Polovtsy became the dominant power of the south-Russian steppe, this trade could not continue and had to be diverted, partly westwards to Cracow and partly to the Volga-Oka region in the north-east.

Tmutorokan. It is plausible that the name Tmutorokan comes from the Turkish *tma tarxan* (commander of a thousand).[27] However, if this was, as Vernadsky believes, the Black Sea capital of the Rus khanate in the seventh–eight century, it begs the question why a Rus or a Russian capital kept its Turkish name. Were the Rus perhaps at that time mixed with the Turks, or were they a Slav tribe dominated by them? At any rate, no site of Tmutorokan has so far been found, and if we accept Vernadsky's hypothesis that it was located at the mouth of the river Kuban, we have to pose another question, namely the distance from other Russian centres and the cohesion of the Kievan state. The only answer to this seems to be that the highly mobile nomadic tribes, who were related ethnically and sometimes politically, ruled the entire 'realm'.

If the bulk of the population had only very few goods to exchange, a money economy had little opportunity to develop. Barter was more likely the general way of business and some small items, like squirrel furs or pieces of cloth, were probably used as a rudimentary currency. McNeill compares Hungary, where peasants had no cash income and where a money economy did not develop, with north Russia, where there were marketable products from the forests, but this, of course, applies to the sixteenth century and after.[28]

In the Kievan period the Hungarian example seems more appropriate, especially if the hypothesis of the scarcity of markets is accepted. Rybakov admits that money trade could only take place in towns where money had a certain purchasing power. Coins found in *kurghans* are in themselves no proof of a money economy.[29] It is highly probable that the early *grivna*, which is mentioned in the sources, was used merely for the calculation of tribute imposed, for example, on the Byzantines after the Russian raids. It is not clear whether it was in internal circulation.[30] In the ninth century tribute was expressed in 'squirrels' and 'martens' alongside silver coins.[31] In the sixteenth century Sweden, where taxes, wages, etc. were paid mostly in goods, a 'natural economy' persisted well into the eighteenth century.[32] J. Pošvář argues that commerce in Great Moravia did not use metallic coins despite the differentiated production of crafts and the high level of agriculture.[33]

In view of what has been said, any theories of widespread use of money and of developed money economy in Kievan Russia should be treated with caution.

To conclude, the towns in Kievan Russia, perhaps with the exception of Kiev and somewhat later Novgorod, were not and could not be market centres; they were garrison posts and administrative centres destined for the collection of tribute from the population. This role they kept until modern times.[34] Kiev itself, however, situated on the edge of the steppe, may have been an important market for the steppe nomads who needed artisanal products and some luxury items, as well as grain, salt and other commodities. The town inhabitants were not burghers in the European sense – with the exception of the short-lived experience of Novgorod and Pskov in the twelfth to fifteenth centuries. They were servicemen of the ruler engaged in various activities on his behalf, partly economic and partly administrative and military. There were few crafts and little local trade. Commerce, especially long-distance commerce, was in the hands of the ruler. There was little money, if any, in circulation and an urban middle class was, at best, rudimentary. The towns were few. Their numbers increased only in the late eleventh and twelfth centuries when the central government weakened and local clans began to establish their own fortified strongholds. It seems that in a later period, with the return of a centralised government, their numbers shrank again and their population decreased.[35]

Nevertheless, there was considerable wealth in the hands of the prince and his immediate family. This wealth came mainly from the slave trade and to some extent from long-distance trade, both import and export. Luxuries thus appeared in the main towns, and it can be assumed that some special crafts also appeared like goldsmiths, jewellers and arms manufacturers. More important, the princes invited master builders to construct buildings of stone and brick, of which the cathedrals of Kiev and Novgorod still provide a testimony.[36]

Chapter 4

Transport

Transport played a crucial role in the economic development of Kievan Russia. The principal means of transport were the boat and the horse. Boats were used for ferrying armies, for example, in the raids on Constantinople, as well as for caravans of goods or slaves. According to some sources, they were also used in slave raids.[1] It is not certain if they were also used for collecting taxes or tribute. The winter timing of the *poludie* would suggest that they were not. The collection of tribute by boat would mean concentrating the goods at certain points accessible by boat. This would then require some kind of territorial administration not likely to exist at that time. In the forested areas where roads were non-existent the boats combined with portages were probably the only suitable means for transporting goods and people alike. Their use would, of course, be limited to a part of the year only.

The horse could be used in the steppe and to some extent in the forest in winter. However, given the small breed of horses then available, they could only be used for riding and pulling of light carts, sledges and sleighs. They would be unsuitable for pulling heavy loads or for ploughing (cf. above). In the 'competition' between the boat and the horse, the advantage of the boat would be the capacity for bulk cargo and easier and cheaper use wherever and whenever water transportation was possible. Its disadvantages were connected with the limitations of the waterways, however extensive these might have been, with the need to use portages, and also with its dependence on the streams being navigable. Given the climate, it was probably less than half the year. It also required human power for upstream pulling. This remained a feature of Russia until the end of the nineteenth century.

For military purposes the main drawback was the limited scope for manoeuvring except, of course, at sea. The disadvantages of the boat were the advantages of the horse. Given the opportunities offered by the steppe and the feather-grass steppe, breeding and feeding would present little difficulty or expense. On the other hand, it might be difficult to feed large numbers of horses in the forests in winter. For the purpose of raids or war the horse had the added advantage of providing the horseman with mobility, speed and tactical power that a foot soldier would be unable to match. The horse was the prime reason of the military superiority of the nomads over the peasant armies fighting on foot.[2, 3]

As for the cost of transport, White finds that in Europe in the thirteenth century overland transport costs added some 30 percent to the price of cargo every 100 miles;[4] Blum says that in sixteenth century Russia it cost 75 percent of the purchase price to ship grain from Moscow to Archangel (650 miles).[5] At the end of the sixteenth century transport costs took almost half of total profits on grain shipments.[6] Grain, however, was of small importance in Russia's trade in the sixteenth–eighteenth centuries. Her chief exports shipped in bulk were hemp, cordage, flax, pitch, and potash.[7]

None of these seemed to play any role in the Kievan period. Nevertheless, Vernadsky believes that 'grain and other food products were supplied by Slavic tribes subjected to the Russes'.[8] If this were the case, transport problems would have to be considered. Rybakov mentions 'episodic imports' of grain or flour in times of bad harvest from Volga Bulgarians and from Western Europe via Novgorod. Rye was bought mainly by Novgorod that could quickly become dependent on 'southern grain-growing countries'. The prince of Vladimir could cut Novgorod's supply route. Rye was shipped (obviously from the Volga region) by boat and cart.[9] Speaking of Sweden, Roberts finds overland transport possible in winter only. In summer it was 'extremely difficult' and wheeled wagons and carriages were introduced very late.[10]

Northeast Russia (Rostov, Suzdal and Vladimir) was separated from Kiev by forests the crossing of which was in the eleventh-twelfth century considered in the *Byliny* 'a heroic venture'.[11]

Turning now to the biggest single transport enterprise recorded, the annual trade caravan to Constantinople, some interesting problems remain to be solved. The journey reputedly took about six weeks.[12] Voronin estimates the ordinary journey to last 35–40 days. Under exceptionally favourable conditions, the mouth of the Danube could be reached in 10 days and Constantinople in 35 days.[13] It included a stretch of almost 1,000 kilometres down the river Dnieper, a dangerous passage through the cataracts with at least one fairly long portage, and a sea voyage from the estuary along the coast to the Bosphorus.[14]

The logistics of such an undertaking would include, first and foremost, the questions of supplies and security. Taking into account the annual contingent of slaves, military escort, boatmen and merchants, the caravan probably numbered several thousand people.[15] Considering that the entire journey between Kiev and the coast led across the steppe where there were no permanent settlements and no local resources of food, the caravan either had to carry sufficient supplies with it or had to be supplied on the way from resources brought to the Dnieper from elsewhere. The first alternative would involve not only gathering a substantial amount of food beforehand (in springtime when it was not easily obtainable), but also ferrying it on some extra ships, transporting it over the cataracts, etc. Even assuming that supplies were available in the settlements along the estuary, the problem reappears again for the stretch along the coast as far as the Byzantine border at Mesembria. In addition, the nomads who inhabited the steppe could be expected to try to make the best of such an important event. For several weeks the riches of Russia were passing through their territory. The same applied for the returning caravan with the even more desirable luxuries of Byzantium. The event was regular, annual, taking place always at the same time. One could see it as an annual feast offered to the raiders 'on a plate'. Could the caravan be sufficiently well guarded to discourage the nomads from attacking it?

The nomads were horsemen and skilled warriors. The guards of the caravan would be foot soldiers burdened with goods, slaves and 'civilians' with no fortifications having only boats as their base. Their mobility and

*A hunting scene, Mongolian.
(Drawing by Den Barsboldt,
from Grollová-Zikmundová,
Mongolové)*

scope of manoeuvring would be minimal and their vulnerability enormous, especially at the portage by the cataract. The fighting superiority of the nomads over foot soldiers has already been mentioned.[16] The caravan therefore had to be accompanied by an army much superior in numbers to that of the nomads – which would complicate the logistics of the enterprise to an impossible extent – or the nomads' 'friendliness' had to be bought for a price equal in proportion to the value of the transported goods. In the sources there is no mention of such a pay-off to the nomads, nor is it known that the caravans were ever attacked. There is merely that rather incongruous remark made in *De Administrando Imperio* that the military escort kept vigilant watch for a possible enemy attack at the portage by the cataract – for 'it is at this point that the Pechenegs come down and attack the Russians'.[17]

The explanation of this puzzle lies in the fact that the Russians were the undisputed masters of the entire stretch of the steppe between Kiev and the estuaries of the Dnieper and of the Danube. Thus both problems concerning the supplies and the security were solved. If the nomads were subject to the Russians, they could be made to bring their herds to the river or to the coast and supply the caravan. The security could be limited to guards against thieves and small bands of marauders.[18]

But could the Russians become the masters of the nomads? According to contemporary sources, the Pechenegs and others before them, just as the Kumans/Polovtsy afterwards, were a force to be reckoned with. They besieged Kiev in 968 and killed Svyatoslav in 972. They were valued allies and dreaded foes of Byzantium.[19] It must be assumed that if they were masters of the steppe along the Dnieper, no 'vigilant watch' could have protected against their attack. Obviously some other deterrent was needed.[20]

Much effort has gone into demonstrating that Kievan Russia was a major naval power. Between the ninth and the eleventh centuries their fleets attacked Constantinople at least four times. There was a strong Viking tradition at least in the earlier part of the country's history. There is evidence (in Gardizi, for example) of their boat raids. There is the fact that the forest area could be penetrated only by water (in summer). And the maritime location of Tmutorokan, if it is accepted, could be that of a powerful naval base.[21] And yet there is much evidence, direct and indirect, that the horse rather than the boat was the mainstay of the Russian way of fighting. The Russians were frequently victorious over the nomads as, for example, Svyatoslav's campaigns against the Pechenegs or the Khazars demonstrate, but these campaigns could not have been conducted from boats. Foot soldiers could not stand up against horsemen without protecting fortifications and these could not be expected in the enemy territory. Boats and horses are mentioned in the campaign of Igor, but the distances and the speed of his movements suggest that the Host was mounted.[22]

In Russian folklore the ship is hardly in evidence but the horse is an integral part of it – in the *Byliny*, in the songs, proverbs, fairy tales, etc. It had an important place in the law: in the *Pravda Russkaya* it is valued more than some humans. It had its place in the funeral rites: 'When a prince died, his favourite horse was buried with him.'[23] There is, so far, no trace of any

Scandinavian-type ship burial in Russia.[24] If much, or most, of the Russian fighting was done in the steppe, the boat was quite unsuitable for it, except perhaps for some ferrying of troops and supplies.[25]

But if the horses were indispensable for fighting, their transport by boat would not have been easy. The boats were fairly small, made of dugout tree trunks.[26] They could be carried or dragged along the riverbanks. It is true that the fifteenth century Venetian, Barbaro, mentions trees which 'being made hollow, serve for boats of one piece, so big that they will carry eight or ten horses at a time and as many men'.[27] But the Vikings never ferried horses in their long boats. The Normans had grave problems in 1066, when they took horses across the channel. And to ferry a horse in a dugout canoe all the way from Kiev to Constantinople is another matter than to ferry it across the Volga (which is what Barbaro saw). And yet Oleg's campaign in 907 (904–5, according to Vernadsky)[28] was also conducted 'by horse and by ship'.[29] Vernadsky considers this 'the first mention in our sources of the use of cavalry by the Russes', and believes that the bulk of it consisted of hired squadrons of the Pechenegs.[30]

This rather tortuous explanation would be unnecessary if the Viking-Rus relationship in the late ninth century was seen in a slightly different light. It seems probable that the Viking conquest did not extend beyond the line of the forests inhabited by Slav peasants. On the edge of the forest and the steppe they would meet the Russes, also of Slav or Anto-Slav origin, who had a long tradition of steppe life behind them. Without going into discussion about the controversial city of Tmutorokan and the extent of the Rus domination of the steppe, it can be assumed that the ruling élite of Kievan Russia was composed of a relatively small element of Norsemen – the House of Rurik – and a majority of Anto-Slav Russes who, in all probability, were nomads. This would explain the use by Kievan Russians both of boats and of horses.[31] It would explain the mastery of the southern steppe by the Russians up to their defeat by the Polovtsy, and the cult of the horse in their laws and folklore. It would also explain the surprise of the Byzantines in 860, so vividly expressed by Photius,[32] when people whom they were accustomed to regard as horsemen all of a sudden descended upon them by sea. Byzantine defences in the Pontic area obviously did not reckon with a sea attack there being, until then, no naval power other then their own. With the weakening of the Viking element, the Russian ability to wage naval campaigns progressively deteriorated.[33] On the whole it seems that the naval enterprises were rather exceptional, whereas steppe fighting on horseback was the day-to-day reality, especially when the incursions of the nomads of different ethnic origin increased and the power of Kievan princes weakened. These nomads, mainly Turkic, challenged the Russes, or Russians, for the mastery of the steppes until finally, some time after the death of Yaroslav the Wise (1054), under the strong pressure of the Kumans, or Polovtsy, the Russians were forced to withdraw to the edge of the forests.

The problem of Russian ships

The earliest mention of Russian ships can be found in the Byzantine chronicle dealing with the Russian expedition against Constantinople in 860 (itself written in the twelfth century); the same event is also mentioned in Masudi's *Golden Meadows*. The Russian (or Rus) armada was led by the Kievan rulers Askold and Dir and had, apparently, 200 vessels each manned by 100 men with a total of something like 20,000 men.[34] At the next raid, in 907 (904), the Russians, led by Oleg, prince of Kiev, had 2,000 vessels with 40 men each, in total 80,000 men.[35] The number of boats taking part in the last Russian expedition of 1043 is given by Michael Attaliates as 400.[36]

An interesting comparison of Arab and Russian ships of that time is made by Leo the Wise in his *Tactica*, written at the beginning of the tenth century: 'The barbarians (Saracens) use larger and slower vessels *(koumbaria)* and the Scythians (Russians) smaller, lighter and faster boats *(akatia)*, because in order to get into the Black Sea through the rivers they cannot use bigger ships.'[37] Constantine Porphyrogenitus, writing in the tenth century, describes in detail the building and equipment of the Russian commercial vessels which he calls *monoxyla* (single-straters). The bottoms of these boats were apparently made of hollowed-out single trees. These boats were floated down the Dnieper, hauled over the cataracts and equipped in the estuary with rudders, masts and sails.[38]

These five descriptions, all dealing with ninth–eleventh century ships, raise the following questions:

1) What *size* of ships? There were obviously differences between naval and commercial vessels. The Byzantine warships *(dromons)* were rowed by up to 200–230 oarsmen, the *pamphylos* by about 160 oarsmen, and the *ousiakos* by over 100 men. The Viking ships, on the other hand, were much smaller. The Gokstad ship had 32 oars and above them hung 64 shields. Presumably, there were two men per oar. The *Anglo-Saxon Chronicle* describes English ships *'with 60 oars and some with more'*, which were 'nearly twice as long' as the Viking ones.[39] This would mean that the Viking vessels had about 30–40 oars. The warships of Harald Hardrada in 1066 had 20–30 pairs of oars with perhaps three men per oar. Thus the crew of a ship may have been 150 men. The army consisted of 200 ships and therefore had some 30,000 men.[40] The 'Long Serpent' of King Olaf Trygvasson in AD 1000 had 34 pairs of oars; 'eight men sat at each oar and 30 stood in the prow making 574 men aboard in all. Such figures [...] have almost certainly been inflated by legend.'[41] Later medieval ship-levies demanded, more realistically, three men per oar: one to row, one to shield him, and one for actual fighting. The fleet of King Olaf had 60 ships, some with 30 pairs of oars, some with 20, and the rest were 'small craft and provision vessels'.[42] The largest fighting ship, the *drakkar*, is believed to have had 80 men at 80 oars.[43] As for the *monoxyla*, Voronin, in his detailed study of Russian boats, comes to the conclusion that they were probably similar to the boats still used by the Dnieper and Don Cossacks in the eighteenth century. They could take 50–70 men, the hull was a hollowed tree trunk, and the sides were heightened with planks and insulated. Oars were preferred but masts and sails could also be used.[44] It seems likely that the boats of the tenth–eleventh century could take about 40 men.[45] There is no evidence of a shipwright craft in Russia similar to that of the Vikings.

2) What *kind* of ships? Byzantine warships were designed for naval warfare and could not go into rivers. The Viking ships, too, were mainly sea-going crafts equipped with a keel; they were capable of penetrating into large rivers, but their use in the upper reaches and shallow streams was limited. For such streams, smaller, flat-bottomed ships with a shallow draught had to be built. Presumably, Viking shipwrights built such craft for exploration, raids and trade in the Baltic area. In addition, these boats had to be hauled on all the numerous portages from one river basin to another and therefore could not be very big or very heavy. It is questionable how suitable such boats were for sea-going operations even if, as Constantine tells us, they were equipped with masts and sails. According to Rybakov,[46] Russian boats were used mostly for transport and rarely for fighting. The Novgorodian raid on Sigtuna in 1188 is a notable exception. And yet Voronin[47] speaks of boats in twelfth-century Suzdal and Vladimir specially equipped for river fighting, with decks, heightened sides and coverings for oarsmen *(nasad)*.

3) The question of *timber.* Vernadsky believes that Oleg's army was composed partly of Kievan Russes and partly of the Rus from Tmutorokan (which Vernadsky sites on the Taman peninsula opposite Kerch). Apart from the fact that no traces of that city have yet been found, the region of the lower river Kuban including the Taman peninsula is mostly steppe and almost treeless. It is difficult to imagine that in the ninth–tenth century it would be covered with forest. So even if we admit that the centre of the Tmutorokan Russes was located on the peninsula, where would they have found sufficient amount of timber for a repeated building of large flotillas of fairly substantial, sea-going crafts?

It is possible to draw several conclusions from the above survey:

– the Askold and Dir ships, if they were built on the Dnieper above Kiev, could hardly have had a crew of 100. This would mean ships too large and too heavy to be pulled overland at the cataracts;

– Oleg's 40 men per boat seems to correspond with the 'lighter, faster' ships of Leo's *Tactica.* It would be possible to get them over the cataracts and also to pull them overland to the Golden Horn.[48] But they could not have been the *monoxyla* of Constantine; rather than the dugout canoes they would have to be constructed, with keel, deck-beams, etc.

And there still remains the question of the Russians' ability to sail on open sea even if only hugging the coastline. Not only does this concern the stability of ships in adverse weather conditions, but also the navigational skills of their crew. Oleg's men may have been skilled warriors, but they could hardly have been skilled sailors. To put masts, sails and rudders on a ship is one thing (if that is what was done in the Dnieper estuary), but to sail such craft along the coasts of the Black Sea down to the Bosphorus is quite another. The only people with necessary seafaring experience who could have provided the crews were either the Tmutorokan Russes or perhaps some prisoners, slaves or mercenary sailors from the Crimea – but there is no mention of either in the available sources.

Thus the combined use of the Russian riverboats for river and sea navigation is something of a mystery. For example, Voronin[49] speaks of light, flat-bottomed boats that were faster and easier to manoeuvre than heavier Greek boats. This seems to have been taken from Leo's *Tactica*. Then[50] he insists that sea-going vessels with deep draught could not penetrate up the Dnieper above the cataracts and could not get into Novgorod. But the Novgorodians used for their Baltic voyages 'boats similar to the Russian *ladia*' made of hollowed trunks with 2–14 oars and 4–28 men. Their fighting ships were 46 metres long, could take 100 men and had shallow draught, oars and sails, heightened sides and even cabins.[51] So, on the one hand, there were river-boats which would make a sea voyage a considerable risk, and, on the other, sea-going boats which could not reach their home ports.

Although portages and cataracts were the main difficulties of river transport, little effort was made to construct artificial waterways to avoid them. Voronin[52] mentions the construction of the first canals in the twelfth century only, without giving any details of their number, length and capacity. The technological difficulties, given the soil conditions, elevation, etc., were certainly not unsurmountable. That little or no such work was undertaken can only mean that river transport, both commercial and military, presented no compelling need for it. Considering that overland transport was even more difficult and expensive, the only explanation could be that the volume of river transport was less than it had to be to make such works economical.

Chapter 5

Army & Warfare

In view of the conclusions reached in the preceding chapters, some established views concerning the army of Kievan Russia require substantial revision. Rybakov[1] believes that the permanent retinue of the prince numbered only several hundred men; large armies were mustered by temporary levies[2] recruited mostly in towns and sometimes including the *smerdy*; there were mercenary units of the Polovtsy, Varangians, Pechenegs, Hungarians and others; the mercenaries were paid with gold and silver, whereas the *soyuzniki* (home troops and allies) were rewarded with land; the army was fighting mainly on foot, only the prince and his retinue were mounted; transport was by boat; horses were used only to a limited extent as they were difficult to ferry by boat; cavalry was a remnant from the sixth–seventh century, still in use in the tenth, but unsuitable for long-distance raids, etc.

First, to face the mounted archers of the steppe nomads, who were the main foes of the Russians, their army had to be mounted too. Foot soldiers could have a role in defensive warfare in fortified positions, but would have no chance in steppe warfare; on the whole, the nomads were superior even in siege warfare.[3] Boat raids in the Viking style could be effective against agrarian settlements and, to some extent, against fortified towns, but they had no place in the steppe. Peasant levies, *smerdy* or other, must be excluded because the absence of manpower in the fields would have an immediate effect on food supplies. Townspeople could supply only insignificant contingents because of their limited numbers.[4] Cavalry, apart from being eminently suited for long-distance raids – as the steppe nomads proved beyond doubt – remained the main arm of the Russian forces until the introduction of gunpowder in the sixteenth century.[5]

Cavalry warfare required more organisation and training than infantry. This is another reason why peasant levies on a temporary basis have to be excluded. A cavalry army had to be a professional army. Such an army could be recruited in sufficient numbers only from the non-farming, that is, nomadic population. The numbers suggested above[6] indicate that it was possible.

Rybakov rather inconsistently stresses the superiority of infantry,[7] but at the same time assigns an important role to mounted archers,[8] and allows both for light and heavy cavalry within the Russian forces.[9] In his view, the fact that Russia had light cavalry in the eleventh century puts it three centuries ahead of Western Europe, where it was introduced only in the fourteenth century.[10] Also, in armour, especially the coat of mail *(kolchug)*, Russia in the tenth century was two centuries ahead of Western Europe, applying the technology of Muslim East, whereas in Europe, Scandinavia, Germany, France, in the ninth–tenth century only leather coats were used, sometimes covered with metal plates.[11]

Contrary to Rybakov, Marc Bloch finds heavily armed horsemen already in the late Merovingian period; they were armed with cuirasses reinforced with metal plates, had helmets, etc. Lightly equipped horsemen *(serjeants)* were part of the host in the Frankish period (eighth–tenth century). The knights at that time had a garment made wholly of metal. The *hauberk*, made of a web of small metal rings – a delicate and expensive work – replaced the *broigne*, which was made of leather or cloth covered with metal rings or plates. The stirrup and the horseshoe were used probably from the tenth century; this made possible the use of pikes and lances. Bloch also stresses the high cost of cavalry in terms of horses and armour and the long apprenticeship necessary to master the required skills.[12] Similar problems were no doubt faced by the Russians. Considering that they had fewer resources and a smaller pool of skilled craftsmen at their disposal, their heavy cavalry was probably rather limited in numbers. To quote Bloch, 'on the one hand there is a body of infantry as ill-equipped for attack as for defence, slow in advancing to the assault and slow in fight and quickly exhausted by long marches [...]. On the other hand [...] are stalwart soldiers, proud of being able to fight and manoeuvre swiftly, skilfully, effectively – the only force [...] which is worth the trouble of counting [...].'

Carpini, who was a considerable expert in military matters, writing about the Mongols in the mid-thirteenth century gives a detailed account of their organisation, arms and armour. The Mongols, who had defeated the Russians in 1221 and overcame their country in 1239, had leather coats covered with some metal pieces and, exceptionally, all-iron ones; these were made of small plaquettes or scales holed and tied together with leather straps. The work required 'skilled craftsmen and quality iron or steel'. There was only one metal plate for a horse; the rest of its armour was made of leather. Their arms were bows, arrows with iron points, axes, and ropes for dragging siege engines. Only some had swords. There were also lances, rafts made of leather for crossing rivers, etc.[13] As defences against the Mongols, Carpini recommends crossbows as a very efficient weapon to penetrate their armour. This would mean that the crossbow had been known neither to the Mongols nor to the Russians, who had been in close contact with them for over a quarter of a century.

Proceeds from trade may have been used to equip and feed the troops. Certainly, any tribute obtained from the peasants could have made only a very modest contribution to the cost of an army. It seems likely that nomadic custom played a role in the way the army was equipped[14]: the maintenance of troops was part of the obligations linked with the *kormlenie* holding.[15]

The organisation of the army was based on the nomadic principle of units of ten.[16] The commander of a thousand *(tysiatsky)* became in the course of time an administrative official (in Novgorod);[17] the units of a hundred *(sotni)* became, also in Novgorod, territorial units.[18] In Muscovy they became commercial bodies.[19] As for the 'mobilisation', the entire retinue *(druzhina)* could, according to Rybakov,[20] gather in 2–3 days; considering the speed of movement he gives for a horse, 50 kilometres per day and a maximum of 120 kilometres in 24 hours,[21] and given the vast territory and the sparsity of the population, this would be possible with a nomadic horde encamped in the vicinity of the princely seat. In Muscovy the nomadic fighting tactics persisted until the sixteenth century.[22, 23]

Chapter 6

The state

According to an older theory, the primitive patrimonial state in some Slav countries, like Bohemia and, earlier, Great Moravia, was a centralised organism ruled from a single stronghold by the prince and his retinue of professional soldiers. The state came into being by conquest when within a given area one tribe achieved domination over the others. This domination, as well as rudimentary administration, was then perpetuated by means of a network of fortresses established in each tribal territory.[1] The main administrative function of such a fortress was to levy the tribute from the population within its area. Therefore the fortress was neither an agricultural centre nor a marketplace. The above-mentioned *burgwalls* seem to fit well into this picture, at least as far as their layout and function is concerned.

This theory has been challenged by some Czech scholars[2] who point out that the early Slav 'state' lacked the essential element of a state, that is, fixed boundaries. There could be no administrative network and the form of government was essentially predatory. Whereas the older theory considered the tribute or tax as a payment by the population for the protection extended to it by the prince *(tributum pacis)*, the later theory prefers the concept of a tribute exacted by the ruler and paid by the subjects to ward off the armed predators, that is a kind of 'ransom'.[3] The boundaries being fluid, the power of the prince expanded as far as it could, the limits being reached when it met an opposition of equal strength, or when for technical or logistic reasons it became unable to exercise effective control over the territory.

At the same time it is acknowledged – and the recent excavations in Bohemia and Moravia of Great Moravian settlements seem to confirm it – that certain Slav tribes led a nomadic, or semi-nomadic life and that the peasant population was ruled by a warrior élite who, with all probability, were horsemen.[4] The role of the *burgwall* thus appears in a different light. While it served to control the surrounding area and to levy tribute, and provided protection for the population against outside incursions, it was also a base for the élite to keep the population in subjection in order to prey on it.

Applied to Kievan Russia, where the nomadic element was much stronger and the scope for expansion much wider, the picture becomes one of tribal territories conquered one by one by nomadic warriors and incorporated into the realm of the prince or *kagan*.[5] Members of the prince's clan were then appointed his governors or lieutenants for the area with the upkeep of military units as their main responsibility. The levying of the tribute served primarily this purpose and only a fraction of it was forwarded to the prince. But the rule of the prince remained personal and these appointments did not represent any kind of territorial 'administration'.

In this respect, the non-existence of an established state and the personal character of the rule also excluded any kind of established legal system. The 'law', as represented, for example, by the *Pravda Russkaya* or by the Great Moravian *Zakon Sudnyi Liudem (Judicial Law for Laymen)*, was not the law of the state but merely an 'ideal programme' inspired by the Church or, to some extent, by Slav tribal custom.[6]

It should be noted that in the system practising rainfall agriculture, whether *podseka* or *fieldgrass*, the state functions would be more fluid and their extent more limited that in an economy based on irrigated agriculture where the régime of water supplies and the construction and maintenance of waterworks had to be centrally organised and controlled.[7] In this lies the main difference between the 'state' of Kievan Russia and other nomadic empires of the Middle East which ruled over sedentary populations practising irrigated agriculture.

EarLy Russian Law

The question of law and justice cannot be considered apart from the character and organisation of the state. Assuming, as mentioned above, that the Kievan state was the personal property of the prince, whose power extended only as far as his military arm, and taking into account the loose character of the administration, the degree of literacy, and the transport difficulties, the early Russian law manuals appear in a rather different light than in the traditional treatment of Kievan history. Centralised legislation and justice is a feature of a fairly highly developed and organised state and requires a fairly long preparatory development. Among its prerequisites are not only a stable and well-established administration, but also some universally accepted cultural and legal customs and values. None of these seemed to exist in Kievan Russia. The prince ruled the country through his retinue of warriors, over whom he maintained absolute and personal power, according to the habits of the steppe. The power of these warriors over the peasant subjects – and this is particularly true of the south and south-east – was again unlimited by anything but local customs.

The first attempts to establish some sort of legal stability and protection must have come from the towns in the interest of trade. This is one of the possible sources of the early Russian legal manuals. The other was undoubtedly the Church, which, pursuing its task of converting the pagan country to Christianity, endeavoured first of all to change the ancient customs and practices connected with pagan religion and to introduce a uniform moral code based on Christianity. Hand-in-hand with it came the attempt to change the legal customs and practices. It has been suggested, for instance, that the oldest Slav legal manual, the *Judicial Law for Laymen (Zakon Sudnyi Liudem)*, which incorporates a number of Byzantine regulations, has been a product of Byzantine missionaries active in the Great Moravian Empire.[8] It was compiled not as a Code of laws of the country but rather as a Church Programme, something which 'ought to be' a desired aim for the converted country rather than a set of legal norms. This *(The Judicial Law for Laymen)* Slavonic adaptation of the *Ecloga* has survived in Russia in many manuscripts and was probably accepted in the pre-Mongol period; by 1280 at the latest it formed part of the *Nomocanon*, used by the Russian Church, and so remains to the present day. In the fourteenth century the East European peoples acquired another collection of Byzantine law of comparable importance – the *Syntagma*. It was compiled in Thessalonika in 1335 and it was intended as a handbook for the use of the clergy.[9]

'The *Nomocanones* and the secular Byzantine law books had somewhat different fates in medieval Eastern Europe. The former was accepted unquestioningly and without change. The impact of Byzantine secular legislation is harder to measure. Few medieval codes of customary law have survived from these areas. Persuasive arguments have been put forward to link the *Judicial Law for Laymen (Zakon Sudnyi Liudem)* with ninth-century Moravia. Of its 32 articles ten are literal translations and nineteen are adaptations of the *Ecloga*; the remaining three are not to be found in the original. The adaptations reveal two tendencies: to substitute enslavement of the guilty party for the mutilation (blinding or cutting off of the nose) decreed by the Byzantine text; and to impose, in addition to the secular penalties prescribed in the original, ecclesiastical punishment in the form of lengthy fasts [...] accompanied by public penance.'[10]

The eleventh-century *Pravda Russkaya* bears the marks of both trends. Apart from penal law, it is concerned mainly with trade and financial matters. It clearly reflects the legislator's concern in the state of the Treasury. 'The first indigenous Russian code was the *Pravda Russkaya* [...]. It is not so much a systematic code as a collection of juridical notes and comments, and is essentially a handbook of customary, and particularly penal, law [...] shows little evidence of being based on a Byzantine model.'[11] 'Nor has any Byzantine influence been detected in the late medieval Russian codes, the most notable of which are the "charters" of Pskov and Novgorod.' *(ibid.)*

The admonishing hand of the Church must be seen in every item where the suggested relations contradicted the harsh barbarian customs of the period. Seen in this light, the absence of capital punishment is not nearly a sign of the humanitarian character of the contemporary justice. Even Byzantine law, which was by far the most civilised system in that period, not only used capital punishment but also a whole series of barbaric mutilations. There is no reason to suppose that a fairly primitive state on the fringes of the Empire would have established a milder and more humanitarian system of law and justice. Not even the early Slav legal practices which lay at the roots of the *Pravda Russkaya* were in any way mild or humanitarian. The idea of the humane and dove-like character of the early Slavs belongs in the same romantic bracket as the idea of their democratic institutions and government. It is far more probable that these legal manuals were simply a compendium of Church advice to the prince on one hand, and an attempt to provide safe conditions for trading on the other.

Real day-to-day justice was probably meted out by local chieftains and military commanders in accordance with the customs of the day, while the interest of the prince's Treasury was to collect as much material benefit from the punishments as possible and, for that purpose, he introduced a scale of fines. The prince probably sat in court in the capital and in some local centres during his annual round-trip, but he certainly judged only some of the most controversial cases. Given the remoteness of provincial centres, the inaccessibility of forest hamlets and steppe-encampments, the difficulties of transport and, most of all, the difference in origin, way of life, economic conditions, and, of course, legal practices in various parts of the country, the idea of a uniform and centralised justice seems plainly unrealistic.

To use modern terminology, it may be assumed that the legal manuals of that period were mainly intended to deal with 'civil' law or, to use Hellie's term, 'horizontal disputes', whereas 'penal' law was still dominated by ordeals, vendettas, blood-money, etc.

It was only much later, when the nomadic ideology of universal power prevailed in Muscovite Tsardom, that attempts were made to introduce a uniformly applied Code of Laws emanating from the ruler's absolute power.[12]

The organisation of the State and the cultural level of the population are not necessarily always on the same level as, for instance, the standard of architecture and of applied arts and crafts, or, for that matter, of literature. It is easier to import an architect with a gang of masons, or to invite craftsmen from a neighbouring, more developed country, or to let missionaries produce literary works than to change the country's cultural pattern, its system of government and above all, its established system of moral values. For example, the rites and beliefs of the pagan religion survived in Kievan Russia throughout its period and long after the Mongol invasion in spite of the official acceptance of Christianity and all the imports from Orthodox Byzantium.

The church

The Orthodox Russian Church was certainly the strongest direct influence of Byzantium in Russia, although there is no real agreement about the depth and extent of this influence among the people. In Byzantium the Church was from the very beginning an official institution. The authority of the emperor imposed Christianity from above, and the Church always enjoyed full government support. That meant that pre-Christian, pagan rites were forbidden and suppressed, but not eradicated. The old beliefs had a more immediate relation to the daily life of the peasants and the population clung to them in spite of official policy. It is known that superstitions and paganism persisted in rural areas of the Empire as late as the twelfth century, and maybe even longer.[13] A similar development may be found in Russia.

The role of the Church was throughout the Kievan period probably much less important than it is generally realised. Hoetzsch is therefore hardly right when he maintains that 'ever since the days of Vladimir I Christianity has penetrated deep into the hearts of the Russian people'.[14] It is far more likely that the bulk of the population, including the early princes themselves, continued to observe their pagan rites including, for instance, the burying of horses and perhaps even human sacrifices.[15] Christianity spread mainly in the cities, where 'a coat of Byzantine civilisation was superimposed over the deeper layer of Old Slavic culture'.[16] It may be apt to quote here from Roman Jacobson: 'Old Russian written literature remained almost entirely subject to the Church; in the "oral" literature the old Russian laity possessed a copious, original and highly artistic fiction – but the only modicum for its diffusion was oral transmission.' The idea of using letters for secular poetry was thoroughly alien to Russian tradition.[17] In the epic poems from the early Kievan period there are traces of old mythological themes. It looks as if Christianity retained, perhaps for centuries, only a superficial hold on the masses, which remained stubbornly heathen in their true convictions and daily practices, incorporating many of their old superstitions into Christianity.[18] The Russian term often used for this situation is '*dvoeverie*', meaning 'double faith'.[19]

On the whole, the impact of Christianity during the Kievan period should be treated with caution. At its best, it probably affected a very thin layer of population: the upper class and the townsmen. As in Byzantium, it was a religion imposed from above, protected and supported by the authorities. The political influence of the Church was therefore much greater than the actual strength of the religion. It may be said that in the Kievan period Byzantine influence was restricted to the ruling and educated class, while the bulk of the population lived spiritually in their pre-Christian, peasant and nomadic traditions.

In another field Byzantine theology and philosophy found little ground on which to grow in Russia and produced no major fruits. Kievan religious writings made a minimal independent contribution to the Christian heritage. Also mysticism remained alien to Kievan soil. The Russification, so to speak, of Byzantine Christianity became gradually apparent in the emergence of Kievan saints.[20]

The probLem of succession

The idea of a hereditary succession never took firm roots in Rome and, consequently, there were very few real dynasties. It represents one of the main ideological differences between Rome and Byzantium, where at least four dynasties held the throne for a total of some 320 years, although there were long intervals between them. The idea of legitimism, such as a claim to the throne by right of birth without actual proclamation and occupation of the seat of government, began to appear in Constantinople as late as the fourteenth century with the aspirations of John Cantacuzene.[21]

On the contrary, the Ottoman Turks remained much closer to the original ideology of the nomads. The old elective principle of sky-worshipping Turks survived in the 'right of the people' to choose and depose the sultan. In practice it was taken care of by the janissaries. No law of succession was laid down, but the tradition that the sultan must belong to the Ottoman clan – or the House of Osman – was so strong that, in spite of seventeen depositions, it was never challenged.[22]

To the Russians, Christ Pantocrator was in the spiritual field what the Great Khan and the King of Kings was in the temporal one, that is, a legitimate ruler of the universe. However, it took more than five centuries before a genuine ideology could develop on this basis. First, the Russian Church was subordinated to Constantinople and, up to the Mongol invasion, the Kievan princes were no match for the Byzantine emperors. During the *'apanage'* period Russia was so split and humiliated that there was again no question of any ambitious ideology. But, by a remarkable coincidence, the Byzantine Empire collapsed and the Mongol yoke in Russia ended almost at the same time. The Russian Church was quick to respond with the theory of the 'Third Rome', by which the universal aspiration of Christianity – in the spiritual field – was passed from Constantinople to Moscow.

In the second half of the fifteenth century Muscovy became by a series of remarkable events the undisputed leader among Russian principalities. After getting rid of the Mongol yoke, the Grand Prince Ivan III began to call himself 'autocrator', at first to demonstrate that he was now a sovereign and independent ruler in his own right. The seat of the emperor of the Orthodox world was now vacant and his role of a spiritual as well as a temporal head of the Orthodox community waited to be filled. Reinforcing his claim by his marriage in 1472 to the niece of the last Byzantine emperor, Ivan III now assumed the title 'tsar' or emperor of all Russia. A coronation and a court ceremonial were introduced, painstakingly copying the Byzantine model. In 1547, at the age of sixteen, Ivan IV decided to be crowned not as a Grand Prince, but as a tsar. Paying minute attention to details in planning the ceremony, he wanted to make it as majestic and awe-inspiring as possible.[23]

The disintegration of the Golden Horde and the conquest of the Khanates of Kazan and Astrakhan gave Ivan IV the proof that he was the rightful heir of the steppe empire as well. By pushing his frontier farther south and east into the steppe, he was claiming his rightful heritage and did, in fact, the same as various nomadic princes had been doing before him: trying to establish by force of arms a world empire of which they claimed to be heirs. Looking eastwards, the tsar-autocrat was the *kagan*, the King of Kings, the true sovereign of the vast empire of the steppes. Looking westwards, he was the head and protector of Christianity – in practical terms of Orthodox Christianity – and he had to behave accordingly.

The Russian Church was never in favour of any rapprochement with Rome. The participation of the Byzantine Church at the Council of Florence in 1439 caused the breach between Constantinople and Russia, and it was not made good before the city's fall. The Orthodoxy had to be preserved intact and the believers protected from any harmful influence. Therefore, when Lithuania and later Poland occupied large areas of former Kievan territory with Orthodox population, Moscow never gave up attempts to bring them back under her protective wing. The idea of Christ Pantocrator and of a Universal Orthodox Empire loomed behind all Russo-Polish wars. Later, when southern Ukraine and the Balkans became Turkish territory, the same justification was given to the numerous Russo-Turkish wars. To liberate the faithful from the rule of the infidel Muslim, or of the heretical Catholic, was the sacred duty of the Moscow tsar. The tsars were ready to intercede on behalf of the Orthodox in the Ottoman Empire at any time – although they had their own spiritual head in the Patriarch of Constantinople.

As for the principle of succession, the Russian system was a mixture of Byzantine and Turkish-nomadic elements. There was no dynasty in Russia until 1797, when, by a decree of Tsar Paul, the monarchy became hereditary, and primogeniture in the male line was introduced. But until then there was no firm rule apart from the condition that the ruler must belong to the House of Rurik (later to that of Romanov). Generally, the eldest male member of the clan was the likely candidate; but on several occasions the sovereign claimed the right to appoint his successor himself, defying the tradition. In case of dispute or doubt, an 'election by the people' was called for. This was provided either by a vote of the *zemskii sobor* – the equivalent of the nomadic *kuriltay* – or by a proclamation of the guards – the equivalent of the Turkish janissaries.[24]

The disintegration of the Kievan state

The Kievan state can hardly be described as a state in the modern sense. The organisation of Kievan Russia tends to be overrated by modern historians, possibly because of its connections with Byzantium. It lacked the backbone of permanent administration, and it also lacked the allegiance of its people to the land. The concept of Russia or Holy Russia wherever mentioned, for instance in the *Byliny*, is not confined to a certain country or region or area of land. It is far more the mystical concept of Mother Earth derived from nomadic ideology rather than a political concept of a Fatherland. The allegiance of the people was personally to the ruler, whose power extended only as far as the operational range of his armed forces. There were no fixed frontiers, these again being defined only by the range of the prince's personal power. There was no fixed pattern of tax collection either, the prince going every year with his retinue on tax-collecting campaigns. In all this the Kievan

State resembles rather the empire of Great Moravia of the late ninth and tenth centuries.[25] It was not yet a fully developed state, but it was not a primitive society either. It can be described as an intermediate formation whose rapid growth was not in pace with the development of its political organisation.

It is interesting to compare the role of eastern and western principalities in the fight for supremacy in the period of decline of Kievan Russia. Almost invariably Novgorod and the western principalities (Galicia and Volhynia) were on the defensive, while the eastern principalities (Tmutorokan, Pereiaslav and Chernigov, and later Rostov, Suzdal, Vladimir and Moscow) were the attackers. This can be explained most probably by their military organisation. Whereas in the west the armies of aristocratic landowners and, in the case of Novgorod, of city militia were trained largely for the defensive, the eastern principalities, with a greater proportion of landless nomads, were much more inclined to offensive warfare.

The nomadic element also gave them a higher degree of professionalism in war – a greater mobility and discipline, and thus became the reason that, for more than a century before the Mongol invasion, a larger part of the Kievan territory was actually dominated by rulers and their retinues from the eastern principalities.

The proximity of Byzantium can be a very misleading point. On the face of it, it looks as if between Kiev and Constantinople was nothing but the sea and empty steppe; consequently, however distant, the two places could still be in close touch, their neighbourly contacts undisturbed by any foreign influences on the way. There were, in addition, Byzantine cities in the Crimea and on the Black Sea coast which were even closer.

The distance between Kiev and Constantinople is about the same as between Denmark and northern Italy and southern Germany. These distances acquire a different meaning when we accept the view that the steppe was not an empty space allowing for free communication without influence and interference. The nomads ruled the steppe from time immemorial and, although communication was physically easy – when the nomads allowed it – it still meant a long journey through nomad-dominated and nomad-supervised lands, with escorts provided and tolls and tributes levied by the nomads. It is therefore quite legitimate to assume that cultural interchange between Byzantium and Kiev was not without some filtration through and mixtures of nomadic influences.

The idea that early Slavs were exclusively agrarian must be considered equally unfounded as the traditional myth of the democratic nature of their institutions and the natural docility and tolerance of their character. 'Research in the social structure of the Slavs in the ninth century was long hampered by the romantic concept of the "democratic character" of the Slavs, a concept which did not admit any deep social differences among them and maintained that this was what distinguished the Slavs from their German and Byzantine neighbours.'[26]

The early Slavs or Antes who lived in the steppes were nomads, while other tribes who lived in the forests were hunters, and yet others practised primitive agriculture. The economy and social structure of the early Slavs was therefore linked with their environment and not with their ethnic origins. Reports of their democratic institutions may simply refer to some forest tribes whose institutions included a degree of consent and consultation.[27] But applying the meaning of modern democracy to these institutions is nothing but an anachronism. As for the character of the early Slavs, there is no reason to believe that it was different from their contemporaries' in a similar habitat. It is known, for instance, that Slavs took part in Magyar raids into northern Italy.[28] We know what reputation the Russians had in Constantinople, and how the Slav prince Andrey Bogolyubsky sacked Kiev in 1169. Here again, it may be safely assumed that the way of thinking and the system of values was linked to their way of life and their economic system rather than to their ethnic origin.

The introduction of the nomadic element with its fluidity and a complete cultural pattern *per se* makes the jigsaw puzzle of Kievan Russia a little more understandable. The emerging administration with its decimal system (*desiatsky*, head of ten, *sotsky*, head of a hundred, and *tysiatsky*, head of a thousand) 'may have originated in the Sarmatian era but it seems more probable to connect its beginnings with the Hunnic Empire'.[29] Taxation had the character of a tribute extracted from the subject population; each member of the ruling clan was given the revenue from a certain district; offices were not hereditary and were not linked with any land-tenure; the whole state was regarded as the personal property of the ruler.

'The organisation of power was first of all based on personal allegiance which was easily established; this is why all state formations organised on these fragile foundations lack stability. Strictly speaking, they do not yet have any state frontiers in the modern sense, but only border zones of influence, or interest. The death of the ruler (extinction of a dynasty) or the dispersal of his retinue could often mean an end of the entire "state". In the society of plundering nomads all capable men took part in the fighting, while in a differentiated society military service became the privilege of a special layer.'[30]

These characteristics, which all nomadic and semi-nomadic formations had in common, can explain the sudden disintegration of Kievan Russia in the second half of the eleventh century. In fact, it was a united state only under St Vladimir and Yaroslav the Wise; both before and after – with the brief interlude of Vladimir Monomakh in the early twelfth century – it was only a loose grouping of principalities ruled by members of the same clan but more often than not at war with each other. The dominant position within the clan was first symbolised by the possession of the city of Kiev; but in the second half of the twelfth century even this lost its significance, after the sack by Prince Andrey Bogolyubsky, and the political prominence shifted to Vladimir-Suzdal, while Novgorod became by far the most important centre of trade and culture.

It would be extremely dubious to apply the institutions of a fourteenth–fifteenth-century Novgorod to an eleventh–twelfth-century Kiev. The differences in development, economy and outside influences have been shown above. They, of course, shared the same language and religion and, to a degree, an ethnically similar population.

And yet, because there is ample information on the later-stage Novgorod and very scanty information on the early-stage Kiev, most scholars are tempted to connect these two areas with a straight development link, as they had once been connected with a straight trade-link.

A further misconception is to apply indiscriminately the modern notion of a nation state to a tenth–eleventh-century formation. A nation state requires clearly defined frontiers and a homogeneous population, something which, for instance, Bohemia with clearly defined natural boundaries was able to achieve only after long struggles at the end of the tenth century. Further, it requires a fairly high degree of abstraction to develop the concept of an impersonal statehood; such degree of abstraction was clearly beyond the capacity of political thinking in a society as little developed as Great Moravia in the ninth and tenth centuries, or Kievan Russia in the tenth and eleventh centuries.[31]

Chapter 7

The society

The society of Kievan Russia was composed of two main groups or classes: the nomadic overlords (the 'warrior élite') and the sedentary peasant subjects. The peasants were sedentary only in a certain way; they tilled the land and they built houses, but the land they tilled changed every few years and their dwellings and settlements moved accordingly.

A. The warrior élite - the prince and his retinue

The nomads were themselves divided into three or perhaps four social groups: the ruling clan, the princely retinue, the ordinary warriors, and, probably to a limited extent, some slaves. The prince, who was the possessor of all land and all people, headed the ruling clan. The office of the prince was elective but it had to remain within the same clan, for example, the House of Rurik.[1] The succession was based on seniority rather than direct family descent. The electors were the heads of the principal clans assembled in a council *(kuriltay)*. Once elected, the power of the prince was absolute. The clan assembly had no other role except that of an occasional war council. Other members of the prince's clan could challenge his power and depositions and assassinations were frequent.

The prince's retinue consisted originally of commanders of military units. This military function contained some administrative aspects, above all the responsibility for the unit's strength, readiness and equipment, and also the collection of tribute. This implied control of a certain area where the 'unit', i.e. the clan or section of a clan, was 'feeding', i.e. grazing its herds. It was eventually combined with the right, originally awarded as a favour for services rendered, to exploit that area for the holder's personal benefit. This right, in Russian called *'kormlenie'* or 'feeding', was based on temporary holding of the area in question. No distinction was made between the holding of land and of people. The leadership of the clan was usually in the hands of one family. The command of the unit as well as the administrative functions connected with it also had the tendency to remain in the same family. In so far as the clan's grazing grounds remained the same, it would appear – but only appear – that the same family had hereditary holding of the land.[2]

People were part of the prince's property as was all land. Pipes' statement that the prince 'laid formal claim to all Russia being his private domain or *votchina* only in the sixteenth century, having previously established a solid base for his authority in his private domain',[3] is open to doubt. The opposite seems to be nearer the truth. The emphasis on the prince's universal right was in fact a re-establishment of his past position which had been eroded by a series of events in the intervening years, like the disintegration of the central authority in the *apanage* period, the growth of *votchina* landholdings, the influence of Poland-Lithuania in the western part of the country, and, to the opposite effect, the Turkish influence after the fall of Constantinople.

There are numerous testimonies of the nomadic character of the Kievan ruling class. The Primary Chronicle describes the way of life of Svyatoslav (mid-tenth century).[4] The ethnographic and archaeological evidence covers the cult of the horse,[5] the horse burial,[6] *kurgan* burials,[7] and the title of *kagan* (or *kha-khan*, the great khan).[8] Some of the Russian or East-Slavic tribes who were under the cultural influences of the Sarmatians had abandoned the Slav custom of cremation and began to bury their dead in tombs, while other tribes continued to practise it. Geographically, those farther away from the steppe, like the Krivichi or the Slavs of Novgorod, continued to cremate.[9] The importance of the horse in early Russian law has already been mentioned. Iranian and Scythian motifs in Russian art and folklore are discussed by Vernadsky.[10]

The famous Russian 'institution' of the *veche* seems to have its origin in the *kuriltay*. Its original function was the election of the prince ('[...] the Kievan veche – in 1113 – disregarding the order of seniority of the Russian princes [...] called to the throne not the senior but the most popular among them [...]'.[11]). '[...] The Novgorodian envoys came to Svyatoslav (in 968) asking him to send one of his sons as their prince. They threatened to find an independent ruler for themselves if he refused.'[12] It is correct, as Pipes says,[13] that 'it is only in the eleventh century, when the Kievan state already showed symptoms of decline, that in the larger cities there appeared popular assemblies called *veche*', which gave the prince advice on important policy questions.[14] But these assemblies did not appear from nowhere; they existed as the prince's advisory organ in the above-mentioned fashion long before and only became 'popular assemblies' when the prince's authority declined and the 'cities' acquired a measure of political importance to vie with that of the boyars.

The tradition of the Greek city states, so often quoted in this connection, could not have played any role whatsoever in Kievan Russia; the autonomous institutions of the ancient Greek *polis* had been by then dead for more than a thousand years; some of the Pontic colonies preserved their municipal institutions under the Byzantines until the introduction of the *themé* system of administration in the seventh to ninth centuries. The last city to be brought in line and to lose its elected magistrates was Kherson in the early ninth century.[15] After that there was no municipal autonomy anywhere in the area. Given the character of the Slav and Russian town, as discussed above, it is most unlikely that any autonomous municipal organ could have developed in Kiev unless it evolved from the nomadic assembly, which, of course, was of an entirely different nature.

In Novgorod and Pskov the situation was different for three reasons. The princely authority was delegated and therefore weaker; the economic position of the two cities was much stronger and, correspondingly, also their political power. And from the twelfth century onwards there was a considerable influence of the Baltic trade, which brought with it the administrative and legal traditions of the West-European trading city.

Unlike Kiev, Novgorod, with its widespread trading interests and its system of landholding, would resemble the great merchant cities of the Baltic, which were part of the powerful Hanseatic League.[16] Municipal self-government with administrative officials answerable to the city council, city militia, legal charters and municipal law courts were institutions with which these cities proudly manifested their independence and power. It is no coincidence that such institutions made their appearance in Novgorod. Although the peak period of its prosperity belongs to the later *(apanage)* period, the roots of its institutions and its rivalry with Kiev go back to the late eleventh and early twelfth century. After the famous expulsion of the prince in 1136, 'the prince of Novgorod became in essence a hired official of the city with strictly circumscribed authority and prerogatives. His position resembled that of the *podesta* in Italian city-states, and made some historians refer to Novgorod as a "commercial republic"'.[17]

Charters were agreed between the princes and the city; the local assembly, or council, the *veche*, controlled the observation of these charters, elected the officials who shared executive power with the prince, and determined the selection of the archbishop. The elaborate judicial system is described by Riasanovsky.[18] Some scholars believe that the *Pravda Russkaya* originated in Novgorod; decisions of the *veche* are only known from Pskov and Novgorod.[19] On the whole, what has been said of Novgorod would also apply to Pskov.

The institutions of self-government and the private ownership of land must be considered the main causes of the destruction of Novgorod and Pskov by Muscovy. The ferocity and thoroughness of that destruction can only be explained by the danger they represented to the ideology of *samoderzhavie* and to the autocratic power of the rulers of Muscovy.

The culture of chivalry

As the Russians apparently had no big horses to compare with those of Western Europe, the armoured knight remained unknown in Russia and with him all forms of chivalry, jousting and also the military tactics of mounted shock-combat;[20] in short, the whole military system which became known as European feudalism did not exist here.

The military tactics of mounted shock-combat with armoured knights on their big horses produced in the course of time a particular set of values, a moral and an aesthetic code of its own.

The young adepts of knighthood were imbued from their childhood with this ideology long before they were first allowed to take part in a tournament. Entertainment of the period clearly reflected this ideology and this set of values.

But chivalric culture did not penetrate beyond the range of Western Europe. The Byzantines, who began to use armoured cavalry already in the tenth century, saw their first tournaments only after the fourth crusade, when the Latin Empire introduced them. Syrian and Egyptian Muslims became acquainted with chivalric culture including tournaments and heraldry after the establishment of the Kingdom of Jerusalem. The mounted shock-combat was essentially an individualistic way of fighting and, consequently, the entire chivalric culture was individualistic. It was valour, not discipline that mattered. It was also a very unequal way of fighting with the privileged, the noble knight doing the honourable part charging against the enemy, and with his followers inferior in armour as well as in birth and social status supplying the humble auxiliary services.[21]

Russia remained completely beyond the range of this influence. There is no trace of armoured knights or of the shock-combat tactics in the history of Kievan Russia. Their military tactic was different, and because their morals and their aesthetic were also based on their military tactics they were also bound to be different. Steppe warfare produced its own ideology and its own set of virtues equally romantic as its West-European counterpart. That is why we find Oriental, mainly Iranian and Turkish motives in old Russian songs and ballads. The romantic flavour of steppe warfare permeates the folk songs *(Byliny)* as well as the large epic compositions like the *Lay of the Host of Igor*.

In Kievan Russia young boys were trained for steppe warfare and imbued with ideology connected with it. Entertainers of that period, itinerant singers and storytellers, complied with this ideology and provided for their audiences romantic stories about heroic deeds and virtues which these audiences could appreciate. If a western troubadour had, by any chance, arrived at the princely court at Kiev, he would have encountered very little response from his audience there. It is very likely that both his stories and his music would be totally incomprehensible because they reflected a completely different culture.

B. The Peasants

The organisation of the peasants was conditioned by the character of the work they were doing. Both *podseka* and *perelog* farming required an amount of labour that exceeded the possibilities of one family unit. Larger groupings were needed to clear the forest, and the frequent shifting of the plots of farmed land required some organisation which would allocate them among the tillers.

In the *fieldgrass* areas the need to share the more expensive implements and animals, and the allocations of land between field and fallow led to similar results. A peasant commune which suited all these requirements thus came into being. It remained the dominant form of peasant organisation until the late nineteenth century, and was recreated after the Revolution in the form of the *kolkhoz*.[22]

The commune became gradually used as an instrument of control and a prolonged arm of the government on the well-known Byzantine principle of collective responsibility for taxpaying. The commune was also made responsible for the investigation and detection of crimes. With the introduction of the three-field rotation system in farming the commune also assumed the role of coordinator in the rotation of crops and the use of pastureland.

The role of the commune elder *(bol'shak)* was in many ways similar to that of the *aksakal* in a Middle-Eastern village. He was not appointed by any authority, but accepted or elected by the people. Only when the commune acquired fiscal responsibilities, probably on the Byzantine model, did the elder become an 'official' responsible for the collection of tribute or tax.

It is also possible that the early commune had a role to play in the delivery of the slaves, just as in later times it was made responsible for the delivery of the contingent of recruits for the army. It seems likely that already in the Kievan period the rulers used the commune to control the movements of the peasants and also to extract from them the tribute and the services they wanted.

Two questions are open to discussion here and a satisfactory answer seems possible only if they are considered in connection with the nomadic domination of the country. One is the curious phenomenon of mobility, or 'freedom to move', which caused so many scholars to believe that there was, in the ninth–eleventh century Kiev, some kind of a 'free society', an *aurea aetas*' which disappeared under the Mongol yoke. Apart from the evident anachronism of the idea – the very notion of freedom was alien to both the period and the area – it must be seen in direct contradiction with the economic interests of the ruler and the ruling class.

It is necessary to bring the phenomenon of mobility into agreement with these interests. This is possible if the value attached to the land is put against the value of the people who are considered a potential source of revenue in the slave-trade. If the latter is higher, then the 'freedom of movement' can be tolerated just as cattle is free to move in its grazing grounds. The peasants could be 'free' to move around in search of land, or even transfer their service from one lord to another, but they still remained the property of the prince who could use them as he saw fit either as tillers, servants or breeders of slaves.

The mobility of peasants was progressively reduced as the value of the land increased. With improved farming methods and increased yields from the arable the balance of the 'land or slaves' competition tilted in favour of the land. For the peasants it meant that they would be less frequently sold into slavery, but they were being kept in their masters' service as tillers. The transition from one form of revenue or exploitation to the other was in no way instantaneous or wholesale. The slave trade was still going on when the peasants were being tied to the land, and its extent fluctuated according to the situation on the markets.

A curious situation arose in the *apanage* period when, according to Pipes, 'the *apanage* prince enjoyed precious little authority outside his domain. The inhabitants in large owed him nothing but taxes, and could move from one principality to another with perfect ease [...] whereas, after approximately about 1150 the Russian princes turned into territorial rulers with a strongly developed proprietary sense, their military retainers and commoners living on their land continued to behave as if Russia were still the common property of the whole dynasty. The former enrolled in the service and the latter rented land wherever they found conditions most attractive.'[23]

We are not told how the prince got his taxes in this system, nor what would be the 'most attractive conditions' for farming and service, and how they could be obtained. Presumably, they would have something to do with higher profits and lower burdens. This would mean a rush to better land and away from a less good one – putting the holder of the latter despite his proprietary sense somewhat at a disadvantage, to offset which he would then lower his income even further and reduce his revenue in order to attract farmers by lower burdens... A real competition for manpower in an era in which manpower was still exported, and in which agricultural yields were still too low to absorb excess labour by increased tillage. Blum is even more explicit: 'The probable explanation [of renting out property by the princes and seigniors] lay in the scantiness of the population and the urgent need of the seigniors for peasants to put their properties into productive use. If the lords had offered less favourable terms, they undoubtedly would not have been able to attract settlers.'[24]

The key words here are 'productive use'. If the yields were marginal, the profit made by the landlord on every peasant would be correspondingly small. If it were in the interest of one landlord to attract more peasants in order to improve the revenue from his land, it would be even more in the interest of the other landlord not to lose them. In this time and place we can hardly expect landlords to respect some 'customary rights' of commoners if it would bring about their own 'bankruptcy'.

The assumption underlying the current theory is that the country was underpopulated. But, as it has been shown in the first part of this essay, there is a close correlation between the supply of food and the population using it, underpopulation meaning that there was more food than people, overpopulation the other way round. It has been demonstrated that the supply of food at that time could not support a large non-producing population.

In the *apanage* period the numbers of non-farming population fell sharply, not so much because of the depopulation caused by the Mongol onslaught, but because the Mongols took over the steppe grazing grounds and thereby deprived the local (nomadic, or semi-nomadic) population of the essential 'other' food supply. The excess population thus produced could still be creamed off by the slave trade, but if the slave market collapsed, they had to be fed and they probably found it possible only by some marginal farming on new lands with a productivity perhaps even lower than in the traditional farming areas.[25]

Obviously, there could not have been much interest in these 'unproductive' people, and a fair amount of mobility probably went on unchecked, and therefore 'free'. Only when the yields gradually began to rise, the interest in land began to awaken and the movements of the vagrants were curbed.[26]

Therefore it seems that it was not the landlords who competed for labour but the peasants who were in search of food and protection that only a well-established landlord could offer. This would explain the preference given to Church estates, because these were farmed more efficiently, and were exempt from royal taxes.

The other difficult problem is the question of landholding and land ownership. For the nomad, land had no direct and concrete value, being used only for grazing. Its value was mystical, emotional, even religious rather then economic. It was used collectively by families, clans and tribes and was never parcelled out to individuals. The prince was the only possessor or owner of all land, but he was also the possessor of everything that lived on it, people, cattle, horses and all.[27] The *kagan*, or the Grand Prince, even made theoretical claims to rule, that is, to own the whole world (each nomadic empire was a world state, potentially, or more than that – a cosmic monarchy).[28]

There are two elements in this ideology: the absolute power of the prince and his exclusive right of possession, and the collective use of the land. In a mixed society in which the nomads are the ruling part nomadic principles and values will apply to the sedentary part as well and will be accepted by it. The allocation of grazing grounds and the military-administrative functions of the nomadic 'aristocracy' have already been discussed. The unit (family, clan, tribe) used these grounds by tradition, from generation to generation, but without any title or claim to its ownership; nor had the commanders, as individuals, any such titles or claims. It was the same with peasants. They were settled on the land of the prince and farmed it without any claim or title. The only difference was that their land was to some extent individualised or delimitated, in so far as it was reclaimed from forests or marshes and turned into fields. But there was no individual holding of the land; the fields were rotated and allocated by the commune, which, in more than one respect, was a tool of the prince or his lieutenant.

Settlements were easily shifted from one place to another without attaching any particular value to this or that stretch of land. Land began to acquire an economic value when agricultural yields began to compete with the yields of the slave-trade, and to some extent when it ceased to be freely available. These two items were connected: when farming began to bring the prince increasing benefits, he became interested in who farmed his land, how much he farmed, and how much could be extracted from him. The result was taxation or tribute system based on land.[29] The fiscal value of better and worse land was recognised, and the availability of new land began to be regulated.

The first breach of the prince's monopoly of land ownership came with the monasteries. The land with which the prince endowed them was ceded 'in perpetuity'; the prince therefore gave up his right to reclaim his possession binding not only himself, but also his successors. Whereas the nobles who were granted land on the *kormlenie* and, later, the *pomestie* basis were interested in exacting from it as much and as quickly as possible, the monasteries were able to farm in a more rational and long-term way. They could invest in their land and combine various types and kinds of production to balance their economy in a way similar to the large estates in the West. Being exempt from tax or tribute, they were able to achieve profitability where the prince's and the nobles' estates were not. The peasants, who could expect a much better deal on monastery land, began to leave the black land and the nobles' estates and flocked to the monasteries. In due course this became a powerful reason for the prince to curb the mobility of the peasants.[30]

In the case of land ceded by the prince to some of his nobles as a reward for their service, the prince's act represented a title to the nobleman's holding. But the prince was careful never to cede his prerogative to own the land.[31] He merely awarded his servant with a temporary use of it which he could rescind at any time. So part of the land was gradually distributed among the prince's retinue, while part remained under his direct exploitation. Originally, the object of such an act was the exploitation of people and herds on the land rather than the land itself. Only when landholding began to be lucrative did direct awards of land for exploitation make economic sense. Historically, it is believed that the private ownership of land began to appear some time in the late eleventh or twelfth century,[32] although Grekov would like to find it already in the pre-Kievan Slav society.[33]

Naturally, there was a strong tendency among the nobles to turn their holdings into permanent possessions, and with a weak prince they frequently succeeded in passing their land on to their heirs. The Polish occupation of Western Ukraine powerfully reinforced this trend introducing Western-type feudalism, individualised farming, hereditary land possessions, etc. A European-type landed aristocracy began to emerge, no doubt transforming the *kormlenie* into a more stable and, to some extent, hereditary type of holding. However, it was never allowed to reach proportions comparable to those of the Middle Ages in Western Europe, when landed aristocrats built their estates into such economic power bases that they could challenge the king's power.[34]

The key here is the attitude to land, or the soil. As Pipes remarks, 'the Russian landlord and peasant looked upon the soil primarily as a means of subsistence, not of enrichment.'[35] This was caused partly by the low profitability of farming, and partly by the temporary character and uncertainty of tenure. The result was a merciless exploitation of the soil on one hand, and lack of investment in its improvement on the other, resulting in a complete absence of integrated estates or large-scale farming enterprises of the West-European type.

This enabled the prince to uphold his position as the supreme owner of all land. Eventually, the trend towards private ownership of land was arrested and, ultimately, brutally suppressed. The *kormlenie* was replaced by another type of temporary holding, the *pomestie*, or service tenure based, with all probability, on the Turkish *timar* holding.[36]

The system of land tenure in Novgorod was basically different from that of Kiev, with the inevitable consequences in political and administrative structure. Land in Novgorod was not the property of the prince, but of the municipality. The town was divided into quarters, or *kontsy*, each of which enjoyed far-reaching autonomy. The *kontsy* possessed separately a part of the *piatina* land, a large area of farmland outside the city boundaries.[37] The large and distant territories colonised by the Novgorodians in the East and North-East were managed by the city as a whole. When, as Blum says, 'the native nobility [in the twelfth century] maintained its separate identity, with its own set of interests that clashed frequently with the ambitions of the princes and their followings',[38] this identity had to be based on a separate and independent power base, which could only be the possession of land; and the interests had to be those connected with it.

The assumption is, of course, that unlike Kiev, there was a marketable surplus of farm produce which was the source of landholders' income. At a later stage, urban landholders joined the nobility. 'In the great trading centre of Novgorod, the Russians who were most active in business and who held the highest offices in the city's government were, apparently, more landowners than merchants.'[39] Although this observation applies to the fifteenth century, it shows that the income from the land was at least as important as the income from trade. There is no analogy to this either earlier in Kiev, or later in Muscovy.

Summary to Part 1

The fringe area of the steppe, the feathergrass steppe and the forest brought two groups of population into intimate contact – the peasants and the nomads. Two basic assumptions are at the basis of this chapter. Low productivity of agriculture on account of poor soil conditions, a short growing season, inclement weather and primitive farming equipment, was able to supply sufficient food only to a limited number of people. It may be assumed that the population increase exceeded the available food supply, even if a contribution of fishing, hunting, gathering and small-size gardening is taken into account. There was, therefore, a relative excess of people which, if left unchecked, would lead to penury and starvation. The size of the non-farming population had to be extremely limited. And yet large armies, priests, numerous traders, etc, are mentioned in the sources, said to be absent from their fields for long stretches of time. That points to another source of food supply, i.e. animal husbandry based on pastoral nomadism in the nearby steppe.

The second assumption, therefore, is that the nomads, being mobile, professional warriors, disciplined and trained, preyed parasitically on the peasants and regularly creamed off the excess population in the form of slave export. Ethnically, the nomads need not have been different from the peasants. The difference lay in their economy and their way of life, not in their ethnic origins. That way of life was not different from other steppe nomads farther east, and reflected, in many ways, their beliefs and traditions, the organisations of their society, their technique of warfare, etc.

In both groups, the society was organised by tribes. There were peasant tribes and nomadic tribes, with the nomads easily dominating the defenceless farmers tied to their fields. Tribute was extracted from them in the form of some forest products (furs, honey, etc.) but mainly in slaves. The towns were mostly fortified enclosures harbouring a military garrison and serving as collection points for tribute as well as a refuge for the population in times of danger. Markets, workshops and the like were outside.

In the 10th century, the Kievan proto-state oscillated for a time between the influence of its two main trading partners, Constantinople and Baghdad. Constantinople prevailed and Prince Vladimir opted for Christianity, he himself being proclaimed, in due course, a saint. The Orthodox Church became part of the Kievan establishment and, in true Byzantine tradition, a faithful supporter of the throne. This does not mean, of course, that the entire country became Christianised – Orthodoxy was merely the official religion and the leading strata of society converted to Christianity, but in the country pagan traditions survived for centuries.

Part 2

APANAGE RUSSIA

Apanage Russia from 1240

FINNS

SWEDEN

Baltic Sea

RUSSIAN STATES

Pskov

Novgorod

Rostov

Suzdal

Moscow

Vladimir

TEUTONIC KNIGHTS

R. Dvina

Smolensk

Tula

POLAND

Orel

BOUNDARY OF KIEVAN RUSSIA BEFORE MONGOL INVASION

KHANATE OF THE GOLDEN HORDE

R. Volga

Vladimir-Volynsky

Chernigov

Kiev

CARPATHIAN MTS.

R. Dniester

MOLDAVIA

R. Kuban

Chersonesus

BULGARIA

Black Sea

BYZANTINE EMPIRE

Constantinople

TURKS

N

© Airphoto International Ltd.

Chapter 8

princes & princelings

If we compare twelfth century Russia with Khorezm, a contemporary Turkic empire near the Aral Sea in Central Asia, we can detect certain similarities. The Seljuk Turks, who were the masters of Khorezm at that time, were originally nomads who ruled over a sedentary population of Iranian descent since the latter half of the eleventh century. Within a hundred years they became sedentary and thoroughly iranised. They were still the ruling élite keeping the centralised system of government, an 'Oriental despotism' based on irrigated agriculture and long-distance trade, but they seemed to have lost their fighting spirit, their quality of warriors. They too became 'lazy landlords' enjoying the fruits of their landholding, and depending for their defence on mercenary armies. Their way of thinking became that of sedentary peoples conscious of the value of their land, and of its wealth-providing potential.

When in 1219, for reasons that are beyond the scope of this study, Chingiz-khan's Mongols attacked Khorezm, the strategy adopted by the Khorezmshah was that of a sedentary ruler. He split his army and decided to defend the fortified towns – which fell to the Mongols one by one. This may have been simply a strategic blunder, but the thinking behind it is symptomatic – instead of a mobile defence, nomadic-style, the invader was met by a static defence typical of agrarian, sedentary population valuing and defending their land possessions. The Seljuks themselves, when they were still nomads, would have dealt with it just as efficiently.

When the Mongols attacked the north-Russian princes of Riazan, Koloma, Suzdal and Vladimir, the princes adopted the same strategy with the same disastrous results and no doubt motivated by the same way of thinking.

The shift of the centre of gravity from the Dnieper area to the Volga-Oka region in the north-east, and the foundation of Russian principalities there in the second half of the twelfth century is commonly attributed to the invasion of the nomads, first the Pechenegs, and later the Kumans (also referred to as Qipchak or Polovtsy) into the south-Russian steppe. This invasion cut the Dnieper trade route and deprived Kiev of its lucrative commerce with Constantinople. The Volga route is seen in this connection as an alternative opening to the Caspian and to Persia, although there is no detailed information about the volume and the nature of the traffic.

But there may be another explanation for this move. The invading nomads deprived the Kievan Russians of their habitual grazing grounds in the steppe, and forced some of them to look for other pastures. They found familiar grounds in the region of the Oka, where Riazan, Suzdal and Koloma were founded. Progressively, as Kiev weakened they became stronger and more independent. The sack of Kiev in 1169 and again in 1204 by the northern princes marked the end of Kievan supremacy, and the beginning of what became known as the 'apanage period' – the authority being dispersed among an ever-growing number of princelings. It should also be noted that the distance between Kiev and Riazan is about 800 kilometres as the crow flies, and it is improbable that the attacks against Kiev could have been made by another force than a host of horsemen.

After the death of Yaroslav the Wise, the last Prince of Kiev who used the title 'kagan', the absolute power of the princes lasted for more or less another century, but around the middle of the twelfth century it began to disintegrate. The prince's relatives who acted as his provincial administrators and tax-collectors became more and more independent. They supplied less money to the centre, and kept more for themselves thus becoming more powerful, and the Grand Prince proportionally weaker. To put it in other words, the nomadic warrior chiefs got used to sedentary life, began to look at the territory they were supposed to run in the prince's name as their own fief, treating the peasants as their own subjects, and fighting wars, mostly with each other, without much respect for some common interest or the prince's superior authority.

There were, according to some sources, 80 civil wars in 170 years between Yaroslav's death and the arrival of the Mongols. Seen from a different angle, the apanage princes *(udel'nye)* became 'lazy landlords'; they lost the purity of poor nomads, developed too many interests of their own, and their fighting skills and spirit deteriorated.

The disintegration of the realm proceeded apace. The princely apanages multiplied quickly until some princes inherited only tiny territories, while some other found themselves with no land at all, and had to find service with more fortunate members of their family.[1] The administrative aspect of the landholding receded, and the hereditary one prevailed. The result was the emergence of a privileged group – the landed aristocracy. However, it was a brief appearance only. The nomadic service traditions were too deeply rooted to allow these landowning nobles to organise themselves into an Estate, and to demand from the ruler some collective privileges and constitutional rights. At the most, they used their wealth and family connections to form a pressure-group at the court, which the Grand Princes quickly countered by creating another privileged class, the servitor princes and the so-called *dvoriane* (courtiers), who received land on a non-hereditary basis as a reward for their services. For this the Byzantine *pronoia* and the Turkish *timar* served as a model. The old traditional principles of personal allegiance to the ruler was never really challenged, and when the Moscow Grand Princes fully established themselves as supreme rulers, the landowning nobles were quickly assimilated to the servitors and the courtiers.

The dvoriane enjoyed obviously more confidence than the *boyars*, for they were assigned important military functions. 'For the Mongol period, the prince's *dvor* (court) must be considered the cornerstone of the Russian army organisation.'[2] The dvor was in fact similar to the *'ordu'* of the Mongol princes – a group of trustworthy commanders with their crack units.

Riasanovsky noticed the transitional character of princely power shifting from that of an administrator to a hereditary landlord-ruler: 'It was during that period that they [the princes] acted largely as managers and even proprietors of their principalities [...]. Princely activities became more and more petty; public rights and interests became almost indistinguishable from private.'[3]

'[...] the "service people" was the name of the class of population obligated to provide service (court, military, civil) and making use, in return, on the basis of a conditional right, of private landholding. The basis for a separate existence of this class is provided not by its rights, but by its obligations to the state. These obligations are varied, and the members of this class have no corporate unity.'[4]

The difference from West-European aristocracy with its hereditary holding of land based on right, its corporate unity, and the ensuing political role could not be put more clearly.

Some authorities, however, emphasise the similarity of the so-called free boyars, or free servants, with the feudal magnates and nobles in Western Europe. The boyars and free servants 'made contracts with their prince, and were at liberty to leave him and seek another master'.[5]

'They acted as virtual rulers of their large estates, levying taxes and administering justice.'[6]

'The feudal institution of immunity exempted from princely jurisdiction and administration (i.e. tax-collecting) another large category of the prince's subjects.'[7]

This is not at all contradictory to the centralised rule of the nomadic state if we realise that under the Mongol domination the prince, or Grand Prince, was not a sovereign ruler, but a mere administrative official of the khan. The magnates, or boyars, were regarded as subjects of the khan, not of the prince, and were levying taxes and administering justice in his name. Only in this way the term 'tax' would make sense; in the West the feudal nobles did not levy 'taxes' for the king from their estates. It is quite possible that some boyars entered into some contractual 'service' with a prince, and then left it and contracted with another, while still being subject to the real sovereign – the khan. The Mongol taxation system did not recognise any sub-infeudation or exemption (except church and monastery estates); the Mongols divided the country on the basis of a census into districts with approximately equal numbers of inhabitants, and appointed a tax-collector for each district.[8] The estate of an apanage landlord usually remained under the jurisdiction of the ruler (read: tax-collector) in whose territory it was located no matter whom the landlord served.[9]

Chapter 9

The Mongols

In the Mongol empire of Chingiz-khan and his successors the idea of a Universal or World Empire found its clearest and most successful expression. Its objective was to establish a system of worldwide peace and a social order based on equality and justice. There would be security for all, but in view of their mutual incompatibility there would be no freedom. As a rule there would be permanent service to the state by everybody. The Mongol law code, the *Yasa*, expressed this principle in no uncertain terms: 'There is equality. Each man works as much as another. There is no difference. No attention is paid to a man's wealth or importance.'[1] Any notion of freedom, independence or individuality was obviously totally alien to this kind of thinking. Some historians saw in the Mongol domination a blessing in disguise. After the dismal picture of the feuding apanage princes the centralised Mongol rule helped to establish a unified Russian nation state. Without it '[...] another hundred years might have passed in princely feud. What would have been the result? Probably the doom of our country [...].'[2]

And not only that. The Mongol rule led to a remoulding of Russian society and of its political and administrative system. 'It can be said with truth, that Russia was really conquered twice: first by the Mongol army and then by the Mongol State idea.'[3] In fact, what happened to the Russians was not exactly new. It was a reversal of the apanage system with its dispersed authority and emerging individual (read: princely and *boyar*) landholding. It was a return to the earlier nomadic system of centralised authority and universal possession by the ruler of land and people, as it existed in the heyday of the Kievan kagans.

The Mongol conquest had another consequence – social. When they took

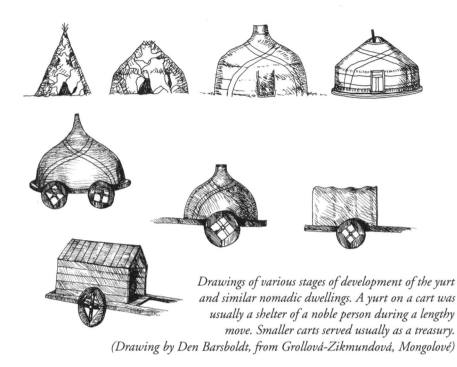

Drawings of various stages of development of the yurt and similar nomadic dwellings. A yurt on a cart was usually a shelter of a noble person during a lengthy move. Smaller carts served usually as a treasury.
(Drawing by Den Barsboldt, from Grollová-Zikmundová, Mongolové)

a town, especially a town which tried to defend itself, they massacred its entire population. Only young women and some craftsmen were spared to be deported. This means that the emerging urban population, out of which eventually a middle-class might have developed, disappeared. In towns like Novgorod and Pskov, which were not destroyed, the development of an urban middle-class – merchants, craftsmen, administrative officials – had a quick repercussion in the political sphere, in the emergence of elective offices, decentralisation of local government, professional bodies, guilds, etc., which existed until they were destroyed by the centralising power of Muscovy.

The immediate effect of the Mongol invasion was that the differences between the three constituent parts of Russian territory became even more pronounced. The east and south became subject to direct Mongol rule. Novgorod and its northern territories were little affected, while the west, Galicia and Volhynia, although occupied for a certain time, were the first to disengage themselves after about a century and, gravitating more and more to the West, became part first of Lithuania and then of the Lithuanian–Polish State.

In the course of the fourteenth and fifteenth centuries their aristocracy became polonised, and took part in the aristocratic-republican politics of Poland. Serfdom was introduced on their estates, and with improved efficiency grain was gradually produced in surplus, and exports were shipped towards the Baltic. The more money these exports produced, the more oppressive became serfdom on the estates, a phenomenon which they shared with Poland proper and Eastern Germany.

The cities in the northwest, in particular Novgorod, in a way benefited from the invasion, because it relieved them from the sometimes oppressive suzerainty of the Kievan princes. They paid tribute to the Mongols, but otherwise the Mongols interfered very little in their internal affairs. Cut off from the Black Sea trade they were nevertheless able to expand their trade relations with the Baltic, and their contacts with northern and western Europe increased rapidly. It was no doubt on the model of the Hanseatic cities that the self-governing institutions of Novgorod and Pskov were established. It was only now that the city assembly or *veche* became a legal organ of the government with the chief executives responsible to it. And whereas in the west the oppressed peasants were leaving their farms to live as free-booters and raiders in the steppes of South Ukraine, the Novgorodians engaged in large-scale colonisation of the north and northeast, penetrating in the course of time as far as the Ural mountains.

It was in the east and south under the Mongol domination where the crucial development took place. The Mongol onslaught was directed mainly against the cities, because ideologically and economically cities represented an alien element in a nomadic empire. While the steppe was occupied by Mongol troops, the forested areas in the northeast were left outside this occupation zone. Also the princely administration was left intact because it was anyway modelled on very similar principles as the Mongol one, and was therefore ready to be taken over. The Mongol and the Russian administrations existed alongside each other for a time.[4] Later, if the princes were willing to accept Mongol suzerainty, they were confirmed in their office and at least some of them were given the task of collecting tributes and taxes for the Mongols.

The rise of Moscow in the first half of the fourteenth century is due partly to the careful cultivation of Mongol friendship by the prince, and partly due to his wealth gained in his capacity as a tax collector for the khan. The princes and their retinues journeyed frequently to the capital of the Mongol khans on the Volga, and it was only natural that the Russian upper class began to imitate Mongol manners. Russians were levied into Tartar armies, and the Russian army later on was based entirely on the Mongol model. All foreign contacts being banned, the Tartar influence became predominant in Russian lands.

By the end of the fourteenth century the Tartars of the Golden Horde gradually abandoned their Mongol shamanism, and were converted to Islam. Through the frequent contacts with Russia described above, Islamic customs made themselves quickly felt among their Russian vassals. New attitudes appeared, for example, in the treatment of women. While in the nomadic society women were equal to the point of military service, the Mongols and the Russians after them now began to practise a strict seclusion. Women were excluded from social life, were kept in a separate part of the home, had to veil their faces, and observe a number of regulations and practices of Islamic law. With the increased influence of Turkey towards the end of the fifteenth century, Islamic and nomadic customs became even more pronounced in Muscovite society to the point that, for example, the Tartar language had become fashionable at the court of the Muscovite princes, and that Russian nobles even assumed Tartar surnames.[5]

Another important field showing the continuity of Mongol traditions was the diplomatic etiquette. Many a Western envoy to Muscovy complained of the stiff and ridiculous formalities of the diplomatic ritual, but at the root of the misunderstandings lay the fact that the Westerners and the Russians followed different bodies of rules. The Russian ceremonial reflected in many respects the Mongol pattern.[6] For example, an ambassador was considered to be a guest of the ruler to whom he was accredited. That ruler had to provide him, and his suite, with free transportation, lodgings, food and drink, and to guard his safety. Especially this last point amounted, in the eyes of the Westerners, to a constant supervision and control. In both Mongol and Muscovite ceremonial much attention was devoted to mutual gifts. No Western envoy was allowed to be armed when received in audience by the tsar. This etiquette, exactly the same as described by Clavijo at the court of Tamerlane, was abolished by Peter the Great, and Western rules were introduced instead.

Moving with a team of yaks. Typical above all in areas of high altitudes.
(Drawing by Den Barsboldt, from Grollová-Zikmundová, Mongolové)

Chapter 10

The society

The security established under the Mongol domination had some positive effects on long-distance trade. The Mongol capital of Karakorum developed into a considerable market centre which attracted caravans from China, Persia and the Mediterranean. Rubruck, in 1255, found Karakorum 'less attractive than the village of St Denis', but there was a Saracen (Muslim) district with markets, a Chinese one where mainly craftsmen lived, several temples (Buddhist), two mosques, and even one Christian church (Nestorian). Outside were separate markets for grain, sheep, cattle and horses.

The Mongols had intentionally disrupted all trade links of the Russian principalities, and diverted the trade routes towards the centre of their own empire. This again affected mainly the towns which were previously the centres of trade and now, after the slaughter, received little impulse for a revival. The development of arts and crafts was brought to a virtual standstill, most craftsmen having been deported by the Mongols.

It seems, however, that agriculture and forest economy was not affected very much. We can assume that because shortly after the invasion, in 1252 and again in 1275, the Mongols decreed a census of the population for the purpose of conscription and taxation. Recruits were conscripted and taxes were levied, which means that the economy of the country was not completely disrupted. Because the Mongol taxation system favoured animal husbandry rather than farming, pastoral economy increased in importance, especially in the southern and south-eastern parts of the territory. This in turn must have slowed down the formation of landed estates and the development of land ownership which, as we have seen, was not fully established in the preceding period and certainly found little encouragement under the nomad domination.

The situation of slave trading is not quite clear, but there are indications that Italian merchant colonies in the Black Sea undertook to supply Byzantium and the eastern Mediterranean with this precious commodity. Some trading perhaps continued, but in the Mongol system itself with its organised labour and a complete lack of freedom of movement, the institution of slavery was of little importance, and war prisoners were the only slaves who could be sold.

Absolute submission to the khan made slavery unnecessary or at any rate unimportant. Rubruck met in Karakorum a goldsmith from Paris, a Frenchwoman who was married to a Russian, and some others who obviously came there as prisoners, but seemed to live without being part of a particular lord's or master's household. On the other hand, Carpini mentions people, men, women and children abducted by the Mongols and made to work for '[…] very bad masters. Worst off are those who are slaves in the house of their lord […].' It seems that the terms 'prisoner', 'slave' and 'servant' were not clearly defined by these authors, and that the treatment meted out to such people differed widely from place to place.

A small upper group of slaves, or *kholopy*, seems to have occupied important positions as managers and administrators of the estates. According to some authorities, court functionaries in the Muscovite principality, and their counterparts in most noble households were originally slaves.[1] This would be yet another proof of Islamic or rather Turkish influence in the emerging Muscovy Tsardom. It was only later, after the disintegration of the Golden Horde Empire, and the occupation of Constantinople by the Turks, that the Crimean Khanate engaged in regular slave raids into Russian territory to supply the Turkish markets. While slavery in Russia continued, it seems probable that slave-hunting under direct Mongol domination may have ceased.[2]

It was during the period of gradually slackening Mongol rule that Russian society underwent some significant changes. First, conscription on the Mongol pattern helped to remove the differences between the warrior and the peasant caste. It has been shown above that in the nomadic system military service was universal. The Mongols extended this system to Russia, conscripting and drafting a percentage of all people into their armies. From the Mongol view the entire population belonged to the khan, and had to serve in the army without exception. The Mongols are known to have used such conquered and subject peoples as 'canon-fodder' in the front line and for the most dangerous tasks, keeping their own crack troops for the decisive charge. Slaves were the only group of the population that was not conscripted, but the Grand Princes had military units of their personal slaves. On the whole, it seems probable that slavery in this period was not very important socially or economically. The entire non-slave population was thus 'levelled in subjection', even the princes being reduced to a status of regional administrators and tax-collectors of the khan. This regional character of their power had some important consequences when the Mongol suzerainty began to weaken.[3]

Chapter 11

mongoL Law & justice

The administration imposed by the Mongols resembled remarkably the system already in existence under Kievan Russia. In Kiev the administrative officers were graded according to a mathematical principle. They were: a head of a thousand, a head of a hundred, and a head of a unit of ten. This decimal system seems to have been an old tradition with both the Turks and the Mongols. The Khazars and the Magyars must have used the decimal system of division in ruling their Slav subjects.[1]

During the Mongol period the population was organised in communes or units of ten; groups of communes corresponded to units of hundred. People belonging to them were known in West Russia as 'hundredmen' and in East Russia as 'numbered men'. Each member of the hundred was permanently attached to his hundred commune. If he wanted to leave the commune, he had to find a substitute who would assume his duties. At the head of the hundred was the 'hundreder'. The hundred was divided in groups of ten. The main duty of the hundredmen was to till land. The 'numbered men' in East Russia were subjects of the Moscow princely clan as a whole, not of any individual prince. Presumably, they had been originally under the direct authority of the khan, who granted the district where they lived to the Grand Prince. The Galician horde-men, like the hundredmen, were organised in communes. The horde performed auxiliary services to the army. The bondage of each member to the horde was permanent and hereditary.[2]

From these two extracts it is obvious that the administration as well as the army organisation in Kievan Russia was based on the traditional nomadic numerical division. The Mongol system did not change it much. It merely improved it. The bondage or the principle of each man 'belonging' to his unit is clearly documented for the Mongol period, but we have every right to assume that in the preceding period it was very much the same. It was clearly the nomadic principle of personal allegiance or rather personal belonging of the subject to the khan that was at the root of this organisation. The administrative principle has also been incorporated into the Great Yasa, or Chingiz-Khan's Code of Law. It states explicitly: 'No man of any thousand or hundred or ten in which he has been counted shall depart to another place. If he does, he shall be killed and also the captain who received him.'

The army was the backbone of the Mongol administration as a whole. Therefore the principle of universal service, with each man having his specific position to which he was bound and which he could not desert, became the foundation not only of the Mongol army but also of the Mongol empire. An important aspect of the obligation of the service to the state was that the burden of it was to be distributed equally among all the subjects of the khan.

Not only men but women as well were bound to the service. 'He [Chingiz-Khan] ordered women accompanying the troops to do the work and perform the duties of men while the latter were absent fighting', wrote Makrizi. The statute of bound service became the basis of the Great Khan's omnipotence.[3]

In criminal law the sanctions of the Yasa were fairly straightforward. 'If a transgressor of such be found among them the lawbreakers are to be put to death.'[4]

As understood by the *Yasa*, the main objective of punishment was physical annihilation of the offender. Not only the offender himself but in some cases also his wife and children were liable to punishment. Punishment by death was prescribed for almost all types of crime, but homicide was punishable by a fine. For horse-stealing both retaliation and a fine in kind were imposed on the offender. The alternative was death.[5] The interesting point here is the mild punishment for homicide. It is in fact a proof of the low value attached to human life in Mongol society. Stealing a horse was, in a way, a greater offence than killing a man.

Similar regulations can be found in the Russian justice of the Kievan period. There were fines *(bloodwites)* for killing people graded according to their importance. This, as we have argued above, does not mean, of course, that there was no death penalty. It simply means that for this particular offence the ruler was content with extracting a fine, leaving it to the clan or tribe of the victim to exact revenge on the perpetrator and his family.

Other offences may have been punished more severely, or the ultimate punishment could be left, in some cases, to somebody else.

As with the administration, it can be legitimately assumed that the spirit of nomadic justice was present already in the preceding period, perhaps existing alongside other systems like the old Slav and Byzantine law. In fact, the Mongols, while introducing the regulations of the *Yasa*, did not altogether abolish the other systems. Obviously, the Mongol law was introduced more fully in the eastern and southeastern principalities than in the western and northwestern parts. In the west it was relatively quickly superseded by Polish law, while in the northwest, in Novgorod and Pskov, the Byzantine legal institutions formed the basis of local legal manuals together with the German Magdeburg law and some old Slav traditions, including ordeals.[6]

A Mongol rider and his horse were almost like a single being. (Drawing by Den Barsboldt, from Grollová-Zikmundová, Mongolové)

Chapter 12

The church

In these circumstances there were in fact only two unifying elements among all three sections of the Russian lands. One was the common language, and the other was the Orthodox Church.

The role of the Church profoundly changed after the Mongol invasion and during the 'apanage' period. As Riasanovsky observed, 'in that age of division, the unity and organisation of the Church stood out in striking manner'.[1] As the authority of the princes declined, the importance of the Church increased. With its enormous holdings and privileged position, it played a major role in the economic and political life of the country.

After the elimination of educated townspeople, it provided virtually the only literate people, and the only cultural influence in an otherwise culturally barren province of the nomad empire. If there were any foreign merchants operating in the country, we may safely assume that they were Muslims and aliens. This may well be the period when certain Byzantine values and traditions became firmly entrenched on Russian soil.

Enjoying the protection of the Government, the Church in Byzantium was committed to supporting the existing system. It therefore developed an essentially non-militant and non-revolutionary character. If something went wrong with the system, repentance and not revolt was the remedy. The Church submitted itself utterly to the ruler of the state, who was the anointed of God. This complacent attitude prevailed also in Russia under the Mongols, only under the rule of the heathen Antichrist more emphasis was laid on repentance and prayer. Ritualism and monasticism were the twin results.

On the one hand, fasting, celebrating of religious holidays, and extremely long and elaborate services were countered on the other by mysticism, asceticism, and by a truly Byzantine sympathy for contemplative life. Missionary work among the heathen tribes was carried on with great zeal. But unlike the Western Church, the Orthodox Church had not only no sense of pleasure, but also no ambition to protest or to improve the condition of life for the people.

When the Grand Prince of Muscovy emerged as the new ruler of Russia in the fifteenth century, the Church immediately resumed its role of a faithful supporter of the throne. The tsar now replaced the emperor as a natural protector of the Church with all its lands and privileges. In return he deserved complete ecclesiastical support. As in Constantinople – and even more so – his authority should extend to all secular matters as well as to Church administration. This doctrine was in the early sixteenth century challenged by the faction of the so-called 'non-possessors' who advocated poverty of the monks, independence of the Church from the state, were against monastic holdings and ecclesiastical wealth, and claimed that the state had no right to interfere in religious matters. Characteristically, at the Church Councils of 1503, 1524 and 1531, the non-possessors were repeatedly defeated by the strength of the Byzantine examples cited by their opponents.[2]

Monastic life in Russia followed strictly its Byzantine model. This differed from West European monasticism in several important points. First, there was not a multitude of orders, but only one order. It was built on the regulations of the Holy Community of Mount Athos and later on those of the monastery of St John Studius in Constantinople.[3]

Monastic life was designed primarily for contemplation and theological research. There were no different regulations, no different aims, and no competition between orders as in the West. There was also no outside Head of the order, the monasteries and abbeys being incorporated in the local Church hierarchy. Second, the monasteries were mostly located in or near the towns. Whereas in the West monasteries fulfilled an important role as colonisers, importers of foreign skills and know-how, and in some cases as manufacturers on a large scale, Russian monasteries were never assigned any similar task. It was only in the later period that some monastic communities were founded in remote areas like the Solovetski Islands in the White Sea. But even there their aim was primarily missionary rather than economic colonisation. Third, in line with the general policy of the Orthodox Church, the monasteries seldom, if ever, intervened in the country's politics. The person of the ruler and his autocratic system of government were sacred, and no churchmen ever dared to question them. Whereas the political history of every western country is full of frictions and conflicts between the Church and the State, and within the realm of the Church between the bishops and the abbots, nothing like this can be found in the Byzantine or, for that matter, Russian Orthodoxy. The only influence, apart from purely literary one, which the monasteries exercised in Russia, was their power as large landowners, a position which they acquired only towards the end of the Kievan period, and in the subsequent times of Apanage Russia until this power had been brutally curtailed by Ivan the Terrible in the sixteenth century.[4]

Chapter 13

The towns
&
the idea of self-government

The history of self-government in Russia begins with the city of Novgorod, which as early as the middle of the twelfth century succeeded in replacing the appointed officials of the Prince of Kiev by locally elected representatives; more than once the city successfully defied the power of the prince – the princely rule being by then in a state of disintegration – and when the Tartar invasion cut it off from the south and east of the country, the city gradually reached the status of an independent city-republic governed by an oligarchy of merchants, not dissimilar from the contemporary cities of the Hanse and northern Italy. Similar institutions developed in Pskov and some other north-western towns.

Clearly, Novgorod had its model in Lubeck and other cities in the Baltic with whom it had frequent contacts. What is not so sure is whether there were any institutions of municipal self-government in Kievan Russia prior to this development in Novgorod which could have served as another model for the northern city's spectacular achievements.

Some authorities maintain that such institution was the town assembly or veche. In Novgorod it was this assembly 'composed of all free householders'[1] that acted in general as the supreme authority in the city. The earliest evidence of its activity is an agreement negotiated with a prince in 1265. It is believed that similar assemblies existed in Kiev and other towns before the Mongol invasion; Vernadsky calls it 'a universal institution in old Russia', and believes that 'the Russian democratic institutions of the Kievan period belong to the classical Greek type – that of immediate democracy'.[2] On the surface, the scanty remarks in the Chronicles would indeed support such a hypothesis; the drawback is that something like 1300 years separates the classical Greek democracy from the Kievan period, and there is no evidence of how and where have these institutions survived the gap. We would have to look for some model, or at least influence which is perhaps less classical, but nearer in time and space.

The Scandinavian *ting* can be eliminated because it was essentially a village or district assembly, not a municipal one (towns were few and insignificant in Scandinavia before the Hanse era). We would have to look to the only country with a developed urban culture in the Pontic – East European area, that is, Byzantium. Byzantine cities indeed enjoyed a large degree of autonomy and self-government until the reforms of Heraclius in the seventh century when the civil and military authorities were merged under the *theme* system. Since then towns were administered by appointed governors, not by elected councils. Local administration and a tradition of municipal autonomy survived in Crimean cities – in particular in Kherson – until the ninth century, when Emperor Theophilus created the *theme* of Kherson, and brought Crimea into line with other imperial provinces.[3] There was some revival of municipal institutions in Byzantium in the twelfth to fifteenth centuries as a result of a new class, the landed gentry, wishing to weaken the central power. Landed aristocracy was the ruling element in these institutions, and merchants or artisans had no say in them.[4]

This may narrow the gap, but there is still a long way from the ninth century municipal authority in Kherson, and an 'assembly of all freemen' in eleventh century Kiev. Perhaps it might be more fruitful to analyse the 'primitive democracy' of the early Slavs rather than the classical mode.

If this assumption is right and the Kievan 'cities' developed from the Slav *burgwalls* – and in Great Moravia of the ninth to tenth century some of them seem to have had a distinctly urban character – then it is just possible that some of the tribal institutions like the gathering of all members might have survived there. This may be supported by the fact that the original 'lands' of the Kievan realm partly coincided with the tribal groups, and each 'land' centred around its capital city.[5] A tribal assembly is, of course, fundamentally different from municipal self-government, although it may resemble the 'immediate democracy' of a Greek city state – for the Greek cities no doubt developed from tribes.

The political institutions of the forest Slavs were weaker and less developed than those of the steppe Slavs.[6]

In spite of the extremely vague character of the Kievan *veche* – which would incidentally confirm that it was an institution of the forest Slavs – it might have been a manifestation of the tribal spirit of the forest people as against the centralising tendencies of the better-organised steppe people.

The steppe Slavs, together with the Varangians and imbued with their nomadic universalistic tradition, came to dominate the Kievan realm from Novgorod to Tmutorokan in the ninth and early tenth century. In their system there was no room for any decentralisation or 'immediate democracy'[7] and even less for a balance of power of any kind. The veche could have come to the fore only when the princely power broke down, for some reason or other, or when it was so threatened that the prince was forced to seek some popular support: 'Popular election [...] remained dormant as long as genealogical seniority worked smoothly.'[8]

After the end of princely power in Kiev, Novgorod and its sister city, Pskov, became the aristocratic republics, not unlike their counterparts in Italy and northern Germany. Novgorod merchants travelled frequently to Gotland, Copenhagen and Lubeck, and maintained factories there. Even before the German merchants established their powerful 'factory' in Novgorod, the city resisted successfully the attempts of the Kievan princes to bring it under their direct rule. As from 1126, the Novgorodians elected the *posadniki* (highest officials representing the prince). After a revolt in 1136 and the expulsion of the prince Vsevolod Mstislavich, the authority of the latter was even more curtailed. The city officials, including the military commander *(tysiatsky)* were elected by an Assembly, or Town Council *(veche)*, whose power was truly outstanding for, according to Riasanovsky, 'it invited and dismissed the prince, elected the posadnik and the tysiatsky, and determined the selection of archbishops by electing three candidates for that position. It decided the issues of war and peace, mobilised the army, proclaimed laws, raised taxes, and acted in general as supreme authority in Novgorod.'[9]

Riasanovsky goes even further, for he claims that a street in Novgorod already had the status of a self-governing unit. 'Several streets formed a *sotnia*, that is, a hundred. Hundreds in their turn combined into quarters, or *kontsy*, which totalled five. Each *konets* enjoyed far-reaching autonomy.'[10] In this case, the organisation by hundreds can go back either to Kiev, or to the Scandinavian *härad*, but the autonomous position of the Novgorod hundreds points rather to the Scandinavian origin.

The judicial system of Novgorod shows a similar composite pattern as in Western Europe. 'The prince, the *posadnik*, the *tysiatskii* and the archbishop, all had their particular courts.'[11] This corresponds roughly to the royal, provincial, municipal and ecclesiastical courts in the West. Judicial combat used in dubious cases may be a relic of ancient Slav practices. Punishments were mild, but the death penalty existed. (This seems to contradict Vernadsky's assertion that the death penalty did not exist in Kievan Russia – see p. 110.) It is hardly probable that the relatively very civilised Novgorod law would be stricter in this respect than the older, less elaborate Kievan law. 'Much evidence reflects the high regard for human life characteristic of Novgorod: the Novgorodian Chronicle at times refers to a great slaughter when it speaks of the killing of several persons.'[12]

Social antagonisms developed between wealthy merchants and landowners on one side, and between the poor layers of the population. This is reminiscent of similar conflicts in Italian cities; in the fourteenth and fifteenth centuries Novgorod became increasingly an oligarchy, with a few powerful families virtually controlling high offices.[13]

While Western Christianity connected with the repeated invasions of the Teutonic knights presented itself in a hostile form, Novgorod witnessed a remarkable revival of cultural activity, especially in architecture and the arts sponsored by the Orthodox Church, and keeping alive the Byzantine heritage.

Novgorod in this period presents an interesting picture of dual orientation. While turning to the Baltic for its economic livelihood and therefore towards Western Europe, its culture remained firmly rooted in its Byzantine past.

Novgorod Church, though canonically dependent on the metropolitan of Moscow, maintained direct links with Constantinople. For this reason when the new Palaeologan art began to spread northwards, it was readily accepted in Novgorod.[14] So it happened that Novgorod became the leading northern outpost of late Byzantine art. Although the Byzantine origins of Novgorod art, especially of wall-painting and icon-painting, are beyond doubt, there are some elements in the murals, reminiscent of late-medieval Gothic painting, while the originality of the fifteenth century Novgorod icons is attributable to local Slav traditions.

Obolensky makes an interesting observation that relates to the personal habits of the Novgorodians.[15] In a treaty signed in 911 between prince Oleg of Kiev and the Byzantine Empire, a special clause stipulates that the Russians 'were to have [in their St Mamas residence] as many baths as they wished: this was doubtless agreed on the insistence of the Novgorodians who, to the ironical astonishment of their south Russian compatriots [...] were addicted to the North-European equivalent of Turkish baths'. The real significance of this little item emerges only when we compare it with what Carpini and Rubruck observed of the Mongols three hundred years later. 'Their hands are very dirty [...] they never wash their dishes [...] they are unclean in eating, drinking and in everything they do [...].'[16] 'They never wash any clothing, because, as they say, it angers their god. They even beat up those who wash and take their washing away from them [...]. They never wash their dishes or cauldrons [...]. If they wash their hands or faces, they take a mouthful of water, then spit a little of it over their hands and wipe their face and their hair with their wet hands [...].'[17] The standards of personal hygiene, at least at that early stage in Novgorod, seem to point towards Scandinavia, while the south Russian ones may have been similar to those of the steppe nomad.

The independent existence of Novgorod and Pskov, with their uninhibited contacts with the West, lasted for more than two centuries from the early thirteenth to the late fifteenth century. But as soon as the Grand Princes of Muscovy emerged from Mongol submission, they felt compelled to reassert their autocratic authority over them. Ivan III destroyed the autonomy of the two cities in 1471 and 1478, and Ivan IV stamped out the last traces of Western influence in 1570 in a bloodbath in which he proved to be a worthy disciple of the Mongol khans.

Meanwhile, in the fifteenth century the influence of a growing power made itself felt in the south. The fall of Constantinople provided no doubt a shock for the pious Orthodox, but its repercussions in the political sphere were even more significant. The rise of Ottoman power brought a new factor into the politics of the Pontic steppes and of the southern and eastern Russian principalities. The rise of Muscovy to a dominant position coincided with the Ottoman rise to power, and it was only natural that the Muscovite princes looked upon the sultan as their nearest and most successful model.

It can be assumed, therefore, that the only case of an institutionalised municipal autonomy, or self-government, with elected officials representing the population (or at least the voting population) were the north-western cities of Novgorod and Pskov. They could develop as such only because there was, at that time, no centralised princely power – and as soon as such power reappeared, by the end of the fifteenth century, its very first act was to curb the autonomy of these cities. A century-long struggle followed, and ended with the destruction of Novgorod, the subjugation of Pskov, and with a complete extirpation of their institutions.

Since then the interest of Russian people in self-government has never recovered. In fact, the Novgorod era being a mere episode affecting only a fraction of the country, it may be said that such interest never had time to develop. So it happened that, when the government 'tried to stimulate initiative, public spirit, and a degree of participation in local affairs among the townsmen by such means as the creation of guilds', and 'when it granted urban self-government in the charter of 1785, as usual, these efforts failed.'[18]

Appendix - some Linguistic remarks

Some linguistic remarks may perhaps be made in this context. Comparing the Czech and Russian words for 'security' and 'danger', we find an interesting difference. Both words are Slav and have the same root, *pas*.[1] In Russian, *opasnost* means 'danger' and *bezopasnost* (non-danger) means 'security'. In Czech, *bezpečí* (no-pas) is the word for 'security' and *nebezpečí* (no-security) means 'danger'. Usually, in most languages, the 'positive' word is used to describe the normal, usual situation, and the 'negative' one is used for the abnormal or unusual one. If we accept this, it would seem to indicate that for a Russian insecurity or danger was the 'normal' state and security an exception, while for the Czech, the opposite would be true: security as the normal state and insecurity as an exception. This could well indicate the difference between the nomadic and the sedentary way of life.

For the comparison of *rab* and *robota* (slave and corvé) in Czech and Russian, see p. 78.[2]

In Russian the absence of the auxiliary verbs in certain grammatical forms, such as *Ia doma* (I at home) or u *menia syn* (at me son) instead of 'I am at home' and 'I have a son' may be derived from Mongolian. (I owe this information to Professor Pavel Poucha from the Oriental Institute of Prague.) According to V. Zikmundová from the University of Prague, this phenomenon is common to all Altaic languages, among them the Kipchaq. The Russians had close contacts with the Kipchaq, or Polovtsy, before the Mongol invasion.

The Russian word *kazna* (treasury) seems to be of Arabic or Persian, not of Mongol origin *(ghazane – treasure, ghazane-dari – treasure-house, in Turkish hazine)*.[3] There are several borrowings from Persian in Russian, but it may be difficult to determine whether they arrived there directly or by way of Mongolian or Turkish. I did not find any special study on this subject.

Curiously, the only non-Slav numeral in the Russian language is *sorok* (forty). Forty is, as mentioned elsewhere, a sacred number in Middle Eastern folklore (meaning 'many') – compare Ali Baba and the forty thieves, or, in Isfahan, the *Chehel Sotun* ('forty columns') Pavilion.[4]

Summary to Part 2

The nomadic invaders in the 11th and 12th centuries deprived the Kievan pastoralists of their pastures, pushed the farming population deeper into the forests and also cut the commercial life-line, the Dnieper route. The entire centre of gravity shifted north-east, to the Volga-Oka region where new commercial contacts and state entities became established. The authority of the Kievan princes was weakened, the provincial governors seized power and began to rule in their own name – and inevitably, to fight each other.

When the Mongols struck, these principalities were unable to offer much resistance. As a consequence, the realm was split into three parts. The south and the east were first depopulated and then ruled directly by the Mongols. The north-western cities were not occupied and were allowed to continue their trade with the Baltic, paying a tribute to the Mongols. The western parts, although occupied for a time, managed gradually to veer into the orbit of the Lithuanian and Polish state.

Whereas the methods and ways of government in Kiev were an amalgam of nomadic and Byzantine traditions, in some cities in the north-west, especially in Novgorod and Pskov, new methods of government appeared, most probably under the influence of the Hanseatic cities and the Baltic trade. Unlike Kiev, the city administration was run by an elected council, the mayor or *posadnik* as well as the military commander were elected officials and even the candidates for the archbishopric were chosen by the assembly.

Another important difference was the land ownership. In Kiev, in principle, the Prince was the sole owner of all land and the only exception were the monasteries which were not only granted land in full possession but also enjoyed important tax exemptions. In Novgorod and Pskov, on the contrary, land could be owned by citizens and the possession of it gave the owners the right to vote in the assembly and to have an influence on the policies of the government. In the subsequent period this was considered an unacceptable breach of the power and authority of the Prince and led to the savage destruction of both cities.

part 3

MUSCOVY
RUSSIA

Chapter 14

The state

The rise of Muscovy to a dominant position among the Russian principalities and its liberation from the Tartar rule coincided with two important events outside the realm, the fall of Constantinople and the rise of Ottoman Turkey to the status of a great power. The Grand Princes of Muscovy were thus from the very start invested with a dual ambition to replace the Byzantine emperor as the head of the Orthodox world, and to imitate and equal the Turkish sultan, who had already successfully replaced the emperor in secular politics. Behind these ambitions was the age-old idea of the universal empire. It was quite in line with this idea that anybody who refused to acknowledge the ruler's claim to universal authority was regarded as an enemy and sooner or later had to be destroyed. An incompatible ideology was considered a far more dangerous enemy than a hostile military power.

This was the reason why Ivan III, after reasserting himself as an undisputed ruler of Muscovy, directed his first blow against the harmless trading city of Novgorod. It was not Novgorod's military power (which was purely defensive), not even its economic wealth which prompted Ivan to this attack, but the city's ideology of free trade, of unrestricted foreign contacts and of a government based on consent rather than autocratic power. Even after Ivan's victory and a severe curtailment of Novgorod's constitution, the city remained a constant cause of concern to the Muscovite rulers until its ferocious destruction by Ivan IV.

Apart from the universalistic ideology, the nomadic heritage has manifested itself in Muscovy in various other ways, ranging from administrative principles and organisation of the army to the contemptuous attitude towards trade and economic enterprise, and to a general lack of

Rise of Moscow, 1300-1533

SWEDEN

FINNS

Semi-dependent Colonies

• Ustiug

• Vologda

Baltic Sea

Pskov • Novgorod

Iaroslavl

Tver • Rostov

KHANATE

• Kazan

OF KAZAN

Vladimir

Smolensk • ★ Moscow

• Great Bulgar

BULGAR

Tula • Riazan

LITHUANIA

Orel •

R. Volga

POLAND

Chernigov •

Kiev •

GOLDEN HORDE

HUNGARY

R. Dniester

MOLDAVIA

BOUNDARY OF LITHUANIA IN 1462

OTTOMAN EMPIRE

Black Sea

• Constantinople

	Moscow 1300 - under Daniel
	To 1389 – Ivan I – Dmitrii
	To 1462 – Basil I, Basil II
	To 1533 – Ivan III, Basil III

N

© Airphoto International Ltd.

artistic creativity. But to the contemporary traveller the most conspicuous one was the unbridled absolutism of princely power and the harsh treatment of subjects.

To the European envoys penetrating sixteenth century Muscovy it appeared as a country governed by an autocrat similar to an Asiatic despot or the Turkish sultan. 'He uses his authority as much over ecclesiastics as laymen, and holds unlimited control over the lives and property of all his subjects. It is a matter of doubt whether the brutality of the people has made the prince a tyrant, or whether the people themselves have become thus brutal and cruel through the tyranny of their prince.'[1]

Giles Fletcher, at the end of the sixteenth century, noticed 'the state and form of their government is plaine tyrannical, as applying all to the behoof of the prince, and that after a most open a barbarous manner'.[2]

The administration of Muscovy was based on the Persian-Mongol rather than the Byzantine-Turkish model. There was no sacred Palace, a combination of the sovereign's private dwelling and the centre of government, as in Byzantine and Turkish Constantinople. A number of administrative departments (known as *puti*) was subordinated directly to the Grand Prince or tsar[3] and resembled the Persian system of *divans*, which had been taken over by the Mongols of the Golden Horde. The word *puti* seems to be a translation from Turkish, which, in turn, took it over from Persian.[4] The officials in charge of the *puti* were sometimes slaves and sometimes *boyars*, but they were always completely dependent on the ruler. They received no salary, and were expected to take as their reward part of the department's income (in Turkey slave officials received their reward in form of gifts from the sultan).

Byzantine influence at the court of Muscovite princes can be found in the elaborate and pompous ceremonial, probably adapted from the Orthodox Church, and also in the curious system of rigid grading of court dignitaries called *mestnichestvo*, according to which each family of courtiers had a fixed and unchangeable place in the court hierarchy based on their genealogical seniority. This 'placed the Muscovite Grand Prince in the curious situation of being unable to allot seats at his own banqueting table among those on whom he could impose summary punishment or execution with comparative ease'.[5]

Land-tenure, which was previously connected more with tax-collecting, was now firmly linked with services to the state, notably with military service. This resembled, in a way, the Turkish *timar* system, and was in fact an expression, on a higher and more institutionalised level, of the old nomadic idea that every member of the community is a personal servant (and property) of the ruler.

With fixed frontiers and the increasing role of agriculture in the economy of the state, the value of land and landholding became gradually acknowledged, while the ruler became automatically identified with the territorial state. The personal character of the service, however, remained unchanged. This is an important difference from West-European feudalism.

Whereas in Western Europe a person had to serve because he held the land, in the East he received the tenure of the land as a reward for his services. The main practical difference was in the inability to inherit the holding. At the beginning the Turkish fiefs were uninheritable. The situation was similar in Muscovy. Only the sons of serving princes had the unconditional right to inherit estates.[6]

A serviceman was given an estate not to develop it, but, in a rather Oriental sense, to exploit it and enrich himself. It was, in fact, the same phenomenon as earlier in history when a nomadic warrior caste lived parasitically off the farming peasants. It can be assumed that many Muscovite servicemen were, in fact, nomads or of nomadic descent (see below p. 177).

The West-European manors and manorial estates grew organically in the period of subsistence farming in order to form a self-supporting unit. Russian estates, on the contrary, were distributed rather haphazardly without any such aspect of economic organisation. Moreover, they came in a period when Russian agriculture was gradually moving into the commercial stage; that means producing for the market rather than for domestic consumption only. (This production was for the internal market. In the sixteenth century Muscovy did not export any significant amount of grain).[7]

Producing for the market meant, of course, a source of revenue for the landlord, and thus another incentive for him to exploit his period of tenure to the utmost. This carried a remarkable similarity with the Turkish system under the Ottoman sultans. On the other hand, and again, similarly to Turkey, this system gave a large scope for village autonomy due to the frequent absence of the landholder either in the army or in court service. A tissue of village communes with the Byzantine element of collective responsibility for taxpaying suited this system very well. Indeed, so well that in the large areas of the north and north-east where gentry estates and serfdom did not develop, the village communes were administered directly by the crown, and later formed the bulk of the so-called state-peasant class.

During the reign of Ivan III and simultaneously with the introduction of non-inheritable fiefs it became a treasonable offence for any nobleman to leave the country. This was yet another logical consequence of a territorial state. In the nomadic system what mattered was the personal service to the ruler regardless of any definite territorial boundaries. Wherever the ruler moved the servitors moved with him. Wherever they moved they still remained his subjects, that is, his property. Now, with the establishment of a centralised territorial state, the frontiers of the state also marked the limits of the sovereign's power. Those who left the state and went abroad defied their ruler's right of possession and were escaping beyond his reach.[8]

The service-state emerging from Ivan III's reforms had some other interesting aspects. The service gentry provided a ready material for the future bureaucratic administration. Under Ivan IV they were running the *guba* and *zemstva*.[9] Also their estates, which were held on a temporary basis, provided the opportunity already contained in the Mongol system of recruiting peasants into the army. Unlike Poland, where aristocratic landowners did not permit their peasants to serve in the king's army in order not to diminish the revenues from their estates, and also not to increase the king's power, the Russian peasant, except those on Church estates, was drafted on a strict and unequivocal pattern with no privileges and very few exceptions. Nor was there to be any privilege between the infantry and cavalry regiments.

Some people may have preferred an economically secure life, and sold themselves into slavery; others had to do so because of debt or for some other compelling reason. There were, according to Hellie,[10] several forms of slavery in Muscovy, and there is no reason why the same or similar forms could not exist already in the preceding period. Apart from hereditary slavery *(starinnoe kholopstvo)*, there was full slavery, which could become hereditary for the slave's offspring, registered slavery for élite slaves, slavery for debt, indentured slavery, which was limited for a certain number of years, voluntary *(dobrovol'noe)* slavery, and perhaps even a limited service contract slavery *(kabal'noe kholopstvo)*, documented only for the period of Muscovy, and which seems to have been a pawnship converted into slavery upon non-payment of the debt. Military captivity was, of course, an important source of slaves.

Slaves were used mainly as domestic servants doing menial work for their masters and enhancing, by their numbers, the masters' social standing. Relatively few slaves were used in productive labour, in agriculture or mines; skilled craftsmen were a special category.

Chapter 15

The army

The organisation of the Muscovite army was taken over from the Golden Horde. The Mongol-type army consisted of two main formations: the right wing or western group, and the left wing or eastern group: the centre presumably consisted of the khan's guardsmen under his personal command.[1] The Muscovite army followed the Mongol set-up. There were five units known as *polki*, grouped as the right-arm division, the left-arm division, the centre, or the big division, with an advance guard and a rear guard.[2] As with the Mongols, the right-arm unit was considered more important. This organisation lasted until the second half of the seventeenth century.

The army usually fought by using age-old echelon tactic with masses of cavalrymen first shooting volleys of arrows, and then attacking the enemy with sabres in hand-to-hand combat.[3] This was the same tactic the Tartars used; also the army equipment was very similar to that of the Tartars.[4]

The Russian cavalryman of the sixteenth century went to war armed much as the military forces of Kiev had been.[5] He had bow and arrows, a sabre and occasionally, a spear or lance.

Artillery was introduced in limited numbers in the time of Ivan III and became a regular part of the army under Ivan IV (according to Hellie, Ivan IV's army had 3,000 artillerists out of a total of some 70,000 men; the *streltsy* (musketeers) numbered 12,000, slaves 17,500).[6] The slaves, however, never reached the fame of the Turkish *janissaries*.

Although it is possible that the Russians first met firearms as early as 1380 when they stormed the city of Bolgar on the Volga,[7] there is no evidence that they ever used them before Ivan III a century later. Handguns (muskets) were introduced when Ivan IV established the first *streltsy* regiments after 1550, although they were known from about 1480. The *streltsy* were also the first standing army units; until then the army reported only on call, usually twice a year for guard duty against Tartar raids, or otherwise in an emergency. The *streltsy* were modelled upon the Turkish *janissaries,* and just like them could engage in trade and manufacturing.

Artillery depended very much on foreign experts, both gun-founders and gunners, and Muscovite princes from Ivan III on invited ever-increasing numbers of experts from West European countries, especially Holland and Scotland. Cannons were at first used in siege warfare only. The practical use of field artillery was hampered by the difficulties of transport. The problems must have been very similar to those of Sweden in the Thirty Years War. Neither Sweden nor Russia possessed great horses, and to pull a cannon in a difficult terrain required an unwieldy number of animals. Therefore the principal way of moving guns was by water.

The problems of financing the army were again similar to those of Sweden of that period. The money economy was not sufficiently developed; taxes had to be collected and armies paid in kind. The Russian solution, similar to that of Turkey, was a system of land-allotments (or grants) called *pomestie*.[8]

Ivan's army was quite capable of defeating the Tartars of the Golden Horde mainly because of its artillery and a better system of recruitment. It had considerable difficulties with the Crimean Tartars, who were better organised and had the support of Turkey; in the West it was no match for Polish cavalry, then at its peak, nor for the Swedish infantry as it emerged from the reforms of Gustav Vasa.[9]

Chapter 16

urbanisation
&
industriaLisation

The lack of towns and the shortage of urban population were reflected, in the field of economics, by the lack of markets, lack of marketable goods, and mainly by the critical shortage of skilled labour. This was so crippling that when more sophisticated equipment of the army became imperative foreign craftsmen and other specialists had to be invited in large numbers and at great cost to the state treasury. There were other fields as well, like the building of stone and brick, in which Russia relied almost entirely on foreign skill. Starting with Ivan III at the end of the fifteenth century, the trend never really stopped. Whereas in Western Europe the towns provided a vast reservoir of skills and techniques, which were the prerequisites of industrialisation, Russia, when industrialisation reached her, had again to resort to foreign help. When manual skills ceased to suffice and education was required to run more sophisticated industries and businesses, or to command larger and more modern armies, foreigners had to be brought in once again to teach the Russians.

The towns which grew in this period were administrative centres and military garrisons rather than manufacturing and market places. In accordance with the concept of the service-state the princes concentrated in these garrison towns the existing artisans, craftsmen and traders, who were then subject to services and taxes imposed by the requirements of the state. The social status of the merchants was correspondingly low; they were just another group of low-class servitors of the state. They were uneducated and inexperienced, and had very little knowledge of the outside world and its products. This was obviously a legacy of almost three centuries of restricted commercial activities during which the Russians seem to have almost forgotten how to trade. No wonder, therefore, that the trade of Muscovite Russia became increasingly concentrated in foreign hands. (The journey of the merchant of Tver, Afanasii Nikitin, to Persia and India seems to have been an exception.)

The principal outlet for foreign trade after the first campaign against Novgorod became the river Don with the trading city of Kaffa in eastern Crimea. The Ottoman navy took this former Genoese colony in 1475, but this event did not interrupt the flow of Russian trade. On the other hand, southern trade required a certain degree of cooperation between the rulers of Muscovy and the khans of Crimea. Alliances were repeatedly concluded between the Muscovites and the Tartars to secure this trade, and also to check the Polish–Lithuanian power in western Ukraine.

Two other outlets were opened during the reign of Ivan IV. In the north the English sailors, Richard Chancellor and Anthony Jenkinson, circumnavigated the North Cape in the 1550s, and established contact with the Russians in the mouth of the Northern Dvina, thus opening a trade route with the intention of replacing the now interrupted links between Novgorod and the Baltic. The conquest of Kazan and Astrakhan by Ivan IV opened yet another trade route down the river Volga, into the Caspian, and further on to Central Asia and Persia.

The extent of this trade seems to have been rather limited and mostly in the hands of foreign merchants who came to Muscovy rather than the other way round. Economic competition has never been allowed to take root in Russia. The system of state-controlled economy and of large-scale state enterprise effectively excluded any free competition. Moreover, there was precious little in the country's economy that could provoke and stimulate competition. It has been shown how long it took before Russian agriculture became commercially viable. In other fields very little was produced for the market – that is, above home consumption – and it was usually taken by the government in the form of taxes in kind to be subsequently exported. Items usually cited in this connection were furs, wax and honey, and later pitch, tar, flax and hemp.

Foreign trade and whatever there was of domestic trade were kept strictly apart. Since the fall of Novgorod foreign trade was government-controlled, and trading concessions were granted to foreign merchants rather than to allow Russians to trade with foreign countries. The government fixed the prices of imported goods, and the tsar had the right of pre-emption.

One reason for the strict separation of the foreign and internal trade was probably financial. Unlike Byzantium, Russia never had an internationally recognised and convertible currency – with the exception of a brief period before World War I when gold coinage was formally introduced. Coinage, whether silver or copper, could only be used within the country. Already in the seventeenth century there were strict regulations that no coins must be taken outside Russia,[1] nor was it allowed to take gold and silver of any description out of Russia.[2] It seems as if the rulers of Russia believed that the currency had a fictitious value, and that by restricting it to domestic use they would protect it from collapse.

Internal or domestic trade run mostly by itinerant pedlars was poorly developed as a result of several reasons, among them low density of population, an undeveloped money economy and difficulties of transport. Manufactured goods were constantly lacking for the same reasons. Crafts were still rare, and most implements and utensils were homemade and wooden. As mentioned above, a craftsman can only make a living if he has a certain market, that is, a number of people with sufficient purchasing power to buy his product, and if he has at his disposal adequate transport to get the product to them at economically acceptable cost. In Russia these prerequisites were lacking, or were insufficient, and crafts – and later manufactures – either did not develop at all, or appeared far too late; even if they appeared, they were usually economically too weak and dependent on government support.

Most crafts and manufactures lived on government orders supplying the army. Prices in such cases were not subject to any market mechanism, but were fixed by the government, even more so, because in most cases the craftsmen were bonded people. In this sector, too, a competitive spirit could hardly develop. 'At market nobody can sell unless the Sovereign's merchandise had first been sold.' In the sphere of domestic trade government functionaries first purchased wax, honey and other items, 'taking them at small prices what themselves list, and selling them againe at an excessive rate to their own marchants, and to marchants strangers [...]. If they refuse to buy them, then to force unto it.'[3]

With the isolation of the domestic from the international market, the value of the currency was fixed by government decree – or by the government's regulation of prices. Apart from such artificial valuing of the currency, money as such had only a secondary importance in the Russian economy. This again was connected with the limited circulation of goods.

Those few items which it was possible to buy and sell were exchanged on a barter basis; taxes were collected in kind (Peter the Great's Head Tax of 1718 was supposed to be collected in money). Administrative officials lived on the *kormlenie*, and armies were mostly unpaid. In 1663, the total wage bill for the active army was around one million roubles per year, of which about 80 percent went to maintain the foreign formation regiments, less than ten percent for the *streltsy* regiments, eight percent for the *dvoriane* and *deti boyarskie* – the *pomestie* service gentry – and less than 0.6 percent for the Cossacks.[4]

Apart from cash, the troops also received an allowance of grain. Money coined by the state was chiefly used for state purchases (arms, etc.), for paying foreign soldiers and specialists, and for eventual government-commissioned building. Little of this money ever got into open circulation. A money economy therefore could not develop, and financial institutions, like banking, credit, accountancy, interest, etc., remained unknown. The idea that 'money can make money' did not seem to have taken root in Russia. Without interest, capital for economic development was not available.

Because of the uncertain situation of land ownership, investment in land never became economically viable; investment in manufacturing appeared only in the nineteenth century, when the government, anxious to foster industrialisation, encouraged foreign capital, and provided state funds either as loans or as direct state investment.

Throughout history, transportation remained one of the major obstacles to economic development. Road building was effectively prevented by lack of stone; thaw and rain made overland journeys virtually impossible for months on end; rivers, the only arteries of transport in most parts of the country, were frozen in winter, while winter was the best season for overland connection between them. Human power was used for hauling boats upstream. Portage was necessary from one river to another; some canals were built under Peter the Great, but large-scale constructions had to wait until the Soviet era. All this combined to make transport difficult, dangerous and expensive.

The effect was that the circulation of goods was restricted to a small range of expensive and easily transportable items, like furs, or some luxury goods for the court and the nobles. Bulk cargoes, like grain and timber, were as a rule shipped downstream to the sea. This is an additional reason against the idea advanced by some historians that 'the grain-producing south supplied food to the unproductive, grain-consuming north'. Grain from the southern areas would have to be hauled upstream for considerable distances before being transferred to one of the north-flowing rivers. Even the rudimentary market of Muscovy and post-Petrine Russia was not impervious to transport costs on this scale, and if such manipulation were true, it would have pushed the price of grain beyond all acceptable limits (see also above p. 92ff).

Russia at the Time of Ivan IV, 1533-98

White Sea

SWEDEN

FINNS

MUSCOVY IN 1533

URAL MOUNTAINS

• Archangel

STROGANOV COLONY

• Novgorod

Torzhok

• Pskov

Tver

Staritsa

Klin

• Nizhnii Novgorod

Vladimir

KHANATE OF KAZAN

Moscow ★

Murom

Smolensk

Kaluga

• Samara

Held by Russia 1558 to 1583

T A R T A R S

Ural River

L I T H U A N I A (POLAND)

• Chernigov

G O L D E N · H O R D E

KHANATE OF ASTRAKHAN

KAZAKHS

River Dnieper

DON COSSACKS

• Sarai

KHANATE OF CRIMEA

• Azov

River Kuban

TEREK COSSACKS

River Terek

Bakhchisarai •

Caspian Sea

TURKOMEN

Black   Sea

Areas taken by Ivan the Terrible, 1533-84; and Theodore, 1584-98

N

© *Airphoto International Ltd.*

Chapter 17

The oprichnina
&
the Non-possessors

Two events in the reign of Ivan IV deserve a closer look. One is the notorious *oprichnina*, which almost every Russian historian has interpreted in a different way. Some saw in it merely a police corps destined to fight opposition and treason. It seems, however, that it was a deliberate or subconscious attempt by the tsar to destroy the principle of hereditary land ownership and to revive the personal bond between the subjects and the tsar – an aspect characteristic of the nomadic system.

On the one hand, the monarch tried to destroy the *boyars* (not as a class but as hereditary landowners); in other words, he was quite ready to accept into his *oprichnina* those *boyars* who owned land as a reward for their services on a non-hereditary basis. It was an attempt to destroy *mestnichestvo* and bring the servicemen to the fore.

It is probable that the *boyars* at that time harboured various ambitions to increase their power in the state at the expense of the monarchy, as they saw it in neighbouring Poland. Hereditary landholding was the main base of their economic strength. Destroying this base, Ivan converted the *boyars* into a harmless group of courtiers wholly dependent on the sovereign.

On the other hand, the creation of the *oprichnina* lands was an attempt to re-establish the sovereign as a sole owner of all land, a prerogative that clearly goes back to the nomadic ideology of the past. It failed because the state in Ivan's time was a territorial entity and not a spiritual one as in the nomadic era. Land ceased to be an abstract idea of something limitless and therefore without value. Territorial boundaries made land a concrete object, and its ownership became a concrete political issue.

The other event is connected with the struggle between the so-called possessors and non-possessors within the Orthodox Church. The possessors believed in a close union of an autocratic ruler and a rich and influential Church. The prince (or tsar) was the natural protector of the Church with all its lands and privileges. In return he deserved complete ecclesiastical support while his authority should extend not only to all secular matters but also to Church administration.

The non-possessors objected to ecclesiastical wealth and, in particular, to monastic landholding; they advocated the independence of the Church, and denied the State any right to interfere in religious matters. This struggle went on for some time, and reached its peak in the reign of Ivan IV. The key to it can be found in the criticism of certain icons commissioned after the great fire of Moscow in 1547. Icon-painters from Pskov were invited to Moscow to paint icons for the cathedral of Assumption. They caused no little stir by introducing their westernised forms into the Kremlin.

Pskov was the sister city of Novgorod in north-western Russia, which lost its political independence in 1510. It had been for some time the bastion of the non-possessors. To counter their influence a number of churches were built in Pskov and in the surrounding area either in the name of the Grand Prince Vassili III, or on the initiative of the Muscovite settlers who had been introduced, as was the Muscovite custom, into the newly-annexed territory.[1] An analogy can be found in the tactics employed by Moscow in Novgorod, which would therefore appear to have been a considered approach of Vassili III to the furtherance of spiritual centralisation of his dominion.

Ivan's chancellery criticised the Pskovian icons for alleged Western influences. However, Pop Silvester, a priest who was a close adviser to the tsar, commissioned the pictures. Obviously, this was a struggle between two concepts of Muscovite politics. The chancellery defended the unrestricted and autocratic power of the tsar, while Silvester, who represented the Novgorod faction, was in favour of a more liberal and oligarchic policy.

To counter such tendencies, Moscow established in Pskov a new monastery

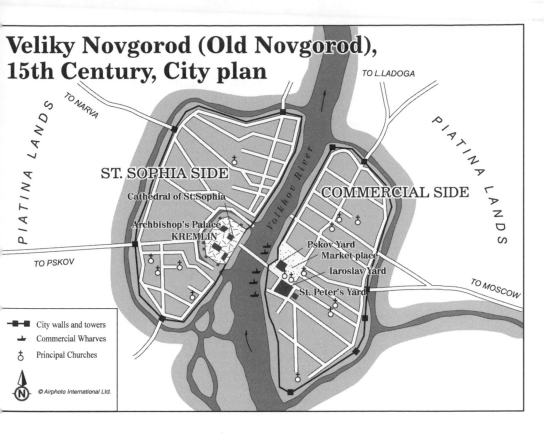

Veliky Novgorod (Old Novgorod), 15th Century, City plan

TO L.LADOGA

TO NARVA

PIATINA LANDS

PIATINA LANDS

ST. SOPHIA SIDE

Cathedral of St.Sophia

Archbishop's Palace
KREMLIN

TO PSKOV

Volkhov River

COMMERCIAL SIDE

Pskov Yard
Market place
Iaroslav Yard
St. Peter's Yard

TO MOSCOW

City walls and towers
Commercial Wharves
Principal Churches

N

© Airphoto International Ltd.

which was to become an outpost of Muscovite Orthodoxy. Muscovite rulers from Ivan IV to Boris Godunov never ceased to honour this monastery with their special protection. Then, in 1570, came Ivan's punitive expeditions against Novgorod and Pskov. The routing of the ideological opponents of the tsar that occurred in Novgorod meant that the churches and monasteries became the property of the tsar. Monasteries lost all their charters. In the case of the Pskov monastery, however, not only the tsar did not touch it, not only he did not instigate any search for traitors, but on the contrary made a rich donation to the monastery, and presented it with several other gifts.[2]

Andreyev analysed these events in a series of articles, and concluded that reforms and in particular West-European influences were detested by Muscovite Orthodoxy, and that, although supporters of reforms occupied for a time the highest places in the Church hierarchy, they were again and again overcome by supporters of unlimited autocracy within the establishment of the State. The Byzantine model of a submissive and pliable Church suited the autocratic principle extremely well, and every attempt at independent thinking had to be eradicated without mercy. The planting of the Pskov monastery in the non-possessor lands, the branding of every foreign influence as treacherous, and the final physical destruction of all opponents or potential opponents can be taken as yet another characteristic manifestation of the universalistic ideology that underlay the Muscovite tsardom.

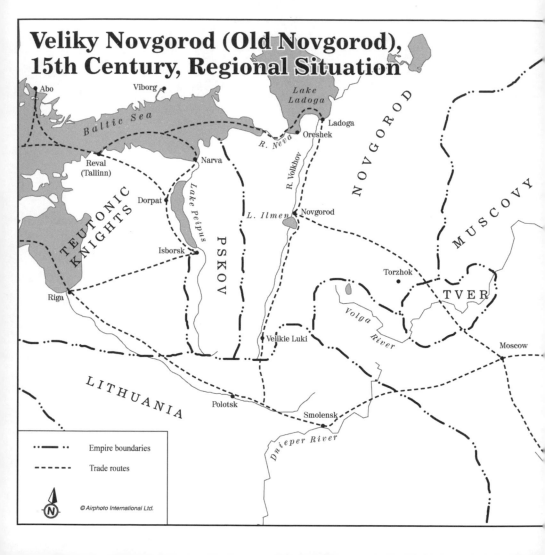

Veliky Novgorod (Old Novgorod), 15th Century, Regional Situation

Abo

Viborg

Lake Ladoga

Baltic Sea

Ladoga

Oreshek

R. Neva

NOVGOROD

Reval (Tallinn)

Narva

R. Volkhov

MUSCOVY

TEUTONIC KNIGHTS

Dorpat

Lake Peipus

L. Ilmen

Novgorod

Isborsk

PSKOV

Torzhok

TVER

Riga

Volga River

Moscow

Velikie Luki

LITHUANIA

Polotsk

Smolensk

Dnieper River

·—··	Empire boundaries
-----	Trade routes

Ⓝ © Airphoto International Ltd.

Chapter 18

The enserfment of Russian peasants

The problem of the enserfment of Russian peasants, probably the most debated one of Russian history, can be explained in a satisfactory way only if we depart from the traditional 'European' viewpoint. We must try to visualise the situation in the context of nomadic-Asian connections, as discussed in the previous chapters.

The contradictions which presented so many difficulties to so many scholars were due mainly to the assumption that Russian peasants prior to the restrictions of their movements were *free*. This assumption has never been seriously questioned. However, if Hellie's view of the Russian civilisation as imitative-adaptive is accepted,[1] somewhere in the fourteenth–fifteenth century a free peasant would have to be found as a model for Muscovy Russia. There were only two such examples: the freemen in Lithuania–Poland, and the peasant freeholders in Sweden. We can find traces of them in *svoezemtsy* in Novgorod, but even there they existed rather as a special tiny group, not as a general rule; we are asked to believe that in Muscovy, where no such special group existed, free peasants were the general rule. And yet the whole nature and traditions of the government in Muscovy would contradict this assumption.

On the other hand, if we accept that the models of Muscovite society, like the models of the Muscovite army, should be sought among the Mongol-Turkish institutions, the picture will become much clearer.

According to the nomadic ideology, all land belonged to the khan, and all people belonged to the khan.

The heads and not acres of land formed the basis of the Mongol system of taxation and conscription, as introduced in conquered Russia in the middle of the thirteenth century. 'The country was divided into military districts (myriads, thousands, hundreds and tens) to facilitate both conscription and tax collecting.'[2] Each numerical division constituted a military–financial district, a territorial unit from which a definite quota of recruits and a definite amount of taxes were required.[3]

'After the decline of the Golden Horde the Grand Princes of Moscow became able to use, whenever necessary, the system of universal conscription established by the Mongols. In Muscovy the basic system of military and financial districts, the *t'my*, was left intact.'[4]

This system did not allow any room for free movement; if a peasant left his unit and his district, he would upset both the military and financial arrangements of which he was a part. But the whole system was based on mobility. The territorial boundaries of the districts were originally very loosely defined. The peasants – and all other people – were not allowed to leave their unit, but could move under the circumstances within the unit's district. If, for example, their land became exhausted, they were moved, or could move, to another plot. There was to be one exemption to this rule – the immunities of the Church lands originally granted by Khan Buyantu in 1316.[5]

In consequence, people on Church and monastery lands ceased to be divided into the myriad system, they were subject to Church jurisdiction, different taxes, and to a less strict conscription system. Indeed, it seems that peasants on Church lands were not conscripted at all. 'The church and its estates were exempted by the khan from taxation and other duties. Hence the peasants on monastery lands were liable only to manorial services for the monastery and not to the state *tiaglo*. In contrast, the peasants on other lands were subject to both tribute and conscription.'[6]

Gradually, the districts assumed a territorial meaning, and their boundaries were finally fixed with the establishment of the territorial state. In turn, all land had to be registered. From the fiscal point, the transitional period was marked by two different viewpoints, taking either heads or land as the basis of taxation. (This conflict reappeared in later periods again and again.) The same conflict existed in the early period of the *pomestia* between the already established landholdings of the monasteries and the magnates, and the temporary tenure of the *pomeshchiki*. The parasitic nature of the tenure quite naturally led to peasant movement – away and into monastery lands. 'Living on monastery lands was the rational choice for peasants because of the frequently more advanced economic level of operation on such properties, more enlightened "personal policies", and probably because of lower rents.'[7] The *pomestie* system itself allowed for a limited degree of mobility, because the *pomeshchik* was granted the financial yield of a group of peasants rather than that of a plot of land; as long as the peasants remained within the district they were assigned to, they could move from one plot to another.

Frequent movement was necessary because of the primitive character of farming. The soil usually became exhausted after 2–3 years; this changed only with the introduction of the three-field rotation system on a large scale. If the peasants moved outside the district, for example, into the monastery lands, they had to be stopped. As long as the *pomestia* kept their personal rather than their territorial character, such stoppages and limitations were not necessarily absolute; but they were gradually tightened when the territorial aspect of land-tenure increased. The competition of monastery lands for peasant labour had to be restricted or eliminated altogether.

The peasants could be forcibly returned or moved without their consent; others, especially those recorded in censuses taken of the grand princely estates, were not to be moved at all.[8] Subsequent restrictions, the Forbidden Years, and the final abolition of this 'freedom' of movement would correspond to the situation of the territorial state now fully established, and with the government being more and more sure of itself and capable of curbing the political and economic power of the Church.

This should be compared with the Turkish system. 'The sultan owned all land in Anatolia, which was not endowed for the purpose of *waqf*, and except with his consent, or that of his representative, no change of tenure was possible.'

'Free movement was discouraged except to take vacant holdings, and the laws generally worked to bind the peasant to the soil; they reinforced established custom and insisted on its observance.'[9]

The term *waqf*, which was an endowment for religious purposes, provides an analogy with Church immunities in Russia.

There is yet another approach to these problems. So far, only the question of 'freedom' and the mobility of peasants has been examined. But from the earliest times peasants were only part of the population of Russia. The non-agricultural population, which no doubt existed in substantial numbers, consisted of forest hunters mainly in the north and north-east, and of cattle-breeding nomads. In the principalities south and east of Moscow, with the expansion of Muscovy, many more were added to the latter, especially in the Volga region. It would be unreasonable to expect that all the nomadic territories that Muscovy conquered and annexed were depopulated and empty. Most of the nomads stayed there and continued their traditional way of life.[10]

This way of life began to clash with the emerging territorial state by the end of the fifteenth century. Lack of pastureland disrupted the nomadic economy, and with the ascendancy of agriculture, the whole machinery of state, administration and taxation alike began to be more land-orientated. Muscovy from Ivan III to Ivan IV can also be seen as a transitional period in this sense, the last phase of a nomadic empire being replaced by an agricultural state.

The once-firm organisation of the nomads disintegrated when they were forced to live in small groupings the size of a clan or tribe; they could not carry on in the traditional rhythm of their economy. The 'land-based' administration certainly had difficulties in controlling and taxing such groups. Therefore it resorted to two quite natural steps.

First it tried to restrict the movement of these nomads and tie them to land where possible. 'Free movement' – wherever mentioned in the contemporary sources – can also refer to these nomadic or semi-nomadic groups; the attempts of the authorities to restrict it, from the *Sudebnik* of

1497 onwards, could be intended not only to prevent the peasants from fleeing, but also to tie the vagrant nomads to a controllable and taxable work, that is, farming.

This applied to a much lesser extent to the forest hunters, whose main products (fur, wax and honey) still constituted important items, especially in the country's foreign trade. The state probably concentrated on improved control rather than restriction of mobility. Little is known about the organisation and taxation of these people, but the nomadic system of decimal units *(sotnie)* and taxation by heads and/or by a percentage of catch probably remained in force for some time.

The other step was colonisation. Here again the attitude of the authorities was fully in line with nomadic tradition. The voluntary element was negligible. Ever since the times of Ivan III the state used forced removal of population for the dual purpose of colonisation and suppression of local disorders. The depopulation of Novgorod lands, mentioned frequently in the sources, can be more easily explained in terms of this policy than by war, epidemics or famine.

Chapter 19

тhe cossacks
& тhe моmads

тhe cossacks

The Cossacks, the famous frontiersmen in the Ukraine, whose nomadic influence in the growth of Russian civilisation must not be overlooked, originated in the partial adoption of the way of life and the social organisation of the steppe peoples by Russians, Ukrainians and Poles; and since many of them were runaway serfs without wives, the intermingling with the steppe peoples was physical as well as cultural. A similar process could be observed in quite recent times, when peasants and Cossacks penetrating into Outer Mongolia were absorbed into the Mongol society.[1]

Hunting, fishing, beekeeping and fighting had been the main occupation of the Cossacks, who first adjusted to the dangerous life of the southern steppe. The steppe, the climate and the economy forced upon these freebooters a way of life which did not differ very much from that of their Tartar enemies, except in one important point. The Cossacks, most of them being refugees from an oppressive serf-system, were essentially individualists and therefore were unable to introduce the rigid discipline of a small nomadic horde. They lived either in small groups of hunters and fishermen, or in tiny settlements with small-scale subsistence farming where leadership depended on personality, and the 'elders' were elected by some informal process of consensus. The highest form of organisation the Cossacks ever achieved was a war-band formed around a particular captain for a particular enterprise.[2]

When, after 1557, these war-bands obtained a rallying centre in the so-called '*sech*' – a fortified island in the Dnieper – their communal life began to be organised on military principles by regiments, hundreds and tens with a council headed by an elected commander, the *hetman*. Provoked by the devastating Tartar slave-raids both Muscovy and Poland tried to organise an effective frontier defence system. 'A series of modest fortifications was supplemented by a system of sentinel posts backed up by "registered" Cossacks, that is to say, frontiersmen who accepted military subordination [...] in return for a small annual payment in cash.'[3]

As a result, the drain of the peasant population into Ottoman slavery was much reduced, and the population of the steppe began to increase very rapidly, being fed by adventurers and rebels from the north who sought to escape the trammels of serfdom by taking up the frontiersman's free life in the south.[4]

After a time, the original aim of defending settled communities receded, and raids and plunder became the main occupation of the band. However, Cossack depredation was directed mainly towards goods rather than the human cattle which Tartar raiders found so attractive. This meant that cities and other seats of civilisation offered by far the best targets for a raid, whereas fellow-feeling with enserfed villagers and the poverty of the peasants discouraged Cossack depredations in the countryside. At the time of the Turkish-Tartar ascendancy city folk preyed upon villagers, whereas in the time of the Cossack apogee villagers attacked cities and city folk. Like the Varangians of old, from headquarters on the Dnieper, interrelated bands operated all the way from the Baltic coast to the walls of Constantinople and from the Volga to the Carpathians: and everywhere booty-raiding and trading went hand in hand.[5]

However, in the end the Poles and the Turks began to cooperate to check both Tartar and Cossack raids. After some setbacks, the Turks managed to bring the Crimean Tartars under control, while the Poles undertook to 'tame' the Cossacks. For a time, the Cossacks became an important factor in the three-power contest between Poland, Turkey and Russia; after a brief interlude of allying themselves to Turkey, they finally opted for Russia. In 1654 'a *rada* (assembly) of the army and the land considered the alternative open to the Ukraine – subjection to Poland, a transfer of allegiance to Turkey, or a transfer of allegiance to Muscovy – and decided in favour of the Orthodox tsar'.[6]

As McNeill puts it, 'the Cossacks had become too closely identified with the defence of Christianity and in particular of its Orthodox variety to be open to Muslim blandishments. Mass conversion of Christian frontiersmen was therefore not resumed in Pontic Europe in the seventeenth century, despite the fact that Turkish institutions allowed far wider local autonomy and were more attuned to the egalitarian authoritarianism of the Cossack hordes than were either the Polish or the Russian polities.'[7]

'More likely, however, this decision was prompted by the strong resentment the Cossacks felt against the land-granting policy of the Polish kings in the Ukraine west of the Dnieper. Russian administration and land grants east of the river did not provoke any such resentment; empty lands were granted to appropriate suppliants who then sought settlers from among desperate and impoverished refugees fleeing from the ravages of the Turkish wars. The squatters' rights and property were not destroyed by the landowners' efforts to forward commercial colonisation.'[8]

In 1731 and the following years, the Russians built a regular defence line to guard the fringes of settlements; from that time the Tartar raiding ceased to be important. Cossack regiments continued to exist, but the fact that European standards of military discipline and deployment had made the old style of unregulated Cossack charge ineffective on the battlefield meant that the Russian government was not anxious to preserve the Cossack military manpower. The old wild-frontier style of life continued to fade rapidly away before the bureaucratised and rationalised organisation of force that had been introduced into the Ukraine by Russian armies and administration.[9] The Agreement of Pereiaslav, whereby in 1654 the Cossacks invited the Tsar of Muscovy to incorporate their lands into his realms, is an interesting proof of how deeply had the age-old nomadic values penetrated the thinking of these 'individualistic freebooters' of yesterday.

According to Andreyev,[10] 'the Cossack leaders looked upon ordinary people – the peasants – as tools in the hands of the Cossacks'. The Cossacks in Khmelnitsky's letter asked for 'an autocrat'. There was no request for autonomy for either the people or the region. The Cossacks made a last-minute attempt to persuade the tsar to take an oath 'to respect the freedom and properties of his subjects'; this was clearly under the influence of the oath the King of Poland had to swear to his Estates. The Moscow envoys refused on behalf of the tsar, because 'Polish kings are untrustworthy and no autocrats'. On the contrary, the Cossacks had to acknowledge the supreme right of the tsar over the lands and the subjects. They had to swear an oath of allegiance, and the tsar 'out of love' promised to fulfil their requests. The agreement which transferred the Ukraine to Muscovy was in no way a 'union', not even a 'vassalage', but pure subjection.[11]

A clear symptom of nomadic thinking is the fact that nowhere in the agreement is there a word about territory. The subjection of the Cossacks was purely personal.[12] The notion of a 'Ukrainian nation' seems to have been completely alien to Cossack thinking, as indeed the idea of nationality was alien to contemporary Russian thinking. Here can be seen almost as in a testtube the development of nomadic institutions. The primitive tribal assembly with its 'government by consent' (though hardly democratic in the modern sense); then the oligarchy of the commanders and the military organisation of the host; and finally the subjection – or unconditional surrender of all liberties – to an autocratic, absolute ruler. Nowhere did the Cossacks attempt to introduce some kind of representative government; and, unlike the American West, their 'individualism' was surrendered too easily to be genuine.

Thus the semi-nomadic steppe people that the Cossacks undoubtedly were decided in favour of a total subjection to a despotic ruler exactly in the tradition of all steppe nomads before them. Obviously, compared with the aristocratic privileges in Poland, Russian oppression seemed more tolerable because it was universal.[13] The choice between the two despots – the sultan and the tsar – went in favour of the latter mainly because of religion. It was Islam and not his despotic rule which made these former freebooters turn away from the sultan.[14]

On the other hand, the aim of Moscow was the unification of 'all Russia'. With this political programme in mind 'Moscow started the war against Poland, her armies entered the territories of White and Little Russia, and on Khmelnitsky's particular request, entered Kiev and several other towns.'[15]

The Nomads

The conquest of Kazan in 1552 and of Astrakhan in 1554–1556 added a number of Muslims, mainly Tartars and Bashkirs, to the tsar's subjects. The Stroganovs, who already held large territories in the north and north-east of Muscovy's realm, obtained after these conquests vast new territories on the upper Kama river and in the foothills of the Urals, which they wanted to open up for trade and colonisation. To break the resistance of the local tribes, which received encouragement from the Khan of Siberia, they sent, in 1581, with the tsar's agreement, a Cossack expedition commanded by the famous *hetman* Yermak, against the Siberian Khan Kutchum. This and subsequent expeditions laid the foundation of Russia's domination of Siberia. At about the same time the Russians pushed south towards the Caucasus and came in touch with local tribes, most of whom were also Muslim.

Although Ivan IV had no intention of destroying Islam, even to the extent of forbidding all forced conversions, the Orthodox Church tried to extirpate all traces of Islam in conquered territories and to replace Muslims with Christians. Kazan became an important centre of Orthodox religion, numbers of churches and monasteries were built, and it seemed for a while that Islam had been broken and silenced. The situation changed only when Catherine II introduced a policy of religious tolerance.[16]

The Tartars, however, resisted the pressure and very few converted to Christianity despite the destruction of their mosques and various discriminations on the one hand, and an energetic Russian colonisation on the other. Paradoxically, as Tartar nobles and aristocrats were forbidden from owning serfs, Tartar peasants and other non-Russians in the Volga and Ural region remained free. Missionary zeal reached its peak in the 1740s, but after serious disturbances during the Pugachev rebellion in 1755, the pressure was relaxed, and in 1773 Catherine's edict promulgated religious tolerance. The Act of Tolerance for Muslims in 1788 organised the Muslim church administration and laid the foundations for Muslim religious education. After their emancipation, the Tartars soon became the leading economic element in Russian expansion. In the Muslim khanates of Central Asia, as well as among the Muslims of the Caucasus, Russian merchants were unwelcome and the Tartars were quick to seize the advantage of their ethnic and linguistic proximity as well as of their religion to concentrate in their hands the bulk of the trade with these regions.[17]

After the conquest of Siberia in the early 17th century, the nomad Kazakhs were gradually absorbed into the Russian state. At the time of the Russian advance, the Kazakhs were organised in three formations, successors to the medieval Golden Horde: the Great Horde in the East, the Middle Horde between the Syr Darya, Tobol and Irtysh Rivers, and the Little Horde between the Syr Darya and the Ural River. The khan of the Little Horde asked for Russian protection (against Mongol incursions) in 1726, the Middle Horde acknowledged Russian suzerainty in the early 19th century and, after the Russians approached the Central Asian khanates in the second half of that century, the Great Horde followed suite and all the Kazakhs were absorbed in the Empire.[18, 19]

Russian Expansion in the 17th Century

SWEDEN

Archangel

Smolensk

★ Moscow
• Tula

ZAPOROZHIAN
COSSACKS

KHANATE OF
CRIMEA

O T T O M A N

Black Sea

E M P I R E

Persian Gulf

Don River

M U S C O V Y   I N   1 5 9 8

Simbirsk •

R. Volga

Caspian Sea

River Ural

URAL MOUNTAINS

KHANATE
OF
SIBIR

K A Z A K H S

River Irtysh

Aral Sea

Lk Balkhash

Arctic Ocean

SIBERIA

River Lena

River Kolyma

River Yenisei

Okhotsk
1647

Iakutsk
1630

Pacific Ocean

STANOVOI MTS.

River Amur

Lake Baikal

Nerchinsk
1654

Irkutsk
1652

Harbin

C H I N A

Beijing

Areas acquired by Russia
in the 17th century

N

© Airphoto International Ltd.

Chapter 20

western influences
in politics

The period of Muscovy Russia can be seen as a struggle between the universalistic autocracy and the oligarchic tendencies of the landed aristocrats. The destruction of Novgorod finished, once and for all, all attempts for municipal self-government; the *oprichnina* deprived the landed magnates of their economic base; the Mongol-Turkish traditions prevailed in the army and in the administration of the state. But the influence of the Western neighbours, especially of Poland, was becoming stronger and more apparent; the Polish constitution, which gave so much power to the aristocracy, could not appear unattractive to the Russian gentry; after the incorporation of the Ukraine, Polish and polonised Ukrainian nobles flocked to Moscow; Kiev was, once again, the most developed city of Russia. Polish fashion began to replace Turkish habits at the court of Muscovy; and Polish and European-style education just began to have some effects in the circles of Russian nobility.

After the death of Ivan the Terrible, when the central power weakened, the rudimentary local administration run by appointed officials – the *guba* and *zemstva* – assumed more authority, if not yet any independence in decision-making; the *zemskie sobory*, which until now had been nothing but advisory *kuriltay*-style councils to the tsar, began to show some political influence; being dominated by the aristocracy, this influence was more often than not in favour of Poland and Polish institutions.

When the central authority finally broke down after the death of Boris Godunov, the power of the nobility culminated with its first and only

Western-style contribution to the history of Russia; inviting the Polish prince Wladyslaw to the throne of Moscow, they imposed on him constitutional conditions, something which has never happened in Russia since the heyday of Novgorod and was never to happen again. After the Time of Troubles, the autocracy quickly resumed its age-old, traditional attitude. The *guba* and *zemstva* disappeared and were replaced by centrally-appointed officials (*voevody*); the *zemskie sobory* resumed their consultative character only to disappear entirely before the Petrine reforms some half a century later.

The Church also made an attempt to reappear as a political factor. Drawing on the ninth century Byzantine theories of shared power between the emperor and the patriarch, the Patriarch Philaret, father of the young tsar Michael Romanov, assumed the title 'Great Sovereign', and ruled until his death jointly with the tsar. The same title was assumed again by Patriarch Nikon (1605–81), who was not content with reasserting the equality of the spiritual and temporal powers, and 'eventually came to assert, in a manner hitherto unknown in Russia, the superiority of the spiritual power and even the subordination of the tsar to the patriarch'.[1]

But the traditions of non-interference in temporal matters, and of submission of the Church to the authority of the tsar proved to be stronger; the theories of Nikon were condemned, and he himself deposed by a Church Council in 1666–67. Nikon 'was the first person in Russia to uphold the papo-caesarist theory of the medieval Roman Church, using essentially the same arguments that had been used by the papist party in the West'.[2]

Thus Western ideology and political theory played, for a short time, a role in the Russian political scene; but with the deposition of Nikon, and with the falling into abeyance of the *zemskie sobory*, this brief episode came to an end. To quote W.H. McNeill, 'Despite tsardom's practical weakness and initial insecurity, the principle of autocracy, rooted deep in the Muscovite past, was emphatically reasserted; and with autocracy, an Orthodoxy profoundly suspicious of all religious enquiry and innovation was also restored'. It was 'far more popular than was the aristocratic Polish regime. The peasants [...] saw a rude sort of justice in the service state which required landowners to serve the tsar just as the peasants were compelled to serve their master, the landowners. Moreover, the holy figure of the distant tsar [...] fitted peasant expectation better than an elective monarchy.' The tsar's oppressions 'were more tolerable because he oppressed everyone, rich and poor, landholder and cultivator, merchant and soldier'.[3]

The old nomadic mentality can thus be detected both in the attitude of the omnipotent autocrat towards the people, and in the people's ready acceptance of it. The picture can only become more complete if we realise that it was the army that acted as the government in periods when the authority broke down; the army brought the autocracy back to power, and again it was the army, and bureaucracy organised on military principles, that helped to keep it there.

Muscovy Russia can be seen as a transitional period in more than one sense. The fluid nomadic state was being gradually replaced by a territorial state; the mobile economy of pastoral nomadism was being replaced by the land-based economy of farming; the nomadic professional warrior caste, which in the preceding period temporarily merged with recruited peasantry, began to re-establish itself as the *pomestie* gentry. All the time European influences and examples worked strongly against the local, deeply-rooted, nomadic traditions, and the 'mad' period of Ivan IV can be seen as either a subconscious or a deliberate attempt to reverse the trend and return to these traditions.

Chapter 21

The 'Politika'
of Iurii Krizhanich

A revealing picture of the Russian economy, society and political system towards the end of the Muscovy period can be gathered from Iurii Krizhanich's '*Politika*'[1]; written in the 1660s, it was intended as advice to Tsar Alexei, the second tsar of the Romanov dynasty (1645–1676). Apart from repeated expressions of outrage against all-pervading and persistent drunkenness and almost pathological invectives against foreigners,[2] there are some surprising statements, for example, about crafts and craftsmen. It seems that in the middle of the seventeenth century implements such as the spinning wheel, the saw or the sword were little used in Russia.

'In Germany women spin thread on the spinning wheel. They spin the wheel by foot, and quite fast. One woman using a spinning wheel spins more than three times what can be spun on a spindle [...] it would be useful if our women could master it' (p. 38). 'No one in Russia is familiar with tridents or carpenters' saws [...]. In other countries people cut boards with saws [...] here, in contrast, boards are cut with axes, and poor ones at that [...]. Axes here are all the same appearance and size, whereas in other countries they vary [...] the number of boards which a hundred serfs can prepare in a month using axes could be prepared in the same period by twenty using saws [...]' (p. 47). 'It is essential to attract craftsmen of all kinds: craftsmen who know how to melt and cast iron, copper, tin, silver and gold [...] produce iron pots, kettles, stoves, presses, cannon balls [...] make iron and copper plates [...] produce good sabres, broad-swords, harquebuses [...] agricultural implements such as scythes, sickles, forks, knives and the like' (p. 39). 'Here, in Russia, I see battleaxe soldiers and a battleaxe system – that is, infantrymen sent into battle with battleaxes only, no other weapons [...]. I believe we employ it only because of a shortage in sabres and swords, or of good iron [...]' (p. 64).

Krizhanich did not have a very high opinion of Russian peasantry. 'Our people are mentally sluggish and unable to discover things for themselves [...] we have no books on agriculture and other enterprises [...] our people are lazy and lethargic and will do nothing worthwhile unless they are forced to' (p. 41). 'The first reason why other nations treat us contemptuously is our illiteracy and our lack of interest in education' (p. 109); '[...] compared with these nations we are not very clean or well cared for: stupid, ignorant in science, and almost completely impoverished [...]' (p. 126). 'Many Russians do nothing out of respect for authority, and everything only because of fear of punishment caused by a cruel government which has made their lives repulsive and without honour' (p. 201).

And yet '[...] there is no kingdom where common people can live as well and can enjoy as many rights as they do here' (p. 179); '[...] this nation has developed so many revolting habits that other nations consider Russians cheaters, traitors, merciless terrorists and killers, foul mouths and slovens' (p. 201).

Nor did he think much of the nobles. 'Nobles and leading merchants live in mansions made of stone. They started building them some thirty years ago. Before this they lived in small wooden houses with only a few insignificant furnishings. Even now they use only three or four earthenware pots and the same number of wooden dishes. Silver utensils are rare. What silver they do have, they make no effort to clean so that even the silver and pewter dishes of the great sovereign [...] looked as though they had not been polished for an entire year [...]. They wear the same clothes to bed that they wear during the day [...]. Husband, wife, children and servants, and sometimes even chickens and pigs sleep together' (p. 118). 'The king of Denmark once made the following remark about our ambassadors: "If these people come often, I will have to build a pig-shed for them, because any place in which they stay becomes uninhabitable for half a year due to the smell they leave behind"' (p. 111). 'When our envoys are sent to Europe, they bring indescribable disgrace upon their people by reason of their coarseness and lack of education' (p. 131); 'Subjects of all ranks must call themselves "slaves of the sovereign"' (p. 117). Slaves represented about ten percent of the population. 'The *boyars* have many slaves on their estates. Some have fifty, or even a hundred in one mansion. These slaves receive payment that barely covers their essential needs [...]. At harvest time, these slaves are sent to cut hay and, near Moscow, they commit violent crimes. Their masters can be considered accomplices, since they give their slaves barely enough to feed and clothe themselves' (p. 117).

Agriculture was for Krizhanich the key sector of the economy. Without an agricultural surplus, resources would not be available for the development of crafts, manufacturing and commerce: '[...] the long winter necessitates an enormous amount of firewood and hay, and supplies for both people and livestock. The summer is short, cold and rainy, so that abundant crops cannot be grown [...]. As a result, it is possible to feed only a small population and to keep only a small number of livestock, which, by the way, is smaller than anywhere else. Moreover, only small horses can be found' (p. 113). 'Our land is one of the poorest because nothing is produced here except grain, fish and meat. Moreover, since we have been unable to develop any knowledge of value, we must learn all science from foreigners' (p. 141).

'Since our people do not have large sea vessels, they cannot sail the seas, and therefore will never be able to establish their own enterprises among the Germans [...]' (p. 144). 'Apparently, we are unfamiliar with marine transport. We should fill the Caspian with our ships' (p. 115).

The Russian system of government was for Krizhanich the crucial problem: 'There are also some very good things in our laws and customs. Of them the first and best is absolute autocracy. A second good custom is the closure of our borders. We deny foreigners free entry and prohibit our own people from wandering outside the borders of the realm without vital reasons' (p. 162). 'No one can free himself from public and national service, be it at court, in government offices or in the military' (p. 162). 'Once the king is anointed and crowned, there exists no other judge above him in the world' (p. 173).

'What should be done should the king be a bitter oppressor, an offender and torturer of the people? The answer is simple: the people should ascribe this misery to their sins, should correct their way of life, ask God for help, and implore the king to have mercy' (p. 173). 'Our greatest political problem is excessive government. Our people do not know how to use moderation. They always stray into fatal extremities' (p. 127). To conclude, Krizhanich recommends to the tsar: 'The first fortress of our tsardom and of the nation has hitherto been the Orthodox faith [...] the second national stronghold is the total *samovladstvo* or humble submission of subjects to their tsar [...] The third stronghold has been the inviolability of the tsardom and its protection from foreign domain. The fourth fortress is the closure of the frontiers [...] Our fifth fortress is the preoccupation of all classes and the prohibition of idleness and unemployment' (p. 226).[3]

Nevertheless, Krizhanich contributed considerably to the idealisation of Russian society, which he saw as an 'exceptional temporal community founded on the ideals of brotherhood, equality and social justice. He was also the first who expounded the ideas of Panslavism, of Slav nationalism and of Slavonic unity under the leadership of Russia.'[4] Some scholars see in him one of the most influential European political writers of his time.[5] Others believe that his 'muddled political ideas had no influence because his treatise was first published, and then only partially, in the middle of the nineteenth century'.[6] Still others take a middle way. According to Letiche-Dmytryshyn, no conclusive proof could be found whether or not Krizhanich had an impact on Russian rulers. It is known that Tsar Alexei had a copy of his book in his library, and that a manuscript of it was found in the library of Metropolitan Paul of Moscow, who died in 1675; 'apparently, the Moscow Printing Office made a number of copies, for the book has also been discovered in the libraries of several key Russian figures of the time'.[7]

Summary to Part 3

The period of Muscovy may be characterised by three, or perhaps four, major changes. The victory of firearms over cavalry, the victory of the peasant over the nomad, the victory of an absolute ruler over the centrifugal aspirations of the gentry and also, last but not least, the penetration of the Ottoman Turks into south-eastern Europe, the first invasion of an Oriental and Muslim people since the expulsion of the Moors from Spain.

It all went hand in hand. The firearms, mainly cannon, helped to defeat the nomads and opened the steppe to colonisation. This in turn was made possible with new and more efficient implements and methods, the heavy mould-board plough, the horse collar, the three-field rotation system, the improved supply of metal, etc. Land ownership was again the key issue. By depriving the gentry of all aspirations to hereditary ownership, the sovereign effectively eliminated all potential alternative power-bases and reverted to the old concept of unlimited possession of the realm. Using a Turkish model, land was given on a revocable basis to military and court dignitaries, thus creating what became known as the service gentry. Deprived of their land holdings the old gentry, the *boyars*, were reduced to powerless and harmless courtiers. Any idea of power-sharing and, especially, any idea of independent land ownership had to be ruthlessly eliminated. And, with the Mongols gone and the Byzantine empire defeated, the idea of a universal empire reappeared quite naturally in Muscovy, whose sovereign now began to call himself 'tsar'.

Territorial expansion was an immediate consequence. The conquest of the Volga khanates and the expansion into eastern Ukraine brought great numbers of nomads under the tsar's rule. Some of them found employment in his armies, but most, not having sufficient pastures and space to move, were condemned to a precarious existence on the fringes of farmed areas. The Crimean Tartars, supported by Turkey, continued to harass the southern borderlands of Muscovy and Poland until they were finally defeated by Catherine the Great in 1783.

part 4

IMPERIAL RUSSIA

Chapter 22

The petrine reforms

Two important international trends provided the background of the development in this period. One of them was the increasing impact of the Reformation on all intellectual activities, while the other was the gradual military ascendancy of the West over the Turks. Although Turkey was still able to score important victories against both Austria and Russia, it became increasingly evident that the balance of power, especially on Turkey's western frontier, was shifting in favour of Austria and her allies. Swedish military principles successfully tested in the Thirty Years War were applied first by Austria and then by Peter the Great. The mutiny of the *streltsy* regiments in 1698 was suppressed by Peter with utter ruthlessness. The old-fashioned regiments which he had inherited from his predecessors were completely destroyed so that no armed and organised defenders of the Muscovite Orthodox and conservative past remained. He then devoted himself to creating a new Russian standing army modelled on the latest and best in the Western practice. Everything had to begin from scratch or nearly so.

'New equipment and factories to supply it, new methods of training and drillmasters to impose it, new concepts of tactics and officers to impart them. And most of all perhaps a new concept of the corporate and personal ethos of the professional military, a new concept of loyalty to the state which was only then emerging in western armies. Monumental confusion was inevitable. The remarkable thing was how quickly Peter's military innovation took root and began to function effectively.'[1]

The whole range of Peter's reforms in the field of government, administration, trade, taxation, and others are sufficiently known, and it is not necessary to analyse them here. In spite of all these apparently

European-style attempts behind the whole impressive structure lay an apparatus of terror economically administered by Peter's political police. A handful of ruthless clerks could call in the army's aid when necessary. Thus 'Russia's remarkable and continuing history as a terrorist bureaucracy effectively began in the pioneering Emperor's reign.'[2]

This, of course, is only partly true. In spite of his reforming zeal and affection for Western-style innovations Peter the Great fits in every respect into the cultural pattern of his country. Other scholars made the same mistaken assessment. 'It was in order to implement his radical reforms that the country had to be strait-jacketed. Peter was so different in his cosmopolitan technological and materialistic obsessions that the chasm between his aims and the parochialism of the milieu he was part of could be bridged only by fiat. His social ideal was thus bound to be the police state and it was precisely as a result of this global reformism that the police came to be the paramount institution in Russian life.'[3]

It is sufficient to look at Peter's methods rather than his aims to get the picture right. 'Though Peter's methods were brutal in the extreme he did not cultivate brutality for its own sake. The suppression of the *streltsy* and later of the Astrakhan mutineers and rebellious Cossacks were more of a scientifically applied deterrent than were the massacres ordained by Ivan the Terrible and Stalin.'[4]

Peter the Great was not all that different either from his predecessors or from his successors. He had a good opportunity to see from the not-so-distant history and from his personal experience in Western Europe that West-European military power was fast becoming more efficient than the Turkish one, and he was intelligent enough to realise that to adopt the western style of warfare with its emphasis on military technology was impossible under the contemporary circumstances in Muscovy. With a characteristic rashness and with a lack of consideration quite worthy of a nomad khan he decided to change all those 'contemporary circumstances' at a stroke, in other words to change the whole Muscovite style of life based on the Turkish and Byzantine heritage, to suit the new requirements of the army.

His principal aspiration was to borrow technology from the West and not civilisation in the wider sense.[5] War was the main preoccupation of Peter and, as a matter of fact, only a few months of his long reign passed without war.[6] Everything in the state had to be subordinated to military requirements; the only difference was that it had to be done in the interest of the state and not of the sovereign in person. But in spite of this far-reaching innovation Peter still continued to call himself 'possessor and autocrat of Russia'. His obsession with war, his treatment of people, friends and foes alike as well as his views of the role of the state and the subjects shows clearly that the ideological background of his thinking was very similar to that of his predecessors. He had the courage to jettison everything he thought to be in the way of his idea of an all-powerful, universal and autocratic state, and he was ready to adopt whatever innovation might help to implement this idea. The Turkish model failed or was failing fast; it was therefore necessary to seek other models, other approaches while putting them into practice with the same methods as before.

Sometimes these reforms were ludicrously inconsistent and mistimed. He insisted, for example, on importing a troupe of German actors at a time when no conceivable audience for them could even have understood the social backgrounds of the German and French plays they put on. There was not even an understandable polite idiom to translate them into. He launched a comprehensive educational programme when there were practically no schools at all in the country.[7]

On the whole, the range and character of the Petrine reforms resembles rather closely the wholesale reception by Russia of the Byzantine and Turkish ways of life in previous periods of her history. In each case the 'revolution' came from above and touched only the upper strata of the society. In each case the ruling and intellectual élite became Byzantinised, Turkicised or Europeanised, while the lower classes remained completely untouched. Similarly untouched remained the methods of the government and the ideology that underlay them.

St Vladimir brought Christianity and Byzantine civilisation to Russia, but his personal behaviour and his methods of government were those of a pagan, nomadic chieftain. Ivan III married a Byzantine princess and invited Italian architects to Moscow, but he ruled his country like a Turkish sultan. Peter the Great had his armies trained and commanded by Swiss and Scottish experts, but when he was faced with a mutiny, he did not hesitate to execute the mutinous soldiers with his own hand equally easily as he shore the beards and pulled the teeth of his courtiers (for this kind of despotic rule Max Weber coined the term 'sultanism').[8, 9]

Nor was Peter the Great the first who tried to westernise Russia. Kiev and some of the West Russian lands had been under Russian rule since 1667. Polonised gentry had a considerable influence at the court of Moscow and during the reign of Peter's half-sister Sophia her favourite, a westernised *boyar* Prince Basil Golitsyn, entertained vast projects of improvement and reform including the abolition of serfdom and education on a large scale. But Sophia was overthrown and Golitsyn banished when a reactionary faction of conservative Orthodox Muscovites led by Peter's mother seized power shortly before Peter himself assumed the reign. 'Revolutionary though Peter's reforms were, Russia had already begun to assimilate European influences long before his birth. He was therefore by no means charting a new course, but violently wrenching the rudder in a direction towards which the country was already veering.'[10]

These European influences received a focal point when Peter founded the city of St Petersburg. Situated at the Gulf of Finland the city had an outlet to western Europe and almost automatically stepped into the older traditions of Novgorod with their tolerance, liberalism, flexibility and internationality. When the city became the seat of government, the westernised, or Europeanised, élite both administrative and intellectual quite naturally concentrated there. But this enforced westernisation, on the other hand, caused an enormous cultural rift between this thin élite and the rest of the population. The new-style gentry and officials had little in common with the benighted *mujiks*, who formed the bulk of the population and who, together with priests and merchants, continued to maintain the antique Muscovite garb, speech and custom.

'If three quarters of a century after the first Tsar-Emperor's death only a small percentage of the Russian population seemed fitted to enter the nineteenth century while the rest, largely peasants, still belonged in spirit to the ninth, Peter must bear much of the responsibility.'[11]

There are considerable differences in the interpretation of some of Peter's reforms. So, for example Pipes, speaking of the Russian civil service, says that 'the administrative order of pre-1917 Russia rested on a system of farming out which resembled neither the bureaucratic centralism nor self-government. Its prototype was the Muscovite institution of "feeding" *(kormlenie)* which gave the civil service virtually free rein to exploit the country.' Under Peter the Great 'only officials in central bureaux in St Petersburg and in Moscow received salaries. Provincial bureaucrats continued to live off the land as before.'[12]

In contrast Riasanovsky, speaking of the reform of the provincial administration, states clearly: 'All officials received salaries; the old Muscovite practice of *kormleniia* went out of existence.'[13] The Table of Ranks *(chin)* promulgated by Peter in 1722, which replaced the traditional *mestnichestvo* setting aside the Muscovite hierarchy of titles and ranks, has been hailed as a novelty based on Western models.[14] And yet we may find almost the same system, just as thorough and detailed in Mughal India, where it was introduced by Akbar in the late sixteenth century.[15]

In Western Europe attempts to break the rule of the Estates and to centralise the government in the hands of the monarch were pursued with varying degrees of success through the seventeenth and eighteenth centuries. The transition was achieved first in Richelieu's France, while in the Austrian Empire a succession of piecemeal reforms was carried out throughout the eighteenth century. In Russia, which had no feudalism and no organised Estates, administrative centralisation was not only much easier, but also the natural way of government.

In the army the part-time militia and foreign mercenaries of the preceding period were replaced, according to the Swedish model, by a peasant army based on a regular draft. The standing regiments of musketeers *(streltsy)* were disbanded after the mutiny of 1698, and replaced by guards; in spite of these innovations, the guards regiments continued to play a similar role like the Turkish *janissaries*, including the staging of palace coups and influencing the choice of the sovereign. This role came to an end only after a new law of succession was issued in 1797 which introduced the dynastic principle of primogeniture in the male line; it eliminated succession wrangles for the next hundred years.

The role of cavalry sharply diminished in favour of infantry and artillery. There was no need to fight the nomads any more, and the equipment and organisation of the army now had to match that of the main foes – the Western neighbours, Sweden and Poland. Turkey, in spite of frequent wars, represented no real threat to Russian heartland, because the Turkish army, still operating without organised supplies, was unable to cross the vast stretches of the steppe in the limited time of their summer campaigns. The Russian army, until Peter's time, had no supply system either, and therefore the first Russo-Turkish conflicts had the character of border skirmishes rather than full-scale wars. Only in the second half of the eighteenth century after the colonisation of the Ukrainian steppe had pushed the Russian supply base sufficiently forward, were the Russians able to deal effectively with the Turks.[16]

The nomadic background of Peter's thinking was most clearly apparent in his tax reform – which, incidentally, proved to be the most lasting of all his reforms. The replacement of the old household tax of 1678 – which in turn amalgamated and replaced the various land taxes – by a single head tax, or poll tax in 1718, was the fiscal acknowledgement of the value of men, as against the value of land.

In the realm of the Church Peter the Great abandoned (after 1700) the Byzantine model of dual authority that existed in certain periods of Muscovy. With the establishment of the Holy Synod in 1721, state authority was superimposed over the Church. Peter may have used the Lutheran countries of northern Europe as his model,[17] but his reform was fully in line with the traditional concept of an absolute and lay state power. Since then, until 1917, the government exercised full control over Church organisation, possessions and policies. Greater religious tolerance and limitations on acquisitions of monastery lands were two other aspects of the same concept.

Chapter 23

The society

If the Time of Troubles and the following decades of the seventeenth century represented a period of growing European influences, the time of Peter the Great can be described in many ways as the return to nomadic thinking. Not only did the territorial expansion incorporate large numbers of nomadic and semi-nomadic population, especially in the Don area and north of the Caucasus; the whole social structure, which had only just begun to differentiate on the European pattern with noble landowners seeking independence from state power, was radically altered by the introduction of the service-state.

By Peter's laws, members of the gentry had to remain with their regiments for life. At the same time the Table of Ranks made sure that advancement in service (including membership of the gentry) was open to all. Both principles, personal military service of the gentry and mobility within the ranks, go back far beyond the Muscovite state; in fact, they were an exact replica of the nomadic warrior caste, or better still, of the nomadic principle that every member of the community is, automatically, a warrior and a servant of the ruler. However, Peter's system in its original purity and rigidity did not last long; in the course of the eighteenth century the gentry gradually escaped from its service obligation, and, at the same time, entry into that class became more difficult.[1]

And yet the principle of service and obedience was so strong that the Russian nobility never seriously attempted to use their estates as an economic base to claim a share in state power, or even to mount an opposition against it. One notable exception, and in fact a second attempt – after the election of Wladyslaw, mentioned above – were the restrictions imposed by the nobles on Empress Anne in 1730. These restrictions resembled in many ways the conditions which formed the constitution of so many European monarchies; the Empress accepted them at first, but shortly after her accession she abolished them and reverted to the traditional autocracy.

Thus the two conflicting trends, the nomadic and the European, discernible in their rudimentary forms already in Kievan Russia, continued to alternate in Russian politics with the nomadic each time gaining the upper hand. Even in the 'enlightened' period of Catherine II, when consent and harmony were acknowledged in theory, the actual methods of the government were based on fear and brutality far more than under the 'enlightened' despots in Europe. The next 'European' wave brought the abolition of compulsory gentry service by Peter III in 1762, and the *Charter of Nobility*, issued by Catherine II in 1785. By this Charter the Russian gentry acquired a corporate status and legal privileges comparable to those of their European counterparts. Among others, members of the gentry were recognised as full owners of their estates, so that, according to some scholars, Catherine the Great introduced the modern concept of private property into Russia.[2]

As for the thorny question of land ownership, Pipes says that during the *apanage* period private property of land was recognised in the form of *votchina*. Possession was later made conditional on service and only in 1785 by a decree of Catherine II, 'the landholders secured clear legal title to their estates and private property in land came once again into being'.[3] The picture, according to Blum, is much more complex. In the *apanage* period the princes considered all land as their *votchina*; even though private individuals had all the rights of proprietors, the concept of the sovereign as the real owner of all land was maintained.

Under Ivan IV all landholders had to perform state service; if they did not, their land could be confiscated. The *pomestia* (land granted to servitors) appeared in the sixteenth–seventeenth century next to allodial properties *(votchina)*, which stood for inherited land, and the *kuplia*, which was purchased land. Ivan IV tried to restrict the independence of the *votchinniki* and reduce their status to that of the *pomeshchiki*. At the end of the sixteenth century *votchina* land could be found only in central Russia. The trend changed again in the seventeenth century, when the *pomestie* gradually began to resemble the *votchina*, and in the latter part of the century there was no real difference between the two. The *de facto* fusion of the two forms was officially recognised in the early eighteenth century and made legal in 1714. By a *ukase* of 1731, *pomestie* was henceforth to be known as *votchina*.

Making a comparison of the Russian system with Turkey, Blum sees as unique to Russia 'that the connection of landholding and service to the state continued during and after the period in which the central power was establishing its supremacy'.[4]

Both essential elements of 'sultanism' were still here: the state together with everybody and everything in it was considered the personal property of the sovereign, and the sovereign himself was the embodiment of law, not merely the source of it.

As already recognised by Kliuchevsky, service formed the basis of Russian society. From 1762, and even more so after 1785, the Russian gentry escaped from this traditional bond and constituted itself as an isolated self-contained clan. As in previous periods, the former warriors became lazy landlords. A new ruling élite had to be formed to take over the army and administration; composed of professional soldiers and bureaucrats, this élite, like its predecessors, was wholly dependent on the sovereign. But at least one clan, the gentry, was now relatively independent from the state power. With little political importance, it soon became the prime factor in the development of Russian culture.

Whereas the French-educated nobles soon became part of the European cultural theatre, the old Byzantine-nomadic traditions survived unchanged in all remaining strata of Russian society. The sovereign, although now dressing and behaving like a European, still treated his country as his property, and all his subjects as his personal slaves. The absolute and universal character of Russian autocracy still remained the same as that of the Turkish sultans or nomad khans. Administration was based on military organisation and run with army discipline; centralisation was complete, and all attempts to create some local self-government failed.[5]

The ruling 'warrior élite', the army and the bureaucracy together with the idle, non-fighting gentry preyed parasitically on the peasant masses. There was still no urban middle class; the numbers of townspeople were insignificant and, with very few exceptions, they were all bonded people. It was not until the second half of the nineteenth century that an urban middle class began to emerge in connection with industrialisation and increasing trade, but by 1917 it did not reach anything approaching political maturity. Meanwhile, steppe nomadism ceased to exist as a viable economy; large sections of the steppe were colonised; the autonomy of the Cossacks was first restricted and later abolished; in the Ukraine they disappeared altogether after an interlude in the eighteenth century, while in the Don, Volga and Kuban areas they retained certain aspects of their administration and military organisation until the end of the Empire and, to some extent, into the Soviet era.

Chapter 24

The end of slavery

Slave-hunting raids by the Crimean Tartars into Muscovy and Eastern Europe continued with diminishing frequency in proportion to the increased efficiency in Russian and Polish defences. They were stopped completely only with Russian annexation of the Crimea in 1783 and the extinction of Tartar independence.[1] Prior to that we find in Ottoman sources descriptions of Russian slaves and their comparison with North African ones. The Russians, apparently, were 'charming, hard-working and obedient, dishonest and unchaste'. In earlier times, says one mid-sixteenth century report, they were famous for their laziness, so that 'a single Tartar could capture many Russians. But today the situation is reversed, and the Russians have subjugated most of the Tartar land [...].'[2]

After the Russian conquest of the Caucasus the supply of slaves from there was much reduced but was not altogether stopped until the sultan's orders against the traffic in white slaves issued in 1854 and 1855.[3] The main reason for the demise of slavery and its merging with serfdom was the need of the state for more manpower and more income from taxes.[4] As the pressure of tax on the peasantry increased, the peasants claimed they were slaves in order to escape it. The government responded in 1679 by ordering all such individuals to be placed on the tax roles. Slaves living outside their owners' household (zadvornye liudi) were after 1679 taxed equally with the peasants.[5]

As for military conscription, slaves who served in the army prior to 1632 usually remained the property of their owners. By about 1720, after the experiences of the Thirty Years War and the Northern War, even house slaves were drafted as infantry soldiers. They could, however, volunteer for the army service and gain their freedom. After Peter's death in 1726 slaves were no longer allowed to volunteer. They had to be drafted like peasants. 'The last loophole that had permitted exit from slave status was closed. The slave was converted into a serf.'[6]

Chapter 25

ReLigion & authority

The key to the role which religion played and still plays in Russia must be sought in the ideology of universalism.

The sky-worshipping nomads believed the 'Eternal Sky' to be the only source of authority; as there was only one sky, there could also be only one authority in the world, extending over temporal and religious matters alike. The people of the chieftain upon whom such authority had been bestowed regarded themselves as superior to all other peoples to whom such privilege had been denied.

The same attitude appears in Islam. As the *Legacy of Islam* puts it:

'This community is different from any other; it is the chosen, the holy people, to whom is entrusted the furtherance of good and the repression of evil; it is the only seat of justice and faith upon the earth, the sole witness for God among the nations, just as the Prophet had been God's witness among the Arabs.'[1]

This view implied both intolerance and exclusivity and, above all, superiority over those of different faiths.

A similar claim of exclusivity was common both to Greek and Latin Christianity. But in the West the Pope's authority in temporal matters was severely restricted; he could claim universal authority only in spiritual matters. In the East, however, there was no distinction between civil and religious authority; the Byzantine Emperor was the supreme authority in both.

Religion and politics could not be separated. In the West the emphasis was laid on personal salvation, while in the East the aim was the redemption of the world.[2] The claims made by Byzantium and the Eastern Church had always been total. No other ruler could equal the emperor, and no other religion could have known the road to salvation. It was only natural that Russia, who saw herself as heir to the empire, assumed also, at least in theory, a paramount role in Christendom. The monolithic regime that emerged in Muscovy thus 'included the Mongol hierarchical authority with all power devolving from the paramount khan, and the religiously inspired quest for a divinely charismatic figure, like the traditional saints'.[3] To put it more bluntly, Orthodox Christianity provided a convenient cloak for the universal power-claims of the sky-worshipping nomads; the 'redemption of the world' thus became in the religious field what the Universal Empire was in the political; the ruler, the tsar, was the embodiment of both.

In a total authority like this there was no room for any weakness, doubt or error. The authority had to rely on a dogma, and the ruler had to prove his infallibility by bending the reality to his purposes. On the other hand, a dogma was necessary to maintain the spiritual discipline which, as in a nomadic system, had to accompany the army-style discipline of the social organisation. The lack of individualism that resulted from the system made such 'disciplined thinking' not only acceptable, but also inevitable. (The connection between religious obedience and fear of an absolute ruler has been noted by Masaryk, *Spirit of Russia*, III).[4]

First, the result was a complete lack of political thought. The official and only ideology was provided ready-made by the joint authority of Church and state, and the totality of the system prevented it from being challenged in any way. Lay philosophy did not exist in Russia at all, and the few religious theories that appeared before the end of the eighteenth century were all rather conformist, derivative and, on the whole, second-rate. There were 'two sets of intellectual and political attitudes, which we shall meet repeatedly in later Russian thought: on the one hand, practicality based on formal discipline and in constant danger of degenerating into ritualism or brutality, and on the other, humane benevolence appealing to inner freedom and toleration and in constant danger of escaping into pure contemplation or abstract theorising'.[5]

It can be argued that these two attitudes reflect yet again the basic duality of Russian society: the discipline and brutality of the warrior élite, and the passive withdrawal of the obedient and helpless masses.

Therefore the Russian system may be characterised as 'ideological monopoly'. As in Eastern despotism, 'the top authority interprets and prescribes the dogma'.[6] The ruler had to be super-human in order to be infallible. To impress his total authority on the subjects and to enhance his own stature, he had to insist on their complete humiliation.

'He that should happen to subscribe his name in the positive degree to petitions or letters to the Czar would be publicly tried for treason. Diminutives must be used [...]. For they deem it greatly derogatory to the supreme rank of majesty not to revere their sovereign with all respect by these humble diminutives of name [...] he ought to write and style himself the Grand Duke's *kholop*, or most abject and vilest slave, and acknowledge that all the goods and chattels he possessed were not his but the monarch's. And in this opinion [...] their sovereign uses his native country and its inhabitants as if power absolute, unbounded, uncircumscribed by any law, lay openly with him to dispose as freely of the property of private individuals, as if nature had produced everything for his sake alone.'[7]

An imperial liturgy copied from Byzantium was used to stress the tsar's religious dignity, but in his treatment of other people, whether his own subjects or foreigners, elements of Oriental, and especially Persian thinking are clearly discernible.

This Byzantine-Oriental humiliation was also characteristic of the Russian way of worship. The tsar and the saints were worshipped in very much the same way. 'It remains difficult to repress an oddly embarrassed feeling on seeing Russians bow to the very ground before altars, relics, pictures of saints, the priests and monks.'[8] The political and ideological significance of such bows and prostrations has been discussed above (p. 41).

For Dostoevsky, 'The Czar is the embodiment of the national organism. Thus – in the last volume of *A Writer's Diary* – we are offered the old, officially sanctioned patriarchal theory, which holds that the Czar is the father of his children... The Czar of all the Russians is no external or exterior power; he is the organic embodiment of all power and might [...].'[9]

'The patriarchal theory of social organisation certainly requires that the people no less than the Czar be heard [...]. Dostoevsky demands that only genuine *muzhiks* be called together [...]. "Let us learn from the people how to speak the truth. Let us learn the people's humility, its realism, and the earnestness of its common sense outlook [...]," [...] the *muzhik* is the very one to tell the Czar the truth and nothing but the truth.'[10] 'Dostoevsky is, in fact, a supporter of theocracy and of the Russian national theocracy in particular; the Church, State and nation become indistinguishable, both conceptually and politically. It obviously follows [...] that authority does not evolve from Christ but rather from the pope-emperor.'[11]

Even in Russian mysticism, which is the product of the individual's search of salvation and peace and of his withdrawal into himself, there is a curious craving for total authority. In Dostoevsky 'a mystical dedication to God, the mystical union with the deity is duly transformed into total devotion to the monk as Russia's only saviour'. In *The Brothers Karamazov* he is more broadly concerned with the institution of the 'Elder' as it is found in Russian and Eastern monasteries. The Elder, whose source of authority is moral rather than hierarchical, wields unlimited power over those who have chosen to subordinate themselves to him. As Dostoevsky puts it: 'The Elder is someone who takes your own soul and your will into his own soul and will; whoever has chosen an elder has abdicated his own will and turned it over to him in complete obedience.'[12]

As Masaryk says: '[...] the institution itself is unquestionably a product of Byzantine absolutism and despotism. It is the quintessence of an aristocratic religion, and therefore a kind of religious slavery since [...] every aristocratic order must and does rest on some form of slavery.'

Dostoevsky's story of the Grand Inquisitor in *The Brothers Karamazov* is perhaps the best description of the negation of freedom and the search for authority in the Russian religious mind.

'Christ wanted to impart a liberal faith and freedom of conscience to mankind. Yet man does not have the strength to be free [...] the masses, in their millions, really do not want freedom at all. No sooner does an individual attain freedom than he seeks out someone to follow and obey. With the growth of freedom there is a parallel tendency to discover someone whom all can follow. The weak person not only wants to obey; he looks to and for the mass idol. Moreover, this need to follow and to obey is quite basic and the genesis of both war and religion. It explains the need for a feeling of universal brotherhood – the craving to be part of a "world-wide ant-heap" – such as achieved by Tamerlane and Genghis Khan.'[13] These paragraphs contain all the basic ingredients: the Oriental philosophy of the individual dissolving and disappearing in the multitude; the Byzantine idea of a total control over the mind by a despotic religious authority; and the nomadic 'world-wide ant-heap' with its total control of the individual's behaviour by a military machine headed by a mass idol, an 'organic embodiment of all power and might'. All in all, it is the thinking of a weak, helpless individual faced with an overwhelming and merciless force – and a result of centuries of conditioning.

Apart from religion, these attitudes began to change in the second half of the eighteenth century under the influence of Europe. The Byzantine ritual and the Persian-style veneration were gradually abandoned; the authority of the tsar remained unchallenged and undivided, but religion became separated from politics. Religious matters became the responsibility of the Holy Synod; through it the government exercised effective control over Church organisation, possessions and policies.[14] The religious universalism and messianism of the earlier times now became transformed into political and military imperialism with growing national undertones. Political dogmatism replaced religious dogmatism and its embodiment became the doctrine of Nicholas I: 'autocracy, orthodoxy and nationality'.

'If Russia and Russia alone is holy, and if only that Russia has the faith which holds the key to salvation, then it follows that the Russian must comprehend his Russianness [...] as something unique, exclusive and quite personal [...] if, in fact, the Russians are a "God-folk", it is absolutely inescapable that they are also unique, and the only ones of their kind. Russian chauvinism naturally over-simplifies itself into a cultural synthesis. If, indeed, Russia has created the only correct foundation for such a synthesis, then the future of Europe belongs to Russia, "because we are mightier than anyone else"' (Dostoevsky, *A Writer's Diary, Polnoe Sobranie Sochineniy*, XI, p. 105).[15]

Chapter 26

Nationalism & Nationality

Russia gradually became in many respects the same multinational empire as the nomadic empires used to be in the past. Yet it is difficult to speak of the nationalism of the nomads. National feelings and nationhood were not sufficiently developed, and tribal differences mattered more than differences of speech, customs and ethnic origin. This goes some way to explain the tolerance of the nomads in national matters. It was usually enough for an alien people – whether tribe or nation – to acknowledge the suzerainty of the khan, to pay tribute and to accept the imperial discipline in case of war. No assimilation in terms of language or customs was required. But this kind of tolerance does not mean that all ethnic groups within the empire were treated as equal. Members of the khan's own tribe considered themselves superior to all others; there was an inner circle of tribes providing the guards and crack units, and the outer circle being used for lesser services. The social standing of these groups was related to the military hierarchy and the non-fighting people, like the peasants or the urban population had no standing at all.

In the Islamic Orient the primary basis of group identity was 'the brotherhood of faith within the religious community, reinforced by common dynastic allegiances. To this day the Western notions of patriotism and nationality have never entirely superseded the older pattern...'.

'Loyalty to a place was known, but it was to a village or a quarter, not a country; loyalty to one's kin was ancient and potent, but it was to the family or tribe, not to the nation. The ultimate loyalty [...] was religion. The next loyalty was political – to the lawful head of the Islamic state.'[1]

In Russia the development was rather similar. The Great Russian nation evolved from the inner circle of the Grand Prince's own followers and those of his relatives and rival princes whom he managed to overpower. This was the fighting élite who in the course of time assumed a superior position towards the nations of the outer circle whether conquered in war or annexed by peaceful means. As in Islam, the prime loyalty was not to the country or nation, but to the religion and the ruler.

As in Turkey, divisions within the empire were cultural and religious rather than national, but were marked with a fair amount of tolerance. The Jews were the only exception, but it may be argued that hostility towards them was of social rather than religious origin. Certainly, nationality coined by Nicholas I to be one of the three pillars of the Empire (alongside autocracy and Orthodoxy) was something substantially different from the nationalism that in Western and Central Europe became the main political force in the nineteenth century. The Russian Empire was, by then, multinational, but the Russians (or the Great Russians) were by no means the ruling nation. The Baltic Germans, Latvians, Lithuanians, Poles, Ukrainians, White Russians, Georgians or Armenians enjoyed more or less the same status; the Asian nationalities were treated as inferior but more in the cultural than in the national sense.

Nicholas' nationality was therefore a fictive one; it was based on the concept of 'Mother Russia' and referred more to the 'Sacred Earth' than to people of the same language or ethnic origin; a similar concept that seemed to exist among the nomadic empires of the past. Through the dual role of the tsar, as an embodiment of the State and of the Church, Orthodoxy and nationality became synonymous. This was a source of inequality because the non-Orthodox subjects, whether Russian or not, found themselves in the 'outer circle'. The pattern, from the point of view of social standing, was therefore rather complex: the Orthodox Great-Russians; the non-Orthodox Great-Russians; the Orthodox non-Great Russians; the non-Orthodox non-Russians. But from the point of view of 'official nationality', they were all 'Russians' whatever their ethnic origins, language or way of life. In literature these views had been most clearly expressed by Dostoevsky.

'Dostoevsky thus equates the notions of nationality and nation (nationality as a form of collective striving and nation as a social whole) with the state no less than with the church and with religion [...]. Russia for Dostoevsky, just as for the *muzhik*, is "Holy Russia"; the Russian people are a "God-folk"; Russia has its Russian God and its Russian Christ. The Russian cannot cease believing in his God because he would thus cease to be a Russian. He has an entirely distinctive church and state. For Dostoevsky, the words "Russian", "Orthodox Christian", "citizen of an autocratic state" – are all synonyms. Hence religion and nationality form a mythical unity for Dostoevsky.'[2]

There is no need to emphasise the role which this idea of nationality played in Russian imperialism. The original tribal superiority of the Great-Russians now acquired a religious sanction. The road was open for all other peoples in the world to achieve salvation by becoming 'Russians' – in other words by accepting the political domination of the Great-Russian tsar. It was a revival, in more modern guise, of the old nomadic multinational empire with its universalistic aims.[3]

The pattern, too, began to change under the influence of Europe. The old fighting and religious relationship with the tsar shifted towards a Western-style nationalism and chauvinism; on the one hand, everything Russian was to be superior; on the other, the non-Russian nationalists were to be helped to achieve this superiority by becoming Russianised. The bond of religion was weakened and that of language and way of life strengthened. A new concept of oneness began to appear: that of Russian nationality *au sens propre*. The oneness of the command structure remained, but the oneness of religion now became what can be labelled the oneness of culture. The European brand of nationalism began to appear only at the turn of the century and its political manifestation, with Great Russian chauvinism on one side, and various separatist movements on the other, had to wait until the Soviet era.[4]

To understand the budding national aspirations of the Asians within the Empire we have to deal with several groups of peoples, most of them Muslims. The question of nationalism cannot, therefore, be separated from that of Islam and its relation to an authority, which was of a different religion as well as of a different ethnic, cultural and linguistic background.

Inevitably, the first stirring of opposition to the Russian colonisation was based on religion. Although the advancing agricultural settlements in the steppe deprived the nomads of their best pastures, they merely pushed them farther away without provoking any major resistance. But, in settled areas, when the authorities under the 'official nationality' policy abandoned their earlier tolerance – or indifference – in religious matters and began to interfere with the teaching of Islam, reducing the number of Islamic schools and even, in some cases, attempting to convert Muslims to Orthodoxy, a pro-Islamic agitation made its appearance, stimulated also, to a considerable degree, by pro-Turkish sympathies in the Crimean war (see also below, chapter 32, on political thought).[5]

There were different attitudes to this movement. The Kazakhs, being rather lukewarm towards religion, were not very enthusiastic over the pan-Islamic slogans of the Tartars. Their language played a part in it, too. Linguistic imports from Turkish suited better the Tartar language than the Kazakh one, which was more distant.[6]

On the other hand, Islam as practised in the Central Asian khanates was far more intransigent and backward. Isolated from the mainstream of Sunni centres of Cairo and Constantinople by the advance of Russia and the Shi'ite Empire of Persia, it became inward-looking and conservative in the extreme, which provided a fertile ground for pan-Islamic and anti-Russian feelings. The first violent manifestation of them was the uprising in the Ferghana Valley in 1898, which was brutally suppressed. The social and political radicalisation which followed the 1905 revolution in Russia left the local population largely unaffected – with the exception of a thin layer of pro-Western intellectuals. But in 1916, following the manifesto decreeing the conscription of Muslims, there was a general flare-up of an anti-Russian revolt, both among the nomads and the peasants.[7]

As late as 1917, the religious feeling among Russian Turks was stronger than the nationalist one. It was only as a consequence of the Jadids' influence in the Communist Party in 1919 that the term 'Turkic' began to replace 'Muslim'. The discussions among various factions of Muslim politicians centred more on cultural or territorial autonomy than on secession from the Empire.[8] The nascent Turkic nationalism of the Central Asians was obscured by their hope for reforming and resurrecting Islam.[9]

In Azerbaijan, the Young Turks' seizure of power in Constantinople strengthened the pro-Turkish sympathies, but according to Zenkovski,[10] the local leaders were more pro-Turkish than pan-Turkic, more interested in Turkey than in the destinies of their Tartar or Uzbek co-religionists. The Tartars, too, had become more definitely oriented towards Turkey but, more pan-Turkic, they worked stubbornly for the unification and the leadership of the Turkic peoples of Russia – in fact, of all Muslims, including the non-Turkic mountain tribes of the Caucasus, the Iranian Tajiks and the Finno-Ugrians of the Volga Region.[11, 12]

Chapter 27

The economy

Trade continued to be hampered by the difficulties of transport. It was difficult to get the farm products to the towns, and the towns themselves could not exceed a size that could be supplied from the immediate neighbourhood. Villages and hamlets continued to be, in most aspects, self-contained and self-supplying communities with very little differentiation of labour and very few local crafts. The town population, 3 percent of the total in 1724, did not rise beyond 4.1 percent by 1796; it was 11.6 percent in 1860 and 14.6 percent in 1914.[1]

As mentioned above, townspeople were mostly bonded serfs, merchants and craftsmen alike. When industrialisation began, manufactures and factories were also worked by serfs – the so-called possessional workers, who were in fact state peasants despatched to work in state-run factories. The lack of an urban middle class and the low status of merchants meant that foreign trade remained in the hands of foreigners; financial institutions, like banking and credit, were also developed by foreigners, and run predominantly by the state. For instance, the entire credit system at the turn of the twentieth century was in the hands of the state. State enterprise, an idea inherited from Byzantium, and existing all the time in the armament industry and state monopolies, as well as in state-run manufactures, expanded rapidly with the beginning of industrialisation. Although private enterprise appeared on a limited scale during the nineteenth century, the state remained the chief source of economic activity until the Revolution. 'It was characteristic also of the Russian tradition that although Witte sought to create the conditions in which capitalists and entrepreneurs of any nationality might freely flourish, he never for one moment doubted that the initiative must come from the state.'[2]

The development of private enterprise was hampered, primarily, by the absence of clear legal title to land ownership. Land could not be used as collateral for credit or source of capital. This must be seen as the foremost reason why, at the early stage of industrialisation, most enterprises were state-owned and run either by the state or by foreigners who brought in the necessary capital.

The colonisation of the Ukrainian steppe in the eighteenth century was made possible by improved agricultural techniques, and security of farming brought about a considerable increase in farm production. It is, however, unlikely that large internal shipments of grain became commonplace even in this period. The idea, mentioned by many historians, that the fertile south was supplying the infertile north does not sound more realistic now than it did in the period of Muscovy or Kiev. More grain was certainly available, and there was also the machinery to collect it, either as dues or taxes or as trade surplus. But transport was still insufficient and unsuitable for bulky commodities; river navigation was still the prevailing means, and the surpluses were shipped towards the Black Sea or Baltic ports for exports rather than being distributed to the population of faraway areas.

Moreover, there was no organisation for such distribution and no adequate price mechanism to make it pay. In most parts of the country the density of the population was still too low to allow the shipment of goods and the establishment of markets to become a viable operation. It is therefore more likely that the more distant areas – distant both from the centre and from suitable river routes – were still dependent on subsistence agriculture in the forests and on domestic manufacture of the necessary implements and tools. Their trade links were limited to easily transportable goods such as furs – which were also used for paying taxes. When the population increased in the nineteenth century, more and more areas reached the density point when markets could develop; but even in the twentieth century internal distribution and transport have been among the main problems of the Soviet economy.

The change came very slowly with the introduction of steam navigation and railways. Steamers appeared on the Volga in the 1820s and later also on other important rivers and lakes. The first major railroad went into operation in 1851, but in the 1850s the network was so limited that 'the Russian army in the Crimea proved to be more isolated from its home base than the allied forces, which were supplied by sea, from theirs'.[3] Nevertheless, rail transport permitted substantial growth of towns, and in the late nineteenth century both the bourgeoisie and the working class began to emerge.

The development of commercial agriculture had one important consequence: there was more money available now for the Treasury to pay for the army and the bureaucracy, which, in turn, provided for a better security of the steppe farmers and for a more efficient system of administration and taxation. The mutual support of army and bureaucracy worked better in Russia than in the increasingly corrupt Turkey and helped, in the long run, to win her a decisive edge over her age-old rival. In contrast to Austria, the third bureaucratic-agricultural empire in Eastern Europe, Russia had the advantage of unlimited centralisation. The national identity and separate political interests of Austria's component parts were too deeply entrenched and had to be taken into account even by an absolutist and centralised state; although the Austrian army and bureaucracy were considerably more efficient than Russia's, the centrifugal tendencies especially in the second half of the nineteenth century weakened the central power and eventually led to its downfall.

The colonisation of the Ukrainian steppe has often been compared with that of the North American continent. However, there were important differences. Whereas the American settlers moved into a country where they did not meet any serious opposition, the Russians were faced with a continuous threat from a formidable and well-organised enemy. Consequently, they could only move in the wake of the army which had to provide for essential security. The whole movement was therefore more organised and less spontaneous than the American one. Moreover, the settlers, in their majority, were not free peasants, but serfs.

'It was not free labour using agricultural machinery on an ever-more elaborate scale that broke the Ukrainian sod, as was later to happen in the

American and Australian wheat lands overseas. Instead the forced labour of serfdom, wielding sickle and scythe with human muscles and driving the plough with animal power, as men had done since early medieval times, was what tamed the Ukrainian plains.'[4]

The security aspect was less important in Siberia, but the character of labour was the same. Serfs and convicts were the main colonisers, and the army provided the backbone of administration. Therefore Russian colonisation lacked two important aspects of the American one: there was no spirit of individualism and no self-government. The authority came from above, not from below, and the colonised lands were simply an extension of the heartland with little or no identity of their own. There was no substantial difference between this colonisation of 'empty lands' and the colonial expansion into the Caucasus and Central Asia in the nineteenth century; there the local population was allowed to keep its religious and local customs, but administratively and militarily the lands became an integral part of the Russian Empire.[5]

Communications between villages were difficult and often dangerous. Trade, except along established routes, was still almost non-existent. Most villages had therefore to rely on their own supply of manufactured goods; but being too small to develop any specialised crafts, this meant that most such goods, utensils, cloths and others, were homemade. Pottery was a luxury and wooden crockery was commonplace until the industrial era. The smith and the carpenter were perhaps the only skilled craftsmen in the village. Among the principal causes of the continuing backwardness of the Russian countryside was the lack of trade and of diversification of labour.

The isolation of the village brought with it an inward-looking spirit, a 'cocoon-like mentality' with an intense in-feeling towards the members of the same group, such as the village inhabitants, and at the same time a xenophobia and strong suspicion towards anybody and anything that came from the 'outside'. Extreme conservatism and parochialism were the result of these attitudes, while within the community closeness of contacts and humanity of feelings, compassion and mutual aid reached an extremely high

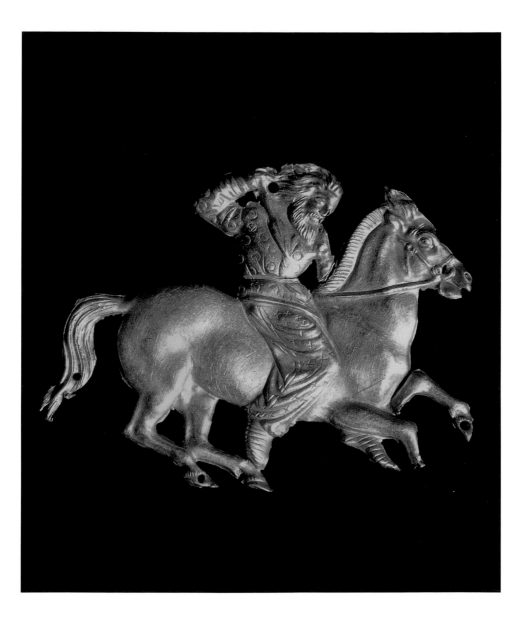

Nomad women, Qashqai tribe, Zagros Mountains, Iran

In a bedouin tent, Jordan

II

Pushtun nomads on the move, Afghanistan

Kazakh yurts, Kyzylkum Desert, Uzbekistan

*Ossetian shepherd,
Northern Caucasus*

*Nomad and horse under a
tree. Golden statue, Scythian,
Altai Region, c.400 BC.
Peter the Great's Collection,
The Hermitage, St Petersburg*

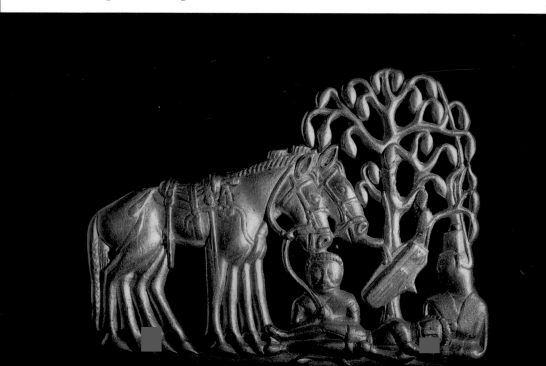

Tajik nomads, Sarykol, Chinese Pamir, Xinjiang, China

Ossetian horseman,
Northern Caucasus

Two Scyths with a loving cup, (rhyton). Scene of fraternization.
Golden statue from Kul-Oba, the Black Sea Region, 4th century BC.
The Hermitage, St Petersburg

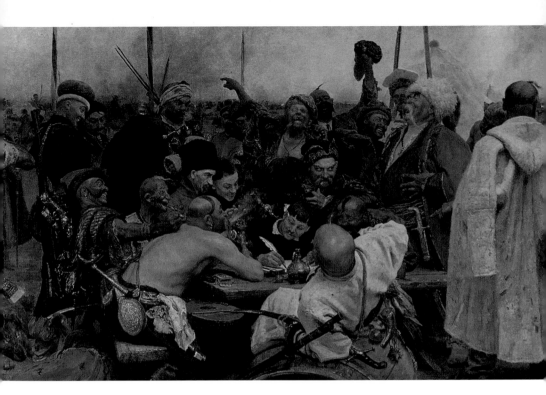

I.E. Repin, 1891: The Zaporozhian Cossacks writing a letter to the Sultan Mehmed IV.
The Russian State Museum, St Petersburg

Golden belt ornaments, Great Moravian artefacts

Tekfur Saray, the Palace of Constantine Porfyrogenitus. 10th century, Istanbul

Investiture of King Ardashir by god Mithra. Naqsh-i Rustam, Iran, 2nd century AD

Sword (gilded bronze) and *Stirrup (iron with bronze admixtures)*
Great Moravia, mid-9th century. Archaelogical Museum, Bratislavia

Cathedral of St Sophia, 11th century, Kiev

Statue of St Vladimir, above the River Dnieper, Kiev

(left) The Church of St George on Pskov Hills, 1655, Moscow.
The golden Byzantine Orthodox crosses on the golden onion
domes is a Russian design going back to the 15th century

The Terem Palace, interior. 16th century.
The Kremlin, Moscow

(left) St Basil's Cathedral. 16th century, Moscow

The Hermitage on the Neva River, St Petersburg, built in the 18th century

Catherine's Palace, Tsarskoe Selo, 17th century. Built by Peter the Great for his wife, the future Empress Catherine I

Poster by V.S. Ivanov, 1965

On the right is the golden dome of St Isaac's Cathedral (19th century)
behind the spire of the Admiralty (19th century)

Apostle Paul. Icon by Andrew Rublev, early 15th century.
Tretiakov Gallery, Moscow

*Hotel Ukraina, one
of the first Stalinist
skyscrapers, Moscow*

level. This inward-looking spirit together with the total dependence on a remote and despotic authority found its expression in a deep religious feeling among the peasants; the teaching of the Orthodox Church went well with their natural passivity, and the Church, with its complacent attitude towards the secular authority, was well-suited to channel eventual discontent into repentance and prayer.

The colonisation of agricultural land in Kazakhstan and Central Asia took place in two main waves: after a crop failure in Russia in 1891-2 and after the revolution in 1905. The land allocated to settlers remained property of the state. The occupation nevertheless led to frictions with the local population, especially with the nomads. These conquests provided Russia with an important source of agricultural produce, mainly grain, cotton and fruit. In the years 1888-1916, raw cotton became the main product of Central Asia and contributed greatly to the expansion of trade with Russia proper. At the end of the century cotton ginneries appeared in Bukhara and manufactured textiles, both cotton and silk, were exported.[6, 7, 8]

Chapter 28

тhe viLLaqe commune

Throughout history, until the present day, the main type of Russian community has been the village. Low density of population was a characteristic feature of Russia until the second half of the nineteenth century, and in large parts of the country it still is today. The village, whether situated in the forests or in the steppe, is by definition an agrarian settlement. The attitude to land is therefore a key factor in shaping the community and its institutions. Links with other communities of the same kind will be another factor, and the vertical communication, or the ways by which the community has been ruled, will be the third.

The fundamental commune principle of periodically dividing the land in proportion to need (repartitional tenure) was in itself a denial of the right to private property in land. The notion of private property did not prevail in the commune.

The lack of individual ownership of land prevented the development of individual farming; the system of collective (communal) farming, which has been the Russian way for centuries, worked consistently against the evolution of peasant individualism with its responsibility for success or failure and the ensuing spirit of enterprise. The Russian commune, while demanding a great degree of discipline from its members, took in effect all responsibility away from them; on the other hand, it gave members a feeling of security unparalleled in any other system.

The commune usually consisted of all heads of households; it administered all land, decided upon the rotation of fields and crops, and was principally responsible to the authorities for the total of taxes levied from the members. This had some important consequences for the mentality of the peasants.

First, there was no profit incentive and no fear of failure. The feeling of security resulting from collective responsibility worked as an inducement to keep the work-level at an absolute minimum. An element of constant coercion was therefore needed to meet the commune's commitments to the authorities. However, little direct coercion was needed from above. The ingenuity of the system was that the members watched and pushed each other.

Inevitably, in a closely-knit community, this excluded any privacy; it can only be imagined that in such circumstances any deviation from communal policies would be ruinous to the perpetrator. Conformity was therefore an essential requirement. A share in the decision-making, the element of consent in running the commune, was of limited importance because all decisions had to be made under pressure from the authorities; the sum of money to be levied was not negotiable, and the threat of punishment to all, if it were not fully met, was only too real.

The result was therefore a kind of 'fatherly despotism' of the commune elders over a passive peasantry, sometimes with bitter inner rivalries and ostracisms, but more often than not with a fatalistic acceptance of the inevitable.

Vernadsky[1] quotes a report from a town elder *(volostnoi starshina)* of Orel province in the late eighteen-nineties describing the institution of a Russian 'family':

'The peasant family in our town consists of several kinsmen, their wives and children, from fifteen to twenty persons in all, who all live in the same house. The elder wields great authority over the family. He keeps the family in peace and order; all of the members are subordinated to him. He assigns the work to be done to each member, manages the farm and pays the taxes. After his death his authority goes to his eldest son [...]. When several brothers live thus in one house [...] they consider all of the belongings the common property of the family, except for the women's clothes, linen and canvas. This is exempt from the commune. Except for these, everything else is managed by the elder. The elder's wife supervises the work of the women-folk [...] All the work is distributed among the men and women according to the strength and health of each.' (Quote from Kovalevsky, *Rodovoi byt.*, I, pp. 32–3.)

D.M. Wallace (Russia, 1877) describes a meeting of the *mir*. A woman is explaining to the meeting that her 'old man', who is at present the '*starost*' (village elder), is ill and cannot fulfil his duties.

"But he hasn't served a year; he'll get better."

"Who knows?" sobs the woman, "the doctor said that he must be brought to the hospital."

"Why has he not been taken there?"

"Who is to carry him? The hospital is 40 *versts* off. If you put him on a cart he would die before he had gone a *verst*. And who knows what they do with people in a hospital?"

"Very well; hold your tongue," says the greybeard of the group. "There is nothing to be done. Whom shall we choose (as a new elder)?" Several peasants look down to the ground; no one wants the honour.

"There is Alexei Ivanov; he has not served yet," says the greybeard.

"Yes, yes – Alexei Ivanov!" shout the peasants. He protests but is not listened to; he has been duly elected.

More important than the elections is the redistribution of the communal lands […]. A man called Ivan is asked how many shares he will take. "I have two sons and myself. I will take three – or less."

"Less! You talk nonsense. Your two sons may get married and so bring you two new female labourers."

"My eldest son works in Moscow and the other often leaves me in the summer."

"But they both send or bring home money and when they get married the wives will remain with you."

"God knows what will be. Who knows if they will marry?"

"You can easily arrange that."

"That I cannot do," says Ivan. "Times are changed now. The young people do as they wish and when they do get married they all want to have houses of their own. Three shares will be enough for me."

"He is a rich *muzhik*: lay him five souls (i.e. five shares of land and burdens)," cries a voice.

"Five souls, I cannot, by God."

"Very well, you shall have four. Shall it be so?"

"Four, four," murmurs the crowd, and it is settled.

Now comes the turn of a woman who has three little boys, only one old enough for field labour, and an invalid husband. "As the *mir* decides, so be it," she says, with downcast eyes.

"Then you must take three."

"What do you say, little Father: Do you hear that, ye Orthodox? They want to lay upon me three souls! Since St Peter's Day my husband has been bedridden – bewitched, it seems. He cannot put a foot to the ground."

"He was in the *kabak* (gin-shop) last week," says a neighbour.

"And you," shrieks the woman, "what did you do last parish fête? Was it not you who got drunk and beat your wife till she roused the whole village with her shrieking."

"Listen," says the old man sternly, "you must take two shares and a half. If you cannot manage it yourself you can get someone to help you."

"Where can I get money to pay a labourer?" wails the woman. "Have pity, ye Orthodox".'[2]

Chapter 29

тhe abolition of serfdom

Serfdom in Russia was not established in 1649, or in 1581. These dates simply mark a confirmation through legal means of a state that existed factually from the very dawn of Russian history, namely that peasants had to work on land which was not theirs, and that the only owner of all land was the all-powerful ruler: whether prince, Grand Prince, tsar or 'the state'. Characteristically, in 1861, when serfdom was legally abolished, land was not given to individual peasants but to communes, which 'divided the land among their members and were responsible for taxes, the provisions of recruits, and other obligations to the state'.[1]

The alien elements in the system, then, were the noble estates which became hereditary in the course of the last two centuries. On a limited scale, peasant ownership of land began to appear in the years before World War I. Between the emancipation and 1905 nearly 24 million *dessyatin* came into peasant ownership.[2] Peasants could also lease land from the landowners, but this practice 'ran clean counter the peasant notion that the land belonged to those who worked it and lived by it'.[3]

This contradicts the complaint of S. Witte in 1905: 'Communal lands belongs to the village commune as a juridical person, but in the eyes of the peasants [...] it belongs to the state which gives it to them for temporary use [...]; [legal relations among the peasants] are regulated not by law but frequently by custom which often "no one knows" [...]; what is an empire of one hundred million peasants who have been educated neither in the concept of landed property nor that of the firmness of law in general [...].'[4]

Economically, there were good reasons for the abolition of serfdom, and the government had been well aware of them for some time, but capitalism in Russia was too weak to force a change by itself. Although it was well known that free peasants were much more productive than serfs, it was still believed that communal farming secured better overall performance, mainly because of the general economic mentality of the peasants which required non-economic coercion to achieve substantial economic results.[5] The commune was very adept in providing such coercion, especially when certain landlords were increasingly reluctant to use punitive methods.

Legally, the lack of peasant mobility was felt as an obstacle to the development of industries which needed a steady supply of labour. In the mid-nineteenth century even a free worker who left his place without authorisation was considered a criminal, on the same level as a runaway serf. In this way, some authors concluded, the economy based on serfdom reached deadlock not because of its low profits, but because it had become impossible to maintain the former level of violence without which the system ceased to be efficient.[6]

In the end, the reform was imposed from above by a government which was itself not convinced about the advantages and desirability of capitalist economy. As a consequence, the legislation established a multiplicity of privileges and obligations, the peasants were not given land but were forced to buy it, often under very unfavourable terms, and most important, the emancipation accentuated the authority of the commune.[7]

The abolition of serfdom in 1861 did not change very much in the position of the peasants. Although they did not 'belong' to individual masters any more, they were still not free to go where they wanted. They were tied to the commune and remained under the unremitting scrutiny of the government. The new administrative unit – the *volost* – grouping one or more villages – functioned as a state institution, quite in line with the administrative principles of the preceding periods. 'To the commune, for example, was assigned the land granted to the peasants as a result of emancipation. The peasant himself only "owned" that portion of the commune's allotment land to which his family responsibilities, as head of a household, entitled him [...] the commune also redistributed periodically the land in accordance with changing family obligations [...] the authority of the commune controlled the individual peasant's freedom of movement. A peasant wishing to relinquish his holding had first of all to obtain permission from the village assembly and the head of the household to which he belonged [...]. Should the peasant's departure from the commune be short-term – in order to work in a factory, for example – then he still remained attached to the commune as a taxpayer, and the head of the household [...] had the right to a share in the earnings of the absent peasant.'[8] 'The members of the commune were collectively responsible for the payment of taxes and also of redemption dues. This circumstance shows how important it was not to lose control of the individual member.'[9]

From these quotations it is clear that collective farming went back to the earliest days of forest agriculture. The old Byzantine principle of collective responsibility for taxes, as well as the nomadic idea that an individual must belong to some community or unit, survived in Russia even in the most westernised period of her history.

Chapter 30

Education & Culture

The level of literacy remained very low. The reform of 1864 made education the responsibility of the newly-created *zemstva*, and the number of schools of all levels began to grow very rapidly. In spite of this the census of 1897 showed that in European Russia only 21 percent of the population could read and write, although among young adults the proportion was 45 percent. The best situation was among the industrial workers in St Petersburg and Moscow, who in the early 1900s were 80–90 percent literate. In 1913 nearly 68 percent of the recruits seemed to be literate, though it is not sure to what level. A system of compulsory education was introduced only after the Revolution.

The political role of the Russian bourgeoisie was insignificant. 'The political impotence of the Russian bourgeoisie corresponded to its inner weakness.' 'This has its reason not only in the social history of the bourgeoisie but also in the whole policy of planning from the top.' Under the system of state enterprise and control 'no independent capitalism could develop, but there was also no need for such development to take place'.[1] As a result the bourgeoisie may be fairly described as a satrap of the regime. There existed 'a firm alliance between the autocracy and capitalism, in which the state, by virtue of its economic policy, was the senior ally'.[2]

Politically, industry remained entirely passive; this was noticed by Herzen already in 1855 and later prompted Marx to his forecast that Russia might bypass the capitalist stage of evolution altogether. This largely explains the failure of the Duma system and the Cadet Party, and why, in 1917, there was no liberal middle-class movement to lead the evolution to parliamentary democracy as in other countries.

The sources of European influence in the field of culture were two-fold.

The westernised regions of the empire, which formerly belonged to Poland and Sweden, like Western Ukraine and the Baltic countries, were the first. Kiev, for instance, during the centuries of Polish rule reached a high standard in education and the arts, and was a full century after its annexation by Moscow still by far the most civilised city in the Empire.[3] The other were Western visitors and immigrants who began to flock to the new imperial capital, St Petersburg. For religious reasons the Protestants came first, and, in the first half of the eighteenth century, the strongest influence was that of the Germans and the Dutch. As the role of the Orthodox Church weakened, the influx of Catholics grew, and in the reign of Catherine II the import of French culture escalated into a Franco-mania comparable to the wholesale reception of Turkish and Byzantine culture in the earlier periods.

In 1767 the English Ambassador, Sir George Macartney, wrote of the 'crowds of French adventurers who daily resort here, and are received into most families with open arms as secretaries, librarians, readers, preceptors, and parasites; though the greatest part of these gentry are equally impudent and illiterate, vagabonds from indigence or fugitives for crimes'.[4]

In 1790 an English traveller, A. Swinton, wrote: 'Russia resembles an heir newly come to his estate [...] the English master is teaching him the art of navigation and commerce, the French [...] to dance and to dress, the Italian is drawing plans for his house and teaching him to sing, the German makes him wheel to the right and left and teaches him all the other arts of war.'[5]

It was during Catherine's reign that the nobles acquired the right to travel abroad: although it was a tiny fraction of the population, it was through them that Europe – especially France and Italy – came to have direct contact with Russia – and the Russians with Europe. Military expeditions during the French Revolution and Napoleonic wars brought more and more Russians into Europe; this time they were common soldiers, not only aristocrats. But it was only the topmost layer of the gentry that could absorb European ideas and cultural currents.

Russian culture, as it began to emerge in the second half of the eighteenth century, was essentially a gentry culture;[6] it became mixed with sporadic middle-class elements only in the middle and late nineteenth century and retained the predominant aristocratic touch until the Revolution. The Europeanised aristocrats not only produced works of art – especially in literature – modelled on and comparable with Western ones; they also viewed Russian reality with Western eyes and implanted into it Western ideas, viewpoints and values. The great Russian literature of the nineteenth century is a typical example: it was a product of a handful of men[7] all isolated by their origin, education and way of life from the broader layers of population and concentrating in their works almost exclusively on members of their own class; others, especially peasants, were seen as if from the outside, as if they were men from a different world – which, in fact, they were.

When Tolstoy was writing *War and Peace*, his characters were in his own words, 'either princes, or counts, and so on, who speak and write in French as though Russian life of that time consisted only of those people. I quite agree that this is neither liberal nor true to life. All I can say is that the life of civil servants, merchants, seminarists and peasants does not interest me and is only half intelligible to me, while for all sorts of reasons I find the life of aristocrats of those days both intelligible and interesting.'[8]

The one exception here is perhaps Dostoevsky, who was able to depict the genuine Russian way of thinking in some of his novels, diaries and journalistic articles. 'No other Russian has ever analysed the spirit of his people so well. No one, apart from Dostoevsky, has made the attempt to see the historical and social realities which confronted him as an expression of the Russian soul and to subject the dynamics of the Russian state and of Russia's national life to such rigorous psychological examination.'[9]

Chapter 31

Art & propaganda

In this chapter the connection between art and the official (State) ideology will be examined as well as the role of state authorities in promoting and directing artistic creations. For that purpose, art in Russia will have to be considered mainly as an importation of the Byzantine Orthodox Church. The influence of the Church in early Russian art has been paramount. All 'official' art had to be religious, sponsored by the Church and serving its purpose. Religious elements in the old pagan art were suppressed and eliminated, and the remnants of the nomadic and peasant traditions of a lay nature were reduced to the level of folk art.

The key issue is the sponsored and programmatic nature of official art, which has become a feature of Russian art ever since. As in Byzantium, the Church had an absolute monopoly of power over the minds of the population. No lay art was permitted. There were no minstrels and troubadours, no bawdy poets entertaining small provincial courts in a highly secular, unreligous way. There were no castles, palaces, not even town hall buildings erected for a secular, non-religious master. The centralisation of secular power in the hands of the Grand Prince or tsar ensured the domination of the Church over everything spiritual and creative.

Thus the messianism of the Church and its religious universalism were brought, in the form of religious art, to support and promote the paramountcy and universal aspirations of the state. Art had to serve a dual purpose: to promote the views and policies of the Church and, by implication, those of the state. There was, at least in theory, no contradiction between the two. It has been said above that wherever the Church tried to establish an independent view from the state, or even a slightly modified view, the state was always able to bring it back to conformity. To use modern terms, Orthodox art served as a propaganda outlet for Church and state policies.

Church literature, music, icons and architecture alike were designed primarily not for spiritual comfort of the believer but to overawe him with the splendour and power of the authority and to reduce him to complete obedience, or, in some cases, to divert his mind into abstract and politically harmless mysticism.

As an example, it will suffice to compare Church architecture of the West with that of Orthodox Byzantium and Russia. In a Gothic cathedral the mind of the believer is carried upwards towards Heaven and God with every architectural element harmoniously combining to bring about the ultimate effect of union between mind and God; the vastness of the space and the simplicity of the decor effectively emphasises the might of the deity while at the same time avoiding to distract the mind from its concentration.

In contrast, the low arches and multiple cupolas of the Byzantine style divide the space with a depressing effect upon the believer while, at the same time, the profuse decor of the interior, the glitter of gold, the vivid colours of the icons and mosaics together with the music, the frankincense and the mystique of the invisible priest are designed not to relieve but to overawe him, to impress upon him his own insignificance before the almighty authority that keeps an eye on him. That eye is, in fact, there; the stern, immovable face of Christ Pantocrator, the Almighty ruler, whose incarnation on Earth is the tsar.

This, then, was the role of Russian art until the late eighteenth century, when, under the influence of Europe, lay art began to appear in the increasingly secularised circles of the gentry. With the urban population still insignificant both in terms of numbers, education and economic importance, this lay art remained almost exclusively confined to the landed aristocracy, and in every generation it was a product of a handful of individuals.

Generally speaking, this was no longer 'official' art; it lacked the sponsorship and the propaganda aspects of the religious art. Religious messianism ceased to be the guideline, but religion began to be linked with nationality, and Russian messianism – or chauvinism – began to appear. Official propaganda was replaced – in this independent, lay art – by the individual message of the artist concerned; with the limited range of philosophical ideas, this message was predominantly either religious or national. Politics and art were never far apart. The work of art was still, as before, a means of conveying a political message; it now served as a vehicle for conveying the artists' views how to save the world, or, at least, Russia and the Russian people. There was still no room for 'art for art's sake' – an idea which, for a Russian layman, was equally abhorrent and despicable as it was unthinkable for the Russian monk.

But the national messianism-salvation of Russia alone was in itself a limited aim which did not satisfy the latent universalistic tendencies of the Russian mind. On the national plan, therefore, it was necessary to extend the salvation at least to all Slavs. On the religious side, with Orthodoxy rapidly losing its appeal, a new universalistic religion had to be found. The Westernisers found it in European socialism – and, in particular, in Marxism.

Meanwhile, official art continued to exist serving the official ideology: Orthodoxy with nationality supporting the autocracy of the tsar. The support of Russian imperialism was the official side of nationalism in art. What distinguished this era of Russian art, whether official or unofficial, was that the propaganda aspect – the promotion of political ideas – was not directly enforced by the authority; it was not claimed as a right by the authority as in the previous centuries, but was an expression of the artist's own conviction (within the limits of censorship).

Secularised painting in the nineteenth century produced only imitations of Western art of non-exceptional value; its heyday came shortly before World War I, when, with artists like Chagall or Kandinsky, Russian painting was on par with that of Europe.

Russian music began with applying European techniques to folk-themes; most composers then leaned on European models until, with Tchaikovsky, they mastered the most sophisticated European style.[1] It was in sculpture and architecture where Russia lagged behind Europe most conspicuously.

Sculpture was, and is even now, virtually non-existent; architecture represented 'the most depressing aspect of arts in nineteenth century Russia'.[2] 'In the second half of the century Russian architects produced doubtless the worst durable buildings: as an ensemble they demonstrated the failure of any native tradition to evolve [...].'[3] This may, of course, be an exaggerated and personal view; but if we look back in history, some revealing explanations offer themselves.

There was no native tradition for either architecture or sculpture; the nomad chieftains had no room for either of them. The tradition of the wooden structures of north-western Russia died with Novgorod in the sixteenth century. Stone and brick architecture was imported since the days of Kievan Russia (with a few exceptions, like the Cathedral of St Basil) mainly for the purposes of the Church. But the Church did not embellish the churches with sculptures, only with icons. And with the weakening of the Church after the Petrine reforms, the tradition of icon-painting withered away, and was not replaced by any other native tradition until the European influence produced its own. In sculpture and architecture this did not happen.

There were attempts, however. When Russia, and especially St Petersburg, became a truly international centre of art, shortly before the outbreak of World War I, modern sculpture and architecture began to emerge, but they both lagged far behind painting.[4] Curiously enough, modern art survived the first decade after the Revolution and, in fact, produced its most notable works in the 1920s before it was stigmatised and suppressed by the new orthodoxy.

Chapter 32

poLiticaL thought

Similarly, there seems to have been little tradition in philosophy and political thought. Until the seventeenth century this was confined almost exclusively to religious problems. The Western philosophy of the Enlightenment, or some aspects of it, was adopted by Catherine II in the early part of her reign and led to some of her – largely abortive – administrative reforms. But this philosophy based on rationalism, liberalism and tolerance soon clashed with Russian political reality; the reaction it provoked was marked with a return to political traditions of old Muscovy and, in fact, of the more distant past.

Formulated in the 1830s, this theory of autocracy, orthodoxy and nationality survived until 1905, if not until February 1917.[1] Orthodoxy meant devotion to the teaching and ritual of the Russian Orthodox Church 'a return to pre-Petrine Russia', while autocracy was being confirmed 'as the basic and permanent feature of Russian statehood'. Nationality was interpreted 'as devotion to the Russian national heritage and the spiritual make-up of the people'.[2]

In a multinational empire this could not be but a fictive concept. The first two principles are clearly derived from Byzantine political philosophy; the old nomadic principle of a lay and absolute state power, as it re-emerged in Peter's era, seemed thus weakened, at least in theory. In practice, Orthodoxy did not mean any political influence of the Church.

Anti-government philosophy was split into various concepts mostly stemming from European thoughts and carried by Europeanised intellectuals.

sLavophiLes and westernisers

The Slavophiles, mostly educated in Moscow, saw their ideal in Kievan and Muscovy Russia, and stressed the agrarian tradition as well as the Slav character of the people; disregarding the non-Slav elements, they rejected the ways and fashions of the West and were often strongly hostile to them; '[…] they rejected the regimentation of the life of the country and also any constitutionalist tendencies.'³ Their orientation on 'the people' – which in practice meant the peasants – was shared by the populists. 'The Slavophile movement's primary concern was not with politics, but the philosophy of history… with Russia's place in the world… and her contribution to the world's civilisation'. 'Their philosophy inexorably led to the conclusion that autocracy as a regime which by definition excludes the people from participation in politics, was the only suitable form of government – not only for Russia but for every nation that wished to enjoy genuine freedom.'⁴

The Westernisers, on the contrary, deliberately accepted West-European political models and split, therefore, into several trends which roughly corresponded to the trends and parties of Western Europe.⁵ In the field of practical politics it can be argued that the Slavophiles and the populists were doomed to failure because the peasant masses were politically inert and did not, or could not, support their movement; the Westernisers of all kinds, including the Social Democrats (Mensheviks), were restricted to a thin layer of Europeanised élite and were using methods which were alien to the Russian political scene and political traditions and for which there were no appropriate conditions in Russia. Political parties of Western types and politics based on representation had no room in Russia; it was not only due to autocracy that repeated attempts to establish some kind of political representation failed; nobody in the country except the tiny élite could understand the purpose of it.

The Marxists

On the left, the most significant were the anarchists and the Marxists; some of the Marxists followed on the whole the theories and political aims of West-European Social Democrats. It is the other section of Russian Marxists who later began to call themselves Bolsheviks, which is of more interest for the purposes of this study.

Certain elements were brought into the Marxist theory by V.I. Lenin, which can be classified as nomadic thinking, namely: emphasis on total power; universalistic claims; quasi-military organisation and discipline; emphasis on equality; emphasis on the dominating role of the community and its control over individuals; emphasis on conspiracy and clandestine operations; and the emphasis on the necessity of total destruction of the existing system. The last two items the Bolsheviks shared with the anarchists; but whereas the anarchists wanted to achieve individual freedom, the Bolshevik ideal was social justice expressed in equality.

The root of the Bolshevik success was that they chose methods and aims wholly compatible with the country's traditional thinking and which fitted the conditions as they found them. In other words, they reversed the trend yet again from the European to the Asiatic, from the Westernising to the nomadic, from the possibility of a government by consent to the reality of government by fear.[6]

Ironically, in the last decade before the fall of autocracy Russia reached her highest point of Westernisation; for eight months, from February to October 1917, she actually had a representative government, however impotent. The extent of Russia's Westernisation in the spring of 1917 was indicated by the political prominence of the middle-class party of the 'Cadets', the peasant party of the Socialist Revolutionaries, and the Mensheviks, all of whom wanted a parliamentary and democratic government.

It was these groups, and not the Bolsheviks, who after the February revolution were supported by the majority of the peasants, workers and soldiers. The bulk of the peasants followed the Socialist Revolutionaries; the bulk of the workers followed either the Socialist Revolutionaries or the Mensheviks. (In April 1917 Lenin admitted that in most of the Soviets of Workers' Deputies the Bolsheviks constituted 'a small minority'.)[7] And among the soldiers, who in the main came from peasantry, the situation was similar.

However, there was not enough time for this popular support to develop into a proper political pattern. The Revolution reversed the trend and was followed by a gradual sliding back into the traditional ways which were fully re-established in the late twenties with such events as the collectivisation of agriculture, liquidation of intra-Party opposition, as well as the foundation of the Third International. The Europeanised classes, the gentry and the urban middle class, were either physically destroyed or left the country. This was not altogether difficult to accomplish considering the small numbers of both. The bearers of European values, of European way of thinking, thus ceased to exist. A class whose views, moral values and political thinking were untouched by European civilisation occupied their place as the country's new élite.

The new industrial working class provided a ready tool, a recruiting ground for the new 'warrior élite'. They had no attachment to the land; mobility was in their interest, and they were ready to accept the organisation by units, army style, which the party offered. They were poor, unattached, mobile, disciplined: they were the pure nomads of their era. An injection of intolerance and hate with a feeling of superiority contained in a militant ideology transformed them into a formidable fighting material: given the organisation and leadership provided by the party, they became a nucleus of an army which not only destroyed the existing machinery of the state, but also defeated Allied intervention and won the civil war.

pan-turkism and islam

On the opposite side of the emerging political spectrum appeared the idea of pan-Turkism and, to a certain extent related to it, the political ideas based on Islam.

The growing Slavophile mood as well as Russia's assumed role of defender of Orthodoxy and her role in the Turkish wars in 1854-5 and 1877-78 not only affected the official attitude towards Muslims but also led to the development of a national consciousness among them. In the forefront of this movement were the Tartars and the Kazakhs, followed somewhat later by the Turkic peoples of Central Asia. The annexation of the Crimean Khanate in 1784 provided the Tartars with another rallying centre, in addition to Kazan, for their cultural and political aspirations. However, unlike Kazan, the Crimea was under strong influence of the Young Turks, who in the second half of the 19th century made their appearance in Turkey. In Central Asia and the Caucasus the locals were similarly exposed to currents emanating from Turkey and from Iran.

It seems that at the root of some of the Tartars' dissatisfaction with the current situation was the medieval, scholastic way Islam was taught at the Central Asian and Turkish madrassas. Education was, therefore, the first controversial issue raised by the Muslim thinkers of the time.[8] The movement – when it eventually became one – developed in several mutually antagonistic ways. On the one hand, there was a conservative brand of Islam, practised mainly by the Volga Tartars and some of the Kazakhs, while, on the other, there were the modernisers taking their ideas from the Young Turks. Interestingly, in the northern part of the Kazakh steppe the nomads were less religious and therefore less conservative than in the south where the influence of Central Asian madrassas was felt more strongly.[9] The two main currents were the Kadimists who took their guidance and inspiration from the 18th century Arab Wahhabists, and the more moderate and reformist Jadids. It was the Jadids who at the beginning of the20th century were more willing to cooperate with the Russian authorities.[10]

The Russian authorities of the time were anxious to prevent any collusion between the conservatives and the moderates. They therefore respected the local customs of the nomads, avoided forceful russification and 'preferred a cooperation aimed at the development of the society towards a modernity combining intellectual progress with respect of tradition.'[11]

It may be argued that what started as a pan-Islamic movement, inspired by the Young Turks, the Slavophiles and the European liberals, developed into a pan-Turkic nationalism which before it could play any significant role on the political scene, was brutally strangled by the Revolution and the Bolshevik régime.

Summary to Part 4

Several attempts at reforms were made during the imperial period. All were prompted by recognised and urgent needs, but none ever fully achieved its objective.

Peter the Great was acutely conscious of the backwardness of his country when faced with powerful enemies, Sweden, Poland and Turkey. He reformed his military establishment, his army, its weaponry and Its military training according to Western models, but he left intact his 'sultanic' way of running the country. He abolished slavery and merged it with serfdom, with the result that the former slaves became subject to tax, to which until that point they had not been liable. He reformed the tax system, but his head-tax was the acknowledgement of the value of men, not of land or property. He did not touch on land ownership or on the freedom of movement of the gentry, treating both as his personal property. He subordinated the Church to the State and created a whole system of ranks and offices, but kept all power untrimmed in his hands. His territorial expansion was fully in line with the idea of a universal empire.

Catherine the Great, a German princess, tried for a time to introduce European-style reforms into the system of government. She gave the gentry their estates in permanent holding and authorised them to travel abroad – a clear breach of tradition. For the first time, estates could be bought and sold, even gambled away, and a section of the population, albeit a very small one, was treated as not being property of the state. This, of course, did not concern the peasants who were treated as part of the land which was frequently not measured in acres but in the number of 'souls' that went with it.

The court and the higher gentry became under her government thoroughly Europeanised – frequently educated to a high standard, familiar with Western, especially French, culture and customs, and widely travelled. The roots of the great Russian literature, music, etc., must be sought here. But the lower classes were largely untouched and the conditions of the peasantry, with the spread of commercial agriculture, became even harsher.

But Catherine's attempts to reform the government failed. When she tried to create a Legislative Commission or even some municipal self-government, she was unable to overcome the immobility and the passive resistance of the traditional institutions. In a way, she may be seen as a 'reluctant autocrat' which of course means no more than that she may have preferred a kind of more or less liberal absolutism in line with other European monarchies. But the country wanted Russian-style autocracy and she had to adapt.

Meanwhile, the empire continued to expand, in the west, in the east and in the south. In the east, it absorbed a number of small nomadic tribes in Siberia and the Far East, most of them shamanist, but also some larger Muslim ones, like the Kazakh and the Kirghiz. Pushing south, the Muslim tribes of the Caucasus were annexed together with the Christian Georgians and Armenians. And, with the conquest of Central Asia, in the second half of the 19th century, the Muslim population of the Empire increased considerably and acquired a particularly backward and fanatical component.

Although the administration of the new territories superficially resembled that of the colonies of other European empires, there was a fundamental difference: they were not 'overseas dependencies', but an integral part of the universal empire. In this respect Russia was more like the other multinational and 'universal' empire, China.

The perennial problems of land ownership and freedom of the individual were not solved with the emancipation of the serfs. Although, in theory, the peasants received allotments of land (against compensation), in practice these allotments were administered and the farming directed by the village commune to which the peasant was tied. He still had to pay the head-tax and could not leave the commune without permission.

The ancient theory of the state being the property of the ruler found a new expression in the 'Official Nationality' of Nicholas I. This confirmed the autocratic powers of the sovereign and the position of the Orthodox Church as the ultimate source and arbiter in all matters of ethics and ideals, but also introduced a new element of 'nationality'. This had little to do with the ethnic and linguistic origins of the various parts of the population. Far more, it was a rather mystical concomitant accompanying and confirming the notion of the universal empire.

part 5

SOVIET
RUSSIA

Part 5A

THE STATE

Russia in World War I – 1914-18

｜ ｜ ｜ ｜ ｜ ｜	Front against German forces, 1918
▬ ▬ ▬ ▬	Front in 1917
├─┼─┼─┼─┤	Furthest line of Russian advance, 1914
─────	Main railway links

© Airphoto International Ltd.

Archangel

Vologda

Baltic Sea

Tallinn (Reval)

Petrograd

Volga River

Tver

Moscow

Nizhnii Novgorod

Libau

Dvinsk (Daugavpils)

Danzig

Smolensk

Minsk

R U S S I A

Brest Litovsk

Pinsk

Gomel

Orel

Kiev

R. Dnieper

Tsaritsyn (Volgogra

AUSTRIA-HUNGARY

Ekaterinoslav

Don River

Rostov-on-Don

BOSNIA

RUMANIA

CRIMEA

SERBIA

Sevastopol

MONTE-NEGRO

BULGARIA

Black Sea

ALBANIA

Chapter 33

The Party & the state

Leninism - theory and practice

The October Revolution marked the return to the traditional attitudes in almost every respect. In Lenin's Communism elements of Byzantine Orthodoxy and of Islam can be found in abundance.

Communist exclusivity is more related to that of Islam; like the Muslims, the Communists regard themselves as the chosen people to whom 'the furtherance of good and the repression of evil is entrusted'. Their doctrine is 'the only seat of justice upon earth', and they are equally intolerant and hostile to other, rival creeds, especially those with similar universalistic aims, that is, Christianity and Islam. Their universalism is more like that of the nomads, or Islam, than that of Christianity. More emphasis is laid on the conquest of the world than on its redemption. In Marxist terms, the reasoning runs on the following lines: social justice ('the redemption') can be achieved only by means of public ownership of the means of production and by eliminating exploitation of man by man. This can be done only by investing the Communist Party with total authority. However, economically, the system can work only when introduced in the whole world (cf 'the capitalist siege'). The first aim must therefore be the conquest of the whole world for socialism – or rather for Communist rule.

Politics in a Communist state embraced everything. Again, as before, there is no separation between religious (or ideological) and civil matters. Both spheres are governed by dogma issued and interpreted by the Party. The need for dogma is the same as in a nomadic society. The army-style discipline of the Party must be accompanied by disciplined thinking; criticism and doubt is not tolerated. Equally, the authority must be infallible, and for that reality can be bent and truth denied without limits.

'It is a cardinal rule of Soviet political life that the Party never errs; the Party, as the apostle of genuine Marxism-Leninism, possesses divine, revealed political wisdom, and is therefore infallible. If mistakes have been made, they are the fault of fallible individuals or factions [...]. The Party itself was, as always, blameless and wholly virtuous; the Party cannot err.'[1]

Communism is a fighting creed, again like Islam; in this respect it reflects the warlike spirit of the nomads, while Christianity was more oriented to the peaceful and passive peasant population. (This is why the peasants became known to the warrior élite simply as 'Krestiane' – Christians.)

The division of the world between the socialist and the capitalist camps is closely paralleled in Islam, which divides the world between the 'House of Peace' *(Dar ul-Islam)* and the 'House of War' *(Dar ul-Harb)*, lands under infidel rule, the two being in a permanent state of conflict.

Communist morale, like that of Islam, is geared for war: if faced with a setback – for instance, when prophecies go wrong – this is interpreted as a challenge to authority, and is likely to lead to confusion within the leadership, to purges, and, eventually, to disintegration. Infallibility of the authority is therefore a means of survival. This leads to another aspect – that of 'monolithic unity'. To be infallible the authority must be total; no challenge can be tolerated. Unity of the system – 'behind the party' – therefore becomes a mystical obligation for the sake of which so many victims of show-trials confessed their guilt.[2]

Every challenge to the total authority will inevitably be treated as a heresy. The religious character of the authority makes overt political opposition virtually impossible. As in Turkey, clandestine factions and cliques within the Party, none of whom will challenge the authority of the Party, will fight political fights.

The religious nature – or rather the religious aspect – of the total authority invested in the Party leads to the phenomenon known as 'the cult of the personality', which is, in fact, only a repetition of the traditional cult of a hero-leader wrapped in a replica of a Byzantine imperial liturgy. 'Since the moment of his death, Lenin has been treated not as a man, but an object of worship [...]. His name is invoked, his memory hallowed, his deeds immortalised, his words quoted and his political message (or whichever of his messages is most appropriate at the moment) is repeated literally a thousand times every day. New books, museums, films, plays, stamps, memorials are planned. His portrait hangs in every office and mass-produced statues and busts are everywhere [...]. Lenin's every gesture, every article of clothing, every word and thought (except those that might embarrass the current Politburo) are the holiest of holy treasures in the Party sanctum [...]. Every moment in Lenin's life (except any unsuitable ones) is told and retold, in tones and terms of the most fervent idol worship. Lenin is with us! Lenin is more alive than living! This whipped-up adoration for a mortal [...] is curiously in harmony with many other aspects of the Russian national character and Russian society. Lenin is the Saviour who explains, justifies and promises sympathy and heavenly reward for all the hardships of life [...]. To change the metaphor, Lenin is an icon, borne aloft by the officials who organise mass propaganda, almost precisely as saints are borne aloft in the feast-day processions of the Orthodox Church while the Russian peasants genuflect [...]. No aspect of Soviet rule is more revealing than this secular canonisation of Lenin. And none more clearly illustrates the continuity – even the reinforcement – of the backward as well as progressive elements in Russian life.'[3]

When Stalin died, 'everybody was absolutely devastated: we all thought it was the end of the world. Life without Stalin was simply unthinkable – unbearable [...]. We all thought of him as a kind of personal god: our great leader, our *rodnoi* [our own dear] Father. Ever since we'd been able to talk and read, we'd talk and read about him. We never had enough to eat, and I remember the wind ripping through my rags; and yet we all chanted, 'Thank you, dear Comrade Stalin, for our happy childhood!'[4]

This is clearly Byzantine. But with Stalin the underlying features of Persian despotism and the Oriental obsession with face reappeared.

The leaders of the USSR still found it necessary to enhance their prestige by humiliating their opponents and by depriving them of the last traces of their human dignity. This could be seen in their treatment of political prisoners, defendants in trials, as well as of rebellious satellites who, like the Czechs in 1968, were not only occupied and crushed, but forced to thank their masters for that 'brotherly help'.

Chapter 34

Nomadic elements in Leninism

Contrary to the subsequent Soviet teaching, Lenin did neither expand nor enrich the original Marxism; far more he deviated from it. 'Marxism-Leninism is a contradiction in itself. The correct concept would have to be Leninism-Stalinism. The break from Marxism came with Lenin [...].'[1]

Marx's thinking was entirely within the context of European philosophy and political theory; Lenin's was an amalgam, or rather, a mixture of views and ideas rooted in Russian political past and reflecting the complex structure of its social, moral and political traditions under a thin veneer of European-styles Marxist slogans. Whereas there is little practical politics in the writing of Karl Marx, there is equally little of what could be called sound theory in the writings of Vladimir Lenin. Lenin's contribution was mainly in providing practical guidance to his followers; in this, he did not hesitate to bend or abandon Marx wherever it suited his strategy or his technical requirements. And it is precisely in this practical guidance, in his strategy and tactics that the traditional Russian views and ideas become most apparent.

'Seen in perspective, Lenin owes his historical prominence not to his statesmanship, which was of a very inferior order, but to his generalship. He was one of history's great conquerors [...]. His innovation [...] was militarising politics [...] to treat politics, domestic as well as foreign, as warfare in the literal sense of the word, the objective of which was not to compel the enemy to submit but to annihilate him.'[2]

It is one of the great paradoxes of Leninism that Lenin's first aim was to lift Russia out of its 'semi-Asiatic barbarism' and by Westernising it as quickly as possible to make it into a vanguard of a progressive, industrial, working-class-dominated society. What he succeeded in doing was to turn it into a totalitarian, single-leader society of the traditional nomadic type which dominated Russian history since the earliest times. One of the more naive utopias of Lenin's universalistic ideology was the progressive 'withering away of the state'. No state machinery will be necessary, he believed, when no class divisions will exist. The management of the state will become so simple that 'every cook will be able to run it'. In reality, he laid the foundations of the most overpowering, all-penetrating state machinery the world has ever known.[3]

Lenin's idea was to bypass the ideology of the industrial working class and to replace it, regardless of the economic conditions of the countries concerned, by the idea of a universal workers' empire ruled from Moscow and using local Communist parties as tools of Russian politics. Leninism was 'Marxism divested of its democratic components and adapted to Russian political conditions'.[4] Marx's objective was the liberation of the working class; Lenin's concern was a worldwide rule of the Communist parties headed, under the umbrella of the Comintern, by the Russian Party. Stalin, using the ideological pretext of the 'capitalist encirclement', pursued quite openly Russian national, or rather, nationalist interests. Communist parties in other countries served merely as tools to subvert capitalist governments, to undermine capitalist economies, and to foster Russian political and economic interests on an international level.

It should be noted, without over-emphasising the fact, that the region in which Lenin was born and brought up was one with a long and uninterrupted tradition of wholly nomadic life. The middle-Volga was the centre of nomadic empires until the mid-sixteenth century, and nomadic life continued there for at least another century and a half. It can be assumed, therefore, that in the days of young Lenin there were still vivid recollections, especially in the country among the people, of the nomadic way of life and its moral and social values. The settled agrarian civilisation, lasting barely a century, was still confined mainly to towns and their immediate neighbourhood.

Communications, steamships and railways were only just beginning to bring these settlements into closer contact with each other.

The boy in Simbirsk and the student in Kazan had, therefore, plenty of opportunity to observe the interaction of the two civilisations as well as the relationship between the ruling class, the Russian bureaucrats and landowners, and the 'underprivileged', the non-Russians, the peasants and the poor.

It certainly conforms with the pattern of nomadic thinking as established above to find how little understanding Lenin had for traditional European values, like individual ownership, especially of land, respect for human life and so on. In fact, the question of peasantry and of land ownership represents perhaps the biggest miscalculation of both Lenin and Stalin. Lenin deviated from orthodox Marxism when in 1905 he thought that the rural and urban proletariat can be combined in an independent class party.[5] The 'revolutionary alliance' of workers and peasants was nothing but a myth; before the Revolution the peasants did not support the Bolsheviks, but the Socialist Revolutionaries. After the dubious carrot of the 'Decree on Land', which, in theory, should have given land to individual farmers, came the requisitions of War Communism and the first wave of terror. 'Two hundred and forty-five peasant risings are officially given for 1918 alone, while ninety-nine are listed in twenty provinces [...] in seven months of 1919.'[6] Then, after the NEP period, came Stalin's principle of state-ownership of all land. The 'collective ownership of the means of production', which is a cornerstone of Communist ideology, is just another facet of the same thinking.

Hand in hand with this went Lenin's lack of understanding for anything individual. His thinking was consistently in vague and abstract terms like class, masses, or people. It never occurred to him that the *individual* could and should be free; his *idée fixe* was to liberate the exploited *masses* from their particular form of exploitation. For this – and for the power of his party – he was ready to sacrifice everything. 'We recognise neither freedom, nor equality, nor labour democracy, if they are opposed to the interests of the emancipation of labour from the oppression of capital.' In 1920 he was insisting that 'revolutionary violence' was essential 'against the faltering and unrestrained elements of the toiling masses themselves'.[7]

'But now one must not pat anyone's little head – they would bite off your hand, and one has to beat their little heads, beat mercilessly, although ideally we're against any sort of force against people [...].' This is how Gorki quotes Lenin in his memoirs; and further he notes that Lenin 'has no pity for the mass of the people', and that 'the working classes are to Lenin what minerals are to the metallurgist'. Bertrand Russell's most vivid impression of Lenin was that of bigotry and Mongolian cruelty. 'His guffaw at the thought of those massacred makes my blood run cold.'[8]

The introduction of compulsory labour – again an old nomadic principle – is entirely consistent with these views. To Trotsky, compulsory labour was the foundation of socialist society.[9] After the Revolution the initial system of workers' control in factories was rapidly changed into a strictly-disciplined and centralised factory system with draconian labour laws; the labour books, which remained the basis of Soviet labour policy ever since, were introduced; penal battalions and concentration camps for slackers followed.[10]

On the international level the situation was similar. Once the Party seized power in Russia, the next logical step was to extend it to the other countries. In line with the universalistic ideology of the nomads the Empire of Communism was destined to embrace the whole world.[11]

Chapter 35

universalism -
the ideology of militarism

There is a fundamental difference between the Marxist slogan 'Proletarians of the world, unite' and the Leninist idea of a worldwide network of Communist parties, supported and financed by the Russian Party and totally subservient to it, the sole aim of it being to subvert all other political systems and to bring about a world Communist empire dominated by Russia. The Communist Manifesto was about the seizure of power by a class – the oppressed, the workers, the proletarians, emphasising at the same time its international appeal. 'The proletarian has no fatherland' – his class interests are everywhere the same, that is, where industrial economy is dominant and the capitalist class exploits the working class.

Lenin replaced Marx's idea of a social movement and of an inevitable revolutionary trend of the exploited classes by the idea of a small elitist group of professional revolutionaries that would, in times, impose the revolution upon the masses.

'Unlike Marx, who tended to think that history itself would make the revolution, Lenin based all his thinking on the premise that revolutions have to be organised.' Directly from this stems his concept of a disciplined political élite organised to lead the mass movement towards the given goal. The élite leads in an authoritarian, or even dictatorial way; the masses are led, but they are allowed to participate, under the guidance and supervision of the Party, in the public life by means of various 'mass organisations' which perform the function of the so-called 'transmission-belts' of Leninist theory.[1] This reflected simultaneously a deep contempt for 'the masses' as unreliable and unable to emancipate themselves, and a belief that they must be led by a small warrior élite who alone knows what is good for them. The idea of a class struggle, based on objective analysis, was built up into a veritable ideology of hate, subjective, emotional and irrational. As Lenin himself put it, in 1907, his methods 'calculated to invoke [...] hatred, aversion and contempt; calculated not to convince but to break up the ranks of the opponent, not to correct the mistake of the opponent but to destroy him [...]'.[2]

Whereas Marx tried to analyse the trends of history and social development and to lay down the objective conditions necessary for a socialist revolution merely adding the 'subjective' element of proletarian political organisation, Lenin put the main emphasis on this subjective element recognising that this applied to the Russian situation while asserting that the objective conditions, too, in Russia had ripened to a degree which made proletarian revolution legitimate.[3]

This had profound implications in practice. Instead of bringing about a spontaneous revolution in an industrialised country by an emancipated working class, it led to a revolution imposed upon a backward agrarian country with a largely illiterate peasantry and a numerically insignificant working class by a tiny élite of professional and mostly middle-class intellectual revolutionaries.

In due course, and quite in accordance with the development of an early society, an 'inner circle' was formed within the Russian party, around its leader. The leader himself assumed unlimited powers, both factually and ideologically. Lenin behaved 'as a Muscovite autocrat issuing on his personal authority ordinances and decrees'.[4] His 'inner circle', the Party high-command which gradually developed into a '*nomenklatura*', had to act as a transmission belt for passing his orders down to the lower echelons of the Party and state organs. The emergence of the *nomenklatura* as a supreme élite within the élite of the Communist Party is connected with the ascendancy of Stalin. It was under Stalin that the Party was reduced to a mere executor of the *nomenklatura*'s will.[5]

From the very earliest time Lenin endeavoured to organise the Bolshevik faction of the Social Democratic Party, and later the Communist Party, on a military pattern, strict discipline and centralisation being the main principles of that organisation. Already in 1903, he urged, in a letter to Plekhanov, '[…] as much centralisation as possible. Autonomy of local committee in local matters, with the right of veto by the Central Committee [...]. District organisation only with the agreement and approval [...] by the Central Committee.'[6] Again, in 1919, he wrote: 'The Party is in a position in which the strictest centralism and the most stringent discipline are absolute necessities. All decisions of higher headquarters are absolutely binding for the lower. Every decision must first of all be executed, and only after that an appeal to the corresponding party organ is permissible. In this sense, outright military discipline is indispensable in the party at the present time.'[7]

In 1921 he applied these principles on an international scale in a Resolution of the Second Congress of the Comintern. 'The main principle of democratic centralism is that of a higher cell being elected by the lower cell, the absolute binding force of all directives of a higher cell for a cell subordinate to it, and the existence of a commanding party centre (whose authority is) indisputable for all leaders in party life, from one congress to the next.'[8]

This principle of electing an organ and investing it with an absolute power while renouncing all means of controlling it is, on a more modern level, the same as that of a nomadic *kuriltay* electing the khan. To the Communist, the 'democratic' element is that of election; 'centralism' means that the orders of the command centre are obeyed without discussion. Only thus could Lenin arrive to his pronouncement of 1918: 'There is absolutely no contradiction between Soviet democratism and the use of dictatorial power by single individuals. How can the strictest unity be ensured? By the subordination of the will of thousands to the will of one.'[9] Clearly, problems like checks and balances, control of executive power or the rights of the individual did not bother him in the slightest.

By this definition, the Soviet system and the political system of the Mongols were equally 'democratic'. The dangers of this system did not escape other European-thinking revolutionaries of the period. Rosa Luxemburg wrote in 1904: 'On the one hand, the sharp separation of the organised bodies of outspoken and active revolutionists from the unorganised though revolutionary active masses surrounding them, and on the other hand, strict disciplines and direct, decisive and determined intervention of the central authorities in all expressions of life in the Party's local organisations. It suffices to note, for example, that the central committee, according to this conception, is authorised to organise all sub-committees of the Party, hence also has the power to determine the personal composition of every single local organisation [...] to give it a set of self-made local statutes, to completely dissolve it by a decree and create it anew, and finally [...] in this manner to influence the composition of the highest party authority, the Party Congress. According to this, the central committee appears as the real active nucleus of the Party, and all other organisations merely as its executive organs.'[10]

'Democratic centralism' was, in fact, from the very beginning designed as a self-perpetuating oligarchy vested with absolute power and responsible only to itself; the margin of responsibility tended to become narrower as the ruling circle narrowed until, finally, it ended in the dictatorship of an individual. Trotsky neatly summed this up in his celebrated remark that '[...] the organisation of the Party takes the place of the Party itself; the Central Committee takes the place of the organisation; and finally, the dictator takes the place of the Central Committee'.[11]

The discipline within the Party was ensured by a tight system of control from above which was similar to that of a modern army – or for that matter, to the social organisation of the nomads. Rank-and-file members were organised in units of ten, headed, or supervised, by a 'leader of ten' who reported to the higher unit which could be either a local or a works committee. The chairmen of these committees in turn reported to the district committee whose chairman, or secretary, was answerable to the still higher unit, the regional committee, and so on, until the top level, which was the Secretariat of the Central Committee, has been reached. This was the body which issued directives that were binding for the whole structure right down to the rank-and-file members. In practice, the elective committees merely approved the actions of their Secretariat. It is therefore not surprising that functions in the apparatus carried more political weight and power than the membership of the Committees, including the highest organ, the Central Committee.

The Party, according to Lenin, was supposed to be 'monolithic', not only in its structure, but also in its views. Whereas the structural unity was preserved by a complete absence of autonomous decision-making at any level, the ideological unity was obtained by a strict ban on factions – which, in practice, meant that even the slightest deviation from the prevailing Party view was branded as heresy and drastically punished. Such theological intolerance, traditional among Russian intelligentsia, has been explained by some (Berdyaev) as a mere self-protection in a hostile world. It can, however, be traced back to two sources.

One is the intolerance of Byzantine Orthodoxy with its hair-splitting arguments and constant recourse to the 'right' texts; its distant and now forgotten political aim was to preserve intact the power of the Empire and, even more, the power of the Church within it. The second source is nomadic. The power position of the khan at the apex of the military structure could be maintained only if every command of his was carried out to the dot. No discussion being permitted, his utterances acquired an almost mythical character of an absolute and indisputable truth; they were collected and later quoted as maxims under the Turkish name *bilik*. The near-magic powers attributed to the quotations of Lenin, Stalin or Mao strongly resemble that of the *biliks* while their 'correct' interpretation was equally important for the present power-holders as it had been for the Byzantine prelates or the nomadic rulers.

According to Lenin, the view that the trade-unions should have any controlling role in industry was non-Marxist, for 'Marxism teaches us that only the political party of the working class, i.e. the Communist Party, is capable of uniting, educating and organising such a vanguard of the proletariat and of the working masses as is capable of resisting the inevitable petty-bourgeois waverings of these masses [...] [and] their trade union prejudices'.[12]

Leaving aside this rather peculiar reference to Marxism (Lenin's own *bilik*) the message is clear enough: only the Party has the right to organise anything in the State.

In Lenin's own time the universal empire was still in the making. As he saw it, the proletariat in a world state, like that of early Russia, had no fixed frontiers. It extended, or was meant to extend, as far as the power of the Comintern, or the Russian Party could reach. The world revolution was expected to topple the capitalist system in one country after another and to establish the proletarian super-state worldwide. When the revolution did not happen, the proletarian empire suddenly acquired fixed frontiers which led, ideologically, to the doctrine of 'socialism in one country'. This did not mean that the idea of a world empire had been abandoned, but that the national or imperial interests of Russia now took precedent over the interests of the working class.[13]

A parallel can thus be drawn between a nomadic empire which is truly limitless – or universal – based on the ideological unity of 'one sky, one khan', and a Leninist super-state based on the ideological unity of one doctrine-one party; we can also recognize a great deal of similarity between a post-nomadic state, like Muscovy, driven to extend its domination by conquest, and a Stalinist empire with fixed frontiers but with ideological as well as political ambitions to become universal. Russian arms became the main tool of expansion helping Communist parties to seize power, to keep opposition at bay and, ultimately, to intervene militarily when the Party's domination was threatened.

Under Stalin the Russian empire, which already was multinational, became an embryo of a potentially world-wide universal empire ruled from a single centre in a totalitarian way in which everything and everybody was deemed to belong to the state. Like in a nomadic empire, the power of the centre personified by the Party and its *'nomenklatura'* had to be total and undisputed. Any challenge to it had to be eliminated – most absurdly, it had first to be invented, like in the Moscow trials, only to be crushed in order to demonstrate the unlimited power of the ruler and his clique. And, like in a nomadic empire, if a challenge was allowed to go on, if it was not crushed immediately, the centre's power began to weaken. The Stalinist Empire survived the challenge of Tito's Yugoslavia, but this was, in fact, the first fatal flaw in its power structure. Hungary in 1956 and Czechoslovakia in 1968 were crushed with merciless brutality even though they did not challenge the Soviet domination as such and merely wanted local ('national') adjustments and a relaxation of the central rule. The Solidarity movement in Poland, which came at a moment when the Soviet power was unwilling or unable to intervene with force, marked the beginning of the end. And the disastrous adventure in Afghanistan in 1979, when the mighty Soviet army was for ten years unable to crush the local guerrillas, was inexorably followed by the disintegration and the collapse of the 'universal empire'. 'The vision of a Soviet commonwealth spanning the globe has had to yield to a more modest programme of securing bases for the military [...] in practice if not in words, Moscow has conceded defeat.'[14]

'The Russian régime that is no longer feared, at home and abroad, will appear to have lost the mandate of heaven and fall apart.'[15]

Thus, the Russian monarchy continued to follow the practices of medieval princely households '[...] a régime which lived in a permanent state of insecurity and fear of collapse.' This, as we shall see, continued unchanged and was even accentuated under the Soviets.[16]

Chapter 36

international communism
- the comintern

In this way, the future proletarian empire would have its warrior élite (the international working class) with its vanguard – the Communist parties, united under the banner of the Comintern and led, or, better still, commanded, by the Russian party. But as the revolution refused to take place and the working class in general showed little enthusiasm to act its vanguard role, a change of strategy had to be devised. On the one hand, it was the Russian Party that assumed the role of the fighting élite. Its leadership of the working class and its 'vanguard' position became purely ideological. In practice, the Party, already tightly knit and used to strict internal discipline, required only an appropriate command structure to become an efficient organ of administration as well as political domination, and a central tool to run the state. The Comintern, on the other hand, was reduced to the role of an extended arm of Russian power-politics supplying the local Communist parties with ideological justification of the tasks they were asked to perform.

The Comintern was founded on the 4th of March 1919. In his '*The Children's Disease of Leftism*', published in 1920, Lenin made clear that the foreign parties were expected to use the Russian experience for 'universal application' in advanced industrial countries.[1]

According to Lenin's 21 conditions of 1920, each party of the Comintern should come under direct control of the Moscow headquarters of the International. 'On paper, the Russian party too had to submit to overriding Comintern authority. In practice, however, the Russian view was invariably decisive. And over the years, the whole organisation was always under effective

Soviet control.'[2]

In the Russian view, Communism anywhere in the world was a matter of Russian interest, and the USSR had the right to intervene in its favour; at the same time Communists, individuals or parties, were answerable to the Russian Party, and it was their duty to obey orders from Moscow in the same way as the Russian Communists did. By definition, 'Only he is a genuine internationalist who carries his sympathy, respect, recognition to the point of practical and maximum aid, support and defence of the USSR by every means and in various forms.'[3]

'Ultimately, [Soviet theorists] envision the new Russia-centred international order as worldwide in scope.'[4]

At the Second Congress in 1920 attempts were made to transform the International into a 'single world communist party', of which the national parties would be sections.[5] The Congress also formulated the strategy for worldwide revolutionary struggle. The first steps to complete subordination of Communist parties to the Russian Party were taken in summer of 1920.[6] This process was carried further at the Third Congress in 1921, which voted that the structure of the Communist parties should be assimilated to that of the Russian party even more than it was demanded at the Second Congress. At the Fourth Congress in 1922 a resolution was adopted which wrote into the constitution of the International 'an almost exact replica of the institutional devices for strict centralised discipline which were at that date being perfected inside Russia'.[7]

The furthering of the world revolution through the Comintern remained at least for some time the ideological aim of Russian politics. Even when the doctrine of 'socialism in one country' was adopted, a period of peaceful coexistence did not mean that promoting the world revolution ceased to be Russia's main objective. Nevertheless, bolstering of the Communist régime within the USSR remained the priority, and the consolidation of trade relations and alliance with the capitalist powers had to be pursued.[8]

The Comintern was dissolved in 1943, when, with respect to the Allies and their aid, the idea of a world revolution had to be shelved at least for the time being. The organisation which replaced it after the war, the Cominform, set up in 1947, was no longer a world organisation committed to the overthrow of the capitalist system. It was limited to the parties of the Soviet Union and its East European allies as well as the parties of France and Italy. Its main purpose was to consolidate the Soviet control over the parties in Eastern Europe, and to enhance and extend the power of the member parties in their own countries.

However, after the break with Tito and his excommunication, the domination of the Communist movement by the Russian Party was no longer absolute, and when the French and Italian parties failed to bring about a revolution in their countries, the importance of Cominform faded until it was dissolved in 1956. In Stalin's last years the deviant party leaders in the satellite countries were tried and executed as 'bourgeois nationalists', but when after the denunciation of Stalin in 1956 riots erupted in Poland, and serious differences appeared within the Hungarian Party, the Soviet Union intervened militarily to keep its dominant position intact and to prevent the empire from disintegrating.

Russian intolerance injected in the international Communist movement meant that 'all other forms of socialist principle and organisation were regarded as heretical, hostile and treacherous'.[9] When the Communist movement began to split after World War II, the dream of the universal empire began to fade: it was replaced by an implacable hostility among the various brands of Communism which again had an analogy in the nomadic past: when the authority of the ruling clan was in any way challenged, there could be no peace between the rivals and no reconciliation.

In almost all countries ever occupied by the Red Army (the only exceptions being Finland and the partial occupation of Austria and Iran) a carbon copy of the Soviet regime was established. In some cases these countries were incorporated in the USSR; in others they became 'satellites' associated with it through a network of treaties – political, military, economic – which invariably were designed to bring about Soviet control and domination. The same principles of organisation and discipline were applied to these countries and, as Hungary, Poland and Czechoslovakia have subsequently shown, every deviation from them was treated as heresy and punished as such. The so-called Brezhnev doctrine of limited sovereignty was just a new guise for the age-old idea of a universal empire; the interest of the USSR was identified with the 'interest of socialism' which in practice meant keeping the local Communist Party in power and in subjection to Moscow.

When extending the 'democratic centralist' party system to apply all over the world, Lenin in fact acted in full conformity with the Russian-nomadic tradition. As Conquest puts it, 'it reflected the feeling that the old Marxist idea of the revolutionary development of the proletariat was not to be trusted, even in advanced countries, and needed to be replaced by subjectivist will-power'. In other words, what mattered was not the 'revolutionary development of the proletariat' but the expansion of Russian Communism – which equals the extension of Russian power. 'More profoundly, in fact, it amounted to the extension of Lenin's own political personality on a world scale. The personal drama played out in Russia, in which it had gradually become apparent that he himself was the only mind and force which could be trusted, was now extended universally to the international scene.'[10]

Thus the nomadic political principles long-buried under the surface of the Russian socio-political scene suddenly became a twentieth-century reality and, in the course of time, one of the dominant factors in international politics.

Nomadic traditions can be found not only in the organisation of the Party, but also in its methods of operation. Here, too, the influence of Lenin was instrumental. We have seen that because the nomads were essentially insecure an important streak of their character was mistrust, suspicion and fear. Mistrust, suspicion and secrecy of operations were perhaps natural while the Party was in opposition and operated illegally facing persecution. But these methods did not change when the Party seized power, when it became the only political party in the country, and when it imposed its own legal system. They remained virtually unchanged until the end of the Soviet régime.

It was impossible to enter any Party secretariat without elaborate security arrangements; Party matters, however low-level, were never made public, and among Party members mistrust and suspicion were far more commonplace than 'comradely spirit'.

The conspiratorial methods which Lenin took over from the anarchists and applied to the Bolshevik Party required that the number of Party members was kept low for security reasons as well as to preserve the character of a 'revolutionary élite'. Even when the Party was in power, it was never interested in becoming a 'mass party'. It always preferred to think of itself as an élitist group; periodical purges became a regular feature of party life and were carried out not only to get rid of heretics, but also to keep the morale high. To belong to the Party was a privilege and, in later days, it no doubt brought considerable benefits in terms of power, status and all sorts of 'extras'; therefore expulsion had the character of a serious punishment, moral and material. The élitist concept of the Party, its exclusiveness and, when it was in power, its privileged position implied that the secrecy and conspiratorial character of its operation were continued.

We thus have here, on a modern level, the classical scheme of a nomadic society: the ideology of a universal empire, an all-powerful leader who decides what is right and what is wrong, and who has the means to put his decisions into practice; his inner circle of faithful followers who depend on him, and who carry out his orders; the outer circle of a wider warrior élite – the upper stratum of society which alone 'counts'; and the lower strata, some more equal than others, like the working class; the peasantry which is theoretically assimilated to the workers, but in reality is reduced to the status of serfs; and the un-persons, the former aristocracy and bourgeoisie which have to be eliminated – suppressed as a class and physically destroyed.

Chapter 37

security

Both tsarist Russia and the USSR have treated neighbouring territories as security zones; the heart of Muscovy required buffer zones east, south and west; when these were colonised and became the heartland themselves, new buffer zones were created beyond them. This security aspect at least motivated most of the expansion in European Russia. Soviet policy before the outbreak of World War II was guided by similar considerations when the Baltic states and parts of Finland, Poland and Rumania were occupied before the Germans attacked. The border territories of the USSR inhabited by non-Russians were treated in many respects as mere buffer zones with strategic considerations overriding all other aspects of development.

After the war the obsession with external danger did not subside. Stalin's programmatic speech of the 9th of February 1946 signalled, in fact, a return to pre-war 'normalcy' or, in Tucker's words, 'back to a time in which a postulated external danger is the primary fact of national life [...]'.

'The historic impulse behind the Stalinist pattern of internal policy [...] was to organise a relatively backward agrarian society, in a short time and by ruthless methods, for total war.'

'The policy pattern was the forced concentration of all resources and energies on preparing the country for a coming conflict. The social pattern was the total subjugation of a society to the direct control of the state [...]. Both had their source in the postulated primacy of the external danger.'[1] Security concerns became paramount everywhere.

Abroad, intelligence-gathering – or spying – was carried out on a large scale. Inside, every foreigner was regarded as a potential spy. Visits from abroad, even of friendly parties, were discouraged except for official purposes, and all visitors were followed and watched. Movements of diplomats were restricted to the capital and its immediate neighbourhood. Russians, too, had their movements restricted. Peasants were forbidden to leave their collective or state farms without a special permission. Foreign travel was banned except on official business or, as an exception, group visits, for which only the carefully screened faithful were eligible – and, even so, a watchdog from the Security service accompanied each group.

Large chunks of the country were declared military zones or restricted areas. Political police acquired much larger powers than under the tsars and, in effect, operating largely outside the laws, it became a state within a state. The old system of snooping and spying on one another has been brought to a new state of perfection based on fear and insecurity. Mutual control and supervision operated earlier by the nomads and by the village commune has now been extended to the urban population; every street and every block of flats had its informer.

The same was in jobs, whether factories, offices, shops or other. The all-powerful propaganda machine fostered the spy-mania among the population at large. Capitalist countries were invariably depicted as war-monger and, especially after the war, fear of an atomic attack was kept alive and omnipresent by all media. In reverse of the Latin proverb, one could say *si vis bellum para pacem*. The peace movement was designed to keep the country on a military alert and on a war footing all the time.

The nomadic xenophobia has become part of the official ideology in all Communist countries. Virtually everything was, or could be, construed as a state secret. In Russia 'something like 95 percent of the country is closed to foreigners [...] any foreigner who tried to drive around it would be instantly detained by the police. On some of the major highways which are open to foreigners, it is categorically forbidden to stop by the roadside even to picnic.'

'We decided to have a picnic a short way off the main road [...]. We have barely opened our boot when three peasants appeared at this strange car which was not of a local make. Without any explanation they rudely gestured that it is forbidden to stop there and that foreigners must not move beyond 50 metres from the main road. Where did this rule come from and how could it be so precisely known to these peasants who seemed to be so far away from all administrative pressure?'[2]

Suspicion sometimes ranged to the grotesque. This writer, for instance, was told in earnest in Czechoslovakia in the early fifties that to make public a directory of government offices would be giving away valuable secrets to the class enemy. Cameras were a veritable bogy to the average security-obsessed Russian.

Like in a nomadic empire, the military aspect dominated everything. 'Militarism is so deeply embedded in the mentality of the *nomenklatura* that it is probably as difficult to be rid of it as it is to change the system of which it is the product.'[3] In theory, Communist ideologues 'have militarised politics and view it exclusively as a form of class warfare'.[4] In Lenin's words 'war is not only a continuation of politics, it is the epitome of politics'.[5]

And yet, having militarised everything within reach, the Soviet régime did not treat its armed forces as an exclusive instrument of warfare. In a truly nomadic way, the whole empire was geared for war; not only its economy, but also all scientific research, public morals, social cohesiveness, political leadership, all had to serve the same overall and universal purpose: to contribute to victory in a modern industrial war.[6] But unlike in a military dictatorship, the army top brass had little say in the running of the country or in the shaping of its policy. From the very beginning the Party insisted on a tight control over the military and the *nomenklatura* jealously guarded its authority against any encroachment by the generals. Ideologically, this was motivated by the fear of 'bonapartism', but the real reason was to keep the power undiluted in the hands of the Party and its leadership.

Chapter 38

Nationalism

Under the Soviets the policy of nationalism underwent several changes. To understand them we have to distinguish between theory – or ideology – and the actual practice, which means the policy of organisation and administration of the state.

In Lenin's imagination a successful revolution would bring about a universal world empire, a classless state that would gradually 'wither away' because of the absence of class struggle. It would be unitary, multinational and national differences would exist in it in a cultural sense only. Obstacles to state unity such as frontiers and national languages would disappear. These ideas were briefly put into practice after the Revolution when the Russian Empire was labelled 'gaol of nations', Great-Russian chauvinism was roundly denounced and all nationalities, however small, were declared equal. As a result, fighters against Russian imperialism became national heroes, the civilising role of Russian culture was decried, the use of Russian was discouraged, etc.

The outcome of this policy was unintended and unexpected. Non-Russian nationalities began to claim the right to self-determination, national Communist parties – especially the Georgians – began to question the leadership of the Russian Party, local nationalism was on the upsurge. As a consequence, the theory of equality within a unitary state was quickly revised and replaced by that of a federal state consisting of a number of autonomous units (republics, regions) based on nationalities. Although the Soviet state was not supposed to be a nation-state, the Red Army reconquered almost fully the territories of the ex-Empire putting an end to all centrifugal tendencies and attempts to establish independent national states in some areas. Soviet power became quickly identified with Russian power.[1]

At this early stage of the Soviet State there was a difference between the concept of Lenin, who was still under the influence of his universalistic or internationalist ideas, and Stalin, who was in charge of the People's Commissariat of Nationality Affairs, and who was more in favour of a centralised state in which the constituent national units would be left with only a limited competence in certain less-important fields.

The Constitution of 1924 was a compromise between the two views. Lenin, in contradiction to his original idea, roundly criticised Stalin for his centralising policy which, in his words, would create 'a single apparatus' that would be no more 'than the old imperial apparatus anointed with a little Soviet holy oil'. In this way 'the right of free secession from the union would be nothing but a scrap of paper, incapable of defending the minorities'.[2] The main difference here was between political and administrative centralism. Politically, the control of the Russian Party was never in doubt. Administratively, against Lenin's preference for some sort of limited federalism stood Stalin's idea of a rigid 'single apparatus' and of separate nationalities coexisting within the Union.

Another change of policy occurred under Stalin in the early 1930s. The nationalism of the non-Russians was now perceived as a threat to the unity of the state and under the label of 'bourgeois nationalism' was condemned and persecuted. Russian history, even the imperial one, was rehabilitated, the civilising role of the Russian culture was emphasised, and former 'freedom fighters' became rebels and bandits. The Revolution was hailed as a Russian achievement, and its benefits for the non-Russians were made abundantly clear. The use of Russian became again universal. In the Muslim republics Arabic script was, for a limited period, replaced by a Latin alphabet on a Turkish model and, in yet another reform, by the Cyrillic script slightly adapted to the local languages. In the years preceding the war Russian nationalism was overtly preached, and during and after the war glorification of everything Russian became the rule.

The national state units created under Stalin's policy of nationalities never acquired any other significance than that they were 'administrative divisions on the basis of language'.[3] On the surface, they were run by local officials who were considered politically reliable. The administration was usually a combination of such 'national cadres' and Russians. Usually, the Russians were in charge of key sectors, though frequently acting as deputy heads with a local person as figurehead.[4] Nevertheless, the national cadres did not always conform to the policies of the centre. As in other underdeveloped countries, the process of self-identification went on among the minority peoples and their national cadres were exposed to considerable pressures. 'One wave after another the national cadres were selected, placed in a position of pseudo-power, eliminated and replaced. The usual grounds for elimination were 'bourgeois nationalism'.[5]

The era of Khrushchev marked an end of Russo-centrism and cultural russification. The importance of national cultures was again recognised, and the excessive power of the Russian administrators was, to some extent, curbed. Local dignitaries could now occupy leading posts in local government albeit usually with a Russian deputy who more often than not pulled the strings behind the scenes. However, in 1959 Khrushchev declared at the XXI Congress that the accelerated march towards Communism would bring about the disappearance of national differences with two important consequences for every individual: the use of Russian as a 'second mother-tongue', and the mobility all over Soviet territory, which such bilingualism will make possible.

In 1960 it became clear that the Party had decided to revert to Lenin's original plan of a unitary multinational state, that is to say, to a state in which there would be no separate 'nations'. 'Nationalities would only exist in a broad cultural sense [...]. The implications of this aim and the process of *sblizheniye* (drawing closer) and *slianiye* (fusion) were made clear in the Party programme adopted at the XXII Congress in 1961.'[6]

Under Brezhnev the unitary character of the state was again emphasised and national differences were not supposed to be tolerated indefinitely. The non-Russians will have the choice either to become at least partially russified or to be left out of public life altogether.[7] The Russian cultural model had to be accepted and assimilated without exception.[8]

Gorbachev, in the final stage of the Soviet era, seemed to return to the original internationalism of Lenin. National differences were regarded as marginal, national susceptibilities were ignored or played down, and the notion of 'Soviet people' replaced that of 'the peoples of the Soviet Union'. Non-Russians, again, were treated on an equal footing with Russians – but this only led to increased influence of the Russians in non-Russian areas, where Russians frequently occupied the best and most influential jobs. Ultimately, it led to the identification of the USSR with Russia.

To summarise, the Soviet attitude towards nationalism and nationalities oscillated somewhat haphazardly between two basic concepts: that of a unitary state with little room for separate nationalities or national autonomy, which appears as a direct heir of the tsarist Western-style idea of a 'Russian – or Soviet – nation' embracing the entire population, in which non-Russian areas would be mere administrative units within a centrally administered state, and that of the old nomadic and early Russian idea of a multi-national, or multi-ethnic, empire with a centralised command structure, with a leader who is an embodiment of both the state and the Party, and with a little more leeway for national diversities and some autonomy for the national areas, mainly in the fields of languages and culture.

The ideological formula expressing both the superiority of the Russian nation and the universalistic aims of the Soviet Union was 'proletarian internationalism'. It implied the acceptance of the world leadership of the Communist Party of the USSR – in other words equality in subjection to the Soviet Union. There are no territorial or ethnic limits to this kind of leadership. It is a class concept – all proletarians are expected to accept the leadership of the first 'proletarian state' in history.

This is why 'bourgeois nationalism' became the most serious ideological heresy. It not only challenged the hegemony of the Communist Party of the USSR, but also clashed with the universalistic claims of the Soviet Empire. The 'bourgeois nationalists' were Communists from the outer circle who refused to accept or began to question the leadership of the Russian Party. If this happened outside the Union, in the satellite states, the danger was that the local Party in power would break away from the Soviet bloc – which is what happened with Tito's Yugoslavia. National Communism is an antidote of 'proletarian internationalism' and, if any national Communism were allowed to survive, the very idea of Communist universalism together with Russian political and ideological superiority would be very seriously undermined.

The Russians behaved towards the non-Russians as a superior race in two ways: as representatives of a superior culture if stressing the unitary state, and as representatives of the most powerful and orthodox nation – the fighting élite of the empire – if stressing the multi-national character of the state. The degree and intensity of russification was bound to be greater when stress was laid on the unitary state; the other concept was more distinguished by Communist orthodoxy and dogmatism.

A paragraph should be added here about an interesting ideological trend which appeared in the 1920s and 30s among the exiled Russian intelligentsia living mostly in Germany, Switzerland and Czechoslovakia. It emanated primarily from the disappointment with the two previous dominant trends, that of the Slavophiles and the Westernisers.

Already, in 1895, a group of political theorists, led by Prince Ukhtomski, saw Russia's destiny in Asia. [9]

Eurasianism, as first formulated by Prince N. Trubetskoy, refused to acknowledge an uninterrupted line of historical progress and to accept the Romano-Germanic culture as a universal cultural base. Preferring the idea of independent cultural types, it arrived inevitably at the conclusion that Russia was exactly such an individual and cultural-historical type, which was subsequently labelled by P. N. Savitsky as 'Eurasianism'. N.N. Alexeev explained this as a reaction to the philosophy of the Westernisers, who saw Russian history basically as part of the Romano-Germanic culture, only somewhat retarded. Therefore the Eurasians found themselves closer to the opposite concept, that of the Slavophiles, but differed from them significantly in what they saw as the Oriental, Asiatic character of Russian history. Refusing to include Western Slavs in the Eurasian world, they did not accept the Slavophiles' belief in the unity of the Slavic world and in any kind of Panslavism. They also did not accept their romantic anarchism, their view of law as basically a Western phenomenon, as well as their tendency towards a certain form of theocracy. On the one hand, the origins of Eurasianism can be found in 'disappointed Slavophilism', on the other hand, among various 'detractors' of Russia. The first emphasized the Oriental and especially Byzantine character of Russia (as can be found, for example, in Dostoyevsky, Blok, Khlebnikov and others), while the second turned the 'Asiatic' character of Russian history against Russia, claiming that it disqualified Russia from the community of European states.

In the view of the Eurasians, the concept of one Europe, which would include both East and West, is absurd (Savitsky). Russia is an independent third continent.[10] The unfortunate policy of Peter the Great reduced Russia to one political factor among many within the framework of a fragile pan-European balance of power. It brought about two false ideas: of Russia as a major European power, and of the superiority of European civilisation (Trubetskoy). Bolshevism will pass and will be replaced by Eurasianism.[11]

Interestingly, whereas in the 1930s the exiled Eurasians split into a number of factions, some of their ideas found their way into the official opinion inside the USSR, which, for a time, emphasized Russia's close links with Asia, whether economic, political or cultural, and saw modern Russia as 'a leader and teacher of the oppressed masses of the East'.[12]

Chapter 39

Law

In the Marxist view, law is a tool of class oppression. The ruling class has always shaped the legal relations to suit its own purposes and to perpetuate its own dominant position. By the same token, when the working class seized power it used law to eliminate its opponents and to enhance its own power. 'Law is what serves the working class' was the accepted definition. In such a class-dominated concept no objective law was possible. The same would apply to the administration of justice, which would become the expression of power of the ruling class, and a tool to suppress all the other classes.

This, of course, is theory, or better still, ideology. In reality, those in power usually do not need courts and the law to have their way. Power itself is enough and objective justice does not exist. In Marxism, and even more in Leninism, objectivity of any kind is labelled 'bourgeois prejudice'. Justice is a manifestation of class-consciousness, and law throughout history has been a mere tool upholding the supremacy of the ruling class. Necessarily, both had to be subjective. A trend towards objective law appeared only in the wake of Europeanisation not before the beginning of the nineteenth century. In spite of the continuing absolutism this trend persisted throughout the century, the tsars respecting more and more their own jurisdiction until Russia was in the first decade of the twentieth century almost within reach of a 'rule of law'.

In this context it is important to consider the agencies enforcing the law and the general concept of justice. In Islam – and more particular, in Turkey – the agencies enforcing the *shar'* (religious or Koranic law) were given much less power than those enforcing the *urf* (secular or state law) who acted as the extended arm of the sovereign. This applied especially to the police and the state officials administering the law. In Russia the police – and especially the

Okhrana – held vast extra-legal powers virtually until the end of tsarism. The courts were separated from the administration as late as 1864, when the judiciary became an independent branch of government instead of constituting merely a part of the bureaucracy.[1] Until then the courts reflected the government policies, and more often than not acted on government instructions. Even after the reform the government tried to influence judges for political reasons; but while the reform of the judiciary could be restricted in application, it could not be undone by the imperial government. At last the government – the tsar – saw himself bound by his own laws. Modern justice replaced arbitrariness and confusion.[2]

In the field of law and justice, as in so many others, the October Revolution reversed this trend towards Europeanisation, and reverted to the more traditional Russian principles and methods of government. 'Given Stalin's ambition, character and policy, the reason why he could indulge in his own kind of bacchanalia was the total lawlessness of the country, and the complete lack of institutionalised responsibility of those who ruled: the foundations for this were firmly laid by Lenin [...]. Lenin destroyed law in Russia.'[3]

In fact, what Lenin destroyed was merely the European concept of the rule of law, the objective system of law and justice and the responsibility of the rulers that goes with it. What re-emerged was the old subjective system of arbitrary rule coupled with equality in submission. Old privileges were abolished and before new ones appeared, the nation could indeed see the fulfilment of its dreams in this summary justice.

The old Islamic duality of *shar'* and *urf* also reappeared. As the Party identified itself with the state, its resolutions had the dogmatic character of the *shar'*, while the government decisions, laws, statutes, regulations, etc., became the Soviet equivalent of the *urf* and as such could be applied, bent or stretched at will. 'The general standard of Soviet law as regards consistency and accessibility is poor. But in the religious field it is absurdly so. Law is thus used in a special sense against religion. In practice, to some extent a locality has its own changeable and arbitrary rules, depending on instructions given by the local representative of the government's Council for the Affairs of Religious Cults. These officials are quite liable to countermand known laws, but only by word of mouth, not in writing; nevertheless, their decisions have to be obeyed.'⁴

As in the past, the police held vast extra-legal powers and the courts became merely a branch of the new bureaucracy responsible to and acting on the instructions of the government. Again as in the past, what is justice, what is a punishable offence, and what should go unpunished was decided by the ruler, that is, by the Party (the same applies to Soviet satellites⁵).

Lenin's concept of law was completely in accordance with his morals. Law was a class weapon – a tool of oppression when in the hands of his opponents, a tool of class justice when in his own. He did not hesitate to take the law into his own hands. As in the long Russian past, to him might was right. And, as in the past, he showed his truly nomadic contempt for the value of human life when he advocated political terror.

'On the 27th of January 1918, Lenin publicly announced – though at this stage about speculators only – that they should be shot on the spot.'⁶

'Life made it necessary to appropriate by revolutionary means the right to immediate executions [...]. Life itself legalised the right of the Cheka to immediate executions'. And Lenin himself said in June 1918 that 'the energy and mass nature of the terror must be encouraged'.

Behind this romantic talk of the spontaneity of terror, life's legalising effect, etc., lies a deep conviction that the enemy has no right to live, that any living enemy, real or potential, is a danger, and that any method that leads to victory is right. It may be added that, again in the nomadic sense, victory was synonymous with survival – for mercy was neither given nor expected.

This disrespect for human life and the emphasis on destruction combined with the élitist thinking of the Party brought about, in the later days, such deliberate destruction of national élites, like the pre-war purge of the army leaders, the notorious Katyn massacre of Polish officers, or the repeated purges of intellectuals both among Russians and non-Russians. Transfer of whole peoples who were considered a threat to security, or had to be punished for disloyalty, was yet another 'method' which has been taken over from the past.

Another facet of this picture was Lenin's tactical flexibility. He was always ready to ally himself with the most improbable partner in order to defeat an enemy, and at the very moment when victory was achieved to turn against his ally and destroy him. The examples here are Russian political parties, both before and after the Revolution, the nationalist movements in the non-Russian areas, as well as the trade-unions. When the one-party state became a reality, and there were no more enemies outside the Party, Lenin's successors, Stalin and Khrushchev alike, were equally flexible in dealing with their intra-Party opponents.

Lenin's ruthlessness in action and his absolute lack of moral scruples were also derived from the Russian and nomadic heritage. In the field of morals the Party took over the old nomadic code. In its concept of politics there were no rules of combat and no mercy for the loser. The aim was not only to destroy the 'capitalist system', but to annihilate all opponents. It is in this emphasis on total destruction where the nomadic streak in Lenin's thinking comes most clearly to the fore.

Lenin was prepared to use any means whatever to forward the struggle – as he put it, 'everything that is done in the proletarian cause is honest'.[7] In the same vein, truth was defined as being 'what suited the working class'. And in Lenin's words: 'Our morality is completely subordinated to the interests of the class struggle of the proletariat [...]. Morality is that which serves to destroy the old exploiting society.'[8] And elsewhere: 'Party members should not be measured by the narrow standard of petty bourgeois snobbery. Sometimes a scoundrel is useful to the party, precisely because he is a scoundrel.'[9]

As for the concept of justice, this, too, must be linked to the concept of the state. In the subjective, despotic system what passes for justice, in the formal sense, can only be the expression of the ruler's will. This would apply equally to sentences and punishments and to the sanctioning by the ruler of otherwise criminal and punishable acts. In other words, in such a system what the ruler declares to be an offence is punishable, while what he sanctions will go unpunished. There can be no equality before the law, because the law will be applied or not applied *ad personam*, and stretched at will. When Solzhenitsyn says: 'The Russians can get by without food and drink – it is justice and right they are after',[10] he has no doubt in mind the lack of equality before the law and the arbitrariness of justice, which was characteristic of Russia throughout the centuries.

But there was another equality – the equality in subjection of the nomadic system. This was able to provide the feeling of a rough justice for the Russian. His craving for justice was therefore often more concerned with abolishing the privileges than with harnessing the arbitrary power of the government. It was this concern that came to the fore in the October Revolution and the first Soviet government.

The nineteenth-century Russian concept of law was basically the same as that of Muscovy, namely as an instrument to regulate relations between people, but not between people and the government. This, indeed, can be detected in the earliest legal documents, like *Pravda Russkaya*. The state was always above the law. Russia, in this respect, resembled rather the ancient oriental monarchies where royal officials dispensed justice as part of their administrative obligations.[11]

Under Nicholas I his chief of the Secret Police, Count Benckendorff, was quoted as saying: 'Laws are written for subordinates, not for the authorities.'[12]

Between 1878 and 1881 legal and institutional bases were laid for a bureaucratic-police regime with totalitarian overtones that have not been dismantled since.[13]

After the Revolution the Communists took over, at least in the early stage, the civil service from the tsarist time, both its organisation and its staff; but whereas in imperial Russia law was beginning to restrain the arbitrariness of the executive, the Communists reversed the trend and 'destroyed all vestiges of this incipient legal order'.[14]

The Soviet system brought another wave of centralisation which equalled and perhaps even surpassed that of the nomadic state. The Party became the governing body and as such it must be equated with the inner circle of the sovereign in the older systems. The organs of the State could be decentralised to the utmost, there could be 'self-governing' republics, any degree of local autonomy, separate courts, trade unions, youth and women organisations, etc. But the entire structure was at every level subordinated to the Party. The Party decided every issue, and it was the structure of the Party machinery that mattered in any discussion on decentralisation. Within the Party there was no local autonomy and no division of power. No Party organ could be elected without prior nominations from above, and it could make no decisions without prior 'recommendations' by the higher organ.

Within the Party there was no separation of civil, military and police matters. As in the times of the nomad khans, every decision had to come from the Centre. The power of the Centre was absolute and indivisible; the Party was organised on a military pattern, and the whole state was run like an army on the move. The Party jargon was only one of many proofs of this. The Party bosses – the 'unit commanders' – were also running the administration and justice in their district, if only from the wings. In an era when democracy was fashionable the 'democratic' facade was upheld – with all such trappings, like a constitution, 'elections', etc. – for mere propaganda purposes. The real power, the real decision-making followed the traditional pattern unchanged since the misty past.

Inasmuch as the Party identified itself with the state it, too, had placed itself above the law. Here again the old nomadic principle can be detected. The ruler, the sovereign, the Party boss, is the embodiment of law, but is not himself bound by it. His 'inner circle', the Party, the *nomenklatura* and the police apply the law and interpret it according to his instructions. Horizontally, the law is used as an administrative device to regulate the relations between people; vertically, the will of the state, as personified by the Party and its boss, is not subject to any rules or regulations.

Decisions concerning the management of the country were presented as taken 'by the Party and the government', indicating the preponderance of the former over the latter. Directives were often confidential, handed down via the intra-party instructions to the *nomenklatura* members who had to carry them out. Even legal statutes were not always made public and openly accessible.

Certain instructions, although having formally a legal character, and not only in the field of criminal justice, were kept confidential to the point of secrecy. For example, in Czechoslovakia in the 1950s regulations governing the practical side of the collectivisation of agriculture were published only as internal documents inaccessible to anybody, except the officials administering the case.

Pipes offers an interesting comparison of 'elastic' paragraphs in the Criminal Codes of 1845, 1927 and 1960.[15] All three include clauses enabling the police to interpret the flexible wording in a way the authorities wanted, and thus turned the police into a supra-legal instrument in the hands of the totalitarian régime. Similar elastic clauses were introduced into the Codes of the Soviet satellites and were used by their régimes to eliminate, like in the USSR, in a pseudo-judicial way all opponents, real or potential. The trials in the early 1950s of political 'deviationists' in Czechoslovakia, Hungary, Bulgaria and elsewhere were carbon copies of the famous Moscow trials of the 1930s. What is less known is that the same 'legal' instruments were used against the politicians of non-Communist parties, Church leaders, industrialists and other representatives of the 'class enemy'.

In one way at least Lenin's vision came true. When the entire economy was state-run and the country was tightly insulated from the outside world, there was no need for any fiscal measures. The budget, the revenues, the outgoings became entirely fictitious, based on the five-year-plan which was set up by the 'Party and government' fiat with little regard for the economic realities. This branch of the state certainly 'withered away'.

To show how persistent are certain traditions in the administration of justice, it may be useful to quote from *The Economist* (June 2001), ten years after the collapse of the Soviet system:

'The days of show-trial, prescripted confessions [...] and justice handed out in the courtyards of KGB prisons may be over, but Russia's legal system still has far to go [...]. Russian courts are staffed by under-qualified judges who see themselves as governmental bureaucrats rather than an independent branch of the state. Prosecutors are lazy, brutal and accountable to no one –

except perhaps politicians and officials. Poverty is pervasive, incompetence the norm, corruption rampant. And acquittal rates in a good year reach one percent.'

'Mr Putin also says he wants jury trials to be introduced throughout the country […]. Arrests and search warrants should be handed out by the courts, not the prosecutors. Defence lawyers would get more rights. At present they are largely helpless observers of the bargaining between judge and prosecutor […]. To insist that [the client] is innocent is a breach of courtroom ethics so serious that is can result in the accused getting a longer sentence just as a lesson in humility for his lawyer […] political opponents do not get sent to gulags for anti-Soviet behaviour but a charge of embezzlement can do the job […].'[16]

Chapter 40

Art & propaganda

The artist's freedom of expression reached its peak in the brief period before and after World War I, when modern art flourished in Russia.

'To the Russian artists, nature is a force hostile to man [...] for the Russian, the machine came as a liberating force, liberating man from the tyranny of nature and giving him the possibility to create an entirely man-made world, of which he will finally be the master. This vision of the machine as a liberating force was one of the reasons for the joyful welcome given to the Bolshevik régime a few years later – a régime which promised a new world, a new society transformed by the machine, by industrialisation.' And so these 'leftist' artists 'leapt to the cause of the Bolshevik Revolution, releasing their frustrated energies in a nationwide propaganda war for the new world which they felt to be imminent'.[1]

But as soon as the Bolshevik régime was established, the concept of official art reappeared. 'Art is a social product, conditioned by the social environment. It is also a means of organising labour [...]. The Proletariat must have its own "class" art in order to organise its forces in the struggle for socialism.'[2]

Meanwhile, the unofficial art did its best to liquidate itself. The 'art for art's sake' was condemned by the Constructivists as a 'speculative activity' to be replaced by 'socially-directed art-work'. The artist 'should concern himself with reality, a hundred times more beautiful than art'. 'The proletarian revolution is not a whipping cry but a real whip which chases out the parasitical from real life [...] tearing oneself from speculative activity, one must find the way to real work [...].'[3]

As soon as the Party was finally in power, the old quasi-religious control over the mind of the people was re-established. No independent thinking was to be tolerated. 'Socialist realism' became the official and only concept of art; its purpose was to promote socialism by supporting the Party line. Once again, the service to the State was declared to be the prime duty of art; propaganda was demanded by the State as of right. The Soviet artist, like the Russian monk, was reduced to a craftsman producing sponsored and approved work. There were to be no other themes except glorification of the Party and its leaders (and vilification of its opponents) and 'realistic' portraits of the Soviet man in his heroic struggle for socialism. The world was once again to be saved by the Russian – this time the creed was socialism and the orthodoxy was Marxism-Leninism.

'From the point of view of the role of the State, the Stalinist harnessing of the country was a repetition of a constant motif in Russian history: the State had always played a key role in the organisation of its people [...]. For just as in literature the socially orientated themes were authorised and indeed enforced by the increasingly monolithic Soviet régime under Stalin, so in the other arts – architecture, music and painting – a wave of uniformity was imposed on all artists from above by fiat [...]. It would be absurd, of course, to consider the Stalin straitjacket a complete innovation in Russian history.'[4]

The propaganda aspect required a degree of conformity in the treatment of themes similar to that of Orthodox art. Once again the Russian artists produced icon-style works suitable to the taste of the public. 'This iconising tendency [...] was devoted to the depiction by fiat of standard episodes in the lives of the leadership, mainly Stalin and Lenin.'[5]

But the nationalist undertones were there, too. 'Soviet patriotism' took over from international Communism when the State was preparing for war. The official ideology was now Soviet nationality and Marxist-Leninist orthodoxy supporting the autocracy of the Party (or, in particular, Stalin). With the victory this was rapidly and conveniently transformed into an ideology of Soviet imperialism. 'Socialist realism' now became more Soviet-orientated, more chauvinistic. The hero-worker became the hero-soldier; the amorphous Party was replaced as mass-idol by the tangible figure of an infallible, infinitely wise *vozhd* – the Leader; and what was formerly the class-conscious, nationless proletarian now became a very nation-conscious Russian – and, even more, Great-Russian.

'Not the least of many paradoxes is that a system which purports to revere culture so profoundly should in effect be so contemptuous of art as to suppose that it can be bureaucratically directed [...] perhaps it is due not to contempt but to fear [...]. Free art, free thought and free expression therefore appear [to the rulers] as highly dangerous, as offensive morally as free love was to the Victorians. The painters and sculptors in the Soviet Union are artists in chains but it would be wrong to blame this entirely on the rulers. Their enslavement could not be so complete were it not for the strange indifference in the Russians for the visual world, and their instinct to coagulate and to conform.'[6]

PART 5B

THE SOCIETY

Chapter 41

The Party & the People

Poverty was a dominant feature of Russian society from the earliest times. As a rule, Russia's neighbours, Byzantium, Poland, Turkey, and in the modern era, Germany and the USA, were far wealthier and their civilisation, or at least certain aspects of it, had therefore to be imitated. In times their military superiority just added to the attraction. Poverty made the despotic government not only possible but also durable. Russia's despotism throughout her history was predominantly of a military character. Commercial and industrial enterprise was discouraged and, at times, downright forbidden. The demographic factor, the low density of population practically throughout the country, did not allow for any 'easily governable areas'. However, people, poor as they were, were generally ready to accept an unusually high ratio of government directive and supervision.

Throughout history, periods of increased stratification alternated with waves of egalitarianism which tried to bring the emerging barriers down. Generally speaking, periods of European influence were marked with a tendency towards stratification, especially with the efforts of the gentry to close its ranks and to establish itself as a class, while egalitarian periods, like that of Ivan IV, of Peter the Great and of Stalin, brought about an increased mobility (cf. under Stalin the workers' origin and Party membership as the main and sometimes the only qualifying principle for virtually any job of significance). This can only be compared with the observation of J.G. Kohl in the 1830s: 'There is perhaps no country in the world where all classes are so intimately connected with each other [...] in no country are the extremes of society brought into more frequent contact, and in few are the transitions from one class to another more frequent or more sudden. The peasant

311

becomes a priest on the same day perhaps that an imperial mandate degrades the noble to a peasant or to a Siberian colonist [...]. Even serfs are more nomadic in their habits than our free German peasants.'[1]

The Soviet reality fits into the picture: all aforementioned criteria can be applied to it without reservation. The Party cadres were poor, unattached, mobile and disciplined; the organisation was quasi-military and centralised to the extreme; the Party interfered with all matters of state, civil and military alike; there was humility within the ranks and a strict separation from the non-party population; there was a feeling of superiority over and contempt for the toiling sedentary peasant; contempt mixed with envy for the money-making, wealthy consumer society of the West; and there was also a rigid code of conduct for the Party members to preserve this superiority and distinction from the ordinary people.

However, the Party bureaucracy showed tendencies to stratify into a self-perpetuating, distinct class and conscious efforts were made from time to time by the leadership to break this tendency by bringing in new people from the outside; a feature of an emerging agrarian despotism was thus continuously thwarted not to gain more popular support, but to maintain the flexibility and efficiency of the nomadic system. 'The autocratic master of the new class society in the USSR exerts supreme control over the ranking apparatchiki by a variety of methods, among them the periodic purging [...] the functionaries' reliability may be expected to be greater, the less they are rooted in any prestige group that preserves elements of social cohesion.'[2]

The principle of the service-state, which was itself a perpetuation of the nomadic system of a complete subordination to a centralised and total power, has been translated into modern terms almost without a change.

A curious paradox developed under the Soviet régime between the official and unofficial attitude to manual labour. Officially, it was glorified. The working-class was hailed as the vanguard of the people, and the worker was the hero. The stakhanovite movement was praised as the most constructive, progressive contribution to the future well-being of the people; miners, factory and *kolkhoz* workers were awarded medals for over-fulfilment of planned quotas, etc. 'I am a miner, who is more?' and similar slogans were supposed to incite people to work more, to feel proud of the jobs they were doing.

On the other hand, there was punishment. The aim of endless purges was to cleanse the non-manual jobs in administration, management or professions of all those who were suspected of insufficient zeal, of lukewarm attitude towards the régime. The sentence was manual labour – officially motivated as 'getting to know the working-class', or 'to do productive work'. For more serious 'crimes' there was the gulag, which again was essentially manual work under slave conditions. In reverse, there was flight from labour into non-manual jobs which were given as a reward to the faithful and the deserving, regardless of their qualifications or abilities. This was motivated, or justified, as 'proletarian justice', or 'safe-guarding workers rights'. An enormous swap of entire classes was thus carried out in the first years of the régime in Russia as well as in the satellite countries. There were worker-managers, worker-judges, but also worker-officers, worker-policemen, and of course, worker-politicians.

Lenin's idea of a 'cook running the state', although quickly abandoned in practice, remained the ideological justification. The aim was to ensure the unchallenged supremacy of the Party, which now became the 'vanguard of the working class', the real warrior élite. Gradually, its role petrified into a new service-class dependent on the leader and his narrow 'inner circle', the *nomenklatura*, which acquired the character of a hereditary class.[3]

In Russia in the years after the Revolution this wholesale destruction of the upper and middle classes, which happened to have been the principal westernised groups, 'permitted the unregenerated Muscovy Russia to float to the surface'.[4] In Czechoslovakia, Hungary and Poland, countries with no 'Muscovy past', enforced proletarianisation brought about a suppression of these countries' cultural traditions, a brutalisation of public life and a general impoverishment in all areas of creativity.

The *nomenklatura*, which in a truly nomadic way preyed as a 'parasitic élite'[5] on the body of the population, was itself relatively poor. In accordance with the established principle that 'only a poor nomad is a pure nomad' its constitutive element was not wealth but power. In fact, the very notion of wealth lost all meaning in a system which abolished private property, and in which the entire wealth of the nation became publicly owned. The totalitarian Party identified itself with the state and occupied alone the entire public space. The public sector and the Party became one and the same thing.[6]

Hand-in-hand with this concept went the attitude of the élite towards the people. In theory there was no difference – the Party issued from the people, consisted of its representatives and was destined to lead it. In practice the people were considered the property of the state and, by the same token, the Party considered itself the rightful master of the whole population. Lenin himself harboured an undisguised contempt of the people, both workers and peasants.[7]

Economically, the monopoly of state enterprise made every member of the community a wage-earner serving ultimately the state. Legally, there was an obligation to work and avoiding it was a punishable offence. Politically, there was no way to oppose the state's total power. The individual was therefore in a similar situation as his forebears of a millennium ago: if he was a member of the ruling 'warrior élite', he was subject to a compulsory service and total obedience to the state; if he was a member of the 'under-privileged', he was tied to his job and saw the ruling élite preying parasitically on his work without having any opportunity to escape this situation or influence the course of events.

To somebody who has grown up in Central Europe it came as a shock to find after the Communist seizure of power that suddenly he was, literally, owned by the state – forbidden to leave the country, assigned to a job, all travel subject to permission – arbitrarily given or refused – with class origin the main qualification for education, job, career, etc. To a Russian, all this was natural.

Chapter 42

The citizen & the state

In the Western sense citizenship means membership of a community which protects its members, while the members take part through representation in running the community. This universal concept evolved from an older one whereby citizenship was restricted to members of a privileged group who ran the community according to their own interest. The community in question, as the name shows, was originally the city – not the state. Historically, the older concept dates back to the Greek city-states; it was extended and considerably deformed in Rome, where a relatively large group of privileged citizens could claim their protection by the state and yet had no say in the running of state affairs. In Byzantium all people were already treated as subjects; the idea of citizenship persisted in connection with municipal authority until the early seventh century, when civil and military administration were merged.

The modern concept began to emerge at first in the medieval commercial cities of Italy, Spain and Flanders – again as that of a privileged group of burghers running the city affairs; it was gradually extended to broader masses of the population, with various qualifying criteria for the exercise of the voting right (householding, income, male sex, etc.) until in most modern democracies it became universal subject only to age and the condition of a minimum period of residence.

In Russia there was no such evolution. Neither the state nor the town had a corporate personality of its own.[1] Municipal autonomy was unknown, except for a time in Novgorod. There has never been a group, or class, of people however privileged who could claim the right to take part in the running of public affairs. 'The cities are not under the jurisdiction of mayors or the worthiest of their citizens; but a *diak* is appointed by the Czar to administer the law.'[2] In fact, one of the most striking phenomena in Russian history is the absolute lack of political privileges. The gentry tried several times, under the influence of European ideas, to become such a privileged group that could share power with the sovereign. But in the Russian view, power was indivisible; the idea of *samoderzhavie* meant that it was firmly vested in the person of the sovereign. All the rest of the population was, by definition, equal in subjection. This was expressed most clearly by Ivan IV in his letter to Queen Elizabeth in 1570: 'We thought that you lord it over your domain and rule by yourself [...] but now we see that there are men who do rule beside you, and not men but trading boors, who do not think of the profit of your safety, honour and lands but seek their own merchant profit. And you remain, in your maidenly estate like a common maid.'[3]

This concept can be traced back to the nomadic past and has its roots in the sky-worship of the nomad Turks. The khan's power was unlimited and universal. It was inconceivable that anybody could share it with him. In such a system there was no room for politically privileged groups. All subjects were equal in their subjection. And yet, there was one important distinction. Members of the khan's own clan, although they had no share in his power, commanded by virtue of their relationship with him the loyalty of the people; they were given key positions in the state machinery (which in practice meant the army) and successors to the khan were as a rule elected from among them.

It was not exclusively the khan's own family which commanded such loyalty, like in the dynastic sun-worship, but the wider entourage of his clan. This is why all Turkish sultans were consistently chosen from the House of Osman, all Russian princes from the House of Rurik, and all early tsars from the House of Romanov (which became a dynasty as late as 1797 under the influence of Europe). Even a usurper like Timur (Tamerlane) respected this tradition insofar as he kept a puppet khan from the House of Chingiz-Khan in whose name, officially, he reigned.

The nomadic system was incompatible with the idea of citizenship for more reasons than one. In the field of law – apart from the corporate personality of the state or town – citizenship presupposes a legal personality of the individual respected by the lawgiver, i.e. the state. This was still possible in Byzantium, where the emperor himself was bound by Law. There were no such limits to the power of the khan, the sultan or the tsar. From another point, citizenship implies that the state is an organism created by the citizens in order to protect them and to serve their interests. A democratic state is a political, not a metaphysical entity. The opposite is true of the nomadic, the Turkish and the Russian state. Here the individual is regarded as the property of the state (to quote Carpini in 1246: 'Everything belongs to the emperor, chattels, cattle and people').[4] The state is a metaphysical creation which exists independently of its inhabitants. It stems from the sky-worshipping idea that the whole world, the 'cosmic monarchy', was given by Heaven to the khan. Therefore an individual can have no rights, no legal position, and no legal claim against the state. The very idea of the individual is quite alien to the system.

Turning to the Soviet system, these old traditions emerge quite clearly. The word 'citizen' *(grazhdanin)*, although occasionally used, was quite meaningless; in a way it was part of the equally meaningless 'election game', for neither the 'citizens' nor the 'election' could have any effect on state power. 'Comrade' *(tovarishch)* was much more accurate, for it at least indicated the equality in subjection. The individual had no rights (in spite of a host of them being declared in the Constitution) and no legal claims against the state. The power of the state was still absolute and indivisible, only it was not vested in a khan or tsar any more, but in the Communist Party, or better still, in its ruling organs, the Politburo, the Central Committee, and the *nomenklatura*.

People were considered to be the property of the state, and as such they were protected by it, but they had no influence on the decision-making. There was no privileged group that could claim, by right, a share in the power of the state. The privileges of the Party members were factual not legal, like those of the khan's clan or tribe in the past. And, as in those days, the successors of the rulers had to be chosen, by tradition, from among them.

This would explain why 'in a system that contains many paradoxes, the central paradox remains that the "supreme law" of the Soviet State – the 1936 Constitution – has been declared by the nation's own leaders, including Brezhnev, to be obsolete and virtually irrelevant to contemporary Soviet society. Despite this, the present leadership left the old document intact and showed no apparent intention of replacing it.'⁵

To command the loyalty of the people the candidates had to belong to the 'House of Lenin'; they had to prove an ideological, if not genealogical, relationship with the founder of the state. Thus attempts were made by every successor to present himself as the 'true heir of Lenin'. This more often than not required a purge, or elimination, of potential pretenders who could cast doubt on such claims or present themselves in a better light. The same happened in the past when pretender families from the same clan tried to eliminate each other.

The Central Committee had a similar function as the nomadic *kuriltay*. It was more a war council than a policy-making body. Decisions were approved not made here. If the Central Committee 'elected' the Politburo, it merely confirmed the existing candidates who either nominated themselves or were nominated by an inner group of a few or even a single person, like Stalin or Khrushchev. The same applied to any other 'election', which invariably was a mere confirmation of a nominated candidate. The whole structure was therefore operated from above, from a single centre in accordance with the theory of absolute and indivisible state power.

Therefore it can be said that the idea of citizenship on state and local level was totally alien to the Soviet system, and has not been part of the Russian political system in any period of history.

Tucker's concept of 'dual Russia', that is, of the state as opposed to the society, corresponds roughly to our division between the warrior élite and the peasantry. The peasants were the unofficial, or 'popular Russia', and from their point of view the autocratic state power was 'an alien power in the Russian land'. 'In Miliukov's formula for the system in Muscovy, there was the "autocratic power" on the one hand and the "population" on the other, the two "more or less imperfectly linked by a system of mediating government organs". This was reflected in the concept of the soviets, cooperatives and other mass organisations such as "levers" of the Party's influence and authority among the population. Thus the outcome of the Revolution, politically speaking, was that Russia had reverted to a situation strongly parallelling the remote past.'6

Chapter 43

тhe individuaL
& the coLLective

The institutions and the way of life of a Russian village hardly changed at all during history except for the brief spell around the turn of the century when the private ownership of land began to emerge. After the Revolution and, especially, after the collectivisation the village life returned to its old traditions.

The supervision from above and the collective responsibility to the state were as tight as ever. The *kolkhoz* board controlled the individual members' lives down to the minutest details. As far as travel was concerned, the villagers were as isolated now as they had been in the Middle Ages. They still had the security provided by the collective, but the lack of incentive to work persisted and so did the mutual coercion.

Even the religiosity remained with the Church having been gradually replaced by the Party. No doubt that the supply of manufactured goods increased, and there was no need any more for homemade utensils; but the amount of trade was still very low, the transport was insufficient, and the communications between villages and between villages and towns remained rather sporadic. In spite of the media, which, in a way, replaced the Church pulpit, the inward-looking mentality still persisted, and every stranger, not necessarily a foreigner, was still regarded with suspicion.

Much less can be said about the urban community in Russia. Towns in the Western sense, autonomous, self-governed polities endowed with legal and economic privileges, did not develop in Russia (with the only exception of Novgorod and Pskov). Russian towns were – and most of them still are – mere overgrown villages with the same way of life and the same mentality. The identity of a Western town was determined by its financial prosperity, its economic enterprise, and its legal safeguards. The walls and the town militia were two symbols of that identity, the third being the town hall with the council of elected representatives. It can be argued that modern Western individualism has its roots in the legal immunities, the economic enterprise, and the self-government of the medieval towns and cities.

Nothing like this happened in Russia. The towns were first and foremost garrison places administered by appointed officials; the fortresses and walls if there were any (usually there was only the fortress) were built by the state and manned by its troops. The townsmen were bonded serfs; skilled craftsmen were concentrated here, often under compulsion, to work on government and especially army orders. The government controlled trade, and merchants had no independent status. Movement of the townspeople was restricted until the era of industrialisation.

Educational facilities, another feature of Western towns, were non-existent in Russia until the Petrine reforms. The only education available until then was in Church schools. Peter's attempt to create a network of schools was short-lived, and lay education appeared to a limited extent only under Catherine II at the end of the eighteenth century. Needless to say, there were no autonomous educational establishments like the universities in the West. An urban middle class therefore could not develop, and began to appear only in the second half of the nineteenth century. All this leads to a conclusion that the Russian town was a somewhat hybrid formation lacking the closeness and the in-feeling of a Russian village, as well as the proud identity of a Western town. But, like other villages, the towns in Russia completely lacked any tradition of individualism and freedom of enterprise.

There was yet a third type of community that deserves attention. Russian frontiers were never – not until the second half of the nineteenth century – entirely fixed, and for most of her history they were uncharted and fluid. Around the hard core of the Kievan and Muscovite territories, the steppes, the forests, the marshes and the sub-Arctic wastes were a sort of sparsely-populated no-man's land where those willing to pay the price of a dangerous and hard life could find refuge from the all-embracing state power.

The southern steppe west of the Don remained open until the colonisation drive and the extinction of nomadism in the eighteenth century. East of the Don the steppes of the Kuban, the Terek and the lower Volga were pacified only at the beginning of the nineteenth century and, except for the Kuban, were only partially colonised; east of the Volga and especially in the Kipchak steppe (present-day Kazakhstan) the nomads were forcibly settled only during the Soviet era; some remnants persist there even today. When in the second half of the nineteenth century the frontier of the Empire was pushed southwards in Central Asia incorporating what became known as Russian Turkestan, colonisation was encouraged in some fringe areas of the steppe along the Syr-Darya and in the Ferghana Valley as well as north of the Tien-Shan Mountains. The latest colonisation attempt was Khrushchev's abortive 'Virgin lands' campaign in the late 1950s.

Colonisation produced a special type of community comparable in some respect to that of the American West. In both cases there were vast open spaces that could be conquered for the plough; there was danger, insecurity and adventure; and it was a way to escape the established authority and the routine way of life. But here the similarity ends. The American settlers were faced with a primitive, weak and disorganised enemy that could match them neither militarily nor culturally. In spite of the dangers and insecurity, the settlers were able to and did help themselves. State power usually followed the settlers and not the other way round. In consequence, the settlers developed a rugged spirit of individualism, independence and mutual assistance as well as a tendency to take law into their own hands.

The nearest the Russians ever came to this type of community were the Cossack hosts before the mid-seventeenth century. They were freebooters, fugitives from law, individualists and adventurers… And we have seen above (p. 194ff) how, after having led a quasi-nomadic life for some time, they opted for the rigid authority of the Russian state. The reason was that the danger they were facing was far greater than in the case of the Americans. The steppe nomads were equally well armed and often better organised than the Cossacks. To survive the Cossacks had to give up their individualism and accept a form of discipline and organisation which would be a match to the nomads; besides, with the then available means they could not profitably cultivate the steppe and had to rely on hunting, fishing, bee-keeping as well as raiding to make their living.

The large-scale colonisation of the eighteenth century was therefore preceded by military conquest and only those areas were colonised which were firmly controlled by the army. This set the pattern for all subsequent colonisation drives. Some settlers were still fugitives from the law or from the oppression of their inland masters; but most of them were serfs commandeered by the authorities to work on lands assigned to them. The voluntary aspect of colonisation was entirely lacking – with the exception, perhaps, of Turkestan, which fell into the period of relative liberalisation and easier mobility between 1870 and 1920, and to some extent Siberia.[1] Soviet colonisation in the steppes of Central Asia or in the forests of Siberia was carried out under the guise of 'persuasion', which means, in other words, Party political pressure, if not outright command.

To conclude, individualism and free enterprise had no room in any of the three communities. The present ideological hatred of these two phenomena is, in fact, the result of the age-old traditions described above. Even the Europeanised intellectuals who claimed freedom from state control for the creative individual would probably hesitate to bring their claim to its logical conclusion, which must be freedom from control also in the economic sphere. But as we have seen, the roots of the collective spirit and authoritarian control go too deep; they form an integral part of the Russian civilisation.[2]

Chapter 44

Moral values

It has been noted already that feudalism in the European sense did not develop in Russia. A set of values which it produced and which formed an integral part of European civilisation was therefore lacking.

The culture of chivalry was of crucial importance for Western Europe. Its way of fighting was individualistic: the armoured knight faced another individual of the same kind similarly bred and trained; they both knew and respected the rules of the combat.

It may be said that the ethics of chivalry reflected an aristocratic culture in a predominantly agrarian society in which the ownership of land provided social status as well as the financial means for the fighting élite.

The Catholic Church supplied the religious counterpart of this 'fighting ethics'.

The sins and virtues as preached by the medieval Church reflected an agrarian society unlike those of the Protestant Churches whose roots were in the urban, commercial, bourgeois societies of the sixteenth and seventeenth centuries. Virtues such as frugality, industry, thriftiness and general emphasis on work, enterprise and wealth as well as efficiency, success and social progress formed part of Protestant ethics that, in its turn, evolved into the spirit of capitalism.

The situation in Russia was altogether different. The nomadic fighting, from which the morals evolved, was collective fighting: an impersonal mass of disciplined soldiers was fighting an equally impersonal enemy. The goal was to annihilate him as efficiently and as completely as possible. This was the pure law of survival; there was no room for anything like sport or fair play. Deceit and cunning were legitimate weapons. Combat had no recognised rules, in fact, it had no rules at all; any stratagem or tactic was permissible as long as it led to victory. There was no gallantry and also no generosity for the defeated; the only alternatives to victory were death or slavery. The very fact that somebody was willing to fight without compulsion was so strange that it provoked suspicion. The Russians thought that 'some Germans of chivalrous mould must be demented when they strive and labour and entreat to be allowed to follow the army into the field [...] such Germans as these they consider either to have little wit, or to entertain fraudulent design against the state'.[1]

With an impersonal mass combat there could be no personal honour. Truth had no moral value at all. Lying was so commonplace that no traveller to Russia failed to notice it. 'They are the biggest liars on earth' (Carpini, about the Mongols, 1246).[2] 'False witness was so prevalent among them that strangers were in danger from it' (Olearius, about the Russians, 1647).[3] 'How their abominable custom of lying and perjury is allowed to go unpunished [...]. For fate hath instituted such a universal perversity of reason in Muscovy, that it is very nearly the index of a superior intellect to be able to cheat.'[4] 'They are shameless and capable of committing any evil; they rely on force rather than reason. Their vices are especially evident when cheating in trade or when, through loans, they place something in someone's hands and accuse him of stealing it. Such deceit is quite frequent among them. Individuals of the more important class are so arrogant and haughty that they flaunt themselves at every opportunity. The coarseness of their customs is evident everywhere.'[5] 'We also have a great inclination to lie, to distrust others, as well as some other vices [...]. The same Slavic people and the same Orthodox faith prevail elsewhere, but there are no such vile habits among the Serbs, the Greeks and in Belorussia. What causes these vices?'[6]

People often lied to please the foreigner rather than to deceive him; it did not occur to them that lying was something wrong. Custine observed that the tradition of cunning and fraud came from Byzantium. 'The Government lives by lies, for truth terrifies the tyrant as much as the slave.'[7] 'No man is free to commit himself to an honest future until he has first been honest about the past. Only the truth can make men free of their own history. But the same perverse conviction which causes the Soviet leaders to regard lying as a legitimate instrument of policy inevitably demands falsification of popular histories.'[8]

'[...] In writing about their phoney statistics I do so not in moral judgement, but merely to point out that it is an essential part of their great scene. They have to deceive both me and themselves [...]. They react as an African [...]. He will always tell people what they most like to hear and those things that will not get him into trouble.'[8] 'There was only one authority, that of the ruler, and it was his task to define good and evil. Moral authority therefore coincided with that of military command. Obedience and discipline were required for military reasons and to ensure them total authority had to be balanced by total humiliation. Pride was synonymous with command, humility with obedience. In the hierarchy of command an individual presented a different picture to his superiors and to his subordinates.'[9] 'Ultimately, good and evil became synonymous with favour or disgrace.'[10] The authority having a monopoly of truth, the result was a strong tradition of right-thinking, of conformity.

The Orthodox Church did not challenge the temporal authority with a separate spiritual system of moral values; far more, it supported the authority of the state by emphasising the sin of rebellion and the virtue of obedience. This Byzantine attitude remained unchanged until the present days.

In line with the military nature of morals, human life had no other value than military. Freedom of the individual had no value at all in a system where the very idea of the individual was unknown. Among the nomads there was no aristocracy and no social status other than military rank. There was no noble birth, no heraldry, and no *parole d'honneur*. In Russia, when aristocracy by birth appeared – under Polish influence –, it never assumed the Western code of conduct and the moral values which accompanied it. Ethically, Russian nobles never really became like the agrarian landowners of the West. Only late in the eighteenth century, in the period of Europeanisation when the West was already largely influenced by the middle-class capitalist ethic, did the Russian gentry begin to behave in a way similar to that of West European aristocrats, but with its extinction in and after the Revolution this brief spell came to an end.

In the field of sexual morals the influence of Turkey and Islam was long dominant. In Islam the system of polygamy led to an absolute domination of men over women. Women were more often than not regarded as mere chattels rather than human beings; they were bought and dismissed at will. Romantic love existed, in Persian poetry for example, but women were not part of society; they were kept secluded in their separate quarters, had to veil their faces when going out, and were supposed to have no other moral obligation and responsibility than to their husband. In Russia, which did not recognise polygamy, these attitudes prevailed, at least in the upper strata of society, until Peter the Great. When Europeanisation affected the upper class, women gradually assumed a similar place as they had in Europe; this applied mainly to the two capital cities, St Petersburg and Moscow. In the country the old system survived much longer.

The peasants did not practice seclusion. Women were regarded as labour force; they were inferior to men, but were part of the village community. In the commune both men and women were expected to serve; this was similar to the nomadic camps where military service applied equally to both sexes.

In the USSR working women constituted just over half the state-employed labour force, but the great majority of them were in the least skilled, least desirable and lowest-paid occupations.

The notion of privacy connected as it is with individualism, seems to have remained virtually unknown in Russia. The accommodation in nomadic yurts and in peasants' huts consisted usually of only one room where the whole family lived together. In the early nineteenth century the habits of the aristocracy were still primitive enough that, as Robert Lyall noticed, they had no bedrooms for their guests. 'The dining-room, drawing room, hall and whole suites of apartments in which we had passed the evening were converted into bedrooms [...] beds were arranged on the floor, some upon chairs, others upon the stoves.'[11] Servants, he notes, lie about anywhere in their lord's house; he even stumbled against them on the stairs. The consequence was a remarkable openness with which the most intimate details of personal and family life were discussed in public, and lack of restraint in their behaviour.[12]

'Another consequence was the inquisitiveness with which the nobles ask the most impertinent questions, with respect to your connections and family, your property and revenues, and your secret affairs and private opinions [...]. But they do not content themselves merely in making enquiries of yourself; they will apply to your servant-women or servant-men, to your lackey or coachman' *(ibid.).* The openness of personal habits – or lack or modesty, as it may be called – as well as the persistent inquisitiveness have been noticed by travellers to the nomads since William of Rubruck described them vividly in 1255. They still exist unchanged among the Mongols in Outer Mongolia.

In the USSR privacy was until recently neither obtainable nor respected. The overcrowded accommodation still more often than not compels the whole family to share one room and several families to share the same kitchen and toilet. It is only recently that the situation began to improve.[13] But the traditional uninhibited inquisitiveness persists among the Russians as it did centuries ago. There is nothing like private life; the authorities can enquire about every detail, and they feel they have the right to do so. The neighbours, fellow-workers, travellers on the same train feel they have such a right, too. It is only the foreigner who feels embarrassed by it; for a Russian it is a natural thing – and he would readily claim the same right to question anybody whom he thinks is interesting enough.

'Every hospital room has two windows, one to the yard where you can see your visitors, one without curtains, leading to the corridor where the staff pass. The toilet is in the room, in full view of the nurses and doctors [...]. All their hospital experiences proved an unbearable contempt for the individual and his elementary psychological components.'[14]

In view of what has been said above, the system of Russian morals corresponds in many respects to that of a militarised society and can be traced back to the steppe nomads. This was the mainstream and the biggest single influence. Islam is still alive in certain parts of Asiatic Russia, and some elements of it survive in villages in Russia proper; European Protestant ethics gained a limited foothold with the advance of industrialisation in the nineteenth century, but both the Orthodox and the Communist morals worked powerfully against it so that little of it now remains. The hostility the Communists show towards what they call 'capitalist morals' or 'petty-bourgeois values' – which can comprise anything from private enterprises to fashionable clothes or hairstyles – is probably due less to Marxism than to the traditional Russian nomadic-egalitarian attitude.

This attitude was clearly reflected in the educational system. 'The most important difference between Soviet and American education is the emphasis placed in the former not only on subject matter, but equally on "*vospitanie*", a word which could be translated as "character education" and which has as its stated aim the development of "Communist morality". The schools are children's collectives and each classroom is a unit of the communist youth organisation [...]. Children are set great lists of behaviour in school, at home, in public places: all the emphasis is on obedience, duties, helping [...]. If one member of the row lets the others down everyone gets together to bring him up to the mark [...]. Older children are taught to report on each other [...]. Parents too are encouraged to report on their children and one of the boy heroes of the USSR is Pavlik Morozov, who denounced his own father [...].'[15]

However repellent one may find this philosophy, Dr Bronfenbrenner says that it produces disciplined, well behaved young people with a deep concern for each other...; he admits they turn out to be very conformist people without much individuality and 'they gave less weight than the subjects from other countries to telling the truth and seeking intellectual understanding'.

Chapter 45

security, equality, freedom

Economic security occupies an important place in the Russian mind. 'To the vast majority of Russians, economic security is more important than economic opportunity, and the reasons are historical and geographical. For lurking in the Russian consciousness is the threat of failure, and until recently failure here has meant not simply not "making it"; it meant famine, starvation and trying to survive the winter without fuel or stores [...]. If economic opportunity – initiative, independence and competition – carries with it the risk of failure, most Russians would rather not take the risk.'[1]

The system of economic command, or planning, virtually excludes any risk of that kind; and as a price, the Russian willingly accepts various orders and directives imposed by it, including compulsory labour.

The character of the individual could not remain unaffected by this situation. He still is, as he has always been, a collective being, submissive, obedient and without much initiative. He easily believes what the authorities tell him, and seldom develops any opinion of his own. More often than not he is simply not interested.[2]

Moreover, he is *egalitarian* by nature and hostile to any kind of privilege as long as it is within his own sphere or stratum. Institutionalised discrimination or privileges do not irritate him. He is ready to accept without protest the privileged Party aristocracy as he accepted the landed or military aristocracy in the past. 'In some ways, Russians are the most egalitarian, least class-conscious people in the world [...]. An unshaven peasant will plant himself at a table in Moscow's best establishment [...] without the slightest self-consciousness about his own appearance [...]. This is an inborn sense of equality – derived probably from the feeling that they are all children of the

Russian earth, and brothers in the Russian family – which the Communist ethic has surely reinforced.'³

Equality and *poverty* are inseparably linked in Russian thinking. It is believed that the only possible equality is that of the have-nots. This again brings to mind the importance of poverty in nomadic society. 'The real Communist is the ordinary worker, who has nothing but his bottle of vodka on Saturday night – which he shares, because his mate's hard up [...]. We believe in equality and brotherhood; that's natural to Russian workers. We don't want to live better than the next person, or live off someone else's sweat. Give a worker the choice between a wad of money and Communism and he'll take Communism every time, even when it means less to eat.'⁴

'Other aspects of the Soviet system, however, have reinforced a caste consciousness so archaic and rigid that it makes a foreigner blush.' 'Many of the privileges Russia's upper crust arrogate to themselves would not be tolerated for a moment under the most unrestrained capitalist economy [...]. No Rockefeller could get away with the kind of disdainful high-handedness taken for granted here. But the "classless" Soviet system is in some ways as class-conscious as the tsarist one, and both surely were derived partially from the Oriental obsession with rank.'⁵

So in one way, the system is still supported by the equality it generates. But it also generates differences, or rather cannot stop them developing. The myth of equality even in subjection still remains, but the growing inequalities, privileged and underprivileged pressure groups, various differences in education and skills, and above all the perks and social status of the new ruling class are undermining the security and eventually will bring about the collapse of the system.⁶

The obsession with equality, spying and total destruction has been nowhere better described than by Dostoevsky: 'He's written a good thing in that manuscript,' Verhovensky went on. 'He suggests a system of spying. Every member of the society spies on the others, and it's his duty to inform against them. Every one belongs to all and all to every one. All are slaves and equal in their slavery. In extreme cases he advocates slander and murder, but the great thing about it is equality. To begin with, the level of education, science, and talents is lowered. A high level of education and science is only possible for great intellects, and they are not wanted. The great intellects have always seized power and been despots. Great intellects cannot help being despots and they've always done more harm than good. They will be banished or put to death. Cicero will have his tongue cut out, Copernicus will have his eyes put out, Shakespeare will be stoned – that's Shigalovism. Slaves are bound to be equal. There has never been either freedom or equality without despotism, but in the herd there is bound to be equality, and that's Shigalovism! [...] To level the mountains is a fine idea, not an absurd one. I am for Shigalov. Down with culture. We've had enough sciences! Without science we have material enough to go on for a thousand years but one must have discipline. The one thing wanting in the world is discipline. The thirst for culture is an aristocratic thirst. The moment you have family ties or love you get the desire for property. We will destroy that desire; we'll make use of drunkenness, slander, spying; we'll make use of incredible corruption; we'll stifle every genius in its infancy. We'll reduce all to a common denominator! Complete equality! [...] Slaves must have directors. Absolute submission, absolute loss of individuality, but once in thirty years Shigalov would let them have a shock and they would all suddenly begin eating one another up, to a certain point, simply as a precaution against boredom. Boredom is an aristocratic sensation. The Shigalovians will have no desires. Desire and suffering are our lot but Shigalovism is for the slaves'.[7]

What can be called the Russian concept of freedom has always had a factual rather than a legal character. It reflected the attitude of a peasant who finds his freedom in withdrawing into spheres where the authority cannot follow him – away from public affairs, into nature and into himself. It was a negative and passive concept of freedom. It did not carry with it any responsibility – and thus, when eventually applied to politics, it led invariably to destruction and anarchy.

This is one reason why anarchism played such an important role in Russian political thought, and why so many artists and writers became obsessed with destruction for its own sake. In practice, this 'negative freedom' will help to explain the 'remarkable absence of conventional standards and pressures to conform' in Russian everyday, private life. 'One is not looked down upon if one is ugly, smells strongly, looks or behaves oddly [...]. And this gives an extraordinary sense of freedom to ordinary, non-political Russian life. Freedom from tension and pressure; freedom from the thousand signals that direct the lives of 'outer-directed' Western man [...] in Russia the conventions permit far greater individual freedom than what the state can grant or take away.'⁸ 'There could never be any individual freedom in the midst of a social organisation whatsoever, freedom was here, in nature, far from everything, far from the regulations. This is our last refuge and here everything belongs to us: no private property, no fence. You can walk as you like in this snow, no one will question you, no on will stop you.'⁹

Laziness often becomes the outward manifestation of such withdrawal and lack of responsibility. 'I've never seen such a negative attitude towards work, or such lackadaisical performance [...]. The objective is to do the minimum, the rules – the unwritten ones – are bent to match the goal. Again, the nineteenth-century novelists give us the important clues to the Russian character: the traditional torpor and procrastination [...] easily predominate over twentieth-century propaganda [...]. Most Russians have worked, or not worked, in this way throughout Russian history, and the general opinion is that the attitudes are so ingrained that generations will pass before they change.'

'One of the reasons Russians work so badly is that they are surprisingly content with their lot [...] most Russians do not want much in the way of material goods (but they want little because they cannot imagine themselves having more [...]). Russian workers have this remarkably low level of expectation and ambition, partly, at least, because they do not live in a competitive society [...]. Their frame of mind is still that of the Russian peasant, to whom the notion of worldly success and riches is as far-fetched as a holiday in Nassau.'¹⁰

The contrast between Russian insouciance and the ambition of the rest of northern Europe cannot be over-emphasised. Russian writers have described it again and again. 'It's a curious thing. The Russian peasant is intelligent, quick and full of understanding. But it's no use at all [...]. He's never developed that – how to put it? – love of work' (One of Turgenev's characters in *A Month in the Country*, 1855).

This 'lackadaisical approach' does not mean that there is no discipline in the system; on the contrary, it is the individual's defence against such discipline. It is still the traditional defence of a helpless peasant against his nomadic warrior-lord.

The political authority, the compulsory labour system, the age-old tradition of service as well as the country's isolation and stringent censorship – all work towards conformity, both in behaviour and in thinking. The product, inevitably, is a collective being unaware of anything like free will, free choice or responsibility for its own acts. The instruments of such conditioning, notably censorship and propaganda, became considerably more effective under the Soviet government than they were under the tsars.

'Take censorship, for example. It's by far the most important and efficient part – the dominant factor – of all our literary world and work. You can't have a label for a vitamin bottle or a toothpaste box printed without a censor's stamp [...]. The control is *total*.'

'It is the politicisation – it is often called 'contamination' – of every aspect of public life that repels [the intellectuals] more than anything, and to escape it, they spin psychological as well as physical cocoons around themselves.'[11]

'Nor can Westerners appreciate the quantity and quasi-religious tone of the political propaganda. The preaching, chanting and twenty-four-hour broadcasting of Marxist-Leninist slogans and jargon is as frighteningly manipulatory as anyone can imagine: it is the Party force-feeding newspeak and doublethink to helpless masses, hypnotising them to love the Party. It is truly Orwellian.'[12]

'The Russians as a nation have a strong tradition of thinking alike. In tsarist times it was abnormal to be a Russian without being of the Russian Orthodox religion. Ordinary people could not understand how a person could be the one without the other. So, although tsarist governments regarded it as one of their primary duties to ensure that the faith and nationality were coextensive, they did not normally need to do much about it. The Communist government has taken over this view of right-thinking, but in respect of its own set of ideas.'[13]

'There is a very strong tendency in the public mental life of the USSR to confuse outward with inward agreement. The *expression* of unanimity on basic philosophical matters has assumed great importance for the authorities [...].'[14]

This conditioning of mind, which appears as uniformity, or at least utmost conformity, on the one side, and as 'negative freedom' or 'absence of conventional standards', on the other, is in fact perfectly logical. It reflects the age-old pressures from 'above' by the authorities, and the individual's reaction, his withdrawal and escape into himself. In the sphere of society over and above the individual's most intimate life, the pressures have always been overwhelming, and it can be argued that nothing like freedom has ever existed here in the whole of Russian history. 'Most people can't conceive of political democracy. They understand quantitative changes perfectly well: more or less suffering, a tighter or looser squeeze, a harsher or more benevolent leader. But only within the system, with someone up above giving or taking back. The idea that they might decide for themselves is simply beyond their comprehension.'[15]

'The Russians are to this day still a relatively primitive people [...] the primitive is a condition of life wherein the instinctive, subjective and collective values tend to predominate: the civilised condition of life is where the rational, objective and individual take command [...] at times in Russia without my upbringing and love of the primitive peoples of Africa I could have felt quite at a loss [...]. The Russians are naturally a communal people because they are basically a primitive people: and a primitive man is naturally collective [...]. I know a dozen or so tribes in Africa which practise in essence the Soviet system [...]. The collective value evolved in prolonged conditions of great danger is entrusted to a powerful central tribal authority [...] just as in the Soviet Union.'

'Property ultimately belongs to the chief on behalf of the whole [...] the phenomenon of violent change brought about from the top [...] is a familiar occurrence in African history. Ivan the Terrible, Peter the Great and Stalin [...] have scores of counterparts on the primitive African scene. Nor is it helpful to blame the despotism of the Russian system on the Tartars. It is a primitive phenomenon [...] the Soviet system struck me as extremely archaic.'[16]

Chapter 46

The militarised society

The duty of every individual to serve the state remained throughout history one of the basic principles of Russian political thinking. At first, it was the 'warrior élite', the gentry liable to service; the service was then exclusively military, but as long as the state administration was organised on a military pattern, the service included administrative duties as well. In historical terms this lasted until the end of the *kormlenie* system and the introduction of a salaried bureaucracy in the early eighteenth century.

By then the idea of service became more or less paramount. Although the gentry managed to escape the actual compulsory service later in that century, for those who did not wish to lead the life of 'lazy landlords', the forces and the civil service were the only two careers open. Meanwhile, the compulsory military service was extended to the masses of population. The conscription system of Peter the Great prescribing a compulsory service for all the gentry and a life-long service for the draftees of other classes thus represented the most thorough repetition of the nomadic system. Those who were not drafted (townspeople and peasants alike) 'served' as bonded people either the state or their landlord.

A certain relaxation of the service system became apparent in the late nineteenth and early twentieth centuries in connection with industrialisation and urbanisation. The extent, however, was limited; commerce and industry had little attraction to the gentry, the urban middle class, who engaged in those activities, only began to emerge, and the peasant masses continued to serve, as they did before, either in the army or on the land. Russian administration followed the military pattern until the modern era. In the eighteenth century bureaucracy replaced the army, but the pattern of organisation and the centralisation remained the same. Neither army nor bureaucracy did develop into a class of their own, and a fair amount of mobility existed within the élite, which remained, of course, strictly separated from the underprivileged subjects.

The Russian obsession with rank is obviously Byzantine. Even the young Vladimir Ulianov, the future Lenin, did not hesitate to claim his hereditary title of nobility to which he was entitled because of the position his father and his grandparents occupied in the state apparatus.[1]

Under the Soviet rule the principle of service was revived and reinforced. With the state being the sole employer and owner of all land, every individual became by necessity a servant of it. The length and rigour of military service in the USSR exceeded those of any other country with, perhaps, the exception of China. Discipline and a hierarchy of command were the principles of organisation everywhere, in the state administration, in the so-called voluntary mass organisation (youth, women, trade unions) and above all, in the all-powerful Party apparatus. Individual initiative was carefully channelled into fields where it could serve the Party and the state; elsewhere it was regarded with suspicion and positively discouraged.

The underlying ideology was based on exactly the same nebulous and mystical ideas as that of the nomadic state. The state is an entity which exists independently of the people. Its authority is never questioned. It is mystical and absolute and is vested in the collective body of the Party. The Party cannot be wrong; its judgement is infallible. Individual leaders may commit errors and may be criticised, tried and executed, even removed from their graves; but the Party is always right. This is clearly a mystical belief which defies rationality; it belongs to the realm of religion rather than politics.

The idea of 'holy Russia' or 'mother Russia' and later the 'Soviet fatherland' shows similar qualities as that of the nomadic 'earth'. It is, in principle, not linked to any particular territory. The Tartar Crimea became 'mother Russia' as soon as it was occupied by the tsarist army; similarly, the attribute of 'holiness' and 'Russian-ness' was extended to any other non-Russian country conquered by the Russian military might. In this sense, 'Russia had no definite boundaries'; it was truly limitless. Like the nomadic empire, its boundaries extended to the limits of the actual state power – for the practical purpose of its military power, as in the nomadic past. This is why the Russian would not understand the meaning of the word 'colony'. For him, what belongs to the state is 'Russia' – or, until recently, the Soviet Union.[2]

The 'earth' thus becomes venerated in an abstract and extremely jealous way. The frontier, for a Russian, is not the territorial boundary of his country; it is the end of the world – and the beginning of another, dangerous and hostile world. An infringement of this frontier – even in a single step across – has therefore the character of a sacrilege – not a legal infringement, but a religious one. Even the proximity of the frontier fills the Russian with certain awe, like the proximity of the World's end. Depopulated and booby-trapped borders and inaccessible frontier zones several miles deep go well with this idea. 'I realised', Custine writes, 'that I was entering the empire of fear. Every foreigner is treated like a criminal on arrival at the Russian frontier.'

'In their movements people seem stiff and constrained. No one seems to be going where he wants to but appears to be carrying out some order [...] everything is gloomy, as disciplined as in a barrack or camp; it is war without its enthusiasm for life. Military discipline dominates Russia.'[3]

As for 'the people', the picture was again similar. It was believed, as in the past, that 'the people's voice shows the will of heaven'. The Party pretended to be ruling in the name of 'the people', but 'the people' had never been asked to take part in the Party's decision-making. The so-called 'democratic centralism' in the Party meant that the lower echelons of the Party were occasionally asked to declare their support for the leadership by voting in favour of this or that decision – always after the event and with no alternative so that any practical meaning of such 'voting' was extremely questionable. The same happened with the 'elections' of the state organs, legislative, administrative or judicial. 'The people' was supposed to show its support of the leadership – again, a declaratory act with little or no political meaning.

And yet, 'the people' figured predominantly in all Party political statements as the sole objective of all its endeavours. 'The people wants...

The people shows its will… The people endeavours' etc. But 'the people', as in nomadic times, is a mystical, not a political idea. The consequence, as with 'the earth', is a religious, not a political attitude. 'The people' acquires a mystical existence that must not be questioned. 'The enemy of the people' is worse than any ordinary criminal. The 'will of the people', usually shown in a mass demonstration, is more than the law.

Thus in the Soviet, as in the nomadic system, the three mystical and nebulous ideas, the state, the earth and the people, formed a coherent whole designed to keep the absolute ruler (the Party) in power. The complex institutions of the Soviet state were hardly more representative than the old and simple nomadic *kuriltay* or the *zemskie sobory* in Muscovy.

Taking into account what has been said above about the military nature of these institutions, the Soviet society was equally – if not more – militarised than that of Peter the Great's Russia or, for that matter, the society of the nomads. The militaristic phraseology used both in the Party jargon and the ordinary Soviet journalese provides just one more symptom of the situation. 'Fight for socialism' or 'fight for higher yields in agriculture' go alongside such slogans like 'the capitalist front' or 'the battle for the grain', 'the enemy within our ranks', 'heroic struggle of the workers' and, of course, with the notorious saboteur – and spy-mania. Other paraphernalia, like the profusion of uniforms and decorations, or the militaristic bombast accompanying every action from harvesting to space missions, from coalmining to the May-Day parade, just complete the picture.

As for the actual conduct of war, nomadic attitudes can be detected in more than one aspect. For example, the Russian armies have repeatedly used the 'scorched earth' strategy whereby the enemy was allowed to penetrate deep in Russian territory and was offered a battle only when his supply routes were sufficiently stretched to restrict his capacity of manoeuvring. Whereas this strategy makes good sense from the military point of view, it implies a complete disregard for the value of the land and the people living on it. Mobility as the main principle of warfare was obviously dictated by the nature of the terrain, from the Scythians of the time of Darius I until World War II;

but whereas the Scythians were sufficiently mobile not to leave any of their people behind at the mercy of the Persians, the Russians had to abandon millions in the territories occupied by the Germans. Land was readily sacrificed; and so were the masses of the population. The only section of the population which was evacuated – or, at least, there were attempts to evacuate it – can be described as the 'warrior élite': members of the Party apparatus, the security and armed forces, and the specialists.

The standards of values applied by the twentieth century Russians would not differ much from those of the ancient or medieval nomads. The same standards can be seen in the use of manpower in battle. Massive charges with massed firepower were used as a rule, while wastage of human material was considered less important than wastage of military hardware. In other words, men were expendable; the value of human life – as well as suffering and other humanitarian aspects – was rated rather low. The same attitude appeared in military planning where considerably less importance was attached to defensive weapons and equipment than to offensive ones. The low standard of ancillary services such as provisioning, medical care or hygiene goes with it. It was by no means chance that first attempts to establish a regular army commissariat appeared only at the very end of the seventeenth century; until then it was assumed that the army would live off the land, like the armies of the nomads.

It is perhaps symptomatic that the static defence has been comparatively rare in Russian military history; in fact, the Russians abandoned their traditional mobile warfare only in the time of their highest Europeanisation: in the Crimean war, in the war with Japan in 1904–5, and in World War I. In each case they decided to dig in and defend the land – and with disastrous results.

But when massive deployment of troops was impossible, when the way of fighting became more individualised, when the enemy was not a regular, easily identifiable fighting force, but an army of irregulars, of guerrillas, like in Afghanistan, the Russians seemed to lack adequate responses. Heavy losses with few tangible results had a profound effect both on the population in the homelands and on the policies of the leadership. In a state which was in fact, if not in name, a military machine, military setbacks were signs of weakness and inevitably brought about a weakening and in the end the collapse of the whole system. A nomadic empire could not face a defeat – if it suffered one, it disintegrated. The infallibility of the leadership began to be questioned, the invincibility of the army was no longer believed, and the casualties were no longer heroes but questionable losses. And, as Pipes justly observed, 'should the Communist authority in the USSR break down, [...] there would be nothing to hold the country together.'[4]

The consequence – or at least, one of several – of Afghanistan was the collapse of the Soviet empire. At the time of writing another guerrilla war drags on in Chechnya with similar inconclusiveness and similar repercussions. Its consequences remain to be seen.

Appendix
The Russian Way of Thinking

'The truth of this country is still in the village; everything comes from the Russian village and the spirit of the village permeates everything. And that spirit is still what we call "dark". You cannot understand Russia unless you know about this darkness: this fatalism, obscurantism and profound religiosity that made our people bow in genuine reverence to an unbenevolent tsar.'[1]

This, however, is only half of the true picture. There is a reverse side to that 'village mentality' which comes to the fore as soon as the humble peasant acquires a position of authority. He then becomes a member of the ruling élite and quickly discovers in himself attitudes and capacities which are far from the relaxed helplessness of the peasant thinking. He begins to behave as he has always seen the rulers of the country behave; he becomes a warrior, a member of a chosen caste to whom all non-warriors are inferior beings. In short, he begins to behave like a nomad assuming the atavistic mentality of those who ruled his country from time immemorial.

As everything in Russian thinking can be reduced to this basic duality, the question is what are the conditions enabling this duality to persist, and what likelihood is there that they will change?

The first item to be considered is the *isolation* of the country. Without any possibility to compare the life in Russia with that of the outside world, there will always be a strong tendency to believe everything Russian to be the best; the authority of those who say it will not be challenged; the obscurantism of the village will remain, and the peasant in every Russian will continue to bow to his unbenevolent tsar. Moreover, given the universalistic streak in Russian mentality, this attitude can be exported; what is good for Russia must be the best for the world, and what is Russian becomes 'the norm' by which everything else is measured. Accordingly, 'normality' means conformity with

343

the Russian model. Isolation is therefore the prerequisite for the village mentality and a means to keep the masses obedient and the regime not only accepted, but also revered.

'[...] The workers themselves are so bored that they often do not bother to inquire about the theme of the meeting [...]. They will raise their hands for the unanimous "yes" vote when ordered, or for the Pravda photographer [...]. They simply couldn't care less about foreign affairs.'

'This state of mind is a reflection [...] of Russia's enduring isolation: the isolation once imposed by vast distances, cruel climate and difficulties of transport, and now by a suspicious, jealous and somewhat xenophobic dictatorship [...]. One is always conscious here of being cut off from the rest of the world [...].'[2]

The second item is *poverty*. This, in turn, is indispensable to keep the warrior spirit alive. As long as the warrior has nothing to lose, he will obey the command, and the power structure built on discipline will survive. As long as the warriors are poor, they are also equal; they can all be subject to the same command; they can be wooed by privileges of status rather than wealth; the membership of the élite being itself the greatest privilege.

The egalitarian principle on which the command system is based would be unthinkable in anything remotely approaching affluence. A 'classless society' can exist only in a state of poverty; a unity of the people in subjection to the command – in other words, the discipline can be achieved only if the people are poor.

'The principal political effect of Communism is to preserve backwardness.'[3]

Isolation and poverty are, therefore, the twin pillars of the system; but they bring with them built-in contradictions. In the world of inter-related economies, a policy of complete isolation would be dangerously counter-productive; in the field of mass-communication it becomes increasingly absurd. Some degree of information and contact is inevitable and it is likely to grow, however reluctantly.

The problem with poverty is that it is the exact opposite of the declared policy of the régime. The official aim of Marxism–Leninism and of the policy of the CPSU was to establish a classless society in order to increase the standard of living of the masses, and to abolish poverty. The emphasis on the construction of heavy industry was a way of making people work for a distant goal while keeping them poor for the foreseeable future. Little improvements could be hailed as great achievements in 'building Communism' while people were still denied most of their work's worth. An enormous economic potential could thus be accumulated by the State and used for spectacular advancements in some narrow fields of research and technology, for furthering its expansionist policies, for armaments, subversion, propaganda, etc.

'This [Communist] dream of building a shining new world, free of all despair and darkness, is itself characteristically Russian: the product of the intolerable misery and despair of Russian life.'[4]

It is well known that one of the biggest difficulties Russian defectors encountered in the West was to cope with choice; when faced with a plurality of possibilities, they were unable to make up their mind and to take the responsibility for their decision. They were so conditioned that everything had been lined up for them that the absence of command, or directive, and the necessity to decide for themselves baffled them to such an extent that many of them gave up and returned home.

THE ECONOMY

Chapter 47

The traditional pattern

The three main branches of early Russian economy have at least one aspect in common. Hunting and gathering, pastoral nomadism and the slash-and-burn agriculture as well as the rainfall agriculture in selected areas of the steppe can all be termed extensive, consuming a disproportionate amount of labour, time and land in relation to the yields obtained. In hunting and pastoralism this is inherent; but intensive high yield agriculture has been known from early times, for example, in irrigated areas where the scarcity of land and the cost of irrigation pressed for constant improvement of methods and techniques.

In Russia such incentives were absent; with a less wasteful farming system and more appropriate tools more land became available, and irrigation was provided by nature. Even when pastoralism and hunting receded in the background and agriculture prevailed in the country's economy, it still remained remarkably extensive and, by Western standards, inefficient and backward. This was partly due to the peasants' and landlords' attitude to land, but mostly to the lack of knowledge and experience with any more efficient methods as well as to the lack of incentives to investigate and improve on the existing situation.

The psychological background can be followed back to the nomadic and Muslim disinterest and fatalism as well as to the lack of a clearly defined title to the land. It was the same psychology of the nomadic Arabs that converted the fields and vineyards of North Africa into semi-desert pastures for goats and sheep; and that of the nomadic Turks that made the Anatolian granary of Byzantium into one of the poorest regions of the Middle East. In Russia the peasants, isolated in their villages and hamlets and ruled economically by the conservative and inward-looking commune, had little chance to learn from the outside, and had little incentive to innovate and improve themselves. Russian agriculture, even in the fertile areas, remained on subsistence level until the sixteenth century and perhaps later. The country was caught in a vicious circle of a low density of population, absence of markets, and lack of trade. The result could only be economic stagnation and backwardness.

To this must be added the tradition inherited from both the nomadic system and from Byzantium of state management of the economy. Little can be added to what has been said above (p. 35) about the economy of the nomads. In their system of rigid discipline and control there was no room for any initiative from below; the state personified by the ruler was the only source of economic activity.

When the Russian economy moved into a more complex stage, the Byzantine model came to the fore. At first, the area of state interference, or regulation, was limited to foreign trade and the management of armament industries; the economic effects of the *kormlenie* system must be added to this. As craftsmen and merchants were bonded people, and agriculture was on subsistence level, there was hardly any possibility of private enterprise. From the times of Peter the Great state and private enterprise existed side by side (from 200 manufacturing establishments founded in Peter's reign, 114 were private and 86 were founded by the state).[1]

In Peter's time state activity also extended into large-scale public building, for example, of canals, and even to grandiose projects like the foundation of St Petersburg. The share of state enterprise increased, paradoxically, with the growth of industrialisation. By the end of the nineteenth century the state was the sole builder of railways, had the monopoly of banking, credit and other financial operations, controlled merchant navigation, manipulated freight rates, etc. Even in the period of highest Europeanisation the state was the biggest entrepreneur in the country, and the views of the Finance Minister Witte in spite of their reforming and Westernised look were, as far as the economic role of the state was concerned, very close to those of the Byzantines.

There are two other phenomena, linked with each other, which may be traced back to the nomadic tradition: the economy of under-consumption, and the parasitism of the ruling élite.

In the nomadic society poverty was the natural and normal state of affairs and at the same time the best safeguard of military efficiency and prowess. This was recognised by the rulers, and conscious efforts were made to keep the warrior élite poor. The best example is the resistance of the state, in Turkey and Russia, to hereditary land ownership. With the weakening of the principle of service, when the *timar* and *pomestie* holders were allowed to become wealthier and to turn into 'lazy landlords', the immediate consequence was a decline in military efficiency.

Confiscations and arrests were another method to curb the growth of wealth. 'Persons of formidable riches are commonly punished by being dragged to prison [...] their goods are handed over to the Treasury and they themselves to exile or death [...].'[2]

The economic effects of a poor élite were manifold. There was no market for luxury goods. There was no inducement for a diversification of crafts. And, most importantly, a poor élite had no interest in increasing the productivity and improving the lot of the subject population. Primitive taxation together with crude exploitation under the *kormlenie* system, and later under the corrupt bureaucracy, kept the purchasing power of the masses constantly so low that circulation of goods, or a 'domestic market' could hardly develop. The economy as such was not incapable of growth; but it was perennially stagnating because of this under-consumption of the masses of population. 'The great oppression over the poor commons maketh them to have no courage in following their trades: for that the more they have the more danger they are in, not only of their goods but of their lives also. And if they have any thing, they conceal it all they can, sometimes conveying it into monasteries, sometimes hiding it under the ground and in woods [...]. I have seene them sometimes when they have layed open their commodities for a liking [...] to look still behind them and towards every doore: as men in some feare, that looked to be set upon and surprised by some enimie'.

'This maketh the people [...] to give themselves much to idlenes and drinking: as passing for no more than from hand to mouth.'[3]

The situation remained unchanged even in the nineteenth century; the purchasing power of the people remained low, despite the fact that a thin layer of wealthy landlords now existed. These, however, preserved the parasitic attitude of their ancestors and were living off the peasantry without any attempt to improve their material situation. 'The Russian, the Great Russian nobility, is not a landed nobility now, nor in all probability was it ever one; it had no castles, it did not pass through a period of knighthood and [private] feuding. It was always a serving nobility [...]. Even today the majority of the Great Russian nobles have no rural residences, no [manorial] economies as we see them in the rest of Europe. All the land that belongs to the noble [...] is left to the village community that works it and pays the lord for it. Even if the lord owns, and lives in, a country house, he still does not have a [manorial] economy, but rather lives like a rentier. Most nobles have country houses, but they live in town and visit the country house only for weeks or months.'[4]

Under the Soviet system the economy of under-consumption persisted. The purchasing power of the masses was kept artificially low for various reasons. Ideologically, it was good to avoid differences in wealth; equality in poverty was still seen as a guarantee of efficiency in the 'struggle for socialism'.

In 1950 an article in *Pravda* condemned the very idea that the Soviet society might at some point move consciously in the direction of material plenty as anti-Marxist.[5]

Without doubt, if the people had something to lose, they would be less interested in fighting for socialism than if they have nothing to lose.

Economically, the state needed to extract from the people as much as possible, in terms of money and labour, for its extremely expensive projects ranging from space missions to economic aid, from armament industries to huge unproductive and parasitic armies of bureaucrats, party apparatchiks, secret policemen and soldiers.

Therefore it had little interest in giving people back any comparable value for their work.

Politically, it was easier to govern a poor and needy population that, under the system of state enterprise, could be tempted and placated with minor concessions and improvements than a consumer society with highly sophisticated requirements.

The drawback was, of course, that in such a system the domestic market was far too weak to provide a real impetus for the economy. The old nomadic ideas of the value of land and people were still at the bottom of the mind of Soviet managers. It was easier to squeeze the maximum out of the people than to provide economic incentives for an increased productivity of agriculture and industry. In most fields and areas the standard of work was still extensive rather than intensive.

The profit incentive being absent, compulsion was needed to keep the machine going. The state being the only employer and entrepreneur, every individual was economically as well as politically at its mercy. The parasitic 'warrior élite' of the Party controlled the whole machine without being economically interested in improving the welfare of the people. Stagnation and backwardness were therefore inherent in the system, and any progress had to be counter-balanced by compulsion and unpaid or underpaid labour.

In the Roman Empire slave labour kept wages of the free population too low and led finally to the complete collapse of the system. In Russia the unpaid labour of the serfs was the chief cause of the stagnation of the economy. In the USSR the situation repeated itself. Masses of slave labour, which were needed to sustain the industrialisation of the country, kept the domestic market stagnant. (For the importance of concentration camps for the construction of massive public works, see note 6.) 'Compulsion is needed to keep people in agriculture and to operate certain branches of industry, like mining. Unpaid labour is used in various *subbotniki* and *voskresniki* (Saturday and Sunday work), farming brigades, and other "voluntary" actions. The result is that the whole economy must be shielded from foreign competition behind impenetrable economic barriers, and would no doubt collapse if these barriers were lifted.'[7]

Chapter 48

Land ownership

Private ownership of land with a clearly defined legal title should be seen as an indispensable condition of economic development, prosperity and progress. It enables one to bring land, which is, potentially at least, a major economic asset everywhere, into the business cycle making it possible for the owner to buy or sell, to lease or pawn, or to use it as a collateral for credit. An absence of private ownership of land or an inadequately conceived legal title – as it still is the case in so many Oriental and Third-World countries – acts as a powerful brake in every field of economic activity.

It has been thanks to the clear definition of private property, and notably to the difference between ownership and possession in Roman law, that the West – and only the West – could throughout the Middle Ages and up to modern times use land as a 'productive asset' which could provide private capital when industrialisation began to require big investments and act as a springboard for rapid development of a capitalist economy.

In the West, where markets and the money economy were more developed as soon as agriculture reached the commercial stage – in some areas as early as the twelfth to thirteenth century – the landlords became interested chiefly in increasing the financial yield of their land; farming became an economic enterprise aiming at profit and using the market mechanism to achieve it. As a by-product serfdom was relaxed until it disappeared altogether, and the peasants became consumers with sufficient purchasing power to sustain a highly diversified system of crafts.

In Russia the economic value of the land was not recognised until the eighteenth century. Farming could not become an enterprise because of the lack of markets, an undeveloped money economy, and the surveillance by the

354

state of economic activity. On the other hand, the old nomadic idea that people were the really valuable property was still very much alive. The tendency therefore was not to increase the productivity of the land, but to squeeze as much as possible from the people, from the peasants. A stagnating economy and serfdom indistinguishable from slavery were the results.

'Plekhanov branded [...] the plan to nationalise the land as potentially reactionary. Such a policy [...] would leave "untouched this survival of an old semi-Asiatic order" and thus facilitate its restoration.' This was the dreaded historical perspective that Lenin alternately designated as 'the restoration of the Asiatic mode of production', 'the restoration of our semi-Asiatic order', the restoration of Russia's 'semi-Asiatic nationalisation', 'the return to the Aziatchina', and Russia's 'Asiatic restoration'.[1]

Plekhanov adhered to Marx's and Engels's idea that under the Mongol rule Russia became semi-Asiatic, and that despite important modification it remained so even after the Decree of Emancipation (1861). He noted that eventually (in 1762) the *pomeshchiki* were made the owners of their former service land without any further obligation to serve the government, while the peasants were still allotted their land (by the State and the *pomeshchiki*). Resenting the striking injustice of the situation, the peasants wanted the old system of state control over the land restored.

Through a restoration of Russia's old economic and governmental order 'the wheel of Russian history would be powerfully, very powerfully, reversed' (Plekhanov, 1906).[2] Invoking the example of the Chinese statesman Wang An-shih, who allegedly sought to make the state the owner of all land and the state officials the managers of all production, Plekhanov exclaimed... 'We want no Kitaishchina – no Chinese system'.

With these experiences in mind Plekhanov fought Lenin's programme to establish a dictatorial government based on a small proletarian minority that could do little to prevent such restoration. Instead he advocated the municipalisation of the land...

Plekhanov certainly was on firm ground when he pointed to Russia's Asiatic heritage, and when he stressed 'the necessity to eliminate the economic foundation through which our people have approached more and more closely the Asiatic people'.[3]

The agrarian reform of Alexander II gave most land not to the emancipated serfs individually, but to the village communes. As mentioned above, the communes had the right to allocate land and to assign peasants to work it. Stolypin's reform of 1906 went a step further by creating a (relatively) small number of individual peasant farmers. But the peasants in their large majority did not give up communal farming, which was to them a guarantee of justice and equality. The individual farmers were not popular, especially where they were successful. One effect of communal farming was that the peasant had little understanding of private property and of the legal rights and obligations that went with it. More often than not he was afraid of it. The task of the Party after the Revolution was therefore rather easy.

The October Revolution promptly returned to the traditional state-ownership by nationalising all land and the wheel of Russian history was duly reversed. The Decree on Land was the second Act of the Revolutionary Government, second only to the Decree on Peace.

By nationalising land and industries the government took over all the country's assets, and 'since the government was in the hands of one party and that party obeyed the will of its leader, Lenin was *de facto* owner of the country's material resources'.[4] He also owned the people. The position of a khan or a sultan could not be defined more clearly.

The peasants who after 1905 were able to raise their voice and make their claims known were after 1917 and even more after 1929 reduced to sullen silence.

However, during the New Economic Policy land-leases and individual farming began to appear again, the more successful farmers being labelled as *kulaks*. This term with its 'connotations of exploitation and greed' is characteristic of the age-old tradition of hatred of the very idea of private possession. In 1927 the collectivisation drive began, and all individual farmers, *kulaks* or not, were 'liquidated as a class'. The commune spirit of collective ownership of land prevailed once again but not without bitter resistance of the peasant masses, especially in the Ukraine. This reveals a curious twist of mentality: 'the commune spirit' worked against individual farmers, especially the successful *kulaks*, while a government-enforced drive into the *kolkhozes*, or communes, was met with desperate resistance.

The explanation of this phenomenon brings us back to the nomadic psychology again. Those who hated the *kulaks*, who opposed individual farming, and who supported the *kolkhoz* drive were the poor, while those opposing the *kolkhozes* were refusing to remain poor. And as 'only the poor nomad is a pure nomad', a section of Russia's poor retained this notion of poverty as something not only natural but also desirable and even honourable. And the ferocity of the 'liquidation of the *kulaks*' can serve as yet another example of the ruthlessness, again dating back to the nomadic past, with which an alien element in the system had to be eradicated.

'At present, the state is yet again the sole owner, as in the nomad times; the communes, renamed collective farms, administer a section of the land while other parts are worked directly by the state as state-farms. The state-peasants are wage-earners and taxpayers, while the *kolkhoz*-workers have a share in their produce and can, under the circumstances, use the produce from their tiny "private plots" for themselves; but not even these plots are their own; they only have the use of them. They have their "right to work" but neither of them is free to leave the land; there is not even a St George's Day, although the *kolkhoz* charters have detailed regulations about the termination of membership. As in the Middle Ages, no movement happens from the individual's free will; if the membership is to be terminated, if the peasant is going to leave the land, the initiative must come from above, from the authority who owns the land. Similarly there is no safeguard against their removal from the land, if the authority so decides; and as in Turkey, the character and tradition of the way the government works makes all legal safeguards look somewhat illusory.'[6]

'The typical member of a *kolkhoz* is a new phenomenon in Russian history. The novelty lies not in his wretched poverty, not even in the extremely heavy exactions imposed upon him, but in the minute state organisation and control of his work and life.'[7]

There were several attempts at reform after Stalin, but none of them tackled the real problem. Khrushchev's Virgin Lands campaign and the creation of huge 'agro-cities' flopped rather quickly; Brezhnev's policy of transforming *kolkhozes* into *sovkhozes*, despite massive financial investment, did not sort out the food shortages either. Gorbachev's *perestroika* tried timidly to loosen the state grip and, as a result, the system fell into pieces.[8, 9]

Chapter 49

Planning

Volumes could be written about the idiocies of centralised economic planning. It is more important to look at the repercussions which total – or totalitarian – planning had in three different and vital fields of the country's life. It has often been said that a capitalist economy is an economy of waste. This is rather a superficial impression based on the fact that capitalism operates with a saturated market. The needs of the consumers – in the widest sense – are anticipated and met with supplies as soon as the demand arises. Competition takes care that there is a choice between products. Sales bring profits, so they are stimulated by publicity and other methods. Reserves are available to keep abreast of the demand. It is the unsold, unused reserves, which make the impression of wastage. But the basic principle is that supply adjusts to demand, is created and stimulated by it, and in expectation of profits, exceeds it. In this way capitalism is an economy of plenty.

A planned economy, which is the essential tenet of socialism, is the exact opposite. Here the market mechanism of supply and demand is suppressed or abolished and replaced with directives arrived at by a bureaucratic process based on political requirement. Demand is straight-jacketed by what the plan decides should be met of it. Reserves are impossible because they cannot be planned. In this way demand always exceeds supply – except where some unwanted goods were produced – and the system operates on the basis of permanent shortages. Labour, paradoxically, is treated as any other merchandise. No reserves of unused labour are tolerated, so unemployment, irregular work or freelancing is unthinkable; anybody without a regular, full-time job is considered 'social parasite' and is liable to prosecution. Salaries and wages are set by the plan and the monopoly, Party-controlled trade union is not supposed to negotiate either wages or labour conditions. Compulsory labour is the norm, and a change of job, unless directed from above, requires authorisation.

Another important aspect is the fictitious role of money. In a planned economy money has not its economic role of balancing supply and demand by means of price. Prices are equally set by decree and remain the same whether there are goods aplenty or none at all. Production is not stimulated by excess demand because the plan does not allow for it. Distribution and services are difficult to plan even in the best of circumstances, and in a production-minded, military-led economy they can only have a secondary importance; hence the queues, black-marketing, corruption and other well known phenomena of a socialist economy.

Socially, economic planning brings about an enormous increase in bureaucracy. Not only are planning offices on every level of administration, culminating in the Central planning office, the Gosplan, but every firm must have its planning department which supplies data to the centre and receives directives from it (for some figures, see Pipes[1]). Bureaucratic management, not enterprise, is the rule, and planners and managers have developed into a new parasitic class – part of the *nomenklatura* élite which contributes nothing to the country's economy, and whose jobs are in most cases totally unrelated to their qualifications or abilities. An inevitable consequence of this is a dominant and often domineering position of the administrative planners, and a difficult relationship between managing directors and planning managers on the enterprise level, but, being both Party members, it is the Party which solves the friction – in the interest of the 'common good'.

The third field where economic planning has important consequences is psychology. When every economic activity has to be planned, is directed from above, there is no room for any initiative from below. Everybody just carries out orders, trying to do as little as possible – managers and workers alike. Nobody has any interest in taking on extra tasks, improving his performance, accepting additional responsibilities.

Ambition does not pay – the reward for an initiative would be negligible, the risk of trouble often considerable – so climbing the Party ladder is a much better, or indeed the only option for an ambitious person. It should be emphasised that in a way Party ranks were quite open to career-minded people who were willing to endorse the Party line and to submit to the necessary discipline. Many of the Party leaders began their careers as factory managers moving from there into the Party apparatus. But the vast majority of the working population remains inert and passive. One outlet of this passivity – and throughout history the most common one – is alcoholism. It cannot be said, of course, that alcoholism is a consequence of economic planning, but it is the consequence of inertia, passivity and frustration, of constant pressure from above, of a feeling of helplessness in face of the authority, which was the same in Muscovy, in imperial Russia, and under the Soviets.[2]

Chapter 50

Trade, money & taxes:
The industries & the unions

As far as trade and transport are concerned, the ideological attitude of the Communist Party in the post-Lenin era reverted to the traditional views of the pre-industrial age. In the earlier part of the nineteenth century 'railways had been feared for their disintegrating effect on Russian life'. In the 1840s, Kankrin, Nicholas I's minister of finance, had called them 'the malady of the age', and accused them of 'fostering excessive mobility and increasing social equality'.[1] Under the Soviets, with the new 'warrior élite' taking over, both mobility and social mixing of people outside the élite were again frowned upon. The immediate effect of state management of the economy was that the planning of transportation assumed secondary importance after production. While in the West more and more commercial and personal transport moved from rail to road, road-building in the USSR remained on a negligible scale.

All commercial aspects being absent, the producing areas all over the country still had very little contact with the consuming areas. This was most evident in agriculture, where perishable and seasonal products were rarely shipped outside the producing areas, and if they were, it was in limited quantities only. Cities were supplied from surrounding areas with a perimeter roughly of a day's journey by lorry or cart. In most cases this meant a continuous shortage of certain foodstuffs, like meat, vegetables and fruit, when the size of the city's population exceeded the supplying capacity of the area.

Trade in the system of planned economy was replaced by a planned distribution of goods. That means that market mechanism was not allowed to operate. The government fixed prices, and the purchasing power of the population was equally planned by government-operated regulation of wages. Goods were distributed according to planned or estimated requirements of the population. Supplies were kept intentionally low because goods in stock were incompatible with the principle of planning. The market, therefore, was generally unsaturated.

Interest was still virtually unknown and private saving almost did not exist. Excess money was more likely to go into the black market than into savings banks, but mostly it was kept 'under the pillow'. Financial transactions existed, if at all, only between industrial enterprises but as these were all state-owned and state-run, the entire field of finance had an air of unreality.

The same applied to taxes. There was little fiscal thinking comparable to that in Western Europe. Disregarding the living standard of the population and not having to reckon with its response, the state simply took what it needed. Direct taxation was insignificant and if it had been abolished altogether, it would not make the slightest difference. The state got most of its revenues from indirect taxation, through price-fixing and, ultimately, by manipulating the currency supply. This is why the Soviet currency had an even more fictitious value than that of Petrine Russia and, as before, the system could operate only in strictest isolation from foreign markets.

'Any competition is incompatible with the principle of planning. There is therefore little incentive to produce more and better goods. The traditional extensive approach to work is still commonplace. There is also no need for advertising. Instead, artificial stimulants of political character, like the "Stakhanovite movement" are currently used and compulsion, direct or indirect, is inherent in the system.'[2]

The last attempt to bring in foreign experts in their numbers – and foreign capital – was the NEP period of the early 1920s. After that suspicion prevailed, and Russia closed her borders to foreigners of whom all were, in the eyes of the authorities, potential or real spies. But the need for foreign know-how was neither satisfied nor removed. Since then until the present-day expert knowledge had to be obtained by espionage or purchase – more often by espionage.

The reasons for Russia's failure to catch up must be explained. Russian towns were never self-governing bodies. Their inhabitants were bonded serfs working mostly on government orders. The reasons why crafts could not develop and differentiate had already been discussed. The system of economy run by the government did not allow for any initiative from below – there were no independent bodies or free individuals, nor was there any room for such initiative. Improvement and innovation became possible only when the government realised the necessity of it and provided the appropriate means to put it into practice.

It is quite obvious that the government, in any period of history, could come to such decision only when pressed by events – that is, trying to catch up with a necessity which had already arisen instead of anticipating it. This policy of satisfying only existing needs had the inevitable drawback that it could not allow for the creation of any reserve pool of skills and capacities. And when all existing resources, home-bred or imported, were tied up with satisfying the actual pressing requirements, there was nothing left to anticipate what other requirements there maybe in the future. State management of the economy could be seen as the main, if not the only, reason for the continuing relative backwardness of Russia.

But state management on such a scale as in the USSR could be possible only if the whole nation had been conditioned to accept it and to live with it. The main purpose of this book has been to demonstrate that this was precisely the case of Russia, where no other system had ever existed. Even in her most Europeanised and liberal period around the turn of the twentieth century state management of whole branches of economy and state running of whole industries was accepted as natural and even beneficial. After the Revolution nationalisation and state planning found the people psychologically ready. There had been little room for private initiative before, so people just continued to live on as they were used to – in the obedient, passive, extensive way the Russian villagers had lived under their warrior lords for the past centuries.

It must be added that the new 'warrior élite' that under the Soviets took over the management of the economy were not entrepreneurs but administrators. They, too, lacked initiative, they were not materially interested in improvements and profits, and acted only when pressed by events. They were not willing to take risks, they were prone to avoid and shift responsibility, and when pressed for results they usually found compulsion to be the easiest way to achieve them. This, again, was completely within the Russian way of doing things and did not provoke any resistance or criticism from below.

Lack of free labour was one of the chief obstacles in the industrialisation of nineteenth century Russia. Some of the factories were owned and operated by the state, and were manned by state peasants who were simply assigned to work there instead of in the fields. Merchants operated other factories, and state peasants were attached to them as 'possessional workers'. They were, in fact, industrial serfs, but belonged to a factory, not to an individual.[3] It seems quite obvious that in such establishments the role of the merchant running the factory was hardly more than that of a manager responsible ultimately to the state, who supplied him with essentials like labour, credit and, in most cases, also with raw materials from state-run mines and forests, and from imports.

Other industries were set up on estates of gentry and used serf labour as well. 'Capitalist' factories using free labour existed alongside the possessional and manorial ones but were mostly able to operate on a limited scale only. Free labour for industry and agriculture was in short supply, and the situation began to change only in the late 1850s, shortly before the abolition of serfdom.

From this brief survey it can be deduced that state management played a decisive role in Russian industry from the very start; private initiative, on the contrary, was very limited. It was tolerated rather than encouraged, and the state always kept powerful control over it through legislation and finance. The similarity with Turkey is, again, striking.

'[...] the doctrine that "the state must take charge" was, in a country like Turkey, an easy and familiar one, well in accord with the inherited traditions and habits of both the rulers and the ruled. To the Kemalist régime, authoritarian, bureaucratic and paternalistic, the idea of state direction and control in economic life came as a natural and obvious extension of the powers, prerogatives and functions of the governing élite. If economic development were really necessary, it would be undertaken by those who were responsible, in this as in all else, for the safety and well-being of the nation. It was far too important to be left to infidel businessmen and ignorant peasants.'

'Étatism thus meant, in effect, the intervention of the state as a pioneer and director of industrial activity, in the interest of national development and security, in a country where private enterprise was either suspect of ineffective.'[4]

From the labour point of view, there was scarcely one generation, prior to the Revolution, of an industrial working class with any experience of organisation and industrial bargaining. Trade unionism was extremely weak. 'In 1907 its membership is estimated to have amounted approximately to 245,555 workers – about one-seventh of industrial labour – divided among 652 unions. Only six unions had more than five thousand members. Three hundred and forty-nine unions had less than one hundred members.'[5]

There was hardly time for the Russian worker to develop any spirit of class-consciousness, solidarity and cohesion. This, in turn, could explain the easy success of the Bolshevik theory and of their revolutionary methods – or rather the lack of resistance against them. They were dealing with an inexperienced mass, largely illiterate, pliable under pressure, with no class traditions and little cohesion, conditioned by centuries to respect authority and to act on command. As Herzen wrote in 1871, 'the masses required apostles, men whose faith, will, convictions and force coincide perfectly with their own [...]. The masses want a social government that will govern for them, and not against them, as at present. To govern themselves – this idea never occurs to them.'[6]

Given the right approach, the right kind of revolutionary propaganda coupled with strong leadership and tight organisation, the Russian workers did not fail to respond. In this the Bolsheviks were noticeably more successful than the Mensheviks, who used Western-style political methods. It is perhaps worth noting that the Mensheviks were most successful in Trans-caucasia, the Ukraine, and the Western provinces, in countries with a longer tradition of settled and urban civilisation, with a stronger cultural cohesion, and with a higher degree of literacy – which is exactly the opposite of Russia proper. In 1907, for example, a line drawn from Astrakhan to St. Petersburg separated the Menshevik areas to the West from the Bolshevik areas to the east.[7]

The Mensheviks 'placed greater trust in the spontaneity of mass action, and therefore thought and worked in terms of a broad party organisation embracing all forms of proletarian mass action, even though it might entail the sacrifice of some degree of party control. Lenin and the future Bolsheviks, on the other hand [...] remained distrustful of untrained spontaneous mass action, fearing constantly that it might degenerate into contentment with the struggle for immediate economic aims. Hence the strictest party control would always remain essential.'[8]

Russian trade-unionism never acquired the characteristic of a labour movement protecting the interests of one class against those of another. After the Revolution the Bolsheviks had no problems in creating a system of nationwide trade unions and integrating it into the machinery of the state as yet another Party and government agency.

Industrialisation led to a rapid growth of the urban population. When the first Russian census was taken in 1897, 106 million people lived in the villages and 18 million in the towns. In 1968 the situation was about 130 million in the towns, while the rural population figure remained the same at 106 million. Of the urban population some 100 million lived in urban developments of the last forty years.[9, 10]

With housing, service facilities and public transport lowest on the list of priorities for most of that time, overcrowding became a problem of unmanageable proportions. Until about 1960 the flats in new state housing were let and in part designed on the principle of one room per family. This was rather in line with the traditional Russian housing: village houses seldom had more than one room which was shared by the whole family, but without the alleviating effect of nature and open spaces the town-dwellers were probably worse off.

Tight control over the individual remained a feature of urban life as much as it was in the villages. Moving into town did not mean that the individual escaped the supervisory power of the commune. He merely exchanged it for a similar supervision by various urban bodies. 'A large housing block or cluster of small blocks or a street of older housing teems with a variety of social organisations, such as a parents' committee connected with the local school, a comradely court for settling quarrels between tenants, etc. In the past few years almost all the new housing and much of the older type of flats have acquired house committees'. The field of responsibility of a house committee is nothing less than the entire social and private life of the occupants. Since the committees operate in large housing units of several hundred and sometimes several thousand families, there are 'stair' or 'entry' councils elected by each group of families. In some places the auxiliary militia detachment based on a housing block has one or two members resident on every stairway that can summon their comrades when necessary or call in the regular militia. In practice the house committees are subservient to the local party organisations. 'By a curious law of 1956, which resuscitated an old Russian tradition, the street committees, and similarly the house committees, when they came into being in 1959, were empowered to convene mass meetings of inhabitants which could order by simple vote the exiling of any neighbour considered to be an "idler" or "parasite". This power was modified in 1965.'[11]

This clearly repeated the age-old pattern of village life with its collective responsibility, mutual aid and control over the individual by a body which, although nominally elected by the members of the community, was in fact responsible to some higher authority. To serve in this body was more a duty than a privilege and was often imposed by the authority. The overall aim was that every aspect of private life was controlled by some such body which would submit reports of it to the authority and, conversely, would transmit the wishes or orders of that authority to the individuals and would be responsible for them being carried out.

Chapter 51

The militarised economy

It has been noted above that Russian imperialism always had a military character – which it owed to its nomadic past. This did not change at all in the Soviet era. It became, if anything, even more pronounced. Under Stalin the entire economy was geared to provide the necessary resources for the military. The prime purpose of the rapid industrialisation and its accent on the heavy industry was to create an industrial base capable of enhancing the country's military potential.[1]

With an economy managed by the government from a single power centre, two factors are highly important to determine its nature: its aims and its methods. Inevitably, a state-run economy must reflect the political objectives of the government. Given the universalistic character of Russian Communism and the complete identification of Party and state, the sole purpose of the economy was to provide an adequate power-base for the politics of the Party. This power was seen in Russia mainly in military terms. Unlike the Western states, there seemed to be little understanding for pure economic power of the state, commercial or financial. Commercially and financially, Russia would not consider herself a super-power; it was her military might which gave her this status. This in a way was quite natural. 'In spite of her vast natural resources, including a wealth of gold, Russia's economy taken out of its protective isolation would prove fundamentally weak.'

After 1991 it became obvious that the value of her currency was artificial and in a state-run economy like hers, the relations of prices and wages, and in fact all economic relations, including employment, had to be necessarily artificial. 'How this system would behave if the barriers separating it from the outside world were removed, is anybody's guess; but the very existence and persistence of these barriers show the government's concern that the country's economy would not be able to compete on equal terms with that of other industrialised countries. This is why Russia's foreign trade must be based on barter, why foreign capital is not allowed into the country (there are a few exceptions, all tightly supervised by the government) and why so much importance is attached to industrial espionage.'[2]

But safe behind the barriers the economy was nonetheless strong enough to sustain the biggest military machine in the world. Everything in the huge economic apparatus was geared to this one purpose only, from direct army supplies to ideological industries like publishing, broadcasting or film-making. In fact, the state and the military machine were identical. The military character of Soviet institutions has been discussed above. The military nature of the economy was complementary to it. The aim being the enhancement of the military power of the state, all economic planning evolved from it. And because every aspect of economic life had to be planned and nothing could exist outside the planned system, this made the aim of military power paramount. There was no room for luxuries or idleness. The armed forces and their requirements, manpower, research, equipment and the like were only one obvious, visible part of the machine. Their position of priority was beyond doubt. The rest may seem like a theoretical construction, but it will become more understandable if the methods of economic planning and of the actual running of the economy are examined.

The entire system was, in fact, a command structure, not dissimilar from an army. The very term 'business' was unknown in Russia. A Russian employee, for instance, never travels 'on business'; he travels on *komandirovka*, that is, on command. Business presumes two equal partners negotiating a deal. In Russia there was no equal partnership and no negotiation. There was only command from above and obedience from below. Even partners on an equal level, one state enterprise buying from another, were acting on command, by the plan's directives. Industrial production was fixed by decree, both financially and in volume. The producing enterprise had little influence on prices of its products; accumulation, which was the socialist equivalent of profit, was fixed by the plan and investment in capital equipment also had to be included in the plan and sanctioned by the central authorities.

Similarly, the farmers in state or collective farms were told by the plan what crops to sow and where, what animals to raise, etc., and the prices they could sell them for. Transportation was also subject to planning, to such extent that, in some areas, to send a parcel by rail – an unplanned action – required a special permit.

Mobility of labour was also planned and enforced or restricted by command. Here more direct coercion than pure economic planning was sometimes required. For example, peasants were not allowed to leave the land; they were not even permitted to travel outside their village without a special passport. School leavers, especially graduates, were 'distributed' to jobs according to the plan. Professionals, like doctors and teachers, were posted where they were needed, and there was no question of disobeying the order. Special 'actions' with political undertones, like the Virgin Lands campaign, were, officially, voluntary, but there was a good deal of pressure and command behind the scene to get the people to the places where they were wanted. Admission to higher education and apprenticeships in less popular jobs were filled by command.

The service industries being the least important for the military objectives of planning were the most neglected. Recreational facilities were recognised only as means to maintain and restore the working potential of the people. Entertainment was primarily designed to keep up 'the fighting morale of the people', in other words, to serve the ideological propaganda purposes of the state and the Party. Consumption was manipulated by the planning mechanism, too; the State Planning Board, according to the requirements of the State, directed from above the supplies of goods as well as the choice.

The reverse of the command is the sanction; and, indeed, a whole system of sanctions, economic and legal, accompanied the command system of planned economy. Non-fulfilment of planned quotas was punished by the withdrawal of bonuses; managers were held personally responsible for the fulfilment of quotas and if they failed, they faced political reprimand with

U.S.S.R. in Europe and Asia - 1962

Arct

NORWAY
★ Oslo

SWEDEN

Stockholm

W. GERMANY

E. GER
★ Berlin

FINLAND
Helsinki

● Murmansk

POLAND

R.S.F.S.R.

Riga

Leningrad

● Archangel

Vorkuta ●

Salekhard

UKRAINIAN SSR

Minsk
BELARUSIAN SSR

ESTONIAN SSR
LATVIAN SSR
LITHUANIAN SSR

Smolensk

Kalinin
(Tver)

● Vologda

RUMANIA

Kiev

Moscow

Tula

Gorkii

● Kotlas

U R A L   M O U N T A I N S

MOLDAVIAN SSR

Kharkov

Kazan

Perm'

Sverdlovsk

Odessa

Penza

Saratov

Ufa

Sevastopol

Donetsk

Kuibyskev

Chelyabinsk

S O V I E

Krasnodar

Rostov-
on-Don

Stalingrad

Chkalov
(Orenburg)

Orsk

R U S S I A N

Omsk

Novosibir

Black Sea

★ Ankara

Astrakhan

Barn

TURKEY

GEORGIAN SSR

Tiflis

ARMENIAN SSR

Caspian Sea

KAZAKH SSR

Baku

Aral Sea

Lk Balkhash

AZERBAIJAN SSR

UZBEK SSR

Baghdad ★

Krasnovodsk

IRAQ

Tehran ★

TURKMEN SSR

Tashkent

Frunze

Alma-Ata

Bokhara

Andizhan

Fergana

KYRGYZ SSR

Dushanbe

IRAN

Persian G

TAJIK SSR

AFGHANISTAN

WEST
PAKISTAN

INDIA

FEDERATED SOCIALIST REPUBLIC

Ocean

Tiksi

Verchojansk

ilsk

Orotukan

Magadan

KAMCHATKA

Petropavlovsk

Ochotsk

Jakutsk

Pacific Ocean

Nikolaevsk

SAKHALIN

Aldan

Sovetskaja Gavah

Kirensk

Skovokomno

Khabarovsk

Krasnoiarsk

Lake Baikal

Chita

Harbin

Vladivostok

vo

uznetsk

Irkutsk

Ulan-Ude

JAPAN

Ulaanbaatar

N. KOREA

S. KOREA

JAPAN

MONGOLIA

Beijing

qi

Baotou

CHINA

Areas acquired by Russia since 1939 (after W.W.II)

Countries under communist control

Principal railways in U.S.S.R.

N

© Airphoto International Ltd.

political repercussions in their political and civil career; even individual workers could be held responsible for wastage and faulty work. A whole range of political, less straightforward sanctions could be attached to economic misdemeanours; from the loss of place on a waiting list for accommodation to demotion and transfer.

Economic planning brought also a set of new legal sanctions ranging from sabotage to misappropriation of state property (which could be anything, bricks, cement, factory tools, typing paper or petrol in a 'borrowed' truck). Collective responsibility was applied to the fulfilment of the plan, on which the bonuses and other rewards depended. As in the Byzantine system of old, this brought with it an air of suspicion, mutual watching and compulsion.

The equation of economic and military power is not new. The tsarist minister Witte was well aware of their close relationship when he argued that 'even the military preparedness of a country is determined not only by its level of military organisation but also by the degree of development of its industry'.[3]

The Communist state brought this idea to its logical conclusion by subordinating the economy completely to the objectives of the military, by equating the state with the fighting machine, and by concentrating all economic management in the same hands as the management of the state and of the army – in those of the Party. By doing this, it reverted to the age-old system of the nomads, where in primitive conditions the ruler (the khan), being the personification of the state, was also the supreme commander of the army and the supreme controller of the entire economy.

This system influenced, as it was, by the Byzantine way of combined state enterprise and state control existed in Russia throughout her history. There were periods of relaxation and others of increased rigidity. On the whole, it may be said that whenever the central power weakened, the system of state control tended to relax and alien elements, like private enterprise or foreign capital, crept in. On the contrary, when the central power was strong, state control stiffened and all alien elements were expelled or destroyed.

PART 5D

DECLINE & FALL

Chapter 52

the coLLapse

If we compare the disintegration of the Ottoman Empire with that of the Romanovs and the Soviets, some interesting parallels can be drawn. First, military parallels. In its long decadence in the nineteenth century the Turkish Empire was unable to cope with the Russian military challenge for at least three reasons. Its fiscal system did not produce enough revenue to meet the requirements of a military build-up; its transport system was woefully inadequate; and the training and equipment of its troops was hopelessly outdated.

The second reason was the inefficient and corrupt bureaucracy subservient to and dependent on the sultan and his court, which was unable to marshal the country's potential when it was needed. The religious establishment was influential enough to thwart the reforming attempts of the sultan, if and when such attempts were made – as, for example, under Selim III – and these were quickly followed by a tightening-up again of the central power under Mehmed II.

But the biggest challenge to the régime came from the non-Turkish nationalities in the Balkans starting with the Serbian uprising and the Greek war of independence. The universal ambitions of the sultanate ended when the sultan's army was twice pushed back from Vienna. With the autonomy of Serbia and the independence of Greece the Turks suddenly found themselves on equal terms with other, previously subject nationalities. Another blow to the Turkish pride was when non-Muslims, Christians and Jews, were granted equality with the Muslims.

The disintegration of the empire led to the emancipation of the outlying non-Turkish provinces into separate states. In Turkey proper the non-Turkish minorities were subject to occasional harassment and even brutalities, whether Christian (Armenians) or Muslim (Kurds).

When the sultan's power was no longer unchallenged, splits appeared among the 'warrior élite' and, although centrifugal tendencies were resisted and more of less brutally suppressed, no formula was found to keep the régime afloat.

Eventually, the sultan was forced to grant a constitution, but this did not mean in any way an abandonment of centralised power, merely a change of a ruling élite. When the sultanate was abolished in 1922, the caliphate was maintained for some time, on condition that the caliph will be chosen from 'the House of Osman'. When the caliphate itself was abolished in 1924, the Turks lost the 'leadership of the Muslim world' and there were fears among the religious opposition that Turkey will become just 'another small and insignificant country'.

In the words of Mustafa Kemal 'the sons of Osman seized the caliphate by force and kept this usurpation for six centuries [...] the Turkish nation has now chased the usurpers to keep the sovereignty and the sultanate in its own hands [...].'[1]

After a short period of chaos when the sultan was deposed and a republic proclaimed, the appearance of a strongman marked the return, in a more modern guise, to the traditional pattern of authoritarian rule. Up to the present the path to democracy has been slow and hesitant with the military playing an important backstage role with frequent seizures of power.

A similar pattern characterised nineteenth-century Russia. The reform period of Alexander II was followed by a stiffening of autocracy under Alexander III and only the defeat in 1905 led to half-hearted attempts at decentralisation and constitutional government. The Orthodox Church was just as conservative and opposed to reforms as the Muslim *ulema* in Turkey. Ignorance of the outside world was the same in both countries; the first critical voices and attempts at reforms appeared when travel restrictions were eased, and also when some educational reforms were introduced – prompted, in both cases, by the need to improve the military efficiency by means of enhancing its technological and industrial performance.

Compared with the Turks, the Russians were considerably more advanced militarily, but when in the Crimean War and again in 1905 against Japan they met with a modern well-trained and well-equipped military machine, their own inadequacy and backwardness became obvious – and nowhere more than in the naval battle off Tsushima where the entire Russian fleet was sunk because it was out-gunned by the Japanese.

In their last phase, both the Ottoman and the Romanov empires had an emerging, weak middle class. In Russia it was wiped out after the Revolution. The Soviet period produced no middle class of independent entrepreneurs, businessmen, professionals, etc. Instead, there appeared a Party-dependent service class of bureaucrats, managers, officers and policemen.

Romanov Russia, too, had its share of nationality problems, especially in Poland, where national uprisings happened in 1830 and 1863, and in the Caucasus, where a guerrilla war was virtually permanent. In the brief period between the collapse of the Romanov Empire and the establishment of the Soviet one, most of the non-Russian provinces made an attempt to gain independence. Some succeeded, like Finland, Poland and the Baltic states, others were reconquered by the Red Army and incorporated into the new-old empire.

The Soviet decline followed a remarkably similar pattern. National 'deviations' in East Germany, Poland, Hungary, Czechoslovakia and again in Poland were suppressed, in the cases of Hungary and Czechoslovakia by a military intervention. Then came the defeat in Afghanistan, which brought about the unravelling of the whole system. It became clear that the Soviet military machine was not up to its task, mainly because it could not deploy masses of troops and armour, and had to sustain an extended period of a guerrilla warfare for which it was neither equipped nor trained.

President Reagan's star-wars project only added to the problem. To match it, massive investment in research and advanced technology was needed for which there simply were no means. To provide them, the government started printing money thereby creating a phenomenon unknown in the planned economy, namely inflation.[2]

An overhaul became imperative, but the economy had to be overhauled first. That required a relaxation of the Party control, less rigidity in planning, and more room for factory managers to run their enterprises. This was resented and opposed by the Party élite, the *nomenklatura*, which felt its position in running the state would be threatened.

Like the long stagnation under Abdul Hamid, the long inertia of the Brezhnev period exacerbated the need for reform. But Gorbachev and his 'young Turks' were first reluctant to weaken the Party grip, and tried to limit their reforms to the economy. However, it quickly became clear that an economic reform was not possible without a reform of the Party and its role in the state. *Perestroika* was followed by *Glasnost*, but it seems that Gorbachev was well aware of the risks involved – and, indeed, it proved that democratising Communism was a contradiction in terms. The system could only function as a centralised dictatorship and once this monopoly of power was dropped, the régime collapsed.

'If, in the end, Communism collapsed like a house of cards, it was because it had always been a house of cards.'[3] But when Malia says 'that an ostensibly advanced industrial nation and superpower should collapse without any large-scale military defeat, after forty-five years of peace, and essentially from internal causes, is unheard of in modern history',[4] he is right only insofar as modern history is concerned. In reality, the collapse of the Soviet empire is a classical case of a disintegration of a nomadic empire where internal causes affecting the monopoly of power were always the prime mover. A military defeat was instrumental only to the extent that it provided reasons to question or attack that monopoly, but it was, by itself, not a cause. Splits within the ruling élite, its inability to defend and keep its hold on power, the distance of the 'inner circle' from the wider service class – which, compared with the rest, ceased to be 'poor' – these were the real causes of collapse and disintegration in ancient, medieval or modern nomadic empires alike. 'The Union was in fact a fraud, an agency, not of its members, but of the Party – and with the Party gone there was no force capable of holding the Union together.'[5]

...and after

After the fall of Gorbachev, the Yeltsin decade was marked with decentralisation and liberalisation on one side, and with chaos, corruption and financial bankruptcy on the other. In the field of economics, commerce, services and small businesses took off rather well; industrial enterprises, which lost their captive markets, were mostly unable to cope with foreign competition when imports became liberalised. Exports were limited to raw materials as virtually the only source of hard currency.

The biggest drawback, however, was the inability of the government to solve the perennial problem of land ownership. Since 1991 private ownership of land has been a classic Russian muddle. A presidential decree of 1993 laid out some basic rules, but a proper land code has never been voted, although, at the time of writing, one is about to be debated by the Duma. Strong vested interests are lined up against it. For the bureaucracy, land is a big source of power and money; for local leaders it means patronage and control to which successful private farming is seen as a threat. 'For the people, land reform is still largely an emotional question. The old, traditional attitude to land as "belonging to all" is still very much alive and so is fear that individual ownership would bring "land-grabbing" from some and impoverishment for all the rest.'[6]

The absence of a financial and banking sector represented another problem for the reformers. The liberalisation of foreign trade showed the fictitious value of the currency, and a succession of imprudent budgets led to the financial crisis of 1998. This, in turn, resulted in cash shortages in most of rural Russia, when the tax collection did not bring in the revenues it was supposed to. The tax laws permitted too much avoidance and evasion, and the state sector, still too large and uncompetitive, could not even pay wages to its employees. Banks were insufficiently regulated and allowed to take on too many bad debts. It is true that the government had to build everything from scratch – having dismantled the system of planned economy, there was nothing to build on, no precedent, no base, and no experience. The European ex-satellites could, to some extent at least, turn to their older legislation, revive their older commercial and tax codes, and adapt them to new circumstances, but in Russia there was nothing of that sort. (This writer remembers that in Czechoslovakia before 1990 there were only two banks, one for internal and one for external businesses, the cheque was an unknown instrument, and people were paid with a bundle of notes every fortnight; no wonder that banks sprouted up like mushrooms and wilted just as quickly.)

Politically, Yeltsin acted radically banning the Party and confiscating its property. This deprived the *nomenklatura* of its power position and pushed it into the arms of radical opposition while in the administration and management, wholly inexperienced people now occupied positions of responsibility. The inevitable result was incompetence, corruption, and, where old cadres stayed in place, only lukewarm implementation of government policies. In the field of legislation, government bills were often emasculated or thrown out by a recalcitrant Duma.

At the time of writing a reappearance of a strongman is again on the cards, just like in Turkey in the 1920s. The tendency to strict centralisation is again gaining ground. People from the security establishments, from the KGB and the army, are appointed to top government posts, arrests and trials smack again of lawlessness. The expansion of state control over the media brings about a 'state of lies'. 'The great lie calls Russia a democratic state'; 'Brought up on lies a society cannot mature.'[7]

In the field of administration, the creation of the *okrugs* headed by government appointees and overseeing provincial governors, the standardising of the constitutions of the national republics, the limiting of the functions of the federal assembly etc., all point again to the restoration of an all-powerful, centralised state. On top of this the protracted and inconclusive Chechen war risks to become another stumbling block in the government's credibility build-up.

History seemed to repeat itself. Again, like at the time of the NEP, foreign experts were called in to advise the government bodies, joint ventures with Western companies were sought (and rarely implemented), foreign managers were called to run Russian enterprises. Foreign loans were requested and readily granted. And yet, after ten years of efforts, *The Economist*, in its excellent and revealing Survey, paints a discouragingly gloomy picture of Russia, both of its present and its near future. And many of its observations seem to prove that the country still is basically the same as it was throughout its history, that little has changed in its mentality, its organisation, its government practices, its social and economic make-up. The authors of this Survey see three contradictory trends in today's Russia – revival, stagnation, and an accelerated decline. The country still has little experience of the rule of law, of private property, and of public participation. In some fields such as tax, security, police and public prosecutors, the government had some success in re-centralising these services and bringing them under control, but bureaucracy still remains the biggest single obstacle to growth and democracy. As in the past, the system works from top to bottom, criticism is discouraged sometimes violently – the media mostly toe the official line for which they are given direct guidance: 'the rule of law is so hazy that even a hermit could be jailed or bankrupt'.

Xenophobia is, entirely within old traditions, state-sponsored and contact with foreigners can be risky. Even in the Academy of Sciences all dealings with foreigners must be cleared in advance. The official attitude seems to be that 'Russia is too big and too backward to be governed exactly like a Western country. Democracy must be managed. The first requirement is order and authority,' and elsewhere, 'Russia is not ready for Western standards of justice. The mentality is different, the perception of justice is different, the respect for law is not the same.'

Aside from its prediction of a slow but accelerating decline in the economy, the 2001 Survey's forecast of an increasing authoritarianism in politics – which would make Russia, it claimed, 'a weaker country with a rather stronger state'[8] – was confirmed by a further in-depth Survey conducted in July 2006: 'Russia's curious path under Mr Putin – assertiveness and paranoia in foreign policy, centralised yet weak government – can perhaps be explained best by an old truth, that Russia is more an empire than a state, its rulers haunted by the fear that their domain will fall apart. Plenty of evidence, such as the widespread admiration for Stalin, suggests that many Russians share Mr Putin's evident belief that authoritarianism is the way to hold the place together. If that ancient conviction is right, and Russia is constitutionally unsuited to democracy, many of its failings are forgivable... Unfortunately, in a country where elections are only a way to legitimize choices made in the Kremlin, it is Mr Putin who will decide who and what follow him if he leaves office...'[9]

As at the time of Peter the Great, Europe is seen primarily as a source of modernisation rather than a model for government and a rule of law.

And, last but not least, there is still the problem of nationalities. All non-Russian nations on the fringe of the Soviet Empire have established independent states – most of them petty dictatorships entirely within their old pre-Russian and pre-Soviet traditions. The only exceptions are – again within their tradition – the three Baltic republics.

All the others have reverted to the Oriental-style despotism, based on tribal or clan loyalties with an autocratic leader who in most cases is an ex-Party boss relying on the revamped Party apparatus for his power. A market economy is allowed to operate in commerce and services, but their industrial production depends on government money, or foreign investment sanctioned by the government, and land ownership is left in a legal limbo. Not too different from the Oriental despotism of bygone days.

But there are still many non-Russian nationalities within Russia – some larger ones who have obtained a degree of autonomy, such as Bashkortostan and Tatarstan, some who are actively seeking it, such as some Caucasian nationalities, and finally those who, like the Chechens, try to break away altogether. What the feelings are among, for example, the Yakuts with their vast and rich territory in Siberia, or the small ones like the Chuvash, the Mordva, and Kalmuks and scores of others, is at the moment difficult to say. What is highly likely, however, is that the question of nationalities is not safely dead and buried, but will play an important role in the country's future. Here again the aftermath of the Ottoman Empire comes to mind: the perennial

Kurdish problem within modern Turkey and the passions and violence among the Albanians, the Bosnians, and the Serbs outside it.

In recent years political ideology in Russia seems to be looking again for inspiration – and, in some respect, to guidance – in Eurasianism. With the collapse of the USSR, Eurasianism reappeared as a doctrine capable of replacing Bolshevism. On the extreme right of the Russian political spectre Russo-centric geopolitics see both Europe and Asia as 'peripheral territories' which must become strategic allies, but culturally must be rejected. For example, Islamic fundamentalism, an enemy of the West, anti-materialistic and anti-liberal, is seen as an important ally. It provides also a ready source of ideas capable of being applied to Russia. Here meet some Russian Islamists ('Islamisation is the only way to prevent Russia's disappearance from the geopolitical map') and neo-Eurasianists, like Vladimir Zhirinovsky ('The best solution would be to divide the spheres of influence along the North-South line [...]. To revive the empire and to re-establish herself as a continent, Russia must expand to the warm seas west and south [...]'). In the eyes of the Eurasianists the priority must be to create a geopolitical alternative to atlanticism.[10]

Against these ideas the new nationalists proclaim that Russia must isolate herself from all Islamic influence, the Caucasian Muslims should be granted independence, and that the main enemy is Turkey. Russia's position is incompatible with a European balance of power.[11]

However, some observers believe that the influence of the Eurasianists is becoming more important than that of the nationalists. Eurasianism, having, in a way, absorbed and replaced Marxism, provides an ideological base for post-Soviet imperialism, whereas the weak spot of the nationalists is that they do not know where Russia's frontiers are, or ought to be.[12]

It remains to be seen if Russia will follow the Turkish model of a slow road towards democracy, perhaps with some nationalistic excesses and military-style interludes, or if it will follow in the footsteps of the Eurasianists towards a more totalitarian, Oriental type of 'sultanism'. [13]

afterthought

Since I first finished my manuscript five years ago, several things happened both in Russia proper and in what the Russians began to call 'the near-abroad', that is in the former parts of the Soviet Union which split off from the empire and became more or less independent. I say 'more or less', because there is a marked tendency in Russia's politics to maintain her influence in those territories and, wherever possible, to increase it using methods ranging from economic blackmail and diplomatic pressure to downright military and strong-arm tactics. It is too early for an historian to draw any valid conclusions from what essentially are no more than journalistic reports and eye-witness accounts (including my own), without any deeper analysis of current or emerging trends and their possible hidden meaning. Nevertheless I would like to bring my book up to date knowing full well that tomorrow some new event can turn my opinion upside down – so everything that I write must be taken with reserve.

The proof that the old imperial thinking and its geopolitical motivation still persist, are the four enclaves of Russian, or ex-Russian territory in or between the newly independent states, which serve to keep Russian influence and her military presence still alive. Kaliningrad (ex-Königsberg) between Poland and Lithuania, a former Hanseatic city and an important port on the Baltic, is 'impoverished, disease-ridden and a prime business location for smugglers and other criminals.'[1] It is linked with Russia by a tenuous transit corridor based on an agreement which will have to be renegotiated should the two neighbouring countries, both now EU members, join the Schengen agreement of free movement of persons. The one attempt to boost the enclave's faltering economy is the project of the Baltic pipeline linking Russia and Germany (and by-passing Poland, to that country's annoyance).

Transdnistria is a strip of land between Moldova and Ukraine, formally a part of Moldova, where Russia keeps in power a separatist regime; it has no viable economy and is wholly dependent on subsidies (and on organised crime). On the territory of Georgia, two enclaves, Abkhazia and South Ossetia, former autonomous regions of the Soviet Republic of Georgia, have declared independence and allied themselves with Russia.[2] This led to a vast exodus of Georgians who represented a substantial part of the population, and a complete economic dependence on their big protector. Sukhumi, the capital of Abkhazia and once a prosperous Black Sea resort, has lost all its former economic assets – harbour activity, tourism and trade with its Georgian hinterland.

South Ossetia, with a kindred population on the north side of the Caucasus, is mostly Christian while the Ossetians of the north are partly Muslims. However, there is no love lost between them and their Georgian co-religionists who are ethnically and linguistically different and are regarded by the Ossetians as opressors. Economically, South Ossetia is a poor agrarian country whose only viable exports used to be grapes and fruit.

The relations with non-Russian peoples inside Russia are also far from settled. The larger ones, being Muslim, were all seeking some kind of independence, but while Daghestan and Bashkortostan eventually accepted a degree of autonomy, Tatarstan and Chechnya opted for secession. Tatarstan, which is completely surrounded by Russia, finished by concluding with Russia a bilateral treaty which gave it, amongst other things, the right to international relations, use of the Tatar language and Islam as a state religion.

With Chechnya, the situation was different. Its declaration of secession was not accepted by the Russian leadership and led to a protracted war which not only claimed heavy casualties on both sides but also had wider repercussions in the spread of all kinds of criminal activity, such as smuggling, counterfeiting, drug-smuggling and mainly Islamic terrorism, when Islamists from other countries joined the Chechens and, on the other hand, Chechen fighters became involved in anti-Western terrorist actions in Afghanistan, Iraq and elsewhere. Some spectacular and bloody actions were, amongst others, the hostage-takings in a Moscow theatre, a school in Ingushetia, in a hospital in Daghestan, etc.

In her relations with the former Soviet republics which seceded from the Empire and became independent, Russia uses a variety of means to maintain her influence. One of them is the pressure Russia can exercise as an important, if not a monopoly, supplier of energy with the ever-present threat of turning off the tap in case of some 'recalcitrant' behaviour. This was, for example, the case of Ukraine after the 'Orange Revolution', which expelled the pro-Russian strongman and installed a pro-Western government (at least for the time being).

Another are the strong Russian minorities in several of the ex-republics, in particular in Latvia and Kazakhstan, but also in Estonia. The requirement to learn the local language is just one element that keeps them looking to 'Mother Russia' and makes them a potentially subversive element in the new countries.

After the confused and unsettled Yeltsin era, the presidency of Vladimir Putin marked in many ways a return to the traditional Russian way of a weak economy and a strong, centralised government with great power ambitions. 'Hardly anyone still hopes that Mr Putin can become the democrat he sometimes claims to be; even 'managed democracy' is no longer touted much'.[3] Some commentators see the most important features of his regime in the redistribution of property and in the unequal application of the law. A symbolic break with the past has been made with an attempt to free the market in agricultural land. However, the question of ownership is still unclear though a law on it now exists. There is no proper land registry and although some 90% of agricultural land is, nominally, privately owned or leased, there is no legal framework for buying and selling and therefore the land-market is small, bureaucratic and murky.[4] It is difficult, if not impossible, to consolidate small plots, borrow money using land as collateral, etc. With urban land, the situation is similar and just as confused. Russian-manufactured exports still amount to little more than guns and vodka. The bulk of her export earnings comes from oil, gas and other raw materials.[5]

The present tendency to use exports of oil and gas as tools of political pressure seems to prove the increasingly authoritarian ways of Mr Putin's government. This was most clearly manifested in the sudden increase of oil and gas prices to Ukraine in the wake of the 'Orange' revolution there (see below). The dismantling of Yukos, the largest independent oil company, the expropriation of its assets as well as the blatantly political trial of its chairman, Mr Khodorkovski, on the one hand, and the privileged position of the state owned giants, Gasprom and Rosneft, the artificially high capitalisation of Rosneft, its access to Western stock exchanges, and its likely acquisition of Yukos' remaining assets, on the other, are in their own field, symptoms of the same trend.[6]

In the field of human rights, the Orthodox Church quite recently stepped in with a declaration adopted at the World Council of the Russian peoples (4–6 April 2006). Guided, no doubt, by the Kremlin, the Metropolitan Kirill, successor designate of Patriarch Alexis II, criticised Western liberalism which 'obscures the division between Good and Evil.' Freedom of the individual leads inevitably to the negation of 'moral imperatives.' The Russian civilisation which, as everybody knows, is unique, is incompatible with political and social standards of the West. Taken straight from the *Brothers Karamazov*, the 'Declaration of the rights and the dignity of man' adopted by the Council, extols 'the supreme values of faith, morality, the sacred and the fatherland.'[7] In its spirit it is thus close to the values of the 'Official Nationality' of Nicholas I, but is also strangely reminiscent of the rejection of democracy and the rule of law in favour of 'Asian values', as declared recently by the ex-autocrat of Malaysia, Mahathir Mohammed.[8]

Turning now to the 'Near-abroad', the first attempt to keep the Empire together in a modified form was the short-lived Commonwealth of Independent States (CIS). However, the member states had different priorities which were often incompatible – some preferred to integrate into a sort of Common Market, while others wanted an opening to the outside world. Russia, which would have liked to have been the leader of the first group, used preferential prices and credit conditions to make her will prevail – which, quite naturally, led some of the republics to form groupings of which Russia was not a member.[9]

After the accession of Mr Putin whose centralising tendencies soon became felt, the CIS disintegrated. Belarus became the last and only true ally of Russia, while Ukraine veered closer to Kazakhstan and Azerbaijian, who could supply her with energy. In the Caucasus, Armenia remained loyal, counting on Russian support in her conflict with Azerbaijan over Nagorno-Karabagh, while Georgia was faced with the 'ethnic cleansing' of her citizens in Abkhazia and also with a rebellion in South Ossetia, both backed by Russia. In exchange of her territorial integrity, she had to accept on her territory four Russian military bases; the dismantling of them is now the subject of difficult negotiations.

The Central Asian republics all became quasi-hereditary fiefs of local strongmen, thus reverting to their traditional pattern of tribal or clan-based government.

Popular reaction to the pro-Russian apparatchiks who became presidents led to anti-Russian movements and eventually to revolutions. Called 'Orange' in Ukraine, 'Rose' in Georgia, they brought to power a young generation of politicians, untainted with Marxism and more open-minded towards liberal economics and free trade. Nevertheless, in Ukraine, the old division between the pro-Russian east and the pro-Western west began again to show and, at the time of writing, the pro-Russian faction, strongly helped by Russia's energy prices and other policies, seems to be gaining influence. The staunchly pro-Russian and authoritarian regime in Belarus has to cope with rising popular discontent and has to use muscular tactics to contain it.

In Kirghizstan, the so-called 'Tulip Revolution' led to a more or less non-violent change of the top personality, whereas in the other republics the authoritarian rulers seem firmly in the saddle. In Turkmenistan, the personality cult is the most blatant, comparable to the heyday of Stalinism or the leader-cult of North Korea.[10] In Kazakhstan, given the oil wealth on the one hand and the strong Russian minority on the other, the regime, although authoritarian, is more open to international relations, both economic and political. The regime in Uzbekistan, although secular, is faced with an infiltration of radical Islamists from neighbouring Tajikistan who were themselves influenced and trained by the Taliban of Afghanistan. In the Ferghana Valley this led to violent clashes and, in 2005, to a bloody skirmish in Andijan with thousands of refugees fleeing across the border into Kirghizstan.

The United States, involved militarily in Afghanistan and Iraq and faced with the nuclear threat from Iran, is paying close attention to this part of the world, which for so long has been regarded as Russia's backyard. The pipeline being built from Azerbaijan via Georgia to the Mediterranean coast of Turkey bypassing Russia; an air-base, first in Uzbekistan and, after a brush with its ruler, moved to Kirghizstan; American investment in oil-drilling and prospecting to Kazakhstan and Turkmenistan; military bases to be installed in Georgia and in Azerbaijan – all this points to an increasing involvement of the United States in the Middle East and to the weakening of Russia's influence there.[11]

It may be concluded that having lost her most Europeanised parts, the Westernising trend in Russian policies and political thinking has again, as so often in her history, been superseded by the Eastern one. With the corresponding strengthening of the Asian pull, the age-old trends and tendencies in Russian thinking have been revived. And, as Mr Putin himself put it, Islam has been accepted as an integral part of Russian history and civilisation. The nomadic and Oriental tradition could not be acknowledged more clearly. As so often before, when the Empire disintegrated, the European tendencies grew stronger, but when it revived and the centralising trends took over, the Asian and the Oriental ones reappeared.

July 2007

Present-Day Russia

NORWAY

SWEDEN

ESTONIA

LATVIA

FINLAND

Barents Sea

Kara Sea

Kaliningrad

POLAND

LITH.

Saint Petersburg

Minsk

BELARUS

Novgorod

MOLDOVA

Kiev

Moscow

UKRAINE

R. Don

R. Volga

R U

S

River Ob'

Yekaterinburg

Volgograd

Black Sea

GEORGIA

Omsk

Novosibirsk

TURKEY

ARM.

AZER.

Astana

Baku

Aral Sea

KAZAKHSTAN

Caspian Sea

L. Balkhash

UZBEKISTAN

TURKMENISTAN

IRAN

Urumqi

KYRGYZSTAN

TAJIKISTAN

AFGHANISTAN

Arctic Ocean

Baring Sea

River Lena

Magadan

A

I

Sea of Okhotsk

Yakutsk

S

River Lena

SAKHALIN

River Amur

JAPAN

L. Baikal

Irkutsk

Vladivostok

Harbin

Ulaanbaatar

N.KOREA

MONGOLIA

S.KOREA

JAPAN

Beijing

CHINA

© Airphoto International Ltd.

N

A short chronology of Russian History

compiled by Bijan Omrani

5th century AD	Settlement of Slavic peoples in the Dnieper and Volga regions
Early 9th century AD	Movement of Varangians (Vikings) from Scandanavia into Slavic territory
860	First Rus attack on Constantinople
862	Varangian Chief Rurik captures Novgorod
880	Oleg (r. c. 879–912), son of Rurik, makes Kiev his capital
882	Unity of Novgorod and Kiev
911	Constantinople grants trade concessions to Rus after Rus attacks
944	Igor of Kiev makes further treaty with Byzantium
965	Prince Sviatoslav I of Kiev (r. c. 942–972) defeats Khazars on the Lower Volga
968	Sviatoslav defeats the Bulgarians
977	Novgorod becomes independent of Kiev
988	Conversion of Grand Prince Vladimir I (r. 978–1015) to Christianity
1037	Yaroslav the Wise (r. 1019–54) begins construction of St Sophia in Kiev
1043	Construction of St Sophia begins in Novgorod
1051	Rus gains the right to elect its own church Metropolitan
1054	Split between Roman Catholic and Byzantine Churches
1103–11	Kiev victorious in campaigns against Kumans
1113	Vladimir II Monomakh (d. 1125) becomes Grand Prince
1136	First election of Posadnik (Mayor) in Novgorod
1165	Novgorod becomes an archbishopric
1169	Andrei Bogolyubsky, Prince of Suzdal-Vladimir r. c. 1157–74 captures Kiev
1223	Battle of Kalka River – first Mongol attack on Kievan Rus
1236	Alexander Nevsky (d. 1263) becomes Grand Prince of Novgorod

1237	Mongols launch full-scale invasion of Southern Russia
1240	Mongols capture Kiev
1242	Sarai established as capital of Mongol Golden Horde; Alexander Nevsky defeats Teutonic Knights on Lake Peipus
1325	Ivan I Kalita (d. 1341), grandson of Alexander Nevsky rules Moscow as Mongol vassal; becomes Grand Prince of Vladimir in 1328
1327	Anti-Mongol rebellion in Tver repressed with help of Ivan I and Moscow; Metropolitan of the Church makes Moscow permanent residence
1359	Assassination of Khan Berdi-bek leads to dynastic conflict and fragmentation of Golden Horde 1360–1380
1380	Dimitry Donskoy, ruler of Moscow 1359–89, defeats Golden Horde at Battle of Kulikovo
1382	Moscow sacked by Tokhtamysh, Khan of the Golden Horde
1391	Tamerlane defeats Tokhtamysh and sacks Golden Horde's capital, Sarai
1392	Moscow annexes Nizhny Novogorod
1453	Fall of Byzantium to Ottoman Turks
1477	Ivan III (the Great, r. 1462–1505) captures Novgorod
1480	Moscow ceases to pay tribute to Mongols; breakup of Golden Horde into smaller Khanates
1485	Moscow annexes Tver
1497	Promulgation of Sudebnik (Law Code) in Moscow
1510	Moscow annexes Pskov
1547	Ivan IV (the terrible, d. 1584) becomes ruler of Moscow; assumes title of 'Tsar'
1552	Moscow conquers Khanate of Kazan
1553	Richard Chancellor's voyage to the White Sea, and opening of commercial relations between England and Moscow
1556	Moscow conquers Khanate of Astrakhan
1564–72	Ivan IV promulgates oprichnina
1570	Expedition against Novgorod and Pskov; Ivan IV massacres opponents in Novgorod
1571	Crimean Tartars attack and sack Moscow

1598	Boris Godunov (d. 1605) becomes Tsar
1610	Poles occupy Moscow for two years
1613	Michael Romanov becomes Tsar after nomination by Zemskii sobor
1630	Establishment of Iakutsk on River Lena
1637	Don Cossacks capture Azov
1639	Cossacks reach the Pacific Coast
1647	First Cossack settlement established on the bay of Okhotsk
1649	Adoption of Ulozhenie (Law Code); Cossack expedition in Amur Basin, and first clash with Chinese troops
1652	Nikon (d. 1681) becomes Patriarch
1653	Nikon's ecclesiastical reforms
1666	Deposition of Nikon
1682	Abolition of Mestnichestvo (system of aristocratic preference)
1687–9	Attempts to capture the Crimean Khanate
1689	Treaty of Nerchinsk establishes border with China
1696	Tsar Peter I (the Great, d. 1725) becomes sole ruler; annexation of Azov
1697–8	Peter conducts grand tour of Europe
1698	Defeat of the Streltsy
1700	Swedish defeat Russian army at Battle of Narva
1703	Establishment of St Petersburg
1705	Establishment of standing army
1709	Swedish army defeated by Russians at Poltava
1712	Peter the Great moves Russian capital to Petersburg
1718	Establishment of poll tax
1721	Establishment of Spiritual college (later Holy Synod) under state control; Russia gains Baltic provinces
1722	Introduction of Table of Ranks; Ukraine deprived of autonomy
1725	Discovery of the Bering Straits
1731	Kazakhs of the Little Horde accept Russian sovereignty
1735–9	Russo-Turkish War
1756–63	Seven Years' War

1762	Charter of Nobility emancipates Russian nobility
1768–74	War with the Ottoman Empire, concluded with Treaty of Kuchuk Kainardji
1769	Russian occupation of Moldavia and Wallachia
1783	Russian annexation of the Crimea
1787–91	War with Ottoman Empire, concluded with Treaty of Jassy
1801	Russian annexation of Georgia
1804–13	Russian war against Persia, concluded with Treaty of Gulistan; Russia gains much of Caucasus, and sole navigational rights on the Caspian
1805	Battle of Austerlitz
1805–7	War against France, concluding in Treaty of Tilsit
1812	French invasion of Russia; Battle of Borodino; burning of Moscow and French defeat
1815	Congress Kingdom of Poland under Russian rule; proposal of the "Holy Alliance"
1825	Decembrist Revolt
1826–8	War with Persia, concluding in Treaty of Turkmanchai
1827–9	War with Ottoman Empire, ending with treaty of Adrianople
1830–1	Polish Revolt
1849	Russian intervention crushes uprising in Hungary
1851	Construction of Moscow-Petersburg railway line
1853–6	Crimean War against Britain and France
1858	Treaty of Aigun further demarcates Russo-Chinese border
1861	Emancipation of the serfs
1863–4	Further revolt in Poland crushed
1864	Establishment of Zemstvos; education reforms
1865–76	Russian conquest of Central Asian Khanates of Kokand and Khiva; Emirate of Bukhara turned into Russian protectorate
1874	Disturbances from Narodnik revolutionaries
1877–8	War against Ottoman Empire, concluded with Treaty of San Stefano; Congress of Berlin and discussion of Balkans
1881	Assassination of Alexander II; emergency measures in reaction
1891–4	Formation of Franco-Russian Alliance

1898	Foundation of Russian Social-Democratic Workers' Party
1899	"February Manifesto" of Tsar Nicholas II starts "Years of Oppression" in Finland
1901	Foundation of Socialist Revolutionary Party
1903	Completion of Trans-Siberian Railway
1904–5	Russo-Japanese War, concluding with Treaty of Portsmouth
1905	Bloody Sunday Massacre in St Petersburg; 1905 Revolution; October Manifesto
1906	"Fundamental Law" of Empire promulgated; State Duma established
1908	Austrian annexation of Bosnia-Herzegovina
1911	Assassination of Prime Minister Stolypin
1914	Outbreak of First World War; Russian defeat at Tannenberg
1915	Russian defeat at Galicia; loss of Poland; Tsar Nicholas assumes command of army
1916	Brusilov offensive against Austo-Hungarians; murder of Rasputin
1917	Riots in St Petersburg; Abdication of Nicholas II; Return of Lenin; Bolsheviks seize power; Cheka established
1918	Treaty of Brest-Litovsk; Murder of imperial family
1920	Russo-Polish War
1924	Death of Lenin
1925	Trotsky removed from Politburo
1927	Decision made on collectivisation of agriculture
1928	Introduction of first Five-Year Plan
1929	Exile of Trotsky
1932–4	Major Famine throughout USSR
1933	Second Five-Year Plan
1934	USSR joins League of Nations
1936–8	Major purges of army and Bolsheviks
1939	Nazi-Soviet Pact; war with Finland
1940	USSR annexes Baltic Republics and Bessarabia (Moldavia); assassination of Trotsky in Mexico
1941	Nazi Germany invades USSR; German Army repelled from Moscow; siege of Leningrad until 1944

1942	Allied alliance with USSR; Siege of Stalingrad until 1943
1943	Battle of Kursk; Stalin meets Roosevelt and Churchill at Tehran Conference; deportation of peoples from Caucasus and Crimea
1944	Red Army advances into Poland
1945	Battle of Berlin; surrender of Germany; USSR enters war against Japan
1946	Soviet attempts to generate Communist separatist movements in north-western Iran thwarted
1948–9	Blockade of Berlin
1949	Establishment of Comecon and Nato; USSR successfully detonates first atomic bomb
1950	Outbreak of Korean War
1953	Death of Stalin; end of Korean War
1954	Launch of "Virgin Lands" Program
1955	Foundation of Warsaw Pact
1956	Khrushchev's denunciation of Stalin; Hungarian uprising crushed; Suez Crisis
1957	Launch of Sputnik
1960	Breakdown in USSR-China relations
1961	Yuri Gagarin first man in space; construction of Berlin Wall
1962	Cuban missile crisis
1963	USSR signs nuclear test ban treaty; agricultural crisis results from Virgin Lands program
1964	Khrushchev succeeded by Brezhnev
1968	Red Army crushes Prague Spring uprising; promulgation of Brezhnev doctrine
1969	Armed clashes between USSR and China over border
1971	Jewish emigration permitted from USSR; USSR launches first manned space station
1975	USSR participates in Helsinki Accords on security and cooperation in Europe
1978	Georgian nationalist unrest in Tbilisi
1979	Soviet invasion of Afghanistan

1980	Western boycott of Moscow Olympics; workers unrest in Poland and establishment of Solidarity Trade Union
1981	Declaration of martial law in Poland
1982	Death of Brezhnev; succeeded by Andropov
1984	Death of Andropov; succeeded by Chernenko
1985	Death of Chernenko; succeeded by Gorbachev; introduction of Glasnost and Perestroika reforms
1986	Chernobyl disaster; nationalist rioting in Almaty
1987	Laws reforming state enterprises; unrest in Baltic republics
1988	Serious friction between Azerbaijan and Armenia over Nagorno-Karabakh
1989	Soviet troops withdraw from Afghanistan; fall of Communist regimes in Poland, Czechoslovakia, Bulgaria, Rumania; fall of the Berlin Wall; uprisings in Tbilisi suppressed.
1990	Soviet troops violently repress Azeri nationalist uprising in Baku; secession of Lithuania from USSR; Soviet blockade of Lithuania; Ukranian Parliament declares sovereignty; Armenia secedes also, and declares sovereignty over Nagorno-Karabakh; Abkhazia secedes from Georgia; reunification of Germany; abolition of media censorship
1991	Soviet troops storm official buildings in Latvia and Lithuania; secession of Georgia from USSR; dissolution of Warsaw Pact and Comecon; failure of Moscow coup attempt; Yeltsin elected executive president of Russia; Ukraine, Belarus and Moldavia secede from USSR; Communist Party of the Soviet Union dissolved; USSR dissolved and Commonwealth of Independent States (CIS) established
1992	Russian dispute with Ukraine over Black Sea Fleet; Chechen parliament declares independence; economic reforms cause serious price rises in Russia
1993	Disputes with Baltic states over former Soviet military garrisons; Yeltsin dissolves parliament after failed armed uprising; elections for a new Russian Duma; new Russian constitution
1994	Russia joins Nato "Partnership for Peace"; Russian forces invade Chechnya
1996	Yeltsin wins Russian presidential election
1997	Russia-Nato Charter

1999   Russia re-invades Chechnya again; Russian opposition to Nato bombing of Kosovo; Russian troops enter Kosovo as peacekeepers

2000   Yeltsin resigns; replaced by Putin

2001   Sino-Russian friendship treaty

2002   Last independent Russian TV station taken under effective state control; nuclear arms reduction treaty agreed with USA; formation of Nato-Russia Council; Chechen separatists hold 800 hostage in Russian theatre siege, also conduct suicide attack against pro-Moscow government in Grozny

2003   Suicide attacks against pro-Moscow interests in Chechnya and North Ossetia; other attacks elsewhere in Russia blamed on Chechens; Russian military base opens in Kyrgyzstan; border disputes with the Ukraine over Kerch Strait and Tuzla; oligarch Mikhail Khodorkovsky, an opponent of Putin, arrested on charges on tax evasion; Putin's political party, United Russia, wins landslide in parliamentary elections

2004   Putin wins second presidential term by landslide; Chechen President Akhmad Kadyrov killed by bomb in Grozny; clashes in Ingushetia blamed on Chechen rebels; assets of oil company Yukos seized by Russian government in settlement of reported tax debts – these assets are later acquired by state oil company Rosneft; further bomb attacks in Russia blamed on Chechen terrorists; 330 die in Beslan school siege

2005   Agreement with Iran over supply of nuclear fuel for Bushehr Reactor; Mikhail Khodorkovsky sentenced to nine years in a Siberian penal colony for tax evasion; Russian state gains control over giant gas company Gazprom

2006   Russia cuts gas supply to Ukraine purportedly over a pricing dispute, during attempts by the Ukraine to move away from Russian political influence; law to monitor and shut down NGOs thought to pose a threat to Russia; tension with Georgia after arrest of four Russian officers on suspicion of spying; murder of independent journalist Anna Politkovskaya in Moscow; poisoning of former security service agent Aleksandr Litvinenko in London; dispute with Belarus over price of gas supplied by Russia

2007   Oil supply to Minsk briefly cut during dispute; demonstrations against Putin in Moscow and St Petersburg broken up by riot police

Genealogy of the Russian Royal Houses – Table 1

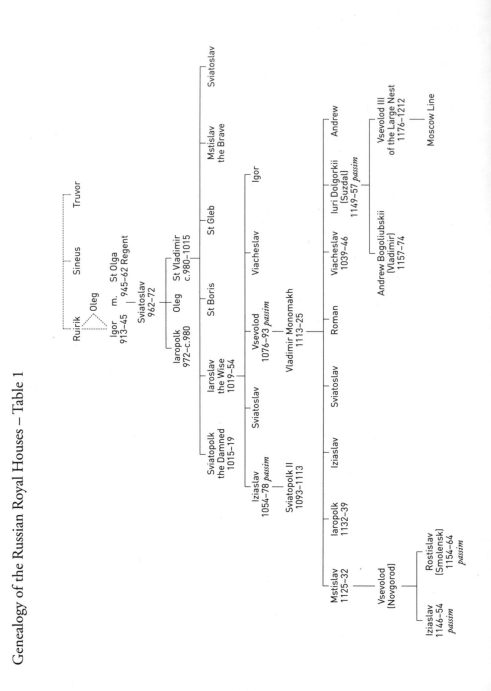

Table 2

Vsevolod III
of the Large Nest
1176–1212

Constantine Boris Iurii 1212–37 Iaroslav 1237–46 Vladimir Sviatoslav 1246–48 Ivan Gleb

Theodore Alexander Nevskii (Novgorod) 1252–63 Andrew [Suzdal] 1248–52 Iaroslav [Tver] 1264–71 Michael Khorobit 1248 Basil (Korstroma) 1272–76

Dmitrii 1277–94 Andrew 1294–1304 Daniel (Moscow) Michael 1304–19

Iurii 1319–22 Ivan I Kalita 1328–41 Alexander Athanasius Boris Dmitrii 1322–25 Alexander 1326–28

Simeon the Proud 1341–53 Ivan II, the Meek 1353–59 Andrew

Daniel Dmitrii Donskoi 1359–89

Basil I 1389–1425 Iurii

Basil II, the Blind 1425–62 Basil the Squint-eyed Dmitrii Shemiaka

Ivan III, the Great 1462–1505

Basil III m. Helen Glinskaia Regent 1533–38 1505–33

Ivan IV, the Terrible m. Anastasia Romanova 1533–84

Ivan Theodore I m. Irene Godunova 1584–98 Boris Godunov 1598–1605

Dmitrii Theodore II 1605 False Dmitrii 1605 Basil Shulsky 1606–10

Table 3

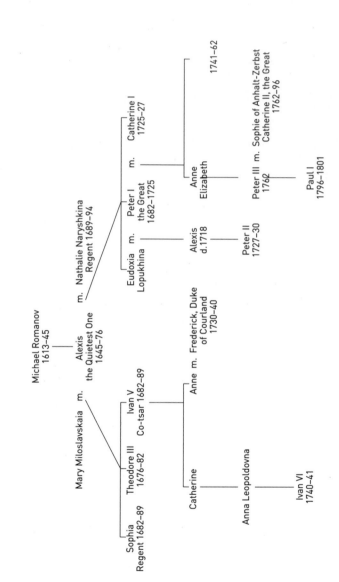

Table 4

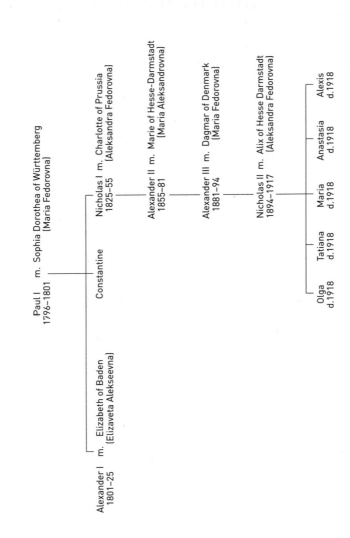

BiBLiography

Aftalion, F., *L'Alerte rouge sur l'Amerique*, Paris 2006

Alderson, A.D., *The Structure of the Ottoman Dynasty*, Oxford, 1956

Alexeev, N.N., *Geschichte und heutiger Zustand der eurasischen Bewegung, Orient und Occident*, 17/1934

Andersson, I., *History of Sweden*, English edition, London, 1955

Andreyev, *Studies in Muscovy – Western Influences and Byzantine Inheritance*, London, 1970

Anon., *A Message from Moscow*, London, 1969

Avrich, P. (ed.), *The Anarchists in the Russian Revolution*, London, 1973

Barber, N., *Seven Years of Freedom: The Hungarian Uprising*, London, 1973

Barthold, V.V., *Turkestan down to the Mongol Invasion*, London, 1928, 1958

Bautier, R.H., *The Economic Development of Medieval Europe*, London, 1971

Bawden, C.R., *The Modern History of Mongolia*, London, 1968

Beazley, C.R., *Texts and Versions of Carpini and Rubruck*, London, 1903

Becker, S., *Russia's Protectorates in Central Asia*, Harvard, 1968

Bednaříková, J., Homola, A. and Měřínský, Z., *Stěhování národů a východ Evropy* (Migrations of Peoples and the East of Europe), Prague 2006

Beranová, M., *Zemědělství starých Slovanů* (Agriculture of Ancient Slavs), Prague, 1980

Bláhová, M. et al., *Pokračovatelé Kosmovi* (The Continuators of Cosmas), Prague, 1974

Bloch, M., *Feudal Society*, London, 1961

Blum, J., *Lord and Peasant in Russia*, Princeton, 1961

Boháček, M., *Scritti in onore di Contardo Ferrini*, Milan, 1949

Boroovka, G.I., *Scythian Art*, London, 1928

Bosl, K., F. Seibt, M.M. Postan, F. Graus and A. Gieysztor, *Eastern and Western Europe in the Middle Ages*, London, 1970

Bréhier, L., *Les Institutions de l'Empire Byzantin*, Paris, 1949

– *La Civilisation Byzantine*, Paris, 1950

Bronfenbrenner, U., *Two Worlds of Childhood*, USA and USSR, London, 1971

Brooke, C., *Europe in the Central Middle Ages*, London, 1964, 1975

Brooke, Ch., *The Structure of Medieval Society*, London, 1971

Brzezinski, Z., *The Soviet Bloc*, Harvard, 1960

Bukharin, N., *Historical Materialism*, New York, 1934

Bush, M.L. (ed.), *Serfdom and Slavery*, London, 1996

Cambridge Economic History of Europe, Cambridge, 1942

Cambridge Medieval History, IV, 'The Byzantine Empire', Cambridge 1966

Carmichael, J., *A Cultural History of Russia*, London, 1968

Carr, E.H., *The Bolshevik Revolution*, London, 1961

Carrère d'Encausse, H., *L'Empire Eclaté*, Paris, 1978

    – *Le Grand Frère*, Paris, 1983

    – *Victorieuse Russie*, Paris, 1992

    – *La Russie Inachevée*, Paris, 2000

    – *L'Empire d' Eurasie*, Paris, 2005

Chadwick, N.K., *The Beginnings of Russian History*, Cambridge, 1946

Chang, J. and Halliday, J., *Mao: The Unknown Story*, London, 2005

Coles, P., *The Ottoman Impact on Europe*, London, 1968

Conquest, R., *The Great Terror*, London, 1968

    – *The Nation Killers*, London, 1970

    – *Lenin*, London, 1972

Coon, S., *The Hunting Peoples*, London, 1972

Čornej, P., *Tajemstvi českých kronik* (The Secrets of Czech Chronicles), Prague, 1987

Cross, S.H., *The Russian Primary Chronicle*, Cambridge, 1930

Cross, S.H. and Sherbowitz O.P., *The Russian Primary Chronicle*, Cambridge, 1953

Deacon, R., *The Russian Secret Service*, London, 1972

Dějiny SSSR (The History of the USSR), Prague, 1953

Dekan, J., *Velká Morava* (Great Moravia), Bratislava 1976, Prague 1980

Deutsch, K.W., *Nationalism and Social Communication*, N. Yorkshire – London, 1953

Deutscher, I., *Russia, China and the West*, London – Oxford, 1970

Djilas, M., *The New Class*, London, 1957

Engels, F., *The Conditions of the Working Class in England in 1844*, New York, 1887
  – *Der Ursprung der Familie, des Privateigentums und des Staats*, Stuttgart, 1921

Fernandez-Armesto, F., *Civilizations*, New York, 2001

Fitzgerald, C.P., *China, a Short Cultural History*, London, 1961

Fitzpatrick, S., *Everyday Stalinism*, New York, 1999

Fletcher, G., *'Of the Russ Common Wealth' in Russia at the Close of the Sixteenth Century*, Hakluyt Society, London, 1856

Frumkin, G., 'Archaeology in Soviet Central Asia', I–VII, *Central Asian Review*, London, 1963–6

Gascoyne, B., *The Great Moghuls*, London, 1971

Gerschenkron, A., 'An economic history of Russia', *Journal of Economic History*, XII, 1952

Gibb, H.A.R., *Arab Conquest in Central Asia*, London, 1923
  – (tr.), *The Travels of Ibn Battuta*, London, 1929

Giles, F.H. (ed.), Fa-Sien, *Travels 399–414, or Record of Buddhist Kingdoms*, Cambridge, 1923

Goetz, L.K., *Das Russische Recht*, 4 vol., Stuttgart, 1910–13

Golden, P.B., 'Aspects of the Nomadic Factor in the Economic Development of Kievan Rus,' in *Ukranian Economic History*, Harvard, 1994

Goodwin, G., *A History of Ottoman Architecture*, London, 1971

Graus, F., *L'Empire de Grande Moravie*, in *Grossmährische Reich*

Gray, C., *Russian Experiment in Art*, London, 1962

Grégoire, H., R. Jakobson et al., *La Geste du Prince Igor*, Paris, 1948

Grekov, B.D., *Krestiane na Rusi*, Moscow–Leningrad, 1948

Griaznov, M.P. and A. Bulgakov, *L'Art Ancien de l'Altaï*, Moscow, 1958

Das Grossmährische Reich (Proceedings of an archaeological conference, Brno-Nitra, 1963), Prague, 1968

Grollová, I. and Zikmundová, V., *Mongolové* (The Mongols), Prague 2001

Grousset, R., *L'Empire des Steppes*, Paris, 1939, 1960

Grunwald, C. de, *Société et Civilisation Russes au XIX Siècle*, Paris, 1975

Haenisch, E. (tr.), *Die geheime Geschichte der Mongolen*, Leipzig, 1948

De Hartog, L., *Russia and the Mongol yoke*, London 1996

Haxthausen, A. von, *Studien Ueber die Inneren Zustände, das Volksleben und Insbesondere die Laendlichen Einrichtungen Russlands*, 3 vol., Hannover, Berlin, 1847–52

Hayter, W., *Russia and the World*, London, 1970

Heissig, W., *A Lost Civilisation*, London, 1966

– *Die Mongolen*, Munich, 1978

Hellie, R., *Enserfment and Military Changes in Muscovy*, Chicago, 1971

– *Slavery in Russia*, Chicago, 1982

Herberstein, S. von, *Notes upon Russia*, tr., 2 vol., Hakluyt Society, London, 1851-2

Hingley, R., *Russian Secret Police*, London, 1970

– *A Concise History of Russia*, London, 1972

Hoetzsch, O., *The Evolution of Russia*, tr., London, 1968

Hookham, H., *Tamburlaine the Conqueror*, London, 1962

Horster, P., *Zur Anwendung des Islamischen Rechts im 16. Jahrhundert*, Stuttgart, 1935

Investigations Archéologiques en Tchécoslovaquie (VII Congrès International des Sciences Préhistoriques et Protohistoriques à Prague, 1966), Prague, 1966

Istoriya Kultury Drevnei Rusi, Moskva–Leningrad, 1948, cited Istoriya

Ivanov-Razumnik, R.V., *Mémoirs*, London, 1965

Jenkinson, A., *Early Voyages and Travels to Russia and Persia*, 2 vol., London, 1886

Julien, S. (tr.), *Hiuan-Tsiang: Mémoires sur les Contrées Orientales*, Paris, 1857

Kaiser, D.H., 'The Economy of Kievan Rus: Evidence from the *Pravda Russkaia*', in *Ukranian Economic History*, Harvard, 1994

Kaiser, R.G., *Russia, the People and the Power*, New York, 1976

Karger, M.K., *Arkheologicheskiye Issledovaniya Drevnego Kieva*, Kiev, 1950

Kehayan, N. and J., *Rue du Prolétaire Rouge*, Paris, 1978

Khazanov, A.N. *Nomads and the outside world*, 2nd ed., Wisconsin 1994; 'Muhammad and Jenghiz Khan compared', in *Comparative Studies in Society and History*, 1993, 35(3)

Khazanov, A.N. (ed.) *Nomads in the sedentary world*, London 2001

Knobloch, E. (tr.), *Putování k Mongolům* (Journeys to the Mongols) – Carpini. Rubruck, Clavijo, Prague, 1964

– *The Art of Central Asia*, Prague–London, 1965

– *Beyond the Oxus*, London, 1972

– *Monuments of Central Asia*, London, 2001

– *Archaeology and Architecture of Afghanistan*, London, 2002

articles:

– *The Art of the Hephthalites* in Czech, *Nový Orient*, 15, 1960

– *The Creed of Ancient Mongols* in Czech, *Nový Orient*, 15, 1960

– *Early Islamic Ornament in Central Asia* in Czech, *Nový Orient*, 15, 1960

– *Uzkend, the City of the Karakhanids* in Czech, *Nový Orient*, 16, 1961

– *The Decline of Central Asian Oases* in Czech, *Nový Orient*, 16, 1961

– *The Land of Ancient Irrigation* in Czech, *Nový Orient*, 16, 1961

– *Chingiz-Khan's Army* in Czech, *Krásná literatura*, 1960

– *William of Rubruck and Mangu Khan* in Czech, *Dějiny a současnost*, 3, 1960

– *Curiosities of the Caucasus, Architectural Review*, 140, 1966

– *Nationalism – Russia's Number One Problem, Contemporary Review*, XIV, 1966

– *Glimpses of Central Asia, Central Asian Review*, XIV, 1966

– *L'architecture islamique en Asie Centrale, Archéologia 6*, 1965

– *Oasis City of Khiva, The Geographical*, 1966

– *The Silk Route Country, The Asia Magazine*, 1966

– *The Uighurs, Contemporary Review*, 102, 1967

– *Survey of Archaeology and Architecture in Afghanistan, Part 1 Afghanistan Journal*, 1, 1981

– *Pir-i Baqran, sanctuaire islamique du XIV siecle, Archéologia*, 371, 2000

Kochan, L., *Russia in Revolution*, London, 1966, 1970

Kolarz, W., *Russia and her Colonies*, London, 1952

Komroff, M., *Contemporaries of Marco Polo*, London, 1928

Korb, J.G., *The Diary of an Ambassador at the Court of Moscow*, 2 vol., London, 1863

Kowalewsky, M., *Le Régime Economique de la Russie*, Paris, 1898

Krofta, K., *Dějiny Selského Stavu* (History of Peasantry), Prague, 1949

Kulischer, J., *Russische Wirtschaftsgeschichte*, Jena, 1925

Landström, B., *Sailing Ships*, London, 1969

Lane, D., *Politics and Society in the USSR*, London, 1970

Latham, R.E. (tr.), *The Travels of Marco Polo*, London, 1958

Lattimore, O., *Studies in Frontier History*, London, 1962

Legg, S., *The Heartland*, London, 1970

Lenin, V.I., *Sochinenia*, 35 vol., Moscow, 1941–50

— *Selected Works*, 12 vol., New York, 1943

Le Strange, G. (tr.), Clavijo, Ruy Gonzales de: *Embassy to Tamerlane*, London, 1928

Letiche, J.M. and B. Dmytryshyn, *Russian Statecraft* (The Politika of Iurii Krizhanich), Oxford, 1985

Levy, R., *The Social Structure of Islam*, Cambridge, 1957

Lewis, B., *The Emergence of Modern Turkey*, London, 1961

— *Race and Slavery in the Middle East*, Oxford, 1990

— *What went wrong*, London, 2002

Lewis, R., *Everyday Life in Ottoman Turkey*, London, 1971

Lloyd, S., *The Art of the Ancient Middle East*, London, 1969

Lot, F., *L'Art Militaire et les Armées au Moyen Age en Europe et dans le Proche Orient*, 2 vol., Paris, 1946

Løkkegaard, F., *Islamic Taxation in the Classic Period*, Copenhagen, 1950

Luxemburg, R., *Ausgewaehlte Reden und Schriften*, Berlin, 1951

Lyashchenko, P.I., *History of the National Economy of Russia to the 1917 Revolution*, New York, 1949

Malia, M., *The Soviet Tragedy*, New York, 1994

Masaryk, T.G., *The Spirit of Russia*, 3 vol., III, London, 1967

Mavor, J., *An Economic History of Russia*, 2 vol., London, Toronto, New York, 1925

McNeill, H., *Europe's Steppe Frontier*, 1500–1800, Chicago, 1964

— *The Shape of European History*, New York, 1974

Medvedev, Z., *Ten Years after Ivan Denisovich*, London, 1973

Miller, J., *Life in Russia Today*, London, 1969

Moravcsik, G., Constantine Porphyrogenitus, *De Administrando Imperio*, English translation by R.J.H. Jenkins, London, 1949

Morin, E., *De la Nature de l'URSS*, Paris, 1983

Nikitin, A., *Journeys Across the Three Seas*, ed. in Russian by V. P. Adrianova-Perets, Moscow, 1958

Noonan, T.S., 'The Flourishing of Kiev's International and Domestic Trade ca. 1100–1240', in *Ukranian Economic History*, Harvard, 1994; 'Rus, Pechenegs, and Polovtsy: Economic Interaction along the Steppe Frontier in the Pre-Mongol Era', in *Russian History* 19, 1992

Norwich, J.J., *Byzantium*, 3 vol., London, 1991

Obolensky, D., *The Byzantine Commonwealth*, London, 1971

Oman, Ch., *A History of the Art of War in the Middle Ages*, 2 vol., London, 1924

Outline of American Geography

Pelikán, J., *The Czechoslovak Political Trials*, 1950–1954, London, 1969

Perdue, P.C., *China Marches West*, London, 2005

Phillips, E.D., *The Royal Hordes – Nomad Peoples of the Steppes*, London, 1965

Pipes, R., *Russia Under the Old Régime*, London, 1974

– *Survival is not Enough*, New York, 1984

– *The Russian Revolution*, New York, 1990

– *Russia Under the Bolshevik Régime*, London, 1994

– *Russian Conservatism and its critics*, New Haven and London, 2005

Plekhanov, G.V., 'On the agrarian question in Russia', Dnevnik Social-Demokrata, No. 5, 1906

Postan, M.M., *Economic Relations Between Eastern and Western Europe in the Middle Ages*, London, 1970

Pošvář, J., *Handel und Währung Grossmährens*, in *Grossmährische Reich*

Poucha, P. (tr.), *Tajná Kronika Mongolů* (The Secret History of the Mongols), Prague, n. d.

Poulík, J., *Archäologische Entdeckungen und Grossmähren*, in *Grossmährische Reich*

Pražák, R. (ed.), *Legendy a kroniky koruny uherské* (Legends and Chronicles of the Crown of Hungary), Prague, 1988

Problems of Communism, 1965–1972, Washington DC

Protokoly – *Protocols of the Unification Congress of the RSDRP*, held in Stockholm in 1906, Moscow, 1907

Rakowska-Harmstone, T., *Russia and Nationalism in Central Asia*, Baltimore and London, 1970

Rashid, A., *Jihad: The Rise of Militant Islam in Central Asia*, Yale, 2002

Rempel, L.I., *Arkhitekturnyi Ornament Uzbekistana*, Tashkent, 1961

Riasanovsky, N.V., *A History of Russia*, New York, 1963

Risch, G., *Johann de Plano Carpini*, Leipzig, 1930

Roberti, V., *Moscow under the Skin*, London, 1969

Roberts, M., *Gustavus Adolphus*, 2 vol., London, 1953

Rockhill, W., *The Journey of William of Rubruck*, London, 1900

Romanov, B.A., *Denghi i Denezhnoye Obrashcheniye*, in Istoriya

Rosenthal, F., *The Muslim Concept of Freedom*, Leiden, 1960

Rostovtzev, M.I., *The Animal Style in South Russia and China*, Princeton, 1927

Rougier, L., *Le Génie de l'Occident*, Paris, 1969

Runciman, S., *Byzantine Civilisation*, London, 1933, 1961

    – *The Fall of Constantinople*, Cambridge, 1965

Russell, B., *Freedom and Organisation*, London, 1965

Rybakov, B. A., *Remeslo Drevnei Rusi*, Moscow–Leningrad, 1948

    – *Remeslo*, in *Istoriya*

    – *Torgovlia i Torgoviye Puti*, in *Istoriya*

    – *Voyennoye Delo*, in *Istoriya*

Salisbury, Harrison E., *The Coming War Between Russia and China*, London, 1969

Sanders, J.H. (tr.), *Tamerlane*, by Ibn Arabshah, London, 1936

Schapiro, L., *The Communist Party of the Soviet Union*, London, 1960

Schultz, L., *Russische Rechtsgeschichte*, Lahr, 1951

Simpson, J., *Everyday Life in the Viking Age*, London, 1967

Slavík, J., *Vznik Českého Národa*, 2 vol., (The Origin of the Czech Nation), Prague, 1946–48

Smith, D., *Russia of the Tsars*, London, 1971

Šolle, M., *Stará Kouřim* (Ancient Kourim), Prague, 1966

Soucek, S., *A History of Inner Asia*, Cambridge, 2000

Spuler, B., *The Mongols in History*, Paris, 1961, London, 1971

Stalin, J.V., *Sochinenia*, 13 vol., Moscow, 1946–51
  – *Selected Writings*, New York, 1942

Sumner, B.H., *Survey of Russian History*, London, 1944

Šusta, J., *Dějiny Evropy* (History of Europe) 1812–70, Prague, 1923
  – *Světová Politika* (World Politics) 1870–1914, Prague, 1931
  – *Karel IV* (Charles IV), Prague, 1946

Szamuely, T., *The Russian Tradition*, London, 1974

Talbot-Rice, D., *Islamic Art*, London, 1965

Talbot-Rice, T., *The Scythians*, London, 1961

Tarshys, D., *The Soviet Political Agenda*, London, 1979

Tauer, F., *Dějiny a Kultura Islámu* (History and Civilisation of Islam), Prague, 1940

Telfer, J.B. (tr.), Schiltberger, J., *Travels and Bondage*, London 1879

Thom, F., 'Eurasianism and neo-Eurasianism', Commentaire, 66/1994, q. from *Politika a společnost*, 1/1995

Titarenko, M.L., 'Eurasianism: A Paradigm of Russia', *Journal of Behavioral and Social Sciences*, 3/1994

Tolstoy, N., *Stalin's Secret War*, London, 1981

Toynbee, A., *A Study of History*, London, 1972

Tretiakov, P. N., *Sel'skoye Khoziaistvo i Promysly*, in *Istoriya*

Trevor-Roper, H., *The Rise of Christian Europe*, London, 1965

Trotsky, L., *1905*, London, 1972 (written 1908–9)

Trubetskoy, N., 'Die Ideokratie als Gesellschaftsordung der nächsten Zukunft nach der Lehre der Eurasier', *Orient und Occident*, 12/1934

Třeštík, D., *Kosmova Kronika Česká* [The Czech Chronicle of Cosmas], tr. K. Hrdina, Prague, 1975

Tucker, R. C., *The Soviet Political Mind*, London, 1963

Utechin, S. V., *Russian Political Thought*, London, 1964

Van der Post, L., *Journey into Russia*, London, 1964

Váňa, Z., *Svějt dávných Slovanů* (The World of Ancient Slavs), Prague, 1983

Vaněček, V., *Počátky Práva a Státu v Československu* (The Beginning of Law and State in Czechoslovakia), Prague, 1946

Vernadsky, G., *Ancient Russia*, New Haven, 1943

– *Kievan Russia*, New Haven, 1948

– *The Mongols and Russia*, New Haven, 1953

– *The Origins of Russia*, Oxford, 1959

– *Medieval Russian Laws*, New York, 1959

Vladimirtsov, B., *Le Régime Social des Mongols. Le Féodalisme Nomade*, Paris, 1941

Voráček, E., *Eurasijství v ruském politickém myšlení* (Eurasianism in Russian Political Thinking), Prague, 2004

Voronin, N. N., *Poseleniye*, in *Istoriya*

– *Sredstva i Puti Soobshcheniya*, in *Istoriya*

Vryonis, S., *Byzantium and Europe*, London, 1967

Weber, M., *Die Protestantische Ethik* (The Protestant Ethic and the Spirit of Capitalism), London, 1930

Wheeler, G., *The Peoples of Soviet Central Asia*, London, 1966

White, L., *Medieval Technology and Social Change*, London, 1962

Wiesehöfer, J., *Ancient Persia*, London, 1996, 2001

Wilson, D., *The Vikings and their Origins*, London, 1970

Wilson, F., *Muscovy Russia through Foreign Eyes*, London, 1970

Wittfogel, K., *Oriental Despotism*, New Haven, 1957

Wittram, R., *Russia and Europe*, London, 1973

Woolley, L.C., *The Art of the Middle East*, New York, 1961

Yakubovsky, A., *La Horde d'Or*, Paris, 1939

Yamshchikov, S. and S. Zimnokh, *Suzdal*, Moscow, 1970

Zenkovsky, S.A., *Panturkism and Islam in Russia*, Harvard

Footnotes

Notes to Preface

1. The interpretations (feudal, Asiatic) of Russian history are discussed by Szamuely, T., *The Russian Tradition*, p. 74f.
2. To Soviet historians, Oriental analogies in Russian history were unacceptable (Szamuely, *ibid.*, p. 90). Some Western scholars seem to share this view.
3. The Marxist view of nomadism is discussed by F. Gellner in his foreword to Khazanov, *Nomads and the outside world*, p. XI.

Notes to Introduction

1. On "slaves and other dependent and exploited groups and individuals" see Khazanov, A.M., *Nomads and the outside world*, p. 159. Wittfogel (*Oriental Despotism*) is probably right when he suggests that the system of irrigated agriculture required centralised despotic government and bureaucratic methods of administration. But he is not aware that despotic government may also be necessary when security of the community is threatened. The methods of rule would then be military rather than bureaucratic and would have nothing to do with agriculture. Even in modern times, in cases of emergency, freedoms are suspended and the government takes on dictatorial powers often exercised by the military.
2. 'The Khan or son of Heaven had two viceroys, one on the left and one on the right hand. The one on the left was his successor designate. Each one of these two had again a "king (*ku-li*)" on his right and left, each "king" had two generals and so on down to the commanders of a thousand, of a hundred and of ten men. The whole organisation was that of an army and indicated also the position of each unit in the field. The general orientation was taken facing south.' (Sseu-ma Tsien, q. by Grousset, *Empire des steppes*, p. 54.) The same system may be found with all the nomads down to Chingiz-Khan's Mongols 1500 years later and could still be traced in the organisation of Timur's army at the end of the fourteenth century.
3. The early tsars practised deportation of disloyal subjects combined with compulsory colonisation of suspect territories by local colonists. Under the tsarist and Soviet system alike deportation could be either punishment under the law or a political security device. The former applied to individuals, the latter was used against large communities and entire nations.
4. On the structure of Islamic Society, see Lewis, B., Islam, p. 33–4.

5. Vernadsky, *Ancient Russia*, p. 64.

6. Vernadsky, *Ancient Russia*, p. 52.

7. Vernadsky, *Ancient Russia*, p. 213; Golden, Nomadic Factor, p. 80, 87, also Noonan, Kiev, p. 107, 144.

8. McNeill, *Europe's Steppe Frontier*, p. 7.

9. Lattimore, *Studies in Frontier History*, p. 149.

10. Lattimore, *Studies*, pp. 153–4

11. Lattimore, *Studies*, pp. 196–7.

12. Lattimore, *Studies*, pp. 61–2.

13. Lattimore, *Studies*, p. 257.

14. Lattimore, *Studies*, p. 550.

15. Carpini, in *Putovani*, p. 36. Collective (corporative) ownership of the land and pastures and – sometimes – also wells and other water resources, are discussed by Khazanov, *op. cit.* p. 125ff. The same author, however, believes that livestock, etc., were held in private ownership (*ibid.* p. 152) leading to property inequality. See also Pipes, *Conservatism*, p.2, 10–11.

16. Vernadsky, *Origins*, p. 29.

17. Lattimore, *Studies*, p. 257. This view is not shared by Khazanov, op. cit., p.70. Security, military organisation, disciplines, etc. are discussed by Khazanov only in connection with conquest (p. 134, 238). On the other hand, mobility "within the boundaries of specific grazing territories" is one of "the most important characteristics defining the economic essence of pastoral nomadism" (p. 16). It is difficult to see how these essential requirements could be safeguarded without an adequate authority. Some chieftains, however, amassed considerable wealth, (Noonan, Pechenegs, p. 319).

18. Lattimore, *Studies*, p. 257.

19. Lattimore, *Studies*, p. 117.

20. *See below*, n.22.

21. Vernadsky, *Origins*, p. 24.

22. Vernadsky, *Origins*, p. 26; Khazanov, A., 'Muhammad and Jenghiz Khan compared', in *Comparative Studies in Society and History*, 1993, 35(3), 464ff.

23. There are exceptions, such as Pipes, *Russia under the Old Régime* or Carrère d'Encausse, *La Russie inachevée*.

24. Pipes, *Old Regime;* McNeill, *Shape of European History.*

25. Cross, *The Primary Chronicle*, pp. 170–1.

26. Vernadsky, *Origins*, pp. 283, 294.

27. Vernadsky, *Origins*, p. 304.

28. Carpini, in *Putovani*, p. 22.

29. Riasanovsky, *A History of Russia*, p. 174; a general characteristic of Islam can be found in Khazanov, *Muhammad*, p. 469–72.

30. Sumner, *Survey of Russian History*, p. 31.

31. The Seljuk advance in Iran is mentioned by Khazanov, *op. cit.* p. 264–5. For the Seljuk's commitment to Islam see Wink, A., in *Nomads in the sedentary world*, p. 291.

32. Cultural similarities between the Russians and the nomads are mentioned in Perdue, *China Marches West*, p. 45.

Notes to Chapter 1

1. Blum, *Lord and Peasant in Russia*, p. 9.

2. Blum, *op.cit.* p. 10; Pipes, *Russia under the Old Régime*, p. 4.

3. Pipes, *Russia under the Old Régime*, p. 6; according to Blum (*op.cit.*, p. 9), the growing season averages 120 days in Archangel, 130 days in Moscow, 146 days in Kazan, 151 days in Kharkov and 161 days in Saratov. Pipes (*ibid.*) gives the average growing season in the USA as more than 260 days in the south and about 100 days in the north. In Western Europe the growing season lasts between 8 and 9 months.

4. Blum, p. 11.

5. Pipes, p. 3.

6. Pipes, *ibid.*

7. Blum, *ibid.*

8. *Cambridge Economic History of Europe*, vol. I. p. 51.

9. Blum, p. 23; Grekov, *Krestiane na Rusi*, p. 51.

10. Grekov, *ibid.* He distinguishes between the *ralo*, pulled by oxen, and the *sokha*, for which horses were required. No reason is given for this requirement. In the German edition (p. 28) the *ralo* is translated as *Holzpflug* while the *sokha* is said to be equipped with an iron point (*Eisenspitze*).

11. Grekov, *ibid.* According to Tretiakov, *Sel' skoye khoziaistvo i promysly*, p. 59, the *sokha* was the implement used in the north while the *plug* and the *ralo* were used in the south. The *ralo* was used in the Ukraine until 1917.

12. *Cambridge Economic History of Europe*, p. 134.

13. According to White, *Medieval Technology and Social Change*, p. 58, the horseshoe was first introduced in Siberia in the ninth–tenth century and became known in Byzantium in the late ninth century. The horse-collar was a Turkic invention in the ninth century and was introduced in Novgorod in the twelfth (p. 61, 63). White, like Grekov, believes that all ploughing in the twelfth century Ukraine was done by horses. He bases this hypothesis on the *Primary Chronicle* (Cross, *The Russian Primary Chronicle*, p. 292, year 1103). In the relevant text we may read:

the retainers remark that hostilities in spring would ruin the peasants and their fields. Vladimir then replied: 'I am surprised, comrades, that you concern yourselves for the beasts with which the peasant ploughs [...] the Polovcians will come [...] seize his horse [...] are you concerned for the horse and not for the peasant himself?' Although horses are mentioned several times in the *Primary Chronicle*, this is the only reference in which they are connected with fieldwork and the connection between ploughing and the horses is indirect. In Grekov's opinion the *sokha* 'presupposes a horse', but to him the *sokha* implied individual smallholding and the horse seemed to provide the only suitable 'individual' pulling power. On the whole, this author appears more concerned with demonstrating the Marxist view of history than with the economics of the period. Tretiakov (p. 58) believes that the use of the horse for ploughing after the tenth century coincides with its diminished use as food. It is rarely found in the excavations dating to the twelfth–thirteenth centuries.

14. McNeill, *Europe's steppe frontier*, p. 4.
15. *Ibid.*
16. *Outline of American Geography*, p. 37.
17. McNeill, p. 5.
18. *Ibid.*
19. Bautier, *The economic development of Medieval Europe*, p. 85.
20. cf. Herodotus' remarks about Scythian farmers in the Dnieper Valley.
21. McNeill, p. 5.
22. Cross, *op.cit.*, p. 92.
23. Blum, p. 22.
24. Tretiakov, p. 51.
25. Grekov, pp. 49–51.
26. Blum, p. 22.
27. Grekov, p. 44–5.
28. Tretiakov, p. 59.
29. In this he agrees with Grekov, p. 45.
30. Tretiakov, p. 62. In Grekov's opinion the rotation of crops began as early as the eleventh–twelfth century (p. 37). In Czech chronicles it is mentioned from the mid-thirteenth century onwards (cf. *Pokračovatelé Kosmovi – The Continuators of Cosmas*, p. 106 and elsewhere).
31. Tretiakov, p. 63.
32. Roberts, *Gustavus Adolphus*, vol. III, p. 12; Tretiakov, p. 52.
33. Roberts, II, p. 12.
34. *Ibid.*

35. Pipes, p. 10.
36. Roberts, II, p. 17.
37. Tretiakov, p. 52.
38. Cf. Knobloch (tr.), *Putování k Mongolum*, p. 92.
39. A not altogether clear hint about horse feed is in the *Pravda Russkaya* (cit. Grekov, p. 34). White (p. 73) believes that surplus of grain, especially oats, made the use of horses possible.
40. Grekov, p. 37; Tretiakov, p. 62; Vernadsky, *Kievan Russia*, p. 110.
41. Riasanovsky, *History of Russia*, p. 125.
42. Pipes, p. 7–8; McNeill (Shapes, 48) uses the same statistics taken from Slicher van Bath, 'Yield ratios 810–1820' in *Afdeling Agrarische Geschiedenis Landbouwhogeschool*, 1963, no 10.
43. Treštík, Kosmova Kronika, p. 11–13.
44. McNeill, p. 13, 50.
45. Hellie, *Enserfment and Military Changes in Muscovy*, p. 255, 256.
46. Pipes, p. 16.
47. *Ibid.*
48. A comparison of the *Primary Chronicle* and the Czech chronicle of Cosmas, which is exactly contemporary, shows that whereas the Czech chronicler frequently mentions farming and is concerned about its conditions and results, in the Russian source fields are only mentioned twice (1093, 1103) and 'locusts eating up grass and grain' only once (1095).
49. *Cam. Ec. Hist*, p. 51.
50. *Cam. Ec. Hist*, p. 59.
51. *Cam. Ec. Hist, ibid.*
52. *Cam. Ec. Hist*, p. 51.
52a. Ten to fifteen times, according to Grekov (p. 49).
53. Blum, p. 22.
54. The estimates of the size of the population differ widely. Blum (p. 120) quotes several sources which vary in their estimates from 2.1 to 9–10 million in the late fifteenth century. In view of the fact that in the Kievan period the yields of agriculture were lower and the area of arable considerably less than in the fifteenth century, the estimate of the peasant population should be correspondingly lower. Gardizi (cited by Vernadsky, *Origins of Russia*, p. 196.) gives the population of Russia as 100,000. This number could apply to the tenth–eleventh century. It seems likely that Gardizi counted only the male population of the nomadic Russes in his estimate, which would give a total of some 500,000–600,000 for the nomadic population alone. If the peasant population numbered twice as

many again, or approximately 1 million, with an unspecified number of forest tribes (Finns and others), the population total of Kievan Russia could well be near two million.

55. According to the estimate of Treštík (p. 12–3), the population of Bohemia numbered about 500,000 in the time of Cosmas. This population could support some 10–15,000 non-farming people and 3–4,000 'lords' or ruling class. Applied to Kievan Russia, one million peasants could support 20–30,000 non-farmers and 6–8,000 'lords', under the same circumstances. These figures have to be adjusted, on the one hand, with regard to the less favourable agricultural conditions and, on the other hand, with the existence of nomads.

56. *De admin. imperio*, p. 56; Vernadsky, *Origins*, p. 286; Pipes, p. 30.

57. Obolensky, *The Byzantine Commonwealth*, p. 62.

58. *Ibid.*, p. 54.

59. Vernadsky, *Ancient Russia*, p. 52.

60. *Ibid.*, p. 85.

61. Ibid., p. 213. On the Khazar kaganate, see Golden, P.B., in *Nomads in the sedentary world*, p. 25-27. Also Noonan, T.S., *The Khazar Qaganate and its impact on the early Rus state, ibid.*

62. McNeill, p. 3, 7.

63. McNeill, *ibid.* Khazanov, op. cit., distinguishes between a food-extracting economy (hunters, gatherers), and a food-producing one (agriculture). Pastoral nomadism "is a single form of food-producing economy which remains different from other food-extracting economies and... also from other food-producing economies" (p. 17). I find this specificity rather difficult to understand, unless we accept its "parasitic" nature.

64. W. Rubruck in Knobloch, *Putování*, p. 78.

65. Vernadsky, *Origins*, p. 267. 'The Russes shall, moreover, not have the right to winter at the mouth of the Dnieper either at Byeloberg or by St Eleutherius, but when the autumn comes, they shall return home to Russia. Regarding the Black Bulgarians who come and ravage the Kherson district, we enjoin the Prince of Russia not to allow them to injure that region.' (Cross, *Primary Chronicle*, p. 162).

66. Hellie, *Muscovy*, p. 318 note 21.

67. Riasanovsky, p. 52.

68. Pipes, p. 36.

69. Rybakov, *Torgovlia*, p. 330, 362.

70. Grekov, p. 35 (German edition).

71. The influence of German law appeared in the Ukraine after the Polish and

Lithuanian occupation in the fourteenth century (Kowalewski, p. 336).

72. Pipes, p. 36.

73. Beranová, M., *Zemědělství starých Slovanů* (Agriculture of ancient Slavs, p. 301, quoting G.G. Gromov, *Podsechnoognevaya sistema zemledelia*, Kiev, 1968, S.A. Semenov, *Proizkhozhdenie zemledelia*, 1974).

74. *FAO Yearbook*, 1978.

Notes to Chapter 2

1. Postan records that in Cordoba, which was only one of many recipients of the human cargo from Russia, the number of slaves at one time in the ninth century exceeded 14,000. In the fifteenth century Pero Tafur – a Portugese traveller – described the abundant volume of slave traffic from South Russia to Caffa (p. 133). The export of slaves is virtually the only well-documented trade originating in the Volga regions (*Economic Relations*, p. 139). According to Carrère d'Encausse, Russian princes sold slaves to Byzantium and Europe and also bought them according to their own requirements. Carrère d'Encausse, *La Russie*, p.91; also see Golden, *Nomadic Factor*, p. 70.

2. The *Russian Primary Chronicle*, year 969, Laurentian text, Cross-Sherbowitz tr., p. 86; Cross, p. 173; *idem* Constantine Porphyrogenitus, *De administrando imperio*, Moravcsik, p. 56–63.

2a. 'Both Ibn Rusta and Gardizi say that the Russes raided the Slavic tribes in boats.' (Vernadsky, *Origins*, p. 196) 'The number of slaves of Slav origin was so large that in the west the word "*slav*" and in Moslem Spain the word "*sakaliba*" in the end came to have the exclusive meaning of "slave".' (Bautier, *The Economic Development*, p. 7).

3. Rybakov, *Torgovlia i torgoviye puti*, p. 322.

3a. Hellie (*Slavery*, XVII) observes that in Muscovy there was no ethnic difference between slaves and slave-owners. Most slaves were natives who sold themselves into slavery. The difference between Muscovy and Kiev may have been merely that in Kiev slaves were hunted by a warrior élite of the same ethnic origin.

4. Rybakov, *Torgovlia*, p. 321.

5. Vernadsky, *Origin*, p. 192.

6. Romanov, *Denghi i denezhnoye obrashcheniye*, p. 374.

7. Cited by Vernadsky, *Origins*, p. 190.8. The fourteenth century Arab writer al-Omari observed that 'in times of drought and famine the Turks (Polovtsy) sell their sons. On the other hand, in times of plenty they would voluntarily give away their daughters, but not their sons [...].' (quoted from Yakubovsky, *La Horde d'Or*, p. 117).

9. Blum, p. 53; also *La Geste du Prince Igor*, p. 126, v.125.
10. Pipes, Old Régime, p. 43–4.
11. Pipes, *ibid.*
12. Pipes, p. 36.
13. Pipes, p. 43.
14. Hellie, *Muscovy*, p. 38, 48.
15. Blum, p. 51.
16. Blum, p. 51; Hellie, *Muscovy*, p. 40.
17. Hellie, *Slavery*, p. 30; also Kaiser, *Pravda*, p. 51, 56; Noonan, *Pechenegs*, p. 314ff.

Notes to Chapter 3
1. Blum, p. 15.
2. Vernadsky, *Origins*, p. 285.
3. Pipes, *Old Régime*, p. 9.
4. *Ibid.*
5. *Ibid.*
6. Cambridge Economic History, p. 57; J. Poulík in *Grossmährische Reich*, p. 38, 44; Šolle, Stará Kouřim, p. 60–2. Princely courts had their own craftsmen who belonged among the *cheliad* (Rybakov, *Remeslo*, p. 169, 180 in *Istoriya*). According to the same author, free crafts developed alongside princely crafts in the eleventh–twelfth centuries. Bonded craftsmen (*kholopy*) belonged also to monasteries and boyars (*ibid.*, p. 167).
7. *Cambridge Economic History*, p. 57.
8. Rybakov, *Remeslo*, p. 173 in *Istoriya*: 'Around the walls of the princely palaces lay the quarters of the craftsmen.'
9. Various points for tax collection are mentioned by Romanov, *Denghi i Denezhnoye Obrashcheniye*, p. 374 (for the twelfth century; only 76 *grivny* out of a tribute of 3,000 *grivny* was passed on to the prince).
10. Pipes, p. 103.
11. Blum, p. 125.
12. Rybakov, *Remeslo*, p. 501–22; Blum, p. 16; Noonan, *Kiev*, p. 108; on commerce, Noonan, *Kiev*, p. 106, 138.
13. Rybakov, *ibid.*, p. 480.
14. Rybakov, *Torgovlia*, p. 350.
15. *Ibid.*, p. 358.
16. Rybakov, *Remeslo*, p. 123.
17. Bautier, 222, Pounds, 320, *Investigations*, 295–6.
18. Clavijo in Putování, p. 282.

19. McNeill, *Steppe*, p. 130.
20. Blum, p. 15; a list of luxury crafts is provided by Noonan, Kiev, p. 108.
21. Rybakov, *Torgovlia*, p. 366.
22. According to Postan, the very quantity of the hoarded gold and silver merely demonstrates how one-sided the Scandinavian traffic must have been; the eastern and western areas of Europe being brought into loose and intermittent contact by trade in slaves, luxuries and bullion (p. 140).
23. Simpson, *Everyday Life in the Viking Age*, p. 110.
24. It seems to have been somewhat earlier than the Dnieper route. It probably developed in the seventh century. This early Arab commerce seems to have been unacquainted with the Dnieper route. The Arabic sources do not refer to the Russes in any connection with the Slavs of the Dnieper Valley (Cross, p. 127, 129). Scandinavian objects found in northern Russia date from the late eighth century, Oriental objects found in Sweden date from the late ninth century, while Russian objects do not appear in Scandinavia before the eleventh century (Cross, p. 12). On trade routes, see also Noonan, *Pechenegs*, p. 320.
25. Ibrahim ibn Yakub (ninth century) speaks of Russian merchants in Prague, trading furs and Byzantine goods. Benjamin of Tudela (twelfth century) also mentions a Russian connection with Bohemia (Rybakov, *Remeslo*, p. 475). Objects of possible Russian origin were found in Czech excavations from the tenth–eleventh centuries.
26. Vernadsky, *Origins*, p. 286.
27. Vernadsky, *Origins*, p. 84.
28. McNeill, *Steppe*, p. 130.
29. Rybakov, *Torgovlia*, p. 365.
30. Romanov, *Denghi*, p. 374, mentions cases in the mid-twelfth century when peasant taxes were assessed in money terms while some town contributions were expressed in kind. In the author's view, the latter was a relic of the past maintained for traditional reasons. On the other hand, the same author seems to believe that the older areas had their contributions fixed in money while newly-acquired ones were assessed in kind, the reason being that the conquering principality took over the system which already existed (p. 375–6). But the expression of the 'smoke tax' in money or furs did not mean that each farmstead actually had to deliver either money or that particular fur. There were 'endless possibilities of converting assessment in money into factual contributions in kind' (p. 377). On *grivna*, see Noonan, *Kiev*, p. 145, also Kaiser, *Pravda*, p. 45.
31. Mainly Arab dirhams: Vernadsky, *Origins*, p. 203; Cross, p. 219; *La Geste*, p. 126.

32. Roberts, II, p. 43, 46.
33. Pošvář, *Handel und Währung Grossmährens*, in *Grossmährische Reich*, p. 279.
34. Pipes, *Old Régime*, pp. 199–2 vol.
35. There were only 63 cities under Ivan III, 68 under Ivan IV and 138 in 1610 (Pipes, p. 200).
36. According to Voronin, *Poseleniye*, p. 182–203, there were some 10 churches in Kiev at the time of Yaroslav the Wise and 4 churches and 3 monasteries in Vladimir on Kliazma in the twelfth–thirteenth century. These are similar numbers to those found in the excavations of Mikulčice and Staré město, sites of the Great Moravia of the late ninth century. In view of this, the number of 400 churches mentioned by Thietmar of Merseburg is an obvious error. Thietmar got his information from some German mercenaries whose mathematical erudition must be doubted (cf. *GM*, p. 261). Considering that 40 is often used in Muslim and Middle Eastern folklore to describe 'many', the information may have been something like 'ten times forty' meaning 'very many'.

Notes to Chapter 4
1. Gardizi, cited by Vernadsky, *Origins*, p. 196.
2. Obolensky, p. 55.
3. According to Rybakov, horses were both exported and imported. The imported ones seemed to be thoroughbreds obtained from or via Constantinople. Some horses were purchased from nomad horse-breeders. From this observation it seems obvious that the Russes themselves bred horses both for their own uses and for export (*Torgovlia*, p. 330). On livestock trade, especially horses, see Noonan, *Pechenegs*, p. 306ff.; Kaiser, *Pravda*, p. 39
4. White, p. 66.
5. Blum, p. 127.
6. *Ibid.*
7. Blum, p. 128.
8. Vernadsky, *Origins*, p. 192.
9. Rybakov, *Torgovlia*, p. 330.
10. Roberts, II, p. 24.
11. Rybakov, *Torgovlia*, p. 340.
12. Obolensky, p. 62.
13. Voronin, *Sredstva i puti soobshcheniya*, p. 285.
14. cf. also Blum, p. 20.
15. Given the fact that the Treaty of Byzantium of 945 stipulated that the merchants were to be allowed entry into Constantinople in groups of fifty at a time, they

must have numbered several hundred (Cross, p. 16).

16. The Pechenegs made proof of it when they killed Svyatoslav at the Dnieper rapids in 972 (Cross, p. 177).
17. Cited by Obolensky, p. 61–2.
18. Rybakov (*Torgovlia*, p. 339) mentions Mstislav's war against the Polovtsy in 1170 to protect the 'Greek route' and he adds: 'In the twelfth century when the princes and their retinue no longer travelled with their goods themselves, it was sufficient to position a strong army at the beginning of the "Greek route" to protect the caravan of ships from raids of the Polovtsy.' Leaving aside the question of whether the princes in earlier times travelled with the caravan or not, this seems to mean that although the Russes in the twelfth century were no longer the masters of the steppe, their army did not accompany the caravan and served only as a kind of deterrent. Considering the distances, the mobility of the nomads and the repeatedly emphasised role of the foot soldiers in the Russian army this assumption makes no sense.
19. cf. Obolensky, p. 174–5.
20. According to Voronin, *Sredstva*, p. 286, the prince's retinue accompanied the caravan up to the twelfth century. Voronin seems to believe that somehow the Pechenegs were only 'on the other side' of the river and 'could not shoot across'. They were also in readiness along the sea-shore as far as the mouth of the Danube 'waiting for shipwrecks'. This seems to imply that the Pechenegs were the masters of the right bank of the Dnieper while the Russes dominated the left bank – a somewhat implausible assumption.
21. Vernadsky, *Origins*, p. 219. It should be noted that the *Primary Chronicle* first mentions Tmutorokan in the late eleventh century (1078, 1079) (Cross, p. 255, 258).
22. La Geste, p. 145.
23. Vernadsky, *Origins*, p. 283.
24. Traces of 'late nomadic funerals' in which the corpse was laid between two small boats were found in the Ukraine (Voronin, *Sredstva*, p. 286). Ibn Fadlan mentions the cremation of Russes in boats, which, according to Voronin, was not necessarily a Norman custom (*ibid.*, p. 287).
25. Rybakov, *Voyennoye Dielo*, p. 405.
26. Obolensky, p. 61; Vernadsky, *Origins*, p. 286.
27. Blum, p. 20.
28. Vernadsky, *Origins*, p. 255.
29. Vernadsky, *Origins*, p. 275; Cross, p. 149.
30. Vernadsky, *Origins, ibid.*

31. Igor's campaign in 944 was also conducted 'by ship and by horse' (Cross, p. 158). In 985 Vladimir attacked the Bulgarians by boat and brought the Torks overland on horseback (Cross, p. 183). Yaroslav attacked the Mazovians by boat; the horses of Vladimir's soldiery died (Cross, p. 227). In 1060 the sons of Yaroslav went against the Torks by horse and by ship (Cross, p. 232). As late as 1103, Vladimir advanced against the Polovcians on horseback and by boat (Cross, p. 292).
32. Obolensky, p. 240–1.
33. Naval campaigns similar to those of the tenth century were unknown in the twelfth–thirteenth centuries (Rybakov, *Voyennoye Dielo*, p. 405).
34. No figures are given for the campaigns of Igor in 941 and 944. The latter, however, is interesting because Igor apparently 'set forth from Kiev by ship and horse' and a detachment of the Pechenegs was accompanying him (Vernadsky, *Origins*, p. 265). The whole phrase reads in Cross' translation: 'After collecting many warriors among the Varangians, the Russes, the Polyanians, the Slavs, the Krivichians, the Tivercians, and the Pechenegs, and receiving hostages from them, Igor advanced upon the Greeks by ship and by horse…' It is therefore not certain that the Pechenegs were the only cavalry in the expedition. However, it can be seen as a confirmation that nomadic horsemen were accompanying – and supplying – boat expeditions, whether civil or military.
35. Vernadsky, *Origins*, p. 219, 259.
36. Obolensky, p. 293; Vernadsky, *Origins*, p. 219.
37. Vernadsky, *Origins*, p. 252.
38. Vernadsky, *Origins*, p. 286.
39. Simpson, *Everyday*, p. 85.
40. Simpson, *Everyday*, p. 86.
41. *Ibid.*
42. *Ibid.*
43. Landstrom, *Ships*, p. 70. 'Drakkar' seems to be a modern word taken from Swedish 'dragon', the Viking one being 'langskip' (longboat).
44. Voronin, *Sredstva*, p. 283.
45. *Ibid.* On Viking ships see also Boyer, R., *Les Vikings* in *Historia Thématique*, 103, 2006.
46. Rybakov, *Voyennoe Dielo*, p. 405.
47. Voronin, *Sredstva*, p. 288–9.
48. *Russian Chronography*, q. Vernadsky, *Origins*, p. 254.
49. Voronin, *Sredstva*, p. 288.
50. Voronin, *Sredstva*, p. 291, 294.
51. Voronin, *Sredstva*, p. 291.

52. Voronin, *Sredstva*. 295.

Notes to Chapter 5

1. *Voyennoye dielo*, p. 400ff.; Noonan, Pechenegs, p. 302, 323.
2. Oleg's campaign, 80,000 men; South Caspian campaign in 912,500 ships with 100 men each, 50,000 men; Svyatoslav's campaign against the Bulgars, 60,000 men.
3. None of the Middle Eastern fortresses could withstand the assault of Chingiz-Khan's Mongols – and there were no comparable fortresses in Russia.
4. In the seventeenth century the towns in Sweden had only about 5 percent of the total population (Roberts, II, p. 20); Blum (p. 123) reckons there were about 150 towns in sixteenth-century Russia, most of which had an average population of a little over 1,000; this would account for a total population of 4–5 million.
5. Hellie thinks town population supplied the infantry (p. 25); in Muscovy, however, the army was mostly cavalry (p. 21), armed with the same arms as the Kievan cavalrymen.
6. cf. p. 45-46 (n.54, 55).
7. Rybakov, *op.cit.*, p. 405; the superiority of cavalry is also mentioned by Golden, Nomadic Factor, p. 80, 81.
8. *Ibid.*, p. 410.
9. *Ibid.*, p. 404.
10. *Ibid.*, p. 404.
11. *Ibid.*, p. 424.
12. *Feudal Society*, I, p. 153–4, II, p. 291.
13. Carpini (cf. Knobloch, *Putování*, p. 39).
14. The Mongols manufactured most of their arms themselves, cf. Rubruck, *ibid.*, p. 81.
15. Riasanovsky speaks of kormlenie holding in the period of Muscovy whereas Vernadsky (*Origins*, p. 248) mentions it already in the tenth–eleventh century as a reward for Varangian mercenaries.
16. For the organisation of Chingiz-Khan's army, cf. Carpini, *ibid.*, p. 39.
17. Riasanovsky, p. 90.
18. *Ibid.*, p. 89.
19. Pipes, p. 197. The Scandinavian *härad* (hundred) could also have played a role here – cf. Anderson, p. 32.
20. Rybakov, *op.cit.*, p. 407.
21. Rybakov, *ibid.*
22. Hellie, *Muscovy*, p. 164.

23. Heavy cavalry (horsemen and horses wearing metal armour) was used by the Parthians (in the battle of Carrhae in 53 BC) and also by the Sasanians. It seems to have been abandoned when the light cavalry used by the nomads (Hephthalites, Turks, Arabs) proved to be superior (cf. Wiesehöfer, p. 147, 197).

Notes to Chapter 6

1. *Cambridge Economic History*, p. 57. Pipes, *Conservatism*, traces the patrimonial type of régime in Europe to the Merovingians and the Carolingians (*op.cit.* p. 4).
2. Slavík, *Vznik českého národa*, I, II (The Origins of the Czech Nation), 1946–8; Vaněček, *Počátky práva a státu v Československu (The Beginnings of Law and State in Czechoslovakia)*, 1946.
3. Krofta, p. 65.
4. Krofta, p. 134; Šolle, p. 84; Graus in *Grossmährische Reich*, p. 188. The following observations may be made on the population of Great Moravia:
a) Nomadic Magyars, pushed by the Pechenegs, advanced into central Europe in search of grazing grounds. They found them in the area of the upper and middle Tisza, which was then held by Great Moravia. In the late ninth century the Magyars occupied this area, which has the character of a steppe to this day. It seems probable that the Great Moravians did not farm it and used it as a pastureland; therefore at least part of that population had to be cattle-breeding nomads. (cf. Ratkos, P., *Die Grossmärischen Slawen und die Altmagyaren*, in *Grossmährische Reich*, p. 227; also Obolensky, *op.cit.*, p. 205, 208).
b) An anthropological analysis carried out by M. Stloukal (*Étude Anthropologique des Anciens Slaves de Moravie, Investigations*, p. 234) on the neighbouring sites of Mikulčice and Josefov brought the following results: A) Josefov was a rural settlement probably inhabited by about 40 people at a time; Mikulčice was a burgwall of considerable size consisting of a princely castle and an extensive suburb with a population probably ten times that of Josefov. The remnants of at least ten churches were found here. B) In Mikulčice there was a 'biologically inexplicable' predominance of male over female skeletons. C) The inhabitants of Josefov seem to have been of a different typological character than those of Mikulčice, perhaps closer to the pre-Slav population of the country.
On the basis of these observations it may be assumed that Mikulčice was a garrison-type settlement with predominance of male (military) inhabitants who controlled the surrounding area of peasant population of a different ethnic type. The inhabitants of Mikulčice were the ruling élite or warrior caste who also used the steppe region of the Tisza as the grazing grounds for their herds, while the people of Josefov were agriculturalists.

5. On the title '*kagan*' see Vernadsky, *Origins*, pp. 184ff.
6. GM, p. 405; Obolensky, p. 411. According to Obolensky, there is little evidence of Byzantine models in the *Pravda Russkaya*; Vernadsky finds traditional Slavic law in the early version of the *Pravda Russkaya*, whereas in the later compilations Byzantine influence prevails (Kievan Russia, p. 292–3); the same author sees Byzantine influences in the three domains: church, art and law (*Kievan Russia*, p. 348).

The earliest version of the *Pravda Russkaya* does not know any system of punishments regulated by the state (*staatlich geregeltes Strafensystem*), Schultz, *Russische Rechtsgeschichte*, p. 51. Hellie (Slavery, p. 3) sees in the *Pravda* mainly a tool for 'horizontal conflict resolution'. See also Kaiser, *Pravda*, p. 55.

The usual punishment for murder, revenge-killing or blood-money, led to continuous fights between families and clans. To reduce it, the oldest Czech legal document, the *Decreta Ducis Brecislavi* of 1039, introduced "expulsion from the realm" (bannitium) which effectively deprived the culprit of any protection. He could be killed, and indeed, should be killed by anybody. If the alleged murderer refused to confess, he was subjected to "Lord's judgment", an ordeal usually by hot iron or water. (cf Boháček, M. in *Scritti in onore di Contardo Ferrini*, Milan, 1949). In this connection see also the decree of the Mainz Council (Concilium Moguntium) of 852 and the legislation of King Canute of 1027-1034.

7. Wittfogel, *Oriental Despotism*.
8. *Great Moravia*, p. 405.
9. Obolensky, pp. 318–9. Also Pipes, *Conservatism*, p.75.
10. Obolensky, p. 318. On the influence of the Church see also Boháček, *ibid*.
11. Obolensky, p. 319; Kaiser, *Pravda*, p.55.
12. Šusta: (in Bohemia) 'At the earlier stage the prince ruled with the help of his court and an armed retinue of his supporters located in certain fortified positions. Later, princely power shifted to new positions: royal towns and royal estates with big castles or forts. Fortified towns and castles were the instrument of efficient government. There was no uniformity in the exercise of state power (in the fourteenth century), which came only as a product of the new era.' (*Karel* IV, vol. I, pp. 55ff).
13. *Cambridge Modern History*, IV, p. 103.
14. Hoetzsch, *Evolution*, p. 58.
15. Vernadsky, *Origins*, pp. 283, 294.
16. *Ibid.*, p. 316.
17. Jacobson, quoted from Vernadsky, *ibid.*, p. 141.
18. Riasanovsky, p. 58.
19. Certain traces of paganism and pre-Christian traditions survived in Russia until

our time. Ritual plays and masquerades were described in central Russia in 1915. Reports may be found from time to time in Soviet learned journals of certain practices described as 'religious fanaticism' which often are a mixture of medieval martyrism and pre-Christian superstitions. This writer remembers an article in one such journal (*Nauka i Zhizn*) about a local prophet who was proclaimed in a central Russian village, not far from Moscow, and was driven around the neighbourhood in a procession, standing in a cart pulled by a group of fanatical naked women harnessed up like horses. Another case described in the same journal was of a young woman, a qualified nurse, who was ordered by the Holy Ghost to sacrifice her baby daughter. She walled the baby alive in the wall of a pigsty where it died.

20. Riasanovsky, p. 58.
21. Bréhier, p. 25.
22. Alderson, pp. 4–5, 59.
23. Riasanovsky, p. 159.
24. Riasanovsky, pp. 209, 269, 272. Soucek, S., *Inner Asia*, p. 162
25. *Great Moravia*, pp. 218–9; see also Lewis B., *What went wrong*, p. 142.
26. *Ibid.*, p. 172.
27. Obolensky, pp. 56–7.
28. *Great Moravia*, p. 241.
29. Vernadsky, *Kievan Russia*, p. 188.
30. *Great Moravia*, pp. 214–5.
31. *Ibid.*, p. 306.

Notes to Chapter 7
1. Schultz, p. 29. According to Golden, one of the most interesting features of governance of the Rus state was the system of succession 'by scales' to the Grand Principate of Kiev. This system seems to have been taken over from the Khazars (*op. cit.* p. 29); also Wink, A. *ibid.*, p. 293.
2. Schultz, p. 31.
3. Pipes, *Old Régime*, p. 21–2.
4. cf. above, Introduction, n.23.
5. *La Geste*, pp. 11, 78, 112.
6. Vernadsky, *Origins*, p. 283, *La Geste*, p. 116.
7. Vernadsky, *Kievan Russia*, p. 312.
8. La Geste, p. 146. The last prince called *kagan* in the texts was Yaroslav the Wise, d.1054. Also Vernadsky, *Origins*, pp. 184ff.
9. *Great Moravia*, p. 260.

10. Vernadsky, *Ancient Russia*, pp. 95, 99; *Origins*, p. 162; Kievan Russia, pp. 250, 263, 364.

11. *Primary Chronicle*, Hypat. text., Cross, p. 319; Vernadsky, *Origins*, p. 206.

12. Vernadsky, *Origins*, p. 287. In 970, according to Cross, p. 171.

13. Pipes, *Old Régime*, p. 31.

14. Schultz, p. 33. Decisions made by the *veche* are attested only for Pskov and Novgorod.

15. Obolensky, pp. 106–13. See also below p. 113.

16. According to Postan, a German 'factory' in Novgorod dominated the trade of the town and drew to itself the entire foreign trade of north-eastern Europe (p. 148). However, a similar 'factory' of the Russians, i.e. Novgorodians, in Visby is not mentioned.

17. Riasanovsky, p. 86.

18. Riasanovsky, p. 91.

19. Schultz, p. 33.

20. Vernadsky, *Kievan Russia*, p. 314.

21. White, *Technology*, p. 28. Also Khazanov, *Nomads in the history of the sedentary world*, p. 2.

22. The situation was different on irrigated lands elsewhere in the Middle East, where joint effort was needed only sporadically for the construction and maintenance of the canals. At the same time water had to be distributed and the supplies controlled by some kind of authority. Fields were laid out permanently and could therefore be farmed individually. This gave rise to strong land authority, corvée labour and small individual holdings.

23. Pipes, *Old Régime*, pp. 45–6.

24. Blum, p. 98.

25. This process began in fact more than a century before the Mongols, when the Polovtsy began to push the Russians out of the southern steppe. The appearance of Russian settlements in the Volga and Oka region precisely in this period is not coincidental.

26. cf. Hellie, *Muscovy*, p. 318. The author attributes the right of movement to the destruction of the commune (Hellie, Muscovy, pp. 10, 13).

27. cf. on this subject Yakubovsky, *La Horde d'Or*, p. 98.

28. Vernadsky, *Origins*, p. 24.

29. On different kinds of peasant holding in the fourteenth–fifteenth centuries with regard to taxation, cf. Yakubovsky, *La Horde d'Or*, p. 114–5.

30. Such restrictions first appeared in the first half of the fourteenth century, and became common in the fifteenth (Blum, p. 108). Gradually, the departure time

was reduced to St George's Day (late fifteenth century), and it was finally abolished altogether at the turn of the seventeenth century. The policy of the first tsars was obviously to do away with the hereditary *votchina* lands, which infringed on and weakened their authority – a policy that culminated dramatically in the *oprichnina* of Ivan IV.

31. It seems that a more or less complete tax exemption was the favourite way rather than a land-holding title – cf. the *yarlyks* of the khans of the Golden Horde, as quoted by Yakubovsky, pp. 111ff.
32. Blum, p. 37.
33. Grekov, pp. 93–4, cited in Blum, p. 31.
34. On the conditions of land ownership and agricultural productivity in eastern Germany and western Poland, cf. Postan, pp. 171ff.
35. Pipes, *Old Régime*, p. 10.
36. *Timar* was uninheritable fief granted to the sipahi, the mounted warrior, in return for his services in war (Coles, p. 113).
37. Riasanovsky, p. 89.
38. Blum, p. 40.
39. Blum, p. 65.

Notes to Chapter 8
1. Riasanovsky, p. 102.
2. Vernadsky, *Mongols*, p. 364.
3. Riasanovsky, p. 131. Pipes, *Conservatism*, p. 15.
4. *Ibid.*, p. 125.
5. *Ibid.*, p. 129. Pipes, *Conservatism*, p. 17.
6. *Ibid.*
7. Utechin, p. 28.
8. Souček, op. cit., p. 236.
9. *Ibid.*, p. 16. Riasanovsky, p. 128. According to Golden, P.B., the nomads formed together with Rus a single political system of Eurasia. The dynamics of Riurikid internal politics cannot be fully comprehended without reference to the steppe people who figured so intimately in their internecine struggles (in Khazanov, *op. cit.* p. 24).

Notes to Chapter 9
1. Vernadsky, *Mongols*, p. 105.
2. Karamzin, *Istoriya*, p. 235.
3. Szamuely, p. 18.

4. Vernadsky, *Mongols*, p. 214.
5. Vernadsky, *Mongols*, p. 383.
6. Vernadsky, *Mongols*, p. 387.

Notes to Chapter 10
1. Riasanovsky, p. 130.
2. Until Peter the Great, when after 1723, it merged with serfdom, (Hellie, *Slavery*, p. 699).
3. "The principalities took on only a few Mongol customs or institutions... The Mongols did not enter into Russian society... Russian princes all too often gave the Mongols a helping hand. The Mongols contributed a great deal to the growth of the Grand Principality of Moscow... The autocracy and despotisms that are characteristic of the Grand Principality of Moscow are only in part an inheritance from the Mongols. The influence of Byzantium is at least as great as that of the Golden Horde." (de Hartog, *Russia and the Mongol Yoke*, p. 163-4).

Notes to Chapter 11
1. Vernadsky, *Kievan Russia*, pp. 187–8.
2. Vernadsky, *Mongols*, pp. 224–6.
3. *Ibid.*, p. 105.
4. *Ibid.*, p. 106.
5. *Ibid.*, p. 107.
6. De Hartog (*op. cit.* p. 164) : "The most important institutions, that the Russian took over from the Mongols were the tax system, the war levy, the military draft and the mounted courier service, the *yam*."

Notes to Chapter 12
1. Riasanovsky, p. 133.
2. *Ibid.*, p. 136 and below p. 219.
3. Obolensky, p. 295.
4. See also Pipes, *Conservatism*, p. 12-14. On non-possessors, *ibid.*, p. 27.

Notes to Chapter 13
1. Riasanovsky, p. 90.
2. Vernadsky, *Kievan Russia*, pp. 185, 186.
3. Obolensky, p. 176, Bréhier, II, p. 208.
4. Bréhier, II, p. 212.
5. Vernadsky, *Kievan Russia*, pp. 173–4.

6. Obolensky, p. 57.
7. Vernadsky, *Kievan Russia*, p. 186.
8. Vernadsky, *Kievan Russia*, p. 178.
9. Riasanovsky, p. 90.
10. *Ibid.*, p. 89.
11. *Ibid.*, p. 91.
12. *Ibid.*, p. 92.
13. *Ibid.*, p. 92.
14. Obolensky, p. 357.
15. *Ibid.*, p. 186.
16. Carpini, *Putování*, pp. 22–3.
17. Rubruck, *Putování*, p. 81.
18. Riasanovsky, p. 314.

Notes to Part 2 Appendix

1. In old Russian, *pasti* (v) means graze, survey the herd (cf. Czech *pásti*, lat. *pastura*); *opas* meant safe-conduct, but also fear. *Obezopasit* (v) which contracted into *opasti* = warm, protect, or in the transitive form, *opastis* = to be afraid, to be on guard.
2. Hellie, *Slavery*, p. 466.
3. Pipes, *Old Régime*, p. 75; Carrère d'Encausse, *La Russie*, p. 61.
4. See also chap. 3 n. 36.

Notes to Chapter 14

1. Herberstein, *Notes Upon Russia*, quoted by Sumner, p. 79. "The Russian monarchy continued to follow the practices of the medieval princely household... a régime which... lived in a permanent state of insecurity and fear of collapse." (Pipes, *Conservatism*, p. 26). Muscovy's close contact with the steppe let it to adopt steppe institutions (Perdue, p. 77). Muscovy princes introduced Mongol political and military institutions on a wide scale (Perdue, p. 76)
2. Fletcher, G., quoted by Szamuely, p. 7.
3. Vernadsky, *Mongols*, p. 361.
4. Vernadsky, *ibid.*
5. Hingley, p. 35. Vernadsky, Origins, p. 31, sees mestnichestvo as similar in many ways to the hierarchy of ranks in Eurasian empires. According to Riasanovsky (p. 207), it was a system of state appointments in which the position of the appointee had to correspond to the standing of his family. It dated formally from 1475, was abolished in 1682 and replaced by a system of ranks, called '*chin*'.
6. Hellie, *Muscovy*, p. 40.

7. *Ibid.*, p. 309, note 70.
8. See also Krizhanich, p. 162, below p. 205.
9. *Zemstvo* – consultative organ of the tsar in the fields of administration, justice and finance. *Guba, gubniye liudi* – local officials charged with administration and justice.
10. Hellie, Slavery, p. 33.

Notes to Chapter 15
1. Vernadsky, *Mongols*, p. 211.
2. Vernadsky, *Mongols*, p. 363.
3. Hellie, *Muscovy*, p. 164. This seems to contradict somehow with Krizhanich, p. 64.
4. There were Tartar units in the army of Ivan IV in his war against Lithuania (some of their descendants still live there).
5. Hellie, *Muscovy*, p. 30.
6. *Ibid.*, p. 267.
7. Vernadsky, *Mongols*, p. 257.
8. Coins, copper and silver, were in circulation, but Krizhanich, in 1659, was still given 40 marten furs on top of an allowance in cash (Letiche-Dmytryshyn, *Russian Statecraft*, XXXVII).
9. A detailed study of the Muscovite army can be found in Hellie, *Muscovy*, pp. 29ff.

Notes to Chapter 16
1. Korb, II, p. 149.
2. Korb, II, p. 154.
3. Fletcher, *Of the Russ Commonwealth*, p. 57.
4. Hellie, *Muscovy*, p. 227.

Notes to Chapter 17
1. Andreyev, *Studies*, p. 322.
2. Andreyev, *Studies*, p. 337.

Notes to Chapter 18
1. Hellie, *Muscovy*, p. 308 note 44.
2. Vernadsky, *Mongols*, pp. 150, 215.
3. Vernadsky, *Mongols*, p. 215.
4. Vernadsky, *Mongols*, pp. 365, 357.
5. Vernadsky, *Mongols*, p. 84.
6. Vernadsky, *Mongols*, p. 375.

7. Hellie, *Muscovy*, p. 42.
8. Hellie, *Muscovy*, pp. 83, 308 note 57.
9. Lewis, R., *Everyday Life*, pp. 164, 165.
10. In the population of Muscovy, Russians and Tartars mixed, Perdue, p. 75.

Notes to Chapter 19
1. Lattimore, p. 138.
2. McNeill, *Steppe*, p. 114.
3. *Ibid.*, p. 112.
4. *Ibid.*, p. 112.
5. *Ibid.*, p. 118.
6. Riasanovsky, p. 199.
7. McNeill, *Steppe*, p. 146.
8. *Ibid.*, p. 146.
9. *Ibid.*, p. 178.
10. *Pereyaslavskii dogovor*, p. 96.
11. Andreyev, p. 97.
12. *Ibid.*, p. 101.
13. McNeill, *Steppe*, p. 84.
14. According to Carrère d'Encausse, the tsar first guaranteed a number of privileges to the Cossacks on which he later reneged. The Cossacks believed they were merely granted a protection by the tsar, whereas he considered 'Little Russia' as his patrimonial estate and its inhabitants his subjects. (*Eurasie*, p. 54-5)
15. Andreyev, p. 101.
16. Carrère d'Encausse, *Eurasie*, p. 36.
17. Zenkovski, p. 15-17.
18. *Ibid.*, p. 56-7.
19. A comparison of the Russian, Chinese and Ottoman way of dealing with the nomads is made by Perdue, p. 128. Souček, *op. cit.* p. 174.

Notes to Chapter 20
1. Sumner, p. 166.
2. Utechin, p. 36. Nikon's doctrine of the dual leadership of the patriarch and the tsar over Russia was based on the *Epanagoge*, ninth century Byzantine law manual (Vernadsky, *Origins*, p. 228).
3. McNeill, *Steppe*, p. 84.

Notes to Chapter 21
1. Letiche-Dmytryshyn, *Russian Statecraft.*
2. Large-scale industries at the time of Krizhanich were established primarily by foreigners (Letiche-Dmytryshyn, XLIX).
3. Krizhanich, Iuri, *Politika,* quoted from *Russian Statecraft;* see also Szamuely, T., *The Russian Tradition,* pp. 61–63. On Krizhanich, see also Pipes, *Conservatism,* p. 46-8.
4. Szamuely, *ibid.*
5. Szamuely, *ibid.*
6. Pipes, *Conservatism,* p. 48
7. *ibid,* p. XIV

Notes to Chapter 22
1. McNeill, *Steppe,* p. 168.
2. Hingley, p. 39.
3. Carmichael, p. 39.
4. Hingley, p. 81.
5. Tucker, p. 72.
6. For the evaluation of Peter's wars, see M. Florinsky, *The End of the Russian Empire: a History and an Interpretation,* New York, 1953, vol.1, p. 335.
7. Carmichael, p. 89.
8. On 'sultanism' see Carrère d'Encausse, *La Russie,* p. 78. Survivals of the patrimonial mentality are mentioned by Pipes, *Conservatism,* p. 64.
9. When Peter the Great was on his visit to England in 1698, he was guest of Admiral John Evelyn in Deptford. When his party departed, 'the house was completely devastated. They slept anywhere, ate anything at any time, respected neither furniture nor paintings. When John Evelyn retook possession of his house he was horrified. Doors and windows had been removed and burnt, curtains torn or soiled with vomit and spit, valuable parquet flooring torn out, canvasses of old masters sprayed with bullets, every figure there having served as a target, flower beds trampled on as if a regiment had camped in the gardens. The admiral had the damages assessed by the court [...]' (H. Troyat, *Pierre le Grand,* pp. 108–9, translated E.K.).
10. Hingley, p. 81.
11. *Ibid.*
12. Pipes, *Old Régime,* pp. 282–3.
13. Riasanovsky, p. 256.
14. Pipes, *Old Régime,* pp. 124.

15. Gascoyne, *Moghuls*, pp. 105–6.
16. A comparison of Russian and Chinese (Ming) defence strategy is made by Perdue, p. 92.
17. Riasanovsky, p. 257. According to Anisimov, E.V. (*The Reforms of Peter the Great*, 1992), Peter prevented the emergence of a capitalist class (quoted by Perdue, p. 540).

Notes to Chapter 23
1. Riasanovsky, p. 261.
2. Riasanovsky, p. 290.
3. Pipes, *Old Régime*, p. 69.
4. Blum, pp. 170–88.
5. Riasanovsky, p. 256.

Notes to Chapter 24
1. Lewis, B., *Race*, p. 12.
2. *Ibid.*, pp. 48–9.
3. *Ibid.*, pp. 79–80.
4. Hellie, *Slavery*, p. 696.
5. *Ibid.*, p. 697.
6. *Ibid.*, p. 702.

Notes to Chapter 25
1. Coles, p. 72.
2. Carmichael, p. 71.
3. Carmichael, p. 73.
4. Masaryk, III, pp. 27–8.
5. Utechin, p. 26.
6. Djilas, p. 76.
7. Korb, II, p. 194.
8. Masaryk, III, p. 27. On Dostoevsky, see also Pipes, *Conservatism*, p. 135-9.
9. Masaryk, III, p. 136.
10. Masaryk, III, pp. 137–8.
11. Masaryk, III, p. 136.
12. Masaryk, III, p. 26.
13. Masaryk, III, pp. 41–2.
14. Riasanovsky, p. 257.
15. Masaryk, III, p. 114.

Notes to Chapter 26

1. On the lack of concept of nationality in Turkey, see Lewis, B., *Emergence of Modern Turkey*, pp. 55 and 323–4; on nationalism, see Lewis, B., *What went wrong*, pp. 119, 170.
2. Masaryk, III, pp. 112–3.
3. On the official nationalism of Nicholas I, see Pipes, *Conservatism*, p. 98.
4. On centralism and national aspirations, see Carrère d'Encausse, *Eurasie*, p. 184ff.
5. At the close of the Crimean War in 1856, about half of the Crimean Tartars left for Turkey. The fever of emigration began to spread to the Volga Tartars. This was the first germ of pan-Islamism and pan-Turkism among the Tartars in Russia (Zenkovski, p. 27).
6. Zenkovski, p. 67
7. Carrère d'Encausse, *Eurasie*, p. 197
8. Carrère d'Encausse, *ibid.* p. 209
9. Zenkovski, *op. cit.* p. 91
10. Zenkovski, *ibid.* p. 103
11. Zenkovski, *ibid.* p. 105
12. Carrère d'Encausse, *op. cit..* p. 208

Notes to Chapter 27

1. Kochan, p. 35; Riasanovsky, p. 313.
2. Kochan, p. 27. The situation was similar in nineteenth-century Turkey, see Lewis, B., *Emergence*, p. 324.
3. Riasanovsky, p. 382.
4. McNeill, *Steppe*, pp. 200–1.
5. According to Pipes, a much larger proportion of Russian inhabitants engaged in trade and manufacture than the official census figures indicate (*Old Regime*, p. 192). On Tartar trade see above Chap. 19. Soucek, *op. cit.* p. 195.
6. Zenkovski, p. 68.
7. 'The growth of trade turned Central Asian economy from an islolated, self-sufficient rural economy into a market-oriented one.' (Zenkovski, p. 80)
8. Under the Soviets the cotton production and industry became a virtual monoculture. This had disastrous effects after the collapse of the Union, when the cotton producers lost their captive market and were unable to compete in the open world markets with the products of Egypt, India, and others, and their economy was not sufficiently diversified to cope with the population's requirements.

Notes to Chapter 28
1. Vernadsky, *Kievan Russia*, p. 133.
2. Quote from Wilson, p. 276.

Notes to Chapter 29
1. Riasanovsky, p. 413.
2. Kochan, p. 56.
3. Kochan, p. 57.
4. Pipes, *Russian Revolution*, p. 120.
5. On the efficiency of serf labour in Russia, see Mironov, pp. 323 ff. According to his statistics, Russia had not reached the British level of productivity of the early nineteenth century even 200 years later (1,773 kg of wheat per hectare as against 1,590 kg per hectare in the USSR in 1986–90).
6. Mironov, p. 339.
7. Bush, p. 61.
8. Kochan, pp. 52–3.
9. Kochan, *Ibid.*

Notes to Chapter 30
1. Kochan, p. 76.
2. Kochan, *Ibid.*
3. Carmichael, p. 91.
4. *An account of Russia in the year 1767*, vol. II.
5. Swinton, A., *Travels in Norway, Denmark and Russia, in 1788, 1789 and 1790*, quoted from Wilson, p. 174.
6. Riasanovsky, p. 386.
7. Carmichael, p. 179.
8. Quoted from the *Sunday Times*, 10 November 1972.
9. Masaryk, III, p. 5.

Notes to Chapter 31
1. Carmichael, pp. 192, 196, 224.
2. Carmichael, p. 197.
3. Carmichael, p. 198.
4. Gray, p. 244.

Notes to Chapter 32
1. Utechin, p. 73.
2. Utechin, p. 72.
3. Utechin, p. 81.
4. Pipes, *Conservatism*, p. 109, 110; Carrère d'Encausse, *Eurasie*, p. 187.
5. Utechin, p. 91.
6. Socialists in multiethnic empires were split as regards methods of achieving the required solutions. The Austrian Social Democrats (Kautsky, Renner, Bauer) preferred the reformist approach, while the Russians, close to Lenin, wanted first of all a radical break with the existing system (cf. Carrère d'Encausse, *Eurasie*, p. 189) For Russian political thinkers who preferred a moderate approach (Samarin, Struve) see Pipes, *Conservatism*, p. 128, 168
7. On the elections to the Constitutent Assembly, see Carrère d'Encausse, *op. cit*, p. 214, Riasanovsky, p. 528.
8. Zenkovski, p. 24, 37.
9. Zenkovski, p. 58.
10. Carrère d'Encausse, *op. cit.* p. 157. On Turco-Tartars in Russia, see Pipes, *Russian Revolution*, p. 143.
11. Carrère d'Encausse, *op. cit.* p. 144. 'As a large part of her newly acquired imperial space was Muslim, Russia, which since the 16th century incorporated Islam in her definition of policy in conquered territories, was able to make it for several decades into an instrument of peace in relations with her subjects.' (*ibid.* p. 146).

Notes to Chapter 33
1. *Message from Moscow*, p. 232.
2. Djilas, *The New Class*, p. 157.
3. *Message*, pp. 163–5.
4. *Ibid.*, p. 84.

Notes to Chapter 34
1. G. Grass, quoted by Conquest, *Lenin*, p. 134.
2. Pipes, *Bolshevik R.*, p. 499.
3. *State and Revolution*, quoted by Schapiro, p. 206.
4. Pipes, *Survival*, p. 22.
5. Conquest, *Lenin*, p. 51.
6. Conquest, p. 96.
7. Conquest, p. 104.
8. Conquest, p. 32.

9. Conquest, p. 96.
10. Conquest, p. 96.
11. For the similarities of the Soviet and Nazi régimes see Aftalion, *op. cit.* p. 298. The list of characteristics is taken from earlier works.

Notes to Chapter 35
1. Tucker, *The Soviet Political Mind*, pp. 10–1.
2. Lenin, *Selected Works*, III, p. 480.
3. Conquest, *Lenin*, p. 116.
4. Pipes, *Survival*, p. 23.
5. Pipes, *Survival*, p. 29.
6. Conquest, p. 43.
7. Resolution of the 8th Party Congress.
8. Resolution of the 2nd Congress of the Comintern.
9. Conquest, p. 46.
10. *Leninism or Marxism*, quoted by Conquest, pp. 46–7.
11. Quoted by Conquest, p. 47, also Tucker, p. 42. For the party above the State, see Carrère d'Encausse, *op. cit.* p. 281.
12. Resolution of the 10th Party Congress, 1921.
13. To Carrère d'Encausse, Russian universalism begins with Peter the Great and Catharine II (*op. cit.* p. 79). On Islamic universalism see Zenkovski, *op. cit.* p 278. According to Zenkovski, 'The Marxist-Leninist dogma of world revolution and the spread of universalist Communist teaching by means of power are not far removed from the universal Islamic expansion and conversion as practised by successful Arabic and Turkish conquests' (*ibid.* p. 278).
14. Pipes, *Survival*, p. 193.
15. Pipes, *Survival*, p. 41.
16. Pipes, *Conservatism*, p. 26.

Notes to Chapter 36
1. Schapiro, p. 196.
2. Conquest, p. 111.
3. Ts. A. Stepanian, 'Neodolimoe dvizhenie k komunizmu', *Voprosy filosofii*, 2, 1948, p. 86, quoted from Tucker, p. 173.
4. Tucker, p. 198.
5. Schapiro, p. 197.
6. *Ibid.*
7. Schapiro, p. 219.

8. Schapiro, p. 351. On the activities of the Communists in the United States, see Aftalion, *Alerte Rouge sur l'Amérique*.
9. Conquest, p. 111.
10. Conquest, p. 112.

Notes to Chapter 37
1. Tucker, pp. 22–4; Fitzpatrick, *Stalinism*, p. 251 (French edition)
2. Kehayan, p. 109, D. Bonavia in *The Times*, 1972.
3. Pipes, *Survival*, p. 114.
4. Pipes, *Survival*, p. 53.
5. Pipes, *Survival*, p. 84.
6. Pipes, *Survival*, p. 86.

Notes to Chapter 38
1. On nationalism among the non-Russians see Carrère d'Encausse, *Eurasie*, p. 238. Souček, *op. cit.* p. 223.
2. Lenin's letter of December 1922, quoted by Schapiro, p. 227.
3. Djilas, *The New Class*, p. 101.
4. Miller, p. 146.
5. Miller, p. 147.
6. Wheeler, *Peoples of Soviet Central Asia*, p. 91. Soucek, *op. cit.* p. 237.
7. Carrère d'Encausse, *Victorieuse Russie*, p. 76.
8. It seems, for a while, that Brezhnev's successor, Iuri Andropov, harboured some reformist ideas like opening to Muslim republics, giving more responsibility to non-Russian leaders, doing away with discrimination of Jews, etc. Unfortunately, because of his early demise, there is little evidence of this (cf. Malia, p. 408).
9. Carrère d'Encausse, *Eurasie*, p. 110.
10. Alexeev, p. 2–3; Trubetskoy, p. 6.
11. Titarenko, p. 202; Thom, p. 6.
12. Quoted by Alexeev, *ibid.* For a detailed study of Eurasianism, see Voráček, *Eurasiánství*.

Notes to Chapter 39
1. Riasanovsky, p. 417.
2. Riasanovsky, p. 418.
3. Schapiro in *The Times*, 1972. Lenin's concept of law was 'Law derives from fact, even if this is the result of violence.' (Carrère d'Encausse, *Eurasie*, p. 243)
4. Miller, Life, p. 183.

5. See Pelikán, J., *The Czechoslovak Political Trials 1950–1954*, London, 1971.
6. Conquest, pp. 99–100.
7. Conquest, p. 42.
8. Conquest, p. 41.
9. Conquest, p. 64.
10. *The First Circle*, p. 1967.
11. Pipes, *Old Régime*, p. 288.
12. Pipes, *Old Régime*, p. 290.
13. Pipes, *Old Régime*, p. 298.
14. Schapiro, p. 229.
15. Pipes, *Old Régime*, pp. 294–5.
16. A more recent Special Report on Russia conducted by *The Economist* (15 July 2006) has found no change in this situation.

Notes to Chapter 40
1. Gray, *Experiment*, pp. 200, 219.
2. Gray, p. 244; *A Proletkult Manifesto*, from Sidorov, *Literaturniye Manifesti*.
3. Gray, p. 271.
4. Carmichael, *Cultural History*, pp. 238–9.
5. Carmichael, p. 246.
6. Van der Post, *Journey*, p. 189.

Notes to Chapter 41
1. Kohl, *Russia*, quoted by Wilson, p. 231.
2. Wittfogel, *Despotism*, p. 362.
3. Pipes, *Survival*, p. 31.
4. Pipes, *Survival*, p. 23.
5. Pipes, *Survival*, p. 50.
6. Carrère d'Encausse, *La Russie*, pp. 272–3. The nomenklatura members had very few private possessions. Their dachas, cars, even furniture, were owned by the state and could be confiscated when the person lost his job, was sentenced, etc. (Fitzpatrick, *Stalinism*, p. 159 (French edition)).
7. Pipes, *Bolshevik R.*, p. 138.

Notes to Chapter 42
1. Lewis, B., *Turkey*, p. 387.
2. Korb, II, p. 186.
3. Quoted from Wilson, p. 41.

4. Carpini, *Putování*, p. 36.
5. Gilison, J. M., 'Khrushchev, Brezhnev and constitutional reform', in *Problems*, Sep–Oct, 1969.
6. Tucker, pp. 80–1.

Notes to Chapter 43
1. 'I have mentioned before how struck I was by the westernness of Siberia. Here in the Far East the people seemed to me more western than ever and the least Asiatic and Oriental of any group encountered on my travels in the Soviet Union.' Van der Post, *Journey*, p. 272.
2. Land ownership of the Kazakh nomads was regulated (and restricted) by the Statute of the Steppe of 1891 and the creation of Land Funds giving the colonisers the right to occupy the best agricultural land (Carrère d'Encausse, *Eurasie*, p. 98).

Notes to Chapter 44
1. Korb, II, p. 142.
2. Carpini, in Putování, p. 25.
3. Olearius, 1647, p. 72.
4. Korb, I, p. 136.
5. Krizhanich, p. 116.
6. Krizhanich, p. 123.
7. Custine, 1839, quoted by Wilson, p. 219.
8. Van der Post, pp. 197, 258.
9. Lyall, 1823, quoted by Wilson, p. 219.
10. Wilmot, 1807, quoted by Wilson, p. 176.
11. Wilson, p. 192.
12. Olearius, quoted by Wilson, p. 73.
13. Miller, *Life*, p. 89, published 1969.
14. Kehayan, p. 156, published 1978.
15. Bronfenbrenner, *'The Two Worlds of Childhood'*, The Times, 1972.

Notes to Chapter 45
1. *Message from Moscow*, pp. 106–7.
2. *Message*, pp. 31–42.
3. *Message*, p. 108.
4. *Message*, p. 180.
5. *Message*, p. 109.
6. Written in 1974.

7. Dostoevsky, F., *The Possessed*, II, pp. 69–70 (London, 1960).
8. *Message*, p. 98.
9. Kehayan, p. 114.
10. *Message*, pp. 99–101, 102–3.
11. *Message*, pp. 208, 236.
12. *Message*, p. 241.
13. Miller, *Life*, p. 1.
14. Miller, *Life*, p. 20.
15. *Message*, pp. 207–8.
16. Van der Post, pp. 284–5.

Notes to Chapter 46
1. Carrère d'Encausse, *La Russie*, p. 150.
2. This is the reason why 'the Russian society remained unaware of the state's having become a multinational empire', and that Russian historiography virtually ignored the subject. Even the great historian V.O. Kliuchevsky 'hardly acknowledged the fact that Russia comprised a multinational polity. 'Thus, the Russians apparently surpassed the English, who had built their empire, it used to be said, in a fit of absent-mindedness – for the Russians failed even to notice that they possessed an empire after they had acquired it' (R. Szporluk, in *Problems*, p. 80, Sep.– Oct., 72).
3. Custine, quoted by Wilson, pp. 219, 221.
4. Pipes, *Survival*, p. 142.

Notes to Part 5B Appendix
1. *Message*, p. 199.
2. *Message*, p. 243.
3. *Message*, p. 212.
4. *Message*, p. 247.

Notes to Chapter 47
1. Riasanovsky, p. 261.
2. Korb, II, p. 163.
3. Fletcher, p. 61.
4. Haxthausen, III, p. 46.
5. Tucker, p. 25.
6. Hingley, pp. 147–8.
7. Written in 1974.

Notes to Chapter 48
1. Lenin, *Sochinenia*, X, p. 303, XIII, pp. 300–303.
2. Plekhanov, *On the Agrarian Question*, 1906, p. 16.
3. Protokoly, quoted from Wittfogel, pp. 393–4.
4. Pipes, *Bolshevik Régime*, p. 504.
5. Carrère d'Encausse, *La Russie*, p. 277.
6. Written in 1974.
7. Riasanovsky, p. 619.
8. There is an uncanny similarity between Stalin's methods of collectivization and those of Mao Tse-Tung in China.

Notes to Chapter 49
1. Pipes, *Bolshevik Régime*, pp. 445–6.
2. On the collapse of the central planning system, the sharp fall in foreign trade, and their consequences, hyper-inflation, etc., see *The Economist*, 5/12/1992.

Notes to Chapter 50
1. Kochan, p. 29.
2. Written in 1974.
3. Riasanovsky, p. 309.
4. Lewis, B., *Turkey*, p. 464.
5. Kochan, p. 161.
6. Kochan, p. 74.
7. *Ibid.*
8. Kochan, p. 73.
9. Miller, p. 86.
10. The Soviet Union's urban population surpassed the rural population for the first time in 1961 and the latter still accounted for 30 percent of the total population in 1985 (Malia, *The Soviet Tragedy*, pp. 357, 365).
11. Miller, pp. 100–4.

Notes to Chapter 51
1. Pipes, *Survival*, pp. 35–7.
2. Written in 1974.
3. Kochan, p. 28.

Notes to Chapter 52
1. Speech of 31.10.1922, quoted by Lewis, B., *Turkey*; see also *What went wrong*, p. 127.
2. Malia, p. 475.
3. Malia, p. 496.
4. Malia, p. 489.
5. Malia, p. 488. On the disintegration of the USSR, see also Carrère d'Encausse, *Eurasie*, p. 380ff.
6. *The Economist*, November 2000, March 2001.
7. Bonner, E., in *The Sunday Times*, 18 February 2001.
8. 'A Survey of Russia', *The Economist*, July 2001.
9. 'A Survey of Russia', *The Economist*, 15 July 2006.
10. Thom, p. 8.
11. Thom, p. 9.
12. Thom, p. 9.
13. The similarity between the disintegration of the Romanov and Soviet empires has also been noticed by Carrère d'Encausse, *op. cit.* p. 419.

Notes to Afterthought
1. *The Economist*, 26th June 2002.
2. Carrère d'Encausse, *Eurasie*, p. 398.
3. *The Economist*, 11th February 2006.
4. *The Economist*, 26th June 2002; also above Chap. 48.
5. *The Economist*, 18th May 2002.
6. *The Economist*, 22nd July 2006; *L'Express*, 29th June 2006. Rosneft's acquisition of a part of Yukos' remaining assets in a rather dubious public auction, changes of government rules of granting licences for oil prospecting and then changing them for trivial "ecological reasons" (Shell in Sakhalin, TNP-BP in Siberia), as well as generous tax concessions to state-controlled companies, Gasprom and Rosneft, all seem to be designed to eliminate competition, both foreign and domestic.
7. *L'Express*, 20th April 2006.
8. *ibid.*
9. Carrère d'Encausse, *op. cit.* p. 435.
10. After the death of President Saparmurat Niyazov in January, the election of his successor, Kurbanguly Berdymukhamedov, this 89% of the vote did not promise many changes of the regime's practices.
11. The obviously politically motivated murder of the journalist Anna Politkovskaya, the mysterious poisoning in London of the dissident Alexander Litvinenko and

the obstacles thrown by the government in the path of the investigation, the recent ban of foreign tradesmen from Russian markets and the clampdown on illegal immigrants, even those coming from the former Soviet republics and, last but not least, the pro-Putin electoral alliance of the recently founded Just Russia political party with the United Russia party (who both claim to be the President's true acolytes) and their strong showing in the March regional elections (held in 14 out of 86 regions of Russia), all this does not augur well for the forthcoming parliamentary election (in December 2007) and the presidential one of the following spring. There are even signs that a constitutional amendment may be voted by the new Duma to make it possible for Mr Putin to stand for re-election. Even if this is not the case, it is most likely that his successor will be approved by the Kremlin and will continue to rule in the same way.

Glossary

Aksakal	(Turk.) White Beard, village elder
Apanage	Orig. province or lucrative office; territorial dependency
Bolshak	(Rus. *bolshoy* – big) Head of family group, village commune
Burgwall	Fortified settlement, Celtic or early Slav
Cadets	Constitutional Democrats, pre-revolutionary party in Russia
Cheka	*Chrezvychainaia Kommissia*, first Soviet Secret Service
Cheliad'	Collective term for "slaves of a master". In contemporary Czech, *čeleď* means "farmhands" (coll.)
Chernozem	Ukranian Black Earth
Chin	System of ranks in Muscovy, established by Peter the Great as the Table of Ranks (*Tabel o rangakh*)
Desiatsky	Leader of ten (Rus. *desiat'* – ten)
Dessiatina	Unit of land, equal to 2.7 acres or 1.092 hectares
Diak	Scribe, government official, administrator
Drakkar (langskip)	Viking fighting ship
Druzhina	Leader's guard, group of retainers
Dvoeverie	"Double Faith", co-existence of Christianity and pagan practices
Dvor	Court, princely or royal household
Dvoriane	Courtiers, members of the *dvor*
Fieldgrass	Belt of steppe with sparse trees and long grass
Field Husbandry	Migratory way of farming
Grazhdanin	Citizen
Grivna	Money unit of variable value (worth 25 marten skins or about one Arabic dirham)
Guba	Local office charged with administration and justice
Hetman	Cossack commander
Hundredmen	(or numbered men) Members of communes under the Mongols

Iurt	Nomadic dwelling, usually round, made of felt and latticework
Jadids	Moderate Islamic party in Central Asia
Kafes	(Turk.) Cage, place of confinement of younger relatives of the Sultan
Kholopy	Forms of slavery (hereditary, voluntary, contracted)
Kolchug	Armour
Kolkhoz	*Kolektivnoye khoziaistvo*, collective farm
Konets (pl. *Kontsy*)	Administrative unit in Novgorod
Kormlenie	lit. "feeding", administrative post in Muscovy whose occupant retained for his own use part of all of the revenues drawn from the temporary allocation of land which he was allowed to exploit
Kulak	(Rus. "fist") independent (private) farmer
Kuplia	Purchase of land (Rus. *kupit'* – buy)
Kurghan	Burial mound of the nomads
Liudi	(Rus. "people") big men, servants of state, military or administrative
Menshevik	Social Democratic Party (Rus. *menshiy* – minor, smaller)
Mestnichestvo	Ranking system of noble families in Muscovy (Rus. *miesto* – place)
Mir	Village commune (Rus. "world")
Monoxyla	Single straters, boats the bottom of which was made of a single log or tree
Nökers	Khan's elite corps, guards
Nomenklatura	Soviet administrative hierarchy
Non-possessors	Orthodox sect objecting to wealth and advocating independence from the state in religious matters
Noyons	Mongol aristocratic commanders
Okhrana	Tsarist secret service
Oprichnina	Royal domain created by Ivan IV and personally managed by him
Oprichniki	Gentry using and living off the *oprichnina* land

Perelog	Farming technique, changing plots every 3–4 years and fallowing
Piatina	Area of farmland outside the city of Novgorod (Rus. "fifth")
Podseka	Farming technique, slash-and-burn
Podzol	Soil in the forest zone (sandy, clayish, stony)
Polki (sg. *Polk*)	Regiments
Poludie	Tax or tribute extracted by the prince directly from the people
Pomestie	Until the 18th century, land held on service or tenure; later, estate held by a noble
Posadnik	City governor in the city of Novgorod, mayor
Promysly	Crafts and other cottage industries
Pronoia	Byzantine temporary land grant in return for the service to the state (11th century), which became the basis of military service
Samoderzhavie	Autocracy
Sblizhenie	lit. "drawing closer"; the trend towards a unitary multinational state
Sech	Island in the Dnieper, headquarters of the Cossacks
Shar'	Islamic religious law
Slianiye	lit. "fusion", see *Sblizheniye*
Smerdy	Peasants on state land, subject to tax
Sokha	Wooden plough, perhaps with an iron point
Sotni	Hundreds, administrative units in Novgorod
Sotsky	Commander of a hundred
Soyuzniki	Home troops in Kievan Russia, rewarded with land
Streltsy	Musketeers
Sudebnik	Muscovite Code of Law
Taliban (sg. *Taleb*)	Radical Islamists governing Afghanistan 1996–2001
Tiaglo	Labour and tax which the commoners owed to the Tsar
Timar	Turkish land-holding based on service
Tovarishch	Comrade

Tysiatsky	Commander of a thousand
Udel'	Semi-independent domain of a prince
Udelnye	Princes of the Mongol period
Ukas	Decree, issued by the Tsarist government
Urf	Islamic secular law
Veche	Municipal assembly in the Kievan period with a consultative function; in Novgorod and Pskov they had legislative power
Voevody	Military commanders, provincial administrators
Volost	Administrative unit, est. 1861, consisted of one of more villages
Volostnoy starshina	Leader of a *volost*, elder
Vospitanie	Education
Votchina	Inheritable land fief; later, land purchased privately
Vozhd'	Leader
Wahhabists	Radical Islamic sect, originating in the area of Saudi Arabia
Waqf	Endowment or religious tax in Islamic countries
Zadvornye liudi	Slaves living outside their owner's household
Zemskii sobor	In Muscovy, an advisory council of the Tsar; in the 19th century, Land Assembly
Zemstvo	Consultative organ of the Tsar in the field of administration, finance and justice

index

zadvornye liudi, serfs, servants, 224,
456
zemskii sobor, assembly, 116, 202,
203, 340
zemstvo, administration office 438,
456
Zenkovski 236
Zhirinovsky, V., 384
Zikmundová, V., 95, 164

Other ODYSSEY travel and history titles include

Distributed in the United Kingdom and Europe by:
Cordee Books & Maps
3a De Montfort Street, Leicester, UK, LE1 7HD
Tel: 0116-254-3579   Fax: 0116-247-1176
www.cordee.co.uk

Distributed in the United States of America by:
W.W. Norton & Company, Inc.
500 Fifth Avenue, New York, NY 10110
Tel: 800-233-4830   Fax: 800-458-6515
www.wwnorton.com

For more information, please visit: www.odysseypublications.com